SHEILA ROWBOTHAM was born in ⸻ Methodist school near Filey in Yorkshire, and ⸻ ⸻ry at St ⸻ College, Oxford. For much of her life she has taught – in technical and further education colleges, comprehensive schools and the Workers' Educational Association. In the early sixties she became active in the socialist movement, and was on the editorial board of *Black Dwarf*. She has been involved in the women's movement since its beginnings in Britain in the late 1960s, and has written books and articles on a wide variety of subjects related to feminism, socialism and history. Her books have become very widely known, and are translated into many languages. *Women, Resistance and Revolution* (1972) and *Hidden From History* (1973) were two early books rescuing hitherto 'forgotten' women from the ravages of history. Later came *Woman's Consciousness, Man's World* (1973), *A New World for Women* (1977), *Socialism and the New Life* (with Jeffrey Weekes, 1977), *Dutiful Daughters* (with Jean McCrindle, 1977) and *Beyond the Fragments* (with Lynn Segal and Hilary Wainwright, 1979).

Sheila Rowbotham has lectured widely in Britain, America and Canada, and in 1981 became Visiting Professor at the University of Amsterdam. She now divides her time between writing and teaching, and lives in Hackney with her son.

This collection, by one of the most original and prolific feminist thinker of the past decade, brings together writings from the 1960s to the present day, and includes unpublished material and some of Sheila Rowbotham's poetry. But people and movements change, and the author has added important new introductions which provide not only a fascinating commentary on her writings but a timely and passionate plea for a renewal of feminism and socialism.

DREAMS
AND
DILEMMAS

COLLECTED WRITINGS

SHEILA
ROWBOTHAM

Virago

Published by VIRAGO PRESS Limited 1983
41 William IV Street, London WC2N 4DB

British Library Cataloguing in Publication Data
Rowbotham, Sheila
  Dreams and dilemmas.
  I. Title
  082   PR6068.0/
  ISBN 0-86068-342-7

Printed in Finland by Werner Söderström Oy,
a member of Finnprint

CONTENTS

Loss

Think back
my mother said
what was it
you were doing?

Think back
my mother said
when you lost
it.

Think back
when I lost . . .
Think back
my mother said
to what it was

was I doing
was I doing
what it was
what is loss?

what was
my mother said

what was
in my head
is loss.

Think back

What was
my mother
doing

dead?

(Autumn 1981)

PREFACE

This book had a somewhat ignoble origin. Bitten by the crisis, shaken out by Margaret and hounded by the bailiffs, I thought: how can I make money faster than it takes to write? Nose in the air, wrote for principles, not for money, until very recently, landing with a bump, permanently broke. The Tories have taught me what my Yorkshire dad tried to tell me: 'If you want to have principles you have to earn money.' Spurred on to endeavour by stalwart materialism, self-help and thrift, and being a good Marxist delighting in contradictions, I reflected upon all those commodious old articles in the cellar. What a nifty little outcome of Tory policy, socialist feminist dreams and dilemmas.

It was not to be so nifty though. I had forgotten how many there were. Carrier bags filled up with rejects, and still 700 pages more. More bags.

Then it was down to the nub of meaning. And it became not nifty at all, squeezing out truths from the spin dryer while the phone keeps ringing with messages and time colliding.

I was walking backwards in the dream through memories and memories of memories. Awake I was still unable to leave well alone, torn, yearning for insouciance, wrenched, unhappy, compelled to go through with it.

There was no slithering in seaweed, escape routes half hidden in rock pools. Out in the clear light of day I was having to put clear markers on regular flowerbeds. 'I said this because', 'This thought means'. When I know and I don't know.

I was prey to doubts. After all, who had appointed me to assemble these bits of me between two covers? It seemed to have been me, myself. There was no-one else really to shoulder the lofty responsibility of this disparate baggage of mine. Moving from ignoble wheeze to lofty implications is a breathtaking transition. It leaves your identity gasping a bit.

I am uneasy in my individuality – a writer. What kind of useful job is that, I ask? 'I write,' I mumble and watch the disbelief peer back. Well, I wrote in between everything else, pulled by political demands and matter of fact. Get it done then. But there was always more to it than that. I want to be needed, to be of service, a popular plan for social need. Let me fashion words, grant me skill in my trade, an honest socialist feminist spinster living off my labour, deftly helping to unpick capitalism. But there is still more. There is that inner resolve, more remotely useful and not necessarily popular. I would echo Thalia Doukas's description of her reasons for writing poetry in *One Foot on the Mountain*. She puts it better than I am able.

'I write because I seem to be compelled to remark, sift, pin certain things down, get past what I ought to think or feel and confront what I believe to be true . . .'[1]

This labour will always be exacting. But in my conception of socialism and feminism it would be neither peculiar nor presumptuous, just necessary. I imagine there will always be some people who incline towards it – as people like to sing, build, garden, knit, solve mathematical problems. I can do none of these at present. Clearly my aptitudes will blossom under socialism and I could enter the building trade. But let me still remark, sift, pin down, get past. And may it be neither falsely valued nor undervalued but equally and justly reckoned. For in capitalism, and it appears in already existing forms of socialism, as the saying goes, writers are lauded for the wrong reasons or despised.

But there is still something not being said. There is something underhand going on. Can it ever *really* become a respectable trade? Are there not grounds for suspicion of dream dancers posing as honest word workers, who woo all comers and seek to dazzle, disarm, flirt, lure, excite, but ultimately let down, because, when you come down to it, and down you must come, it's all fantasy and show. What would happen if such dream dancers were let into affairs of state or trusted to guard morality by the hearthside? Where would illusion and reality be, left to these dealers in entrancement and images?

For how can we write and not yearn to make the words dance, to pound out the arguments until the head spins, making lyrics and melodies of sober plans and reputable programmes. Well perhaps a tension will remain for as far as we can imagine. Writers, like all artists, are not clearly useful for organisation and analysis. They sling arbitrary tightropes between thought, feeling and fancy, and demand to be needed. They want fuss, bring confusion and reach for the heart.

I would not write though for writing's sake. Twiddling words is fun. But there is too much injustice in the world not to be in earnest.

I still feel a tug to look round for grown-ups or princes, heroes, saints, anybody really who is not me. I know it to be a false search. Reluctantly I am responsible. A bit tardy, I am forty after all. A bit shame-faced, sheepish, gormless in parts. But advantaged because with many other women through women's liberation we have caught a rare and precious glimpse of a shared free commitment.

All those who have been there will find much that is familiar, accounts of equal pay demonstrations and strikes, the struggle of women to become bus drivers, 'Miss World', the night cleaners' campaign, the Family Allowance Campaign, Women's Aid, the Fakenham occupation, Imperial Type-writers, the origin of the Working Women's Charter, the organisation of nursery workers, the abortion campaign, sharing childcare, attempts to gain community control over the welfare state, the first black women's liberation conference in Britain, the alternative economic strategy, workers' plans, *Beyond the Fragments*.

From outside Britain, France in May 1968, the anti-authoritarian childcare centres set up by German students in the late 1960s, the impact of the American movement for black civil rights and the emergence of women's liberation in the United States.

And whether you were there, somewhere else or too young to be bothered, there are general questions which have arisen from all these to consider, for example the interconnections between memory of conscious-ness, class and sex, women and the trade union movement, feminism and motherhood, socialism and feminism. What do we mean by patriarchy? How does history relate to modern politics? When is the personal not political? What kind of socialism do we want? How do we start to make it?

You will meet a varied troupe of companions as you ponder, Marilyn Monroe, Karl Marx, Ada Nield Chew, Anna Coote, Rudolf Rocker, Agnes McLean, Loretta Lynn, R.D. Laing, Sue Oppenheimer, the Woodcraft Folk, Charlotte Perkins Gilman, Lenin, Billy Liar, Lil Bilocca, Evans Pritchard, Bea Campbell, Talcott Parsons, Myra Garrett, Emma Martin, Kentucky miners and their wives, Lucy Lippard, Edward Carpenter, James Dean, Linda Gordon. Confused? I did warn you about writers.

Curious? Now read on.

ACKNOWLEDGEMENTS

Acknowledgements and thanks for permission to reprint to: *Black Dwarf*, *Cutlasses and Earrings*, *Hackney People's Press*, *History Workshop Journal*, *Islington Gutter Press*, *The Leveller*, Merlin Press, *The Miner*, Onlywomen Press, Pantheon Press, Penguin Books, *New Society*, *New Statesman*, *Radical America*, *Radical History Review*, *Red Rag*, *Spare Rib*, Stage 1, Spokesman, *Wildcat*, *Women Speaking*,

Thanks to Rose Ades, Sally Alexander, Paul Barker, Anna Coote, Tony Gould, Susan Gyarmati, Kerry Hamilton, Ruth Petrie, Raphael Samuel, Julia Vellacott, and Gareth Steadman Jones, who edited some of these articles, to Ros Baxandall, Adam Ganz, Jean McCrindle and Sue Sharpe for reading the introductions, and to Ursula Owen for help in editing the collection.

PART ONE

BEGINNINGS: THE ORIGINS OF WOMEN'S LIBERATION

INTRODUCTION

Turning the pages of yellowed newspapers, in the stiff formality of a library or crouching to read them under old lino while decorating, I have often wished myself behind the print. If only one could have been there to get the full story.

Yet to have been involved in the beginnings of a movement does not necessarily mean that you have tales your granddaughter or indeed anybody else might want to hear. Participation and perspective can be contrary partners.

The focus of personal memory is too near. Detail disintegrates into angles of variance, a stroke, a point, a nuance, a moment without contour and context.

'We suddenly began to talk to one another in a different way.' But why do people seek one another in new ways? And at the same time?

In the deepest most general sense it would be fraud to say I knew. Moreover, in our own particular case, in the context of a movement I helped create, I do not know. We were only dimly conscious of embarking upon a historical process. The intensity, the need to talk, to be with other women, the discovery of self in a new relationship with others, the opening of understanding, the strength of trust and the mutuality of communication were immediate delights. Well they happened. They left marks and are too valuable to be forgotten.

I long to communicate these memories, but not in a spirit of nostalgia, not so that they are revered or crammed for academic examinations. How do we hand on more than the outer husks of history?

Craft skill involves a recognition of one's limits. My closeness means I could not adequately distinguish, assess, constitute. I am too encumbered by the particular to move with grace and delicacy between subjective experience and the broad sweep of social relationships. I cannot merge, knead, and emerge with history. But this is not so sad if I know that there are others listening, recording, assimilating memories. One day there will be tales for our granddaughters, rich, complex, stark, demanding. Meanwhile I can join the dance of memory myself, give history a nudge, drop a few hints and leave a paper chase for the future.

First, hints and clues from me as a craftswoman. A history of the emergence of women's liberation would need to take account of those large changes in capitalist society, population, sexuality, work, welfare, consumption, education, the media and the rest. It would need to trace the impact of past feminist movements. It would examine cultural attitudes. Ah, how many fashion magazines and government reports, surveys, old films, statistics, coroners' reports, biographies, letters, embroidered handkerchieves can be studied in a lifetime?

It would require a knowledge of intellectual currents and of radical political movements in quite different countries in order to reflect upon the shaping of discontent. In 1964 Casey Hayden and Mary King, both active in the American Civil Rights Movement which was 'the borning struggle' for women's liberation, produced a mimeographed declaration.

'It needs to be made known that many women in the movement are not happy and contented with their status . . . women are the crucial factor that keeps the movement running on a day-to-day basis. Yet they are not given equal say—so when it comes to day-to-day decision making.'

When this declaration was discussed Stokely Carmichael responded with an historical joke which still echoes. 'The only position for women in SNCC is prone.'[1]

In Paris during the 1968 May Events this poster appeared:

> Student
> who questions everything
> the relations of the worker to the employer
> the relations of the pupil to the teacher
> have you questioned
> the relations of man to woman?
> Girl students
> who take part in the revolution
> don't be duped again
> do not follow others
> define your own demands.

In September 1968 Helke Sander exploded at the German socialist student conference in Frankfurt – 'Comrades your meetings are unbearable!' She began to define the womens' demands for a political context in which open and democratic communication was possible, for a recognition of the interconnection of personal, sexual life and public participation in politics, for a new relationship between theory and experience, for a transformation in the material circumstances of everyday life and the conscious creation of non-hierarchical relations between adults and children. She also noted how these demands were regarded by the men as 'frontier-trespasses'.[2]

Even in its origins women's liberation shifted boundaries, crossed zones, made politics into something else.

So it leaves headaches for historians. Where are the limits of evidence? There is after all existentialism, Talcott Parsons, Reich, Laing, Marcuse, de Beauvoir, Lessing, Mercer, James Dean, Marilyn Monroe, the Beatles, Bob Dylan, changes in the law on prostitution, militant strippers, the Pill, the preschool playgroups, homosexual law reform, the Vietnam war, the student movement – the dialectics of liberation indeed. But where does a collective consciousness of oppression come from?

Search me. I remain inwardly silent amidst the external chattering of facts. I could trace kinship, describe meetings, talking to this one and that one in the 'ladies', or I could wear my heart on my sleeve and outline sociological trends. But I would not be honest if I pretended to history. I do not know how my private memories plait with those of other women. I am too much within these personal recollections to spread out a wider pattern.

Unable to pattern the particular I cannot maintain the tension between my myriad moments of individual experience and the outer shifts which can be surveyed like 'more married women in paid employment' or even labelled clearly as 'the politics of experience'.

It is becoming too daunting. A history, like a culture, is not the word made finite but the culling and coaxing of available material. In the end we present honest approximations. How fine the tension, wrought the craft, in labouring for the nicest approximation. What excitement in timing the inspired leap. Such slithers of delight in history.

But the dust has to settle a bit. Meanwhile I'll sit here, my toes dabbling the sea of time, making pebbles into piles and shells into circles. One day along will come an enterprising gang of granddaughters, pick them up, kick them over and tell what happened.

1. Women's Liberation and the New Politics

'Women's Liberation and the New Politics' was written in spring 1969 and published by the socialist grouping, May Day Manifesto. It became a Spokesman pamphlet and appeared in a slightly amended form in the first British women's liberation anthology edited by Michelene Wandor, *The Body Politic*', Stage 1, 1972.

When it was written there were only a few small women's groups and not a women's liberation movement. I could not imagine then that learned debates were to develop about the housewife. With hindsight, my dismissal of liberal feminism and condescension towards utopias appears mistaken and oversimple. My description of lesbianism as a retreat is clearly silly. All three indicate fears and defensiveness which were part of my attitudes at the time. The growth of a movement has been a good way of learning.

I have changed some phrases which in retrospect do not read clearly. But I am still tussling with the relation of theory and experience, with how consciousness changes, with the inner and outer bondages, the historical interconnections between socialism and feminism.

The so-called women's question is a whole people question. It is not simply that our situation can only be fundamentally changed by the total transformation of all existing social relations, but also because without us any such transformation can be only partial and consequently soon distorted. The creation of a new woman of necessity demands the creation of a new man.

Recently E.E. Evans-Pritchard pointed out that the position of women and the relationship of the sexes called into question also those between parents and children, brothers and sisters, teachers and pupils, managers and workers, citizens of one country and citizens of another.

'In so far as the problems of the relations of the sexes are not those just of sex as such, but of authority, leadership, control, cooperation and competition, they are problems which occur in every sort of society; and they cannot be solved by an insistence on absolute equality but rather by recognition of differences, exercise of charity and acknowledgement of authority.'[1]

The case is most beautifully put. The domination of women is at once the most complex and the most fundamental of links in the chain. Accordingly

5

in moments of acute social unrest the question of our position leaps to the surface.

Consistently from the right comes the implicit commitment to the smothering of the women's revolt. Our uprising is the most terrible to the conservative, precisely because it is so important for the revolution. The opposition to the women is always more intense than that towards any other group, and it is always expressed in the most hysterical terms. The imagery too becomes sexual almost immediately.[2]

Now while the left has always included 'the women problem' and 'equal rights for women' on the agenda, it has placed them rather far down. There is a hesitancy and a hopelessness about the issue, a tendency to 'if' and 'but' and 'of course'. This is expressed in a curious fear that the subject is 'diversionary'. Of course it is diversionary. It is one of the largest diversions that could possibly be made – the diversion of one half of the human race towards social revolution. Partly the matter is very concrete. It is about 25p an hour and the suicide rate, about nursery schools and legal discrimination. All these need to be studied. But there is another important aspect to 'the women problem' – how it feels in the head. If the external social situation subdues us, it is our consciousness that contains us.

The attempt here is to explore the nature of women's containment, to examine the ways out and to see how these ways out relate to total social transformation. At the same time it is necessary to try and understand the awkwardness with which Marxism has touched upon the situation of women, which of necessity involves questioning the emphasis of some species of Marxism. To think of providing final answers would be absurd. But hopefully it should be possible to begin enquiry.

On containment

The first question is why do we stand for it? The oppressed are mysteriously quiet. The conservative answer is 'because they like it like that'. But the revolutionary can't afford to be so sure. He has learned to be doubtful about the 'happiness' of the exploited. He knows that containment cannot be directly related to quietness. The subordination of women only achieves perspective when it is seen in relation to the mechanism of domination. The way in which we are contained only really becomes comprehensible when it is seen as part of the general situation of the oppressed. In order to understand why those in control stay on top and the people they use don't shake them off it is necessary to trace the way in which the outward relationship of dominator to dominated becomes internalised.

'But they are happy like that.'

'Can't you see they enjoy it?'

Superficially there is a complicity between the subordinated and the authority figure. But this is in fact the mutuality of whore and pimp. They associate because of the way the game is rigged. She continually keeps back a percentage, he continually steals her clothes and beats her to survive. Deceit and violence are the basis of their relationship, and continue to be so until the external situation is changed. However the conception of change is beyond the notions of the oppressed. They are confined within the limits of their imagination of the possible. For the dominated without hope the relationship is habitual. There is neither the memory of a different condition in the past, nor the possibility of difference in the future, but an always world of dominating and dominated without moral belief in change or the means of effecting it.

The oppressed in their state before politics lack both the idea and practice to act upon the external world. Both coherent protest and organised resistance is inconceivable. They do not presume to alter things, they are timid. Life is cyclical, weary, events happen, disaster impinges, there is no rational order in the universe, to the authorities properly belong the business and responsibilities of government. They play dumb and the superior people assume they have nothing to say, nothing to complain of. Those in power conclude their 'inferiors' must be a different order of people. This justifies their subjugation. The impression is confirmed by their inability to take the advantage offered to them, by the shrugging off of responsibilities, by the failure to take initiatives. They refuse to help themselves, they are their own worst enemy. But meanwhile they survive. They are skilled in collaboration and subterfuge. They do not compete, they resort to indirect, sly methods. Like Br'er Rabbit they lie low.

All these characteristics can be detected amongst oppressed groups before they have created a political movement. They are also most common among those women completely dependent on men. The same mistake has been made about these traditional women as the rest. Because they do not articulate their complaints in terms recognised by those in control, they are presumed to be happy.

Women have been lying low for so long most of us cannot imagine how to get up. We have apparently acquiesced always in the imperial game and are so perfectly colonised that we are unable to consult ourselves. Because the assumption does not occur to us, it does not occur to anyone else either. We are afraid to mention ourselves in case it might disturb or divert some important matter he has in hand. We are the assistants, the receivers, the collaborators, dumb, lacking in presumption, not acting consciously upon the external world, much given to masochism. We become sly − never trust a woman − we seek revenge, slighted we are terrible; we are trained for subterfuge, we are natural creatures of the underground. Within us there are great gullies of bitterness, but they do not appear on the surface. Our wrapped-up consciousness creeps along the sewers, occasionally emerging through a manhole. After death, hag-like spirits roam the earth, the symbols of frustrated unfulfilled desires. But in life our spirits are contained.

On the language of silence

The revolutionary who is serious must listen very carefully to the people who are not heard and who do not speak. Unless attention is paid to the nature of their silence there can be no transmission of either memory or possibility and the idea and practice of transformation can accordingly not exist.

Movements develop in the process of communicating themselves. The forms of communicating consequently define considerably their shape and direction. Communication for people who have no name, who have not been recognised, who have not known themselves, is a difficult business. For women it is especially difficult. We have accepted for so long man's image of himself and of ourselves and the world as his creation that we find it almost impossible to conceive of a different past or a different future. MANkind is his, WOMANkind is his, huMANity is his. We have not even words for ourselves. Thinking is difficult when the words are not your own. Borrowed concepts are like passed-down clothes: they fit badly and do not give confidence; we lumber awkwardly about in them or scuttle off shamefacedly into obscurity wondering whether we should do our/their flies up for us/them.

First there is the paralysis. Their words stick in your throat, their setting causes you to flounder. This is of course not peculiar to women. It is part of the common condition of the subordinated. In the 1848 revolution in France the people stormed the Assembly. A fireman adjusted his helmet and leapt onto the rostrum as if it were a roof. The people cheered him and told him to speak. But he stood there dumb, unable to cope with the constructions of those who had been his masters for so long. He was dragged down in shame and disgrace.[3]

There is not only the paralysis, there is the labour of making connections. Theory and the removed language in which it is expressed presents a means of going beyond the immediate. It crystallises innumerable experiences, it puts a canopy over the world which enables it to be regarded as a relating whole. It makes reality intelligible. But this theory is constructed from the experience of the dominators and consequently reflects the world from their point of view. They, however, present it as the summation of the world as it is, their model of existence, ideology, to reaffirm their position. Thus the struggle to take hold of definitions, the tools of theory, and to structure connections, model-building, is an essential part of the politicisation of the oppressed. Without this it is impossible to shatter the hold of the dominators and storm their positions of superiority.

But the struggle becomes a kind of agony. In the making of the working class in Britain the conflict of silence with 'their' language, the problem of paralysis and connection has been continuous. Every man who has emerged through the labour movement expressed this in some form. The embarrassment about dialect, the divorce between home talking and educated language, the otherness of 'culture', their culture. It is happening now in the relations between teacher and pupil in every working-class school. The intensity of the degree of accommodation has varied. It has meant sometimes a stilted borrowing from the culture of the ruling class, even at the point of denouncing their political and economic hold most fiercely; or it has resulted in a dismissal of theory as something contaminated by belonging to the rulers. The persistent elevation of understanding through direct experience has become both the strength and the weakness of British working-class politics. It provides security in the defence of existing strongholds, and weakness in the creation of an offensive strategy.

Similarly relevant is the understanding of the movement of Black Americans.[4] For an oppressed group to successfully challenge those who control them they have to be able to create, to construct a total alternative kind of being. Such an alternative does not drop neatly from the sky. It has to be hewn out through suffering, in struggle, over time, and with thought.

In order to see how this relates both to the situation of woman in a traditional state of complete social dependence and to the situation of the woman in the process of casting off this dependence, it is necessary to consider the ways in which these women understand the world, and the ways in which they communicate their understanding. While such a study requires, in fact, volumes of empirical research, some impressions will have to do for us now. The first mistake of superior people is to equate the silence of the oppressed with stupidity. The second is to assume the 'inferiority' of experience-knowing to theoretical understanding because the former has been associated with those lower down. Those few who rise from the ranks before any cultural or political movement exists tend to fall into a similar misconception. This is not surprising because it was that very instrument of the oppressors, removed language, that enabled them to 'make' themselves. It is necessary both to understand how the oppressed refine and develop their capacity to apprehend directly what is going on, and at the same time to see how this reinforces their defensive outlook on the world.

Most important is observation. If you are safe and sound you don't need to keep a sharp look out and if you have absolute power you don't need to take into account the feelings and reactions of those you control. Consequently the self-consciousness of a dominant class or group increases as they become less confident. As for the weak, they excel in perception. The traditional woman who knows the ways of a man, who can meet him with flattery, who can delight him, will be successful. Her ability to succeed is inseparable from her capacity to excite his desire and to entangle him in obligation. This woman-lore is a delicate art, half imparted by other women, half learned from experience. She attunes herself to him, she picks up the slightest quiver of resentment, nurses his vanity with tenderness, follows the flow of his speech, responds to his rhythm. She accordingly is able to distinguish precisely and exactly the difference between what is said and what is meant – intention does not exist for her in the word alone. After all, what he says with his pants on invariably does not relate to what he does with them off, and the consequences are very real for her. Not surprisingly the weakness of her position makes her unwilling to state exactly how she feels; she takes refuge in ambiguity, cultivates mystery. In response to forthright questioning she becomes devious and dumb. She avoids direct and open confrontation, preferring to get her opponent in the dark. Her tactics are manipulative. She takes pride in her subtlety and her ability to get things from the man deviously. We women have our ways.

To locate this more exactly, think of three characteristics especially associated with women and often regarded as marks of inferiority: giggling, gossip, and old wives' tales. All three make considerable sense in the environment of the dominated. Girls giggle at the moment of taboo. It is a way at once of making a point and of avoiding the issue. It precludes criticism and does not give the game away. A guerrilla tactic rather than a head-on encounter, it irritates in moments of weakness. Gossip provides another important way of perceiving and describing the world. In an underground and rather subversive way it communicates through anecdote. In a more reflective and elaborated form it has become the novel. For the woman dependent on men it provides also a powerful form of social control over the behaviour of other women. Gossip can determine who is within the protection of society and restrict other women from moving over into self-determination and giving the game away. It is specifically directed against any manifestation of liberation, sexual or otherwise, and is designed to prevent women scabs taking on some of the powers of the men. Not surprisingly it is most common amongst the older, more established women and is aimed at the younger ones yet to find a settled place. The greater the institutional bondage, the more gossip becomes a fine art. Related to gossip is the old wives' tale, which presents a series of myth warnings within which forbidden subjects can be contained. This satisfies curiosity and restrains young girls from wandering out of the protected territory of dependent womanhood.

Experience-knowing is thus characterised by symbol, myth, allegory. The dominated can tell stories, they can fantasise, they can create Utopia, but they cannot devise the means of getting there. They cannot make use of maps, plan out the route and calculate the odds. The dominators continue to hold ideology. Thus while the traditional woman is able to defend herself, she is unable to create the conditions which would make such defence unnecessary. Moreover she has no separate identity because she has no way of defining herself or her condition. Experiencing herself in isolation she can only know herself in the situation in which she is put, as object. She has only article awareness. Her highest aspiration can be to become merely his most elaborate commodity, clothes-pegging the proof of his wealth about, or playing intellectual foil to his thinking, her leisure the confirmation of his ceaseless striving to accumulate, her passivity the proof of his ability to subdue the world. This fragmentation, isolation and lack of identity makes it impossible for her to relate her own situation to that of any other oppressed group, or to seek a way out. Trapped, she turns round and repeats the process of domination within her own group. She translates the outer authority inwards, repeating what is done to her by men to other women. The woman of the upper class despises the working woman, the married distrust the unmarried, the old suppress the young. The conflicts between women are well known, the war between wife and mother-in-law, or in polygamy between the wives, or between wife and concubine. Most venomous are the feelings of the dependent toward the emancipated. This causes the free woman to view the rest with a mixture of contempt and fear; she feels at once superior, i.e. more like the man, and insecure, accused of being incapable of being a woman. While feeling more able to fend for herself, she has shed many of the traditional defences, and in a society structured for men can become suddenly very defenceless. If the traditional feminine woman presents no alternative and exhausts herself in internecine conflict, those who become 'free' are at once uncertain of their position and inclined to rush off down blind alleys.

The anxious object[5]

The girl who for some reason breaks away intellectually is in a particularly isolated position. She finds herself straddled across a great gulf, which grows wider, while she is pulled both ways. A most perilous and lonely condition, comparable to that of a black or working-class militant. In the process of becoming interested in ideas, she finds herself to some extent cut off from most other girls and inclines naturally towards boys as friends. They do more interesting things, discuss wider topics. She really defines herself as a boy. Other girls appear curious and rather boring, passive and accepting. She has little to say to most of them. The social contempt in which women are held confirms this. She is constantly being told she is 'quite good for a girl'. Femininity becomes synonymous with frivolity, stupidity and narrowness. It seems obviously better to be a man. Doesn't she feel like a man, do their things, talk their talk? It is natural for her to define her situation in terms of a kind of sub-manness.

The image is constantly reaffirmed. The books she reads and the films she sees are almost invariably by men. The women characters created by them, however sympathetically and with whatever intuitive understanding, must of necessity be the projection of their responses towards women. One is simply not conscious of *men* writers or *men* film-makers. They are just writers, just film-makers. The reflected image of women they create will be taken straight by women themselves: these *characters* 'are' women.

Throughout this process the educated girl probably takes her 'emancipation' as being beyond question, not worth even stating or discussing. The suffragettes happened a long time ago.

Men will rapidly accept her as different, an exception, an interesting diversion. She lives in fact as a man. There might be a hint of strain over her virginity, a flicker of doubt, the discovery of a strange duplicity lurking still in men. But no connection is obvious. She cannot see a condition of women. It is not until she becomes older, grows less decorative, has babies, that the rather deep cracks in the gloss of 'emancipation' appear. She has the rest of her life to explore the limits and ambiguities of her 'freedom'. And what a spurious freedom. We walk and talk and think as living contradictions. Most of us find the process too painful and, not surprisingly, settle for limited liberated areas. We give up struggling on every front and ease into a niche of acceptance. We become the educated housewife desperately searching for dignity and fulfilment through ever more elaborate cooking recipes or constant redecoration schemes, suspicious and defensive about women who are unmarried or women who work. Or the occupational variant of this: doing a womany womanness to a very male style. These two responses are described as mature integration. They are of course simply avoiding the issue in a peculiarly complicit and false way.

Obversely we become the popular (distorted) image of the suffragette. A tweedy, sensibly shod battle-axe with a severe hairstyle and a deep voice, advancing aggressively on the male world and the board room. The sexual corollary of this is the retreat into lesbianism. Both share a profound distaste for the male. Emancipation is doing without men.

Our other retreat is into sexuality. Because women have traditionally been deprived of the power to make 'free' choices, our bodies have been part of somebody else's belongings, we prove that we have control, that we are liberated simply by fucking. But if the definition of our constraint is not extended beyond sexuality we are only entrammelled in a greater bondage. We may not be choosing but reacting, ironically under the compulsion of our real subordination. We could be expressing in our sexual life the very essence of our secondariness and the destructive contradictions in our consciousness, through the inability to meet and communicate and love with a man on every level. The same 'free' woman could still expect men to pay for her, buy her expensive presents. She must of necessity be excessively pre-occupied with her appearance and regard other women's men as fair game. After all she needs constantly the reassurance that she is wanted and beautiful, because only through these is she capable of defining her freedom.

We shelter as well as retreat. We take refuge behind the privilege of class and education, using the manner and accent of the rulers to secure respect and serious consideration: a protected dignity at the expense of the working class, and a protected liberation based on the underpaid labour of an au pair. Most of us live a combination of these or run the whole gamut knowing them for subterfuge – at certain moments struggling through and beyond them all. However they are peculiarly stultifying, peculiarly paralysing. They present neither the possibility for the individual woman nor for women as a group to emerge in a redefined and whole way. They never go beyond confirmation or denial of what men say we are, and they ignore the infinite acceptability, the infinite absorbability of exceptional individuals and privileged elites, from an oppressed group with no real effect on the position of the rest. In their existing form such 'emancipations' can no more provide a means of transforming the situation of women than the dreams of the traditionally dependent women. Consciousness is atomised, the situation is met at the moment of psychological aloneness. The free woman merely exchanges fantasy for neurosis. Schizophrenia and psychosomatic illness are the real expression of her condition. Not surprisingly, too, such a false freedom is never attractive to the vast mass of women, even those whose position of class privilege would attain to it. They see the emancipated woman as a kind of fake male, as someone playing at being a man. They feel a certain revulsion and do not trust her.

In reality the simple 'abstraction' between 'unfree' and 'free', 'traditional dependent' and 'emancipated' cannot be maintained. Under closer examination such polarisation dissolves. Rather like the innocent idea that there are girls you can sleep with and girls you marry, clearly defined categories can only be observed from a distance. Individuals weave between the two poles in an infinitely complex manner, but the freezing of reality in this way helps to indicate what is happening.

On men

Amidst such ambiguity and confusion it is not surprising that men are unsure how to act. There is the assumed superiority but there is also the suspicion of the traditional dependent woman. They notice most women seem incapable of behaving like men and quite naturally assume this implies inferiority. They feel the dependent woman clings to them, that she cannot relate to them in certain ways. They turn to the 'free' woman, expecting to find at once a kind of forbidden fruit and a decent chap. Few women can sustain these roles together. Even if they could there would still be dissatisfaction and unease. The free woman seems to switch from their game back to the behaviour of the traditional woman or she brings competition into bed. He wants her to be independent, but fears she might outstrip him. Such anxieties make even the most benevolent of men unwilling to let go of the certainties retained within their external control of the traditional relationship. The origins of the fears would seem to be partly sexual, partly the terror of dissolving identity – with nothing fixed in the world – but also the whole social pressure within capitalism to compete, to prove yourself by subduing nature, by grappling with existence and in the process dominating others. Men as the makers of the world are subjected to these pressures most intensely. The emergence of women thus creates a tension. Any break-through must occur dialectically. As women's situation becomes more defined, the conditions will be created in which men can clarify more exactly the nature of these fears. At the moment of clarification such anxieties begin to dissolve, and a new process of release will begin for both men and women.

While individual men and women are obviously engaged in this now, in order for there to be a significant shift in the social sense, the beginning of a new series in the process of change, there has to be the intensification of experience which takes place when individuals combine and collectively create their consciousness together. In other words there must be some kind of interaction – discussion and action – interlocking-organisation. If this is not to defeat its own purpose the initiative must come from the group most immediately concerned – women themselves. A movement is thus an essential form of group expression. It is the means of finding a voice.

On breaking the silence

There is nothing like learning from example, apart from doing it yourself. We are fortunate to live in a time when all manner of people who had previously been trodden in the dirt, people with no place in society, people with no right to speak have audaciously lifted up their heads and taken power into their hands.[6] We are thus able to learn from their audacity.

It is possible to trace a dialectic in the breaking of silence. Most important at first have been those amongst the rulers who cut themselves off from their own kind to take up the cause of the 'inferior' people in an ideal or moral sense. For instance, the enlightened aristocrats before the French Revolution, the intellectuals in the Russian and Chinese Revolutions, the white liberals in America. They are able to communicate possibility to the oppressed. Not all of them can withstand the time when the dominated use the tools they gave them *against* them. Some of them retreat. Then there is that section of the subordinated who break away under their encouragement. At first they will be only a few isolated individuals, immediately absorbed within the dominant culture. However, as the rate of migration intensifies, entrance becomes limited, and under certain specific conditions the possibility of a mass movement from below emerges. Such a dialectic can be seen working in the making of the proletariat, in the struggles for national liberation, in the history of the black people of America. An important speeding-up process is the relating of one struggle to another. To know someone else has made it, however far away, can be a most powerful encouragement.

Various phases of consciousness can be observed. First there is the simple moral protest against oppression, as against religion or common humanity. Secondly there is the more material demand of the privileged among the inferior to be allowed to compete equally with the dominant group. This is conceived as equal rights. The oppressed are still able to define themselves only according to the terms of the domination. The black man must still want to be white because white represents power over the world. Thirdly there is the realisation that the real liberation of the oppressed group can only be achieved through the transformation of the economic base and of social relations – i.e. that it consequently affects others who are dissatisfied. This is the discovery of Marxism. Fourthly and closely related is the realisation within Marxism of the interlocking nature of oppressions and the significance of hegemonic control.

In order to locate the situation of women more exactly, it is necessary to examine what kind of movement has been created in the past, what relevance it has now, in the present, and, finally, how Marxism relates to our liberation.

On feminism

It is most important to be clear about the way in which we use 'feminism'. There are two possible interpretations, one ideal, the other historical. Feminism can be seen as the conception of a society in which the roles of dominator and dominated are reversed, and in which women take over the superior status of men. It can also be seen as the demand for equality for women made on religious or ethical grounds: this feminism wants to compete more fairly with men and is expressed in the struggle for equal rights.

Feminism in the first sense is utopian – i.e. it exists in the realm of stories and visions, not as a political movement. Detailed study of the myths would be illuminating. There is for example an Anglo-Norman poem, *Des Grantz Geanz*, probably composed in the mid-thirteenth century. Thirty daughters of the king of Greece plotted to murder their husbands. None of them wanted to have a master and to be in subjection. Each wanted to be her own mistress. Their plot discovered, they were punished by being set adrift in a boat, and arrived very seasick on a desert island. Albine, the eldest, took possession of the land, which was called Albion after her. The sisters learned to trap animals, they grew 'big and fat' and began to want human company. Incubi or bad fairies came to satisfy their needs. These incubi were both invisible and undemanding. Together they bred giants, who flourished until Brutus conquered the island and called it Britain.[7] Again in a Chinese novel written in 1825 by Ju-Chen a hundred fairy folk turned into women and oppressed the men, binding their feet and generally holding them in subordination.[8]

Utopian feminism found an existential gesture when Valerie Solanas tried to shoot off Andy Warhol's balls because 'he had too much control over my life'. Her S.C.U.M. Manifesto (Society for Cutting Up Men) is a kaleidoscopic vision of the ways in which modern capitalism crouches in the inner crevices of the psyche, combined with an acutely myopic political perspective. S.C.U.M. could never get mass woman appeal. For a start S.C.U.M. can't cope at all with sexuality. The S.C.U.M. female has to 'condition away her sex drive' in order to be 'cool', 'cerebral' and 'free'. Nor can S.C.U.M. present anything but the reversal of domination and the elimination of first men and then women. Not much to make a social revolution for. S.C.U.M. gives women the chance to cut off men's balls to fuck up our own cunts.[9]

What about the more sedate kind of feminism? It is possible to trace two phases: the emergence of the religious and moral idea of the individual worth and dignity of women, and the movement for specific reforms, legal, educational, the vote, etc. To relate this more precisely to Britain, the first glimmering assertions were expressed not surprisingly in religious terms. Religious mysticism undoubtedly provided a shelter in a situation where it was impossible to conceive any alternative. For example, Margery Kempe, a fourteenth-century mystic, saw devils after a difficult childbirth, communed with heaven, and subsequently 'never desired to commune fleshly with her husband, for the debt of matrimony was so abominable to her that she would rather have eaten or drunk the ooze and muck in the gutter than consent to any fleshly communing save only for obedience'.[10]

It was no coincidence that the effect of man's questioning his relationship to God created an element of doubt about the nature of his relationship to women. All were, after all, equal in the eyes of the Lord. Within the puritan sect women could find a certain degree of self-expression. But the division of loyalty produced some confusion. Women not only preached and prophesied as handmaidens of the Lord, they divorced their husbands for spiritual deviation.[11] However, the puritan woman was as yet incapable of feminist justification. The women petitioners of Parliament against popish lords and superstitious bishops reassured the gentlemen of the Commons in 1642: 'We do it not of any self-conceit or pride of heart as seeking to equal ourselves with men, either in authority or wisdom.'[12] But by the late seventeenth century on the 'authority' of 'reason and good sense' the case that woman was 'as good as the Man' was being argued.[13] The grounds were now that given a similar external environment women would prove themselves intellectually as capable as men. Not surprisingly this took the form of demanding education. 'Had we the same literature they would find our brains as fruitful as our bodies.'[14] Richardson's novel *Clarissa Harlowe* marks a further stage in this moral revolt. Clarissa resists an arranged property marriage, remains 'pure' despite being raped, and is able to extend her experience with the generalised reflection on 'one half of humanity tormenting the other and being tormented themselves in tormenting'.

Corresponding with Richardson a woman brought the radical nature of his position home to him. Lady Bradsheigh declared the laws of society were made by men 'to justify their tyranny', argued for equality in sex relationships, and said of the views of the Old Testament Patriarchs, 'if they took it into their heads to be tyrants, why should we allow them to be worthy examples to imitate'.[15]

Mary Wollstonecraft's *Vindication*, often taken as the 'beginnings' of feminism, was really the important theoretical summation of this moral phase. Along with William Thompson's *One Half of the Human Race* in 1820 it put the case firmly on the secularised basis of equal rights, though Thompson's work is more radical in emphasis because when Mary Wollstonecraft wrote it was still necessary to justify the woman's right to self-development on the grounds that it would make her a better mother.

While radical theory played an important role, there were good economic reasons for the development of the movement in the second half of the nineteenth century which tried to improve the legal status of woman and enable her to be educated and enter the professions. The increasing prosperity of the middle class released many women from housework into aristocratic leisure. But it also deterred men from marrying young, as the conspicuous display of the household increased. For the unmarried gentlewoman on the capitalist labour market the only hope was to become a governess. The vote seemed the obvious way of carrying into effect a general improvement in the position of women.[16]

There were two crucial weaknesses in feminism in its liberal-radical political phase. First it could not come to terms theoretically with social class. Secondly it could not define itself except in terms of the dominant group. The New Woman was in fact merely the upper-middle-class man in a peculiar kind of drag. These weaknesses made the split with Sylvia Pankhurst and the patriotism of World War 1 inevitable. It was a case of anything they can do we can do better. There was no alternative social vision.

The feminist movement at this stage consequently failed to produce any prospect for a real social emancipation which could include all women, or to create a consciousness through which women could appreciate their identity as a group.[17]

Now

Liberal-radical feminism expressed the way in which women could see themselves in a particular context. But it obscures the real contradictions of the woman's position now. It cannot contain within it the possibility of real change for the woman with a family, it cannot speak for the exploitation of the working woman, it cannot comprehend the process of objectification. It cannot break the silence.

Certainly the struggle phrased in terms of equal rights effected a vital and necessary exposure. It laid bare one level in the structure of domination. But like a snake's skin, as one idea system is peeled off another forms beneath it. Liberal-radical feminism is now only the shrivelled skin of a past reality shed on the ground. It is no good waving cast-off skins. We are concerned with the living creature.

Because of the inadequacies in the liberal-radical feminist approach there has been a tendency to dismiss 'emancipation' as such, to conclude that there is something peculiarly immutable about our position. Instead of course we should examine the real conditions from which change could develop. It is necessary to look more closely at the situation of the housewife in the family, at the position of the woman at work and the means by which women are thingified in the head, here and at this moment, in order to begin to find out what can be done. Such a separation is for convenience only, in fact they are completely intertwined.

Housewife

The housewife is not considered much except by those who want to make sure she stays put. Yet here social secondariness is experienced most intensely. It is here that the real contradiction in the woman's situation is most clearly expressed. Susanne Gail in the Penguin *Work* describes this.

> It was never a burden to me to be a woman before I had Carl. Feminists had seemed to me to be tilting at windmills; women who allowed men to rule them did so from their own free choice. I felt that I had proved myself the intellectual equal of men, and maintained my femininity as well. But afterwards I quite lost my sense of identity; for weeks it was an effort to speak. And when I again became conscious of myself as other than a thing, it was in a state of rebellion that I had to clamp down firmly because of Carl. I also grew very thin and I still do not menstruate.

The pregnant housewife is not only unable to escape from her femininity, she is economically, socially and psychologically dependent on the man – from this point 'free' choice becomes impossible. Think of the social position of the housewife with a family. In order to clear up the confusion it is necessary to place the housewife socially. There is much conservative cant about the respect due to motherhood. Imagine these benevolent gentlemen if all mothers demanded a wage from the state for their important work and threatened a general strike if this was not granted. A hairdressing day-release class, using the criteria of cash and respect, created a model of social stratification:

The Queen
pop singers (various grades)
employers
principal of college
vice-principal of college
teacher
hairdressing students
black people
mothers

It is no coincidence that mothers came at the bottom. Firstly consider the housewife as a producer. Rather than producing marketable commodities her function relates to the development and sustenance of people. Those who make people rather than things are not valued very highly in our society. The relationship to production is connected very closely to the relationship in distribution. This is obscured because the housewife who does not work receives money from the husband. In other words the society pays him to pay her. If the housewife wants to 'improve' herself, she has in fact to 'improve' the situation of her husband. She has to translate her ambition into his person. Thus the respect due to her is delicately adjusted by the respect due to him. The more of herself she pours into her image of him the more she loses herself. The relationship is at once that of economic, social and psychological dependence. It is exploitative: in terms of cash she undoubtedly puts in much more than she receives back. The individual man will vary in what he demands or extracts from the woman in labour, as will her ability to bargain with him personally.

But the exploitation of women at home only becomes clear when it is seen in a social way. The individual man acts as a kind of middleman or channel through to the rest of society. The domestic work of the housewife is socially vital: recognition is shown by paying the woman through the medium of the man. Any individual man – especially the working-class man – is unable to avoid this, whatever his private intention. Both the work situation and social assumptions are too rigid for him to experiment with a different division of labour. Essentially the woman gives her labour to the community and the community gives her nothing in return. She is a social attachment.

In the situation of poverty such reflected 'exploitation' is clear and apparent. In the case of many working-class women it is easy to locate the way in which the family situation reflects in microcosm the deprivation of the man at work. He translates the alienation and frustration he finds in the external world into the home. The woman experiences a reflected alienation. But it is a mistake to conclude that the alleviation of poverty will solve this. Increased affluence merely enables the less immediate problems to emerge. After two centuries of conditioning, teaching us to value worth in terms of money, we are now having to learn that it is possible to have enough money to live comfortably and have no sense of worth. Production for waste does not only apply to things, it applies to people. As modern capitalism devises ever newer and more ingenious waste-disposal schemes a great revolt of the useless begins. Student unrest is only the anticipation of the malaise of vast numbers of lower managerial, white-collar and skilled workers who receive high material 'rewards' but who have little fulfilment or control at work. They spend their time in tasks which do not seem whole, which they do not believe in and cannot take hold of. Such expenditure of self cannot be measured neatly. It is close to the situation of the middle-class housewife. She will actually seek for more and more tasks. She will lose herself in work – either inside or outside the home. This loss of self is the only way in which she can achieve a sense of virtue, of worth. The more she puts of herself into the objects around her, the more the objects come to dominate her. Such alienation will also be experienced by the working-class woman, especially after her children grow up. So far 'welfare' capitalism can only shovel aside the useless who express their futility in neurosis, by putting them into cold storage until they emerge tranquillised.

The woman at home is thus a victim of the reflected alienation of the man's work situation and also of an alienation of her own. Only significant structural changes can radically affect this. The production relations of the man would have to change, the woman would have to be paid directly by the community, and the social division of labour would have to be transformed. Such changes would necessitate social ownership as well as control.

No such total immediate solution can be envisaged yet, but there are specific, concrete ways in which the sheer drudgery and monotony of house-work can be alleviated, and possible means by which women could have more sense of fulfilment and more control over their external environment. There are firstly particular improvements like more nurseries, launderettes, good cheap municipal restaurants in all areas, better housing and imaginative architecture which takes the needs of the people as a prime consideration (look at the space considered necessary for the working class, compared to the space in middle-class areas, as though being working class meant you needed less air to breathe), cheap council flats for teenagers who want to live away from home. Eventually we should make detachable, enlargeable dwellings, because while most people settle in a relatively stable way in couples to bring up children that doesn't mean they want to be falling over one another all the time. Under socialism it should be possible to build for much greater personal flexibility, so the environment would be quite literally both living and moving.

Meanwhile though, 'improvements' are not enough. The important way in which reforms become a means to more substantial transformation is when they are consciously made by the struggle of the people who benefit from them. When women take part in tenants' campaigns, in squatting, in sit-downs for zebra crossings, in demonstrations with dirty washing for more council launderettes, when they organise cooperative playgroups in their street or flats there are the beginnings of the possibility of breaking the silence. It means that people in groups are creating and controlling aspects of their immediate environment. At this point socialism can make sense as the natural and necessary development of such control.

The way in which the family has developed in capitalism is so closely related to the system of production which has emerged through the private ownership of capital and the growth of factories, that certain changes are bound to appear under a system of social control. As the society takes over some of the functions of the individual family this makes possible a changing relationship between men and women. Most important is the independent social security of the woman.

Although we have the advantage of the experience of the socialist countries, these indicate more the complexity of the family relationship and the primitive level of our thinking about it rather than a clear guide. In order to replace it by a more honest way of living we should remember the reasons for seeking to transform it, rather than making a fetish of its form. The objection to the bourgeois family is the necessary dependence and isolation of the woman, the internalisation of the competition and struggle for dominance, the tension and the possessiveness of man and woman directed towards the children. Rather than presenting only the institutional form of the state nursery school, which is by no means a complete answer, we should agitate for innumerable ways of reducing the drawbacks to the family. We should produce a multiplicity of practical schemes for social living, some of which we can achieve immediately, which would at once liberate individuals and enable them to see that a socialist society would mean more choice and would allow people real alternatives.[18]

Worker

It would seem then that any real change for the woman at home would have to be social. It would involve a fundamental recreation of the structure of society and the ways in which people relate to each other. When the position of woman as worker is considered the case becomes conclusive.

Here again the contradiction between the 'role' as woman and the 'role' as sub-man is most marked. The woman has to run the home and go out to work as a sub-man. The more privileged can avoid this by hiring other women, but the working-class woman is forced to carry the double load. An immediate way of lessening this, apart from a determined campaign for better facilities in the home situation, is for the unions to press for a much more flexible attitude to part-time work, convenient hours, for more crêches at work (why not for men as well as women, with time off work to play with the children so the child would have continuing contact with parents of both sexes). As for the future, when we talk about work in the socialist society we should consider in a positive way the breakdown of the specialised division of labour between men and women. It is simply no good to avoid any positive thinking about these things and trust to some magic 'revolution' to create completely new forms of living; the depth of revolutionary change will be considerably dependent on the conscious conceptions and struggles formed in the old society.

The working woman is subordinated both as a woman and as a worker. Her demand for equal pay[19] carries profound economic and social implications. Firstly, it's going to cost someone a lot of money – anything between £600 and £1000 million. The question is, of course, who? Within the terms of the Labour Party's incomes policy, 'equality' would mean a readjustment between men and women workers, i.e. it would be contained within a struggle between two groups of workers divided only by the intensity of their rate of exploitation. It is apparent that equal pay must be phrased in terms of the social redistribution of wealth. Even so the securing of equal pay alone won't solve the problem unless the whole social subordination of women is challenged. This is summed up in the phrases 'women's work', 'girl's work'. When men and women are not working side by side it is possible to define work customarily done by women as work which does not require skill. The other aspect of this is the refusal to admit women into the more highly graded and paid jobs. At Fords in 1968 the Court of Enquiry into the dispute revealed that whereas one man in four was on grade C, only two women in 900 amongst the machinists were receiving pay at this rate. Yet when they went for the job the women had to pass a test on the three machines. If they failed, they weren't employed. Indeed at Fords the real issue was over the question of grading.

The assumption is really that women exist through their husbands, and the whole work situation is geared to this. Consequently innumerable attendant secondarinesses arise. Women on the buses are not only not allowed to drive them, they have to wait five years before they can get sick pay. Men get it after only one year. Similarly the inequalities in training opportunities – only seven per cent of girls enter apprenticeships (predominantly hairdressing), compared with forty-three per cent of boys. Very few girls get day release in Colleges of Further Education. Employers are reluctant to let clerical workers have day release, partly because they can't be spared from the office, partly because they leave quite soon to get married.

Equal pay then is a vital demand, not because it will solve the situation of working women, but because it will expose more clearly the nature of their oppression. The inequality of women at work is inseparable from our inequality in society as a whole. Given our real situation, we have to demand *unequal* rights, i.e. the concept of equality has to leave the realm of moral abstraction and become concretised in the existing social situation. Fords employers justify discrimination against women on the grounds that women have to take time off to have children. Unequal rights has to take this kind of thing into account.

Even when the class disadvantages don't exist, the middle-class women experience a special and peculiar secondariness. The socialisation, education and opportunity for development and expression of women is a preparation for a complementary role. In terms of work there exists great difficulty still in securing jobs which require considerable initiative and responsibility and at the same time are not just extensions of the familial role. Even more significant is the fact that women won't apply for such jobs even when they have a chance of getting them. Part of secondariness is the assumption of it.

Nor is this something that is confined to work. It penetrates right inside the labour movement. There are only five women amongst 151 men trade unionists on the industrial training boards. Half the members of U.S.D.A.W. are women, but only an eighth of the executive. When Lil Bilocca and the fishermen's wives campaigned against the unsafe conditions on the trawlers they met considerable hostility and ridicule.[20] Girls who are students are not at work and relatively free from the domestic situation, but the assumed subordination remains. Glance at any left theoretical journal or go to any large meeting, you won't find many articles either by or about women and you won't see many women speaking. Think of the way women relate to the left groups. Very largely we complement the men: we hold small groups together, we send out reminders, we type the leaflets, we administer rather than initiate. Only a small number of men are at once aware that this happens and take positive steps to stop it. In fact in some cases they positively discourage women from finding a voice. Revolutionary students are quite capable of wolf-whistling and catcalling when a girl speaks; more common though is tolerant humour, patronising derision or that silence after which everyone continues as if nobody had spoken. The girl in the process of becoming interested in socialism is thus often treated as an intruder if she speaks or acts in her own right. She is most subtly once again taught her place. She drops back again, lets go, settles into a movement as somebody's bird. None of this develops confidence. Ultimately this 'politics of the gangbang' cannot secure deep commitment from most women.[21]

In terms of organised power, the militant action of women at work is obviously crucial; the demand for equal pay would be merely paper resolutions unless there was the possibility of grinding things to a halt. But there is also the need for a political campaign for equal pay. This would be most effective if it acted as a means of coordinating industrial activity and circulating information about the various struggles. A respectable main body working through traditional channels would be accompanied by less orthodox action by a smaller group. In the short run, by struggling on specific issues which express the ways through which we are contained, it will be possible to generate a confidence and enable more women to act consciously to change the world. . . . It will also be possible to make reforms of a social nature which will make more obvious the potentialities of a fundamental social transformation. Ultimately this social transformation must be a revolution in both the domestic and the work situation of women. Marxism has customarily gone this far. In the experiments with house communes, the discussion of attitudes to sex in the 1920s, in the real improvements in the position of women in the Soviet Union, in the communes in China, and in the general raising of women's position in Cuba it is possible to see some of the potentialities. But there is still very much to be done.

Structural changes will interact on the way the woman can see herself and call into question the assumption of social secondariness. But unless the internal process of subjugation is understood, unless the language of silence is experienced from inside and translated into the language of the oppressed communicating themselves, male hegemony will remain.

Without such a translation, Marxism will not be really meaningful. There will be a gap between the experience and the theory. This will make a movement impossible, it will lead people to say 'women are reactionary'. By this they mean only that the revolution has proved itself unable to relate to what is happening. Marxism will prove incapable of speaking for the silence in the head, for the paralysis of the spirit. If women are to be convincingly mobilised it is necessary for Marxism to extend into unexplored territory. The struggle is not simply against the external mechanisms of domination and containment, but against those internal mechanisms. It is the struggle against the assumption that men make and define the world, whether it be capitalist or socialist. Unless this is made explicit and conscious, revolutionary politics will remain for most women something removed and abstracted.

Really because the movement which demands at once social revolution and the possibility of creating a new woman is still politically embryonic it is difficult to visualise clearly the means of effecting this. This recent brief experience of revolutionary women's groups provide some clues. Discussion is vital. At this stage this is the way in which the individual woman is able to stop experiencing her situation as neurosis. The confidence is essential too. The decision to exclude men should be made on the basis of the experience of each group. It may be necessary in the early stages for women to discuss the situation without men because their nervous hostility or benevolent patronage are precisely the points at which we become hysterical or dry up through lack of confidence as a group. However there are considerable dangers in continuing on a separatist basis. Some women may simply drop into the 'male' aggressive role. Also the interaction between our situation and that of men under capitalism can be forgotten. The way is not open for men to redefine themselves. This can create a polarisation. Most dangerous, too, is the tendency for us to see our struggle as proving we are as good as men.

This competitive achievement approach is obviously a problem for both the working class and black people, but if it becomes predominant it can eat a movement away. All the competitive and egotistical characteristics of capitalism penetrate the attempt to transform it, and the same authoritarianism, the same projection and elevation of individuals starts to happen. There is danger too, however, in dogmatic opposition to groups which consist only of women. There can be considerable dishonesties at work here. A refusal to explore the real situations of women, a desire to straitjacket our consciousness by a talmudic obsession with the 'correct' texts taken out of their particular historical context. Such a response is frequently one of fear. It is the deep-seated feeling that people have to be school-mastered/mistressed into socialism. Such paternal maternalism is misplaced. A Marxist approach to the situation of women can be justified only on its ability to illuminate our position and the way out, not as some kind of moral imperative.

It is necessary not only to learn more about our social position and the means of changing it: to communicate we have to find the symbols which express our oppression. The Spanish peasants destroyed Virgins in the churches; the Chinese put paper hats on the local gentry; in a more abstract way the exam is a symbol for the student movement. The symbol has to carry a whole complex of experience within it. Thus women in the States located Miss America as a symbol; in Britain we located in a tactical way the Ideal Home Exhibition, the ICA women's exhibition, the Nelbarden swimwear campaign which is based on women experiencing themselves as objects. These express in a fragmentary way some aspect of thingification, women as sex objects, as consumer dustbins, as rarefied art objects, woman as unreal unless she is being regarded by men.[22] Such spheres of consciousness are both intangible and complex. This means they need to be thought out more, not less. Object-consciousness is the common condition of all women, it is our normal state of mind.

A peasant woman in Fan Shen in China said, 'Our husbands regard us as some sort of dog who keeps the house. We even despise ourselves.'

A West-Indian woman in Dalston, London, said, 'We women are just shells for the men.'

An English woman in Guildford said, 'When I'm in the bath it's the only time I'm myself.'

An American girl said, 'Really being a groupie is like borrowing a series of lives from people and thinking you can be them. It's not something you can do.'

It is not a question of simply rational enlightenment. Intellectual awareness of what is going on does not mean object-consciousness dissolves. When I go out without mascara on my eyes I experience myself as I knew myself before puberty. It is inconceivable to me that any man could desire me sexually, my body hangs together quite differently. Rationally I can see the absurdity of myself. But this does not mean I experience myself in a different way.

The naïve belief that institutional change will automatically penetrate the concealed pockets of the psyche, that it is not for Marxists to be bothering their heads about such airy-fairy nonsense, still prevails. Not only does such myopic mechanicalism screen itself from understanding what has happened in the countries which have made revolution, it ignores the explicit warnings of innumerable Marxists. Of course no single idealist liberation is capable of personalising this object-consciousness, of course revolutionary changes in the fabric are essential. The way sexual 'freedom', despite its liberatory implications, has been grotesquely distorted under capitalism is the most convincing proof of this. There is a cruel irony in the way the assertion of the dignity and honesty of sexual love has become the freedom for the woman-object to strip to sell the object-commodity, or the freedom for the woman-object to fuck her refracted envy of the dominator man.

But this doesn't make transformation simple. Modern capitalism beguiles with flickering lights, it mystifies with a giant kaleidoscope. We lose ourselves and one another in the reflected images of unrealisable desires. We walk into a world of distorting mirrors. We smash the mirrors. Only pain convinces us we are there. But there is still more glass. Your nose is pressed against the glass, the object suddenly finds herself peeping at herself. There is the possiblity of a moment of illumination. The feminine voyeur finds her identity as pornography. The 'emancipated' woman sees herself as naked buttocks bursting out of black suspenders, as tits drooping into undulating passive flesh. WHO ME? Comprehension screeches to a halt. She is jerked into watching herself as object watching herself. She is being asked to desire herself. The traditional escape route of 'morality' is blocked. She can either shut off the experience or force some kind of breakthrough.

Revolution must relate to both the means and the nature of this breakthrough. There must be the acceleration of collective demystification accompanied by the conscious dismantling of the external framework, there must be the connection with the experience of the other oppressed groups, there must be a political alternative, a way out which relates to all the groups. Object-consciousness cannot be shattered by individual rationality, it cannot be simply eliminated by external change, it cannot be bypassed by psychological or cultural concentrations. It demands social revolution and it demands it whole. It demands release from the inner and the outer bondages. It is not to be fobbed off with an either/or. Which brings us all back again to Marxism and the whole people question.

On the whole people question

Well, here we all are then, millions of us, our situation demanding a fundamental redistribution of wealth, a profound social transformation in the ways people relate to each other and an end to alienation. Communism is the necessary condition of our freedom. A communist society means having babies in a state of social freedom. It means you don't starve when you're helpless to fend for yourself or have to be a dependent. It means the possibility of such communication that human beings share the pains of labour and the ecstasy of creation. Real comradeship involves the end of subjugation and domination, the explosion of sadomasochism and the climax of love.

However, there are a few inescapable points to be considered before we make it.

The subordination of women cannot be ended simply by reducing it to class or to our exploitation at work. These exploitations are only part of the oppression of some women. The full extent of our oppression is not fully revealed by the isolation of these particular forms of exploitation. The woman question is not comprehensible except in terms of the total process of a complete series of repressive structures. Thus the particular form of domination changes but the process operates in both pre-capitalist and post-capitalist society. The function of revolutionary theory is to keep track of the moving shape of these subordinations. Such a revolutionary theory is compelled to be continually reforming and recreating itself. It has to understand the way capitalism subdues us as consumers as well as workers. It has to follow the particular experience of domination not only of the worker but also of the student. It has to understand the condition of blackness as well as the condition of womanness.

Thus while the working class is undoubtedly the most crucial force in modern capitalism for creating a new society, this does not mean that the specific experiences of other oppressed groups are in any way invalidated. It does not imply they must relate to socialism simply as an abstract idea or merely project their own situation onto that of the working class. Every group has a particular struggle coming directly from the position in which it finds itself. It accordingly has a particular consciousness of oppression.

Not only is it consequently possible to mobilise many more people, it is possible to mobilise them at several levels. Capitalism has to be resisted not only at work but in the home, not only in the institutional apparatus of government but in the head. The revolutionary struggle is thus extended and sustained in a multistructural, multidimensional way. As well as the macro-theory, which is about systems at war, about a mass movement for political power, Marxism has to explore the way human beings relate to one another. This means noticing all the little unimportant things which revolutionary theory tends to regard as not worthy of attention. Like how we live with one another and how we feel and regard each other, how we communicate with each other. We are contained within the inner and outer bondages and unless we create a revolutionary theory of the microcosm as well as the macrocosm we shall be incapable of preventing our personal practice becoming unconnected to our economic and institutional transformation. We will consequently continually lose ourselves in the new structures we have created.

In order to comprehend this it is necessary to replace a mechanical model of social change (base/superstructure) by a complex and interrelated self-regulating revolutionary model. It also means that some forms of action will be directed specifically towards transforming people's perception and comprehension of themselves and the world, as well as being concerned with material change. The so-called women's question is thus a whole people question not only because our liberation is inextricably bound up with the revolt of all those who are oppressed, but because their liberation is not realisable fully unless our subordination is ended. Nor does the particular experience of women speak only for itself. Like the consciousness of all the people who are kept down it brings its own species of implication for the revolutionary struggle. Trotsky's comment on the complaint of Russian working women, 'You only think about yourselves,' is most apt.

'It is quite true that there are no limits to masculine egotism in ordinary life. In order to change the conditions of life we must learn to see them through the eyes of women.'[23]

Such a leap in consciousness would undoubtedly shatter whole layers of comfortable paternal authoritarian assumptions within the revolutionary movement.

But that, comrades, is another story . . .

2. The Beginnings of Women's Liberation in Britain

◆◆◆◆◆◆

'The Beginnings of Women's Liberation in Britain', *The Body Politic*, ed. Michelene Wandor, Stage 1, 1972.

This account was written in 1971 along with unpublished impressions of the emergence of the movement in France, Italy, Germany, Holland and the North and South of Ireland. I had learned a bit about lesbianism in two years, but 'men' still carry 'girls'.

◆◆◆◆◆◆

In the autumn of 1968 vague rumours of the women's movement in America and Germany reached Britain. We had only a hazy idea of what was going on. No-one I knew then had actually read anything which had been produced by the women's groups. All we knew was that women had met together and had encountered opposition within the left. Some of the ideas discussed in Germany and America had already percolated through. In the diary I kept during 1967 there are persistent references to incidents I'd seen and books I'd read from a women's liberation point of view. I can remember odd conversations with women who were friends of mine, and particular very intense moments when I was hurt and made angry by the attitudes of men on the left. But it was still at an intellectual level. We didn't think of meeting consciously as a group, far less of forming a movement. We were floundering around. The organisational initiative came from elsewhere.

A women's rights group formed in Hull in the spring of 1968 around the campaign led by Lil Bilocca and the fishermen's wives to improve the safety of trawlers after two ships had been lost in bad weather in January 1968. Mrs Bilocca had fantastic courage and resolution. She was ready to take anyone on. She said if the ships sailed without proper safety precautions, 'I shall be aboard and they will have to move me by force.' It was unusual to see a woman fighting publicly and speaking, and men on the left listening with respect, tinged admittedly with a touch of patronage. The response from the trawler owners was predictable, a combination of class insolence and sexual contempt. Said the secretary of the Hull Trawler Officers Guild, 'Mrs Bilocca has not enhanced the image the public may have of fishermen's wives. . . . The idea of forming a women's committee to fight battles for the men is to my mind completely ludicrous.'

The wives of the fishermen and particularly Lil Bilocca encountered hostility also from some of the other women and men in the fishing community. Mrs Bilocca received threatening letters and couldn't get a job. Out of this opposition and the connections it had also for left middle-class women came the Equal Rights Group in Hull. Though the working-class women drifted off, it continued as a group and later organised a meeting for all the sixth-formers in the town on women's liberation.

When the sewing machinists at Dagenham led by Rose Boland brought Fords to a halt, it acted in a similar way to make women on the left feel they could do something. The women wanted the right to work on machines in C grade because although they had to pass a test on these machines they could only work on the lower-paid grades. This developed into a demand for equal pay. It lasted for three weeks and received the full glare of publicity: the papers called it the 'Petticoat Strike' and the women received the usual sexual banter which any action taken by women provokes. It imposed a great strain on their personal lives; Rose Boland said she hardly ever saw her husband and son in the whole three weeks, 'they never knew whether I was in or out'. The strike came out of the particular conditions in Dagenham; in Halewood the women weren't so interested. Rose Boland believed that this was because 'they've got a different way of life up there really, up there the man is the boss. Not so much now with the younger generation but more with people of my age. The youngsters of today won't have it, they want it on an equal basis.'

The Fords strike sent a tremor of hope through the trade union movement. Women who had fought hopelessly at TUC meetings for equal pay took heart again. There followed a period of industrial militancy among women workers which has only been sporadically chronicled in the socialist press, and has never been seriously studied. Rose Boland was undoubtedly right when she said, 'I think the Ford women have definitely shaken the women of the country.'

Out of the Fords strike came a trade union organisation for women's equal pay and equal rights called the National Joint Action Committee for Women's Equal Rights, which organised a demonstration of trade union women for equal pay in May 1969. NJACWER's membership was mainly older trade union men and women in the Labour Party and Communist Party, who were often heavily involved in committee work. It remained rather an official body which had an impressive existence on paper but only tentatively got off the ground in practice after the demonstration.

A small group of women in a Trotskyist organisation, the International Marxist Group, went to the early NJACWER meetings and helped to set up the first NJACWER groups. Interest in the position of women had appeared earlier when IMG was called the Nottingham Group. After Juliet Mitchell's article appeared in *New Left Review* they held a joint meeting with NLR. But it was the initiative of the trade union women which meant the IMG women could raise the topic in their organisation without being dismissed. Although they had some connections with the American movement, their approach to the position of women was a traditional Marxist one. They were terrified of being called feminists at first. In Nottingham and London Socialist Women groups were formed and produced a journal, *Socialist Woman*. Not all the women in Socialist Women groups were in IMG, but the journal had a broad Marxist perspective. The first number announced, 'We are not anti-male, a charge often thrown at those concerned with the woman question. We are opposed to private property, the alienation of labour under capitalism, the exploitation of the entire working class, we are opposed to men who do the "gaffer's" job and assist him to do the dirty on women workers – whether in the home or in industry.' (*Socialist Woman*, February, 1969)

The Fords women also helped to make the question of women's specific oppression easier to discuss on the left. At first the men would only admit that working-class women had anything to complain about. Very defensively at first and with no theoretical justification, only our own feelings, women on and around the student left began to try and connect these feelings to the Marxism they had accepted only intellectually before. Out of the first faltering attempts at these connections came an edition of the revolutionary paper *Black Dwarf* in January 1969. There were articles about being an unsupported mother, how to get contraceptive advice, women in trade unions, and Marxism and psychology (by a man) and a thing by me trying to relate how you encountered sexual humiliation to Marxism. They all appear very obvious now, but at the time it was very hard to make the connections, and just having something down on paper meant you didn't feel either a hopeless bitter rage or as if you were a completely neurotic freak. I remember one left man coming up to me and with a pitying air saying he supposed it had helped me to express my personal problems but it was nothing to do with socialism.

Completely separately another group had formed in London. They were predominantly American and in their mid-twenties. Some of them had been active in Camden Vietnam Solidarity Campaign, most of them had husbands who were very deeply involved in revolutionary politics. Many of them too had small children and felt very isolated both as housewives and as foreigners. They started to meet in Tufnell Park and were later to have an extremely important influence, particularly on the London Workshop.

> It was tremendously exciting. We felt like we were breaking through our conditioning and learning new things each week. Maybe small groups have this same experience now, but I think there was probably more tension and emotion because of the newness of it all — no-one else seemed to have heard of Women's Liberation — we were freaks. I used to be exhausted and exhilarated after meetings and used to lie awake thinking — couldn't stop. We argued a lot with each other. We were mostly political, mostly not Marxists because our experience and identification was American new left of the first half of the sixties type, i.e. before Marx and Lenin. I'm glad it was that way. We all felt Women's Liberation at a gut level and for me at least it led to reading (starting to anyway) Marx and Lenin . . . because we were confused and unclear in some aspects of our politics the way was clear for us to admit the truth and feelings of Women's Liberation into ourselves and then try to work it all out. . . . We were really concerned with whether we could change our lives at all in view of our involvement in Women's Liberation. We wanted to be able to break down the barriers between private personal life and public political life. We admired and discussed Helke Sander's statement to the German SDS conference. That piece

also influenced our attempts to organise something for our own children and we met a number of times as adults and as adults with children with German SDS people in Golders Green. (Letter from member of the original Tufnell Park group, June 1971)

Shortly after the issue of *Black Dwarf* came out, the women at Essex University arranged a discussion of women's liberation as part of a revolutionary festival there. The atmosphere of Essex at the time was fraught with impotent isolated revolt. The festival was broken up continually by a group of students who regarded any structured discussion as a violation of their 'freedom'. The meeting on women's liberation was in a lecture hall. There was a very tense feeling around. A man carried a girl in on his back. Someone messed about with the lights. Branka Hoare, who was connected with the *New Left Review*, started to read a paper in a very quiet, nervous-sounding voice. There were occasional interruptions and then a curious silent coalescing of the women in the room. We felt a most profound collective urgency. But we couldn't communicate it very well in the discussion that followed.

At various times it seemed as if the meeting would go over the edge and end in acrimony and ridicule. A very clear intervention by a man from the German SDS describing what had happened in Frankfurt and warning the men not to make the same mistakes was important because it prevented it from being just a women's case against the men. For a moment the women's resentment focused on a man who made a speech about political priorities. He said very self-importantly that in a revolutionary movement you couldn't waste time on trivia, and the fact was that women simply weren't capable of writing leaflets. In the smaller meeting we held later a girl hissed venomously through her teeth, 'I always change his fucking leaflets when I type them anyway.' When we held the little meeting we didn't have any definite commitment to being an all-woman group. A few men came and could be said to have played a historic role. One was a ponderous and patriarchal Maoist who lectured us endlessly on Marxism-Leninism, another was a twitchy young man who said we were like a mothers' tea-party because we kept on giggling.

The next meeting we held we decided not to have men because we wanted to work things out amongst ourselves. One man came in fact to this meeting and kept saying we must have a theoretical reason to exclude him. We said we didn't have one but we were fed up with being told by men what we ought to think about ourselves and them. This meeting was very long and rambling. People were going on about shopping hours and nurseries and Mao on consciousness. There was a girl from the SDS there who told us about the Kinderladen, and people from the Tufnell Park group. It didn't occur to us to form discussion groups just to talk. We were very grandiose about doing things immediately. I don't think any of us realised we were starting a movement.

Three permanent groups started, one in Essex and two in London, including the Tufnell Park group. The first newsletter came out in May. The next issue was called *Harpies Bizarre* and reported response from leafletting the equal pay demonstration and the formation of a group in Peckham. 'Meeting of a group of housewives and students from Morley College. The group grew out of Juliet Mitchell's classes at the Anti-University.' (*Harpies Bizarre*, no. 2, June 1969)

The third newsletter was called *Shrew* and the name stuck, with the principle established that the editing should pass from group to group. This issue reflected the disparate influences which went into the London Workshop. It included accounts of meetings with older feminists and a vehement denunciation of the Maoists in the Revolutionary Socialist Students Federation who had criticised feminism. 'I do not intend to ask permission from Peking before proceeding. I do not intend to neurotically consult Marxengelslenin before baring my teeth or my teats. I do not intend to give ladylike (read suck ass) reassurance to radical chauvinists during the course of this struggle, even if it means losing their friendship (i.e. patronage).' (*Shrew*, no. 3, July 1969)

But in the same issue Irene Fick wrote, 'While fighting for economic and social equality in general, under the present capitalist society, women must oppose male chauvinism and domination in personal life.' Only with the ending of 'class society' was women's liberation possible. The Workshop had from the start a cheerful eclecticism. Any woman was welcome, 'communists, along with Maoists, Trotskyists, syndicalists, Seventh Day Adventists, nuns, anarchists, Labour Party members, etc., in short feminists.' (Irene Fick)

The women who came in fact tended to be young housewives who were only mildly left-wing. But there was at least one link with an older feminist tradition. A woman of 78 who was a pensioner wrote in the September *Shrew*, 'It has been pointed out that no exercise of power is ever relinquished voluntarily. It always has to be overcome by overwhelming force – not necessarily physical force, but the force of public opinion. In my view it is futile for women to rely on men to fight their battle for them. They must do it themselves – even at the risk of being dubbed "battle-axes" or any of the traditional moves to discourage revolt.'

When the Tufnell Park group produced *Shrew* in October '69 they raised questions which have continued to be discussed by many other groups since. They presented them in conversational form. They hinged on the old problem of how explicit the aims of any organisation on the left must be.

'Do we present ourselves as socialists? I think we should work with women in any action which is relevant to them as women, not necessarily as socialists.'

'No, this could lead to manipulating people: it is using a common problem to mobilise people under false pretences. To organise as many people as possible at the expense of hiding half our ideas is dangerous and is ultimately going to backfire.'

'We have to make it explicit from the start that women's common problems can only be solved by means of a radical social change in the framework of the existing system.'

'If we had a mass movement of women who were aware of their common problem, but never got beyond that, I wouldn't be interested in them as a political movement. Women have to understand the causes of their oppression. . . . Women have to believe that revolution is necessary for themselves, not just for some abstract group of people called the working class. They have to feel that they are part of it, and that they can participate.'

The Workshop remained open and theoretically only vaguely defined. There was an instinctive emphasis on politics from below, a trust in personal experience, a suspicion of theory, and a belief in the small group as a basic organising point.

By this time other groups had started in other towns. There was a Socialist Woman group in Nottingham, for example, and a group in Coventry which had originated in the University but spread to include some working-class women on a local council estate. In autumn 1969 a few of us held a completely informal meeting at Ruskin College in Oxford during a meeting on working-class history, to suggest having a similar meeting on women's history. An American girl from Coventry who was in International Socialism said we shouldn't have an academic history meeting but a general meeting on women's liberation. We planned this for February 1970 and met several times in London to organise, though a small group of women in Oxford bore the main strain.

We thought perhaps a hundred women would come. In fact more than 500 people turned up, 400 women, sixty children and forty men, and we had to go into the Oxford Union buildings because Ruskin was too small. I'd never seen so many women looking so confident in my life before. The night we arrived, they kept pouring into Ruskin with bags and babies. The few men around looked rather like women look at most large predominantly male meetings – rather out on a limb. The reports on the Friday evening session were the most interesting, because you felt part of a movement for the first time. This was captured again in the Saturday evening workshops but tended to go during the very large open sessions when there were papers on the family, crime, work, and history. The National Coordinating Committee was set up with a very loose structure in order to circulate information round the groups. (This was dissolved at the national conference at Skegness in September 1971 and replaced by a more workable structure.)

It was really from the Oxford conference in February 1970 that a movement could be said to exist. The earliest activities had been propagandist and educational, speaking in schools, leafletting the Ideal Home Exhibition, demonstrating outside the Miss World competition in 1969. During 1970 all the new groups faced the problem of sudden growth, combined with rapid turnover of membership. Inevitably this forced the organisation of groups, informally, upon a few women who came regularly. There were very few women with experience in organisational initiative. Even the ones in political groups had tended to take action on the cue of the men. We went off into leafletting-type political work very quickly, often as a result of the enthusiasm of apolitical women to do something, and the guilt impressed on the Marxist women about simply talking to other middle-class women.

In contrast to America where the movement in some places became very inward-turning because of exhaustive consciousness-raising, in England we rather overreacted against this and have never built up the independent strength they achieved. We have not solved the problem of translating the personal solidarity of the small group into external action either. We made obvious beginners' mistakes. The Sheffield group, for instance, gave out leaflets on contraception at a factory gate at six in the morning. Not surprisingly, the women teased them mercilessly, 'Sex at this time in the morning. You must be joking.' York organised a meeting on equal pay without contacting trade union women thoroughly first. Nobody came.

Although the movement is nationally committed to four demands, equal pay, improved education, twenty-four-hour nurseries, free contraception and abortion on demand, action for these, apart from the demonstration of March 1971, has been very localised and groups have taken up issues as they came up. The Liverpool group for instance was involved in opposing the Catholic lobby for making abortion illegal. Birmingham worked with the Schools Action Union to support the woman school teacher who was sacked for appearing masturbating in a sex education film for schools. The initiative for the four national campaigns came from the Socialist Woman groups and the Women's Liberation Front (Maoist). They were concerned that the movement would disintegrate into 'psychological' discussions of problems. The difficulty about these campaigns was that they didn't grow out of real organisational developments from below. They floated down from documents prepared by little groups. They are handy as answers for us when we don't know how to reply to the question, 'But what do you want?' But they did not come from any understanding of how our movement had come into being and what our strategy should be. Instead we found ourselves caught between being a new movement which is still essentially for mutual education and propaganda and, at the same time, a movement trying to organise without any explicit theory, of where our strength lies within capitalism and thus of how we can act, how we relate to other left groups, what is distinct about the ideas in women's liberation. It is true, of course, that you learn too through doing. But it takes time to collect and circulate information and experience from which to draw any conclusions. We are only just beginning to establish ways of getting information through.

Although the first groups tended to consist of students, later on they became less important. The women who have joined tend to be still predominantly middle class, in their twenties and thirties, housewives and white collar workers. A few groups include men – Liverpool and Leeds for example. The real growth came after the demonstration in March 1971. Groups have formed more slowly in Scotland and Wales. Many of the women who join have no previous political experience and only very vague political ideas.

All the revolutionary left organisations have had an awkward relationship to women's liberation. The personal and emotional emphasis and its middle-class membership put them off. But its growth and its appeal directly to the women in left organisations, often almost despite themselves and against all their training, makes it difficult to ignore. From the start a small group of Maoists, almost exclusively based in the London area (Women's Liberation Front, later Union of Women for Liberation), and the IMG women in Socialist Women groups, of which there are several throughout the country, have each worked as an organised political tendency in women's liberation. The Maoists have been the least successful. Their somewhat talmudic approach to Marxist texts and their intense conservatism about any new idea for fear of dogmatic heresy have meant that they consistently fail to communicate. Their initial strength lay in their zeal for attending committee meetings, and their prolific duplication of unintelligible documents which terrified people into believing they must be very high-powered because they were so difficult to understand. The IMG women have worked more flexibly and have consequently gained more support. They have had a strong activist emphasis which has attracted people, and they stressed the importance of working with women in industry: their meetings are relatively formal. It is evident, however, that there are certain tensions between being members of an international Trotskyist organisation and being members of the unaffiliated Socialist Women groups, whose members are united simply by accepting the name 'Socialist'. This has already produced a split in the Socialist Women groups, and it raises the whole question of an organisation with its politics clearly formulated working as a tendency in an ill-defined movement.

International Socialism, a semi-Trotskyist group, and the Communist Party haven't encountered this problem as explicit tendencies because their members entered women's liberation as individuals without official backing. The official attitude in IS has shifted from joking incredulity to grudging support. The change has been a result of pressure from IS women, at first only a handful, mainly in Coventry and London, who argued for women's liberation from the start. The initial response was to OK political activity with working-class women and an admission that women weren't playing their full role in the organisation of IS. But as more women got involved they have started to push the implications of women's liberation home. At the first IS women's conference in summer 1971 the question of how revolutionary organisations should relate to movements like Women's Liberation, of the connection between sexuality and personal attitudes to political consciousness, and of the lack of any Marxist analysis to explain the position of women who work as housewives were raised.

Within the Communist Party there was more attention to women's issues, and more of a tradition of a limited kind of emancipation, than in the more recently formed Marxist groups. There is a women's organisation and a women's organiser in the Party. But the official line tended to favour safe questions – equal pay, nurseries – and avoid any discussion of the family or sexuality. When a small group of young women in the Communist Party raised these issues they provoked uproar but also gained quite a lot of support, and controversy trickled into the *Morning Star*.

Unfortunately, most working-class and trade union women know about women's liberation mainly from the media, except in particular cases where people from women's liberation have supported them, as in the Night Cleaners' Campaign which started in autumn 1970. The only way their suspicion can be broken down is by us explaining ourselves and giving them practical support. At present women's liberation as a movement is very mysterious to them. They have noticed it seems to grow, but it rarely enters their lives in the shape of people they know. Many of them have been campaigning for equal pay and nurseries for years and feel understandably suspicious of publicity suddenly given to young, middle-class women. At the same time, women's liberation has communicated itself rather as a symbolic slogan of defiance, particularly to young working-class girls.

Sandra Peers who is in IS describes a discussion at a TUC school in Newcastle on equal pay when women's liberation was raised.

> All the women had doubts about it, and some were very hostile. By the end most were won over, though I doubt if any of them will ever join women's liberation organisations for reasons of time as much as anything. . . . Their chief objections were the glorification of outside work as a means of liberation, the anti-men image and the bra-burning image – most of which derive from TV interviews rather than from actual positions taken within Women's Liberation. The chief argument that won them over was that it is largely the attitudes of women (and, to a lesser extent, men) to women's role in society that holds back militancy, and most of them eventually agreed that Women's Liberation had at least got a useful propagandist role to play in getting at these attitudes. One thing that rather surprised me was the extent to which the women accepted without any show of concern that monogamous marriage and the present family structure are on the way out, and supported abortion on demand. And half of them agreed with it. (Report on a TUC weekend school on equal pay, *IS Women's Newsletter*)

It has been easier in America for women's liberation to relate and develop in practical activity with other movements. In Britain the student movement was collapsing as women's liberation started, and the Vietnam Solidarity Campaign was already dead. The real political initiative has come from the labour movement, in the struggle against the Industrial Relations Act, and opposition to unemployment and wage cuts, in which the Communist Party had the most influence but where even the small revolutionary groups were better equipped to intervene than women's liberation. The structure of women's liberation serves an educational propagandist function but is difficult to mobilise. Also it is almost impossible to act in a concerted way without any clear agreement of what your aims are. The fact that working-class opposition to the Tories' economic policies is predominantly male makes it more removed from the experience of women who are not left-wing in women's liberation. Accordingly the response has been limited to supporting demonstrations, organising meetings to discuss the Industrial Relations Act, or trying to communicate to working-class housewives about trade union rights and rising prices. Particularly the Northern groups though are aware of the way in which the economic situation is going to affect women's militancy, especially at work.

Gay Liberation started in England in the autumn of 1970. It was started by two men and influenced strongly by the American movement. The men took the initiative and tended to dominate the movement in the early meetings. As it grew, some of the women decided to meet on their own as well, although other gay women opposed this, identifying with the men. Unconsciously the men manoeuvred the women, just as the straight gay world in prison reproduced 'masculine' and 'feminine' characteristics in relationships between people of the same sex. Gay women are in a complex and intricate dilemma.

> We share the experience of our gay brothers but as women we have endured them differently. Whereas the men in GLF (Gay Liberation Front) partake of the privileges of the male — you have been allowed to learn to organise, talk and dominate — we have been taught not to believe in ourselves, in our judgement, but to act dumb and wait for a man to make the decisions. As lesbians, 'women without men', we have always been the lowest of the low. Only through acting collectively can we overcome our own passivity and your male chauvinism so that together we — the whole of GLF — can smash the sexist society which perverts and imprisons us all. WE'RE WOMEN. WE'RE LESBIANS. WE'RE OPPRESSED. WE'RE ANGRY. (*Come Together*, Gay Liberation Front, Women's Issue)

At the same time women in GLF feel uncomfortable often in women's liberation because straight women are suspicious and afraid with them. They have also noticed a 'liberal silence' which opens up whenever a gay woman starts to speak. This is how a member of the first lesbian group in the British women's liberation movement put it.

> One of the great aims of women's liberation has been sisterhood. All women are oppressed so all women must join together. Given this view lesbianism can be seen as particularly important or attractive because it can be viewed as the epitome of sisterhood — women completely together. It is important for women to learn to love and trust each other because like other oppressed people we have been divided against ourselves, taught to denigrate each other and so ourselves. However, sisterhood cannot be an end in itself. So more and more women come together, so there are more and more sisters — so what?
>
> There is also the temptation for straight and gay women to think that by being or by becoming gay they achieve a more revolutionary position. But abandoning the privilege of the oppressors, in this case the straight world (in all senses) is of itself no more revolutionary than going into holy poverty, dyeing one's skin black, or putting on a donkey jacket and spitting on the floor to kid yourself you're a worker. . . .
>
> I think one's relationships with other people, and the sexual responses must be an integral part of all other responses, must spring out of one's relationship to society. And basically the question here is whether the relationship is one of attack or passive surrender. One is not attacking the system by hopping from one oppressed category to another.

3. Diary in the Life of Sheila Rowbotham

'Diary in the Life of Sheila Rowbotham' was published in the socialist feminist paper, *Red Rag*, in 1968. It is based on a diary I kept between 1967 and 1969. It is more personal than the account of the origins of the movement. It is still a vexed question as to when the personal is political or the personal remains personal, and how the personal connects with the political.

I decided to base my account of 1968 on a diary I kept spasmodically between 1967 and 1970. But reading it over I felt that the demarcation I'd remembered between 1967 as an inner year of exploration and the external explosion of 1968 was too simple and that for me 1968 had already begun in the autumn of 1967.

I wrote there was a big anti-Vietnam demonstration that October of 'grown-up CND'ers' and strikes at the Barbican of building workers. Both had a new mood of militancy about them.

I was surprised at how many comments I'd scattered through it about myself as a woman. Juliet Mitchell's article *Women! the Longest Revolution* had appeared in 1966. But these were more personal and confused.

In October I wrote of a relationship with a man I had begun to love in the spring of 1967.

'*Our non-communication lately has been total. I find it quite impossible to talk to him. I feel he has deliberately made that so. My words freeze and congeal in the air. He feels our thing to be exploitative. I am masochistic and suicidal, he is an imperialist, a colonizer.*'

Then again in December I'd evidently seen the film 'Room at the Top' again. The book had affected me much earlier because it was set in parts of Yorkshire I'd grown up in. This time I was irritated by the narrow options of womanhood presented by John Braine, '*State of being a woman seen through the eyes of men.*' This is so obvious now, but then it was a struggle for me to see this.

Looking back after eleven years, I may be marginally wiser but I feel much more tired – especially after nineteen months with a non-sleeping infant. Even allowing for age and sleeplessness I seemed then to have had an enormous sexual energy and an incredible ability to maintain infinities of emotionally fraught relationships with men.

I was aware of the false option of 'free' fucking. I felt this involved me in '*A kind of inverted devaluation, a tendency to use some men for simple physical needs. How far emancipation simple inversion of men's attitudes? Conflicting thing to be as a man. Why do I want to be like you?*' A persistent inability of several men I fucked with to get erections made me question my breezy matter of factness which would be called sexist now.

But I thought the two women who had been my closest women friends were becoming enmeshed through the hippy movement in another false option of becoming goddesses, princesses in the high tower. Yet I could see we were all dependent on men though not economically.

There was no sense of a conscious relationship with other women as a group then. It seemed to me that most women asserted a limited area of independence but within the 'attributes given by men'. Women like me and my friends were able to *observe* this but we could find no way out. We were in a men's world and thus helpless and cut off from most other women. There is the beginnings of recognising some shared predicaments among us 'observers' though.

'*Only our kind who operate in men's world can acquire a marginality which makes it possible to ascribe limits and areas to the assumptions somehow inherited. We become in fact half men.*'

This was the price of observation, denial of our womanhood. My last comment at the end of the year was, '*I would HATE to be anyone's* wife.'

Early in January 1968 I noted that during a Vietnam Solidarity Meeting in Hackney, the men talked to one another not to any of the women. My two close women friends told me they'd 'always felt subordinated to men. If they didn't they found the men a drag.' I felt shocked and isolated again. But I wondered if I was only passionate and assertive about equality in my relationships with men because I concentrated all my feelings of subordination into sexually handing over my body without my head in fucking. In my fantasy life subordination had a dark masturbatory hold.

I became preoccupied with trying to find a pattern in these masochistic masturbatory fantasies and menstruation. I'd been reading Karen Horney that January. I tried reversing my fantasy male-female roles but didn't seem too convinced.

The seriousness of external events seemed undeniable. But I felt deeply alienated from the sectarian left. I couldn't bear what I expressed in images of 'hard-backed', 'sheathed in correctness', 'waxwork cadres'. Nonetheless force of circumstances was pulling me back into the left.

On May 1st some dockers spat at me and a socialist woman friend, when we tried to give them anti-racialist leaflets. They surged towards us behind a police cordon with such hatred I think they would have torn us apart if they could have got to us. But they were only a hard core of intransigents. Another old docker who was active in a tenants association was sincerely upset. He wasn't a racialist he told a middle-class Indian student. But you could only 'fill a cup so far'.

I spoke very badly at an anti-fascist meeting through a megaphone in Ridley Road Market the following Saturday. We all had to take our turn. I had no gift for street talking. The megaphone was not for me. There must be more effective ways of communicating. I started talking to people about this including a teacher at the Further Education College, who came from Northern Ireland. 'Back projector screens in vans,' he kept saying. We got very excited about how socialism had to be a 'social movement', not just political groups propagandising.

After this conversation I began talking to other people. There appeared to be something in the air. It seemed suddenly possible to act clearly and turn socialist ideas outwards in all kinds of ways.

I also became involved in the new paper *Black Dwarf*. I thought the *Dwarf* could become a socialist paper which would not express sectarian positions. I was enthusiastic – posting the early copies and selling it. In the excitement after the French May Events I was beginning to meet new women friends who were socialists. Some of us were to travel into women's groups together. These new friendships were very important to me because of the sadness of my earlier friendships breaking. Part of the breaking had been about the choices between inner and outer journeys.

I felt a much deeper pull outwards. It was 'a sense of significance outside myself'. It was as if the power of people to act together in Vietnam and France was transmitted. I realised my own actions were important. We were all capable and responsible for our politics. I think such a feeling was peculiar to 1968 – perhaps a faint glimpse of what must be the subjective experience of a revolutionary process which is why people with revolutions in their history can rise more easily than those without.

Towards the end of July I banished my distrust of left groups in a rhyme.

> Comrade, comrade through your teeth
> Talk of life and growth and love,
> The revolution's all sewn up
> Your tendency has got the brief.

And I joined I.S. (not a very successful recruit).

In September I wanted to cut all my hair off and wear no make-up. I went off and spent money buying clothes. Still when I met a man I'd lived with for whom I felt affection, but no longer love I felt *'a terrible internal friendship. It was as if I'd been his wife.'*

So I had been a wife after all. But I'd not seen I had.

I'd noticed that in the rows which marked the end of this relationship with the man I'd lived with 'this blind dissolving suffering panic which came in those rows with my father. The same inability to retaliate with aggression.

The same inturning of the feeling which might have been aggressive into myself and consequent sapping of the centre emotional core.'

Another kind of estrangement and sadness occurred with older socialists I knew who felt we were irresponsibly playing with violence and that this would have dangerous consequences.

On October 27th there was the enormous demonstration in support of the Vietnamese liberation front. I was moved at the 'flags flickering over Waterloo Bridge'. I went to Hyde Park not to Grosvenor Square.

There had been the Equal Pay strike at Fords and a trade union group to fight for women's rights was formed. There were arguments on *Black Dwarf* about women. A suggestion was made that we should put in pin-ups to increase sales. I was upset and wrote an angry poem I pinned on the wall.

It was decided to do an issue of *Black Dwarf* about women. I was coopted onto the editorial board. Fred Halliday was asked to be responsible for collecting articles because he knew about Reich. I assisted him with such zeal I collected all the other articles and wrote one myself in a burst of feeling after one of the most sensitive of my engineering students told me he would only marry a virgin.

I felt something changing in my conversations with women friends towards this time. There was a pent-up intensity. One friend told me revolutionaries made her want to cry. I knew what she meant but it was muddled for me with affection.

After *Black Dwarf* came out early in 1969 it began suddenly to be possible to express feelings which had been private before. Small groups of women had been talking to one another already. We were suddenly together. It felt as if all that blocked love and understanding could flow outwards. But that – as they say – is another story.

4. Oh Watch the Ways of a Man

◆◆◆◆◆◆

'Oh Watch the Ways of a Man' was written in a bad temper in 1968. Perhaps it might serve now as a homily for the young — but I doubt it. And me? I've certainly grown in wisdom. I wouldn't sleep in a bath again. On the other hand. . . .

◆◆◆◆◆◆

He came very late with an old black hat,
'There's no place in my bed,' he said.
'We could meet next week,
but there isn't a seat,
I've a Liverpool girl
and I can't take two,
so that means I leave you.'

Refrain
Oh watch the ways of a man
If you can
Oh watch the ways of a man.

The following week we managed to meet
the Liverpool girl was there.
'I've got a disease and ruptured knees
and too many girls to possibly please,
I'd turn you out
but you'd probably shout,
so you might as well stay here.'

Oh watch the ways of a man
If you can
Oh watch the ways of a man.

Well I lived in the bath for a day and a bit
and finally figured it was time to split
Then he wrote and told me to stick around
Perhaps one day he'd be coming to town.

Oh watch the ways of a man
If you can
Oh watch the ways of a man.

49

5. The Little Vanguard's Tail

◆◆◆◆◆◆

'The Little Vanguard's Tail' is an anti-Leninist joke, unpublished, written 1968 or 1969.

◆◆◆◆◆◆

Once upon a time there lived a little vanguard. It was only very small but it was very hard. It was so tightly packed with cadres that there was no room at all for revision or deviation. No sinister ideas from outside ever penetrated inside the vanguard. All the cadres were carefully streamed and graded and taught not to step out of line. Consequently the vanguard was always extremely pure and correct. Sometimes there were bits who broke away. But they always ended up by deviating or revising something or other and the little vanguard used to shake its point over them. 'No-one is as correct as the vanguard,' it would say to itself.

Nonetheless sometimes the vanguard became lonely. It would sometimes long to put its bottom up and give its point a rest and not bother to penetrate or inject correct ideas anywhere. It got so puffed raising the level of consciousness. In moments such as these the vanguard thought how nice it would be to go all soft and floppy and not poke or pull at all. But where would a soft floppy vanguard get you? It might even find itself mistaken for a tail and start to wag or straggle. Everyone knew that any self-respecting vanguard had to be hard. A floppy vanguard was a contradiction in terms.

The vanguard's job was to poke about until it found some unorganised lumps and clusters. Then it had to inject them with the right ideas and turn the people in the lumps and clusters into cadres. Unfortunately the people were often unresponsive. They did not want to become cadres or receive the correct ideas. The vanguard got blunt with all the poking and injecting. It became lethargic and developed lassitude. It was obviously suffering from routinisation.

One day there was a terrible rumbling among the cadres. Splits were appearing in the vanguard – the cadres were no longer so tightly packed. One lot were completely fed up with the lumps and clusters. 'Where do we get with all our poking and prodding? We get puffed and blunt. The lumps and clusters never move. They just sit in a lump watching TV. It was alright for all those vanguards in the past. The masses weren't so dozy in those days.'

These cadres became nostalgic and went off to join the ruling class.

Another lot started to send each other papers on organisation. They began to question the structure of the vanguard.

'You better watch out with that kind of talk,' said the top cadres. 'If you're not careful you'll find the vanguard will disappear altogether and where would we be then, indistinguishable from any old lump. If there's anything worse than a soft vanguard it's one that's lost its cadres.'

But the bottom cadres were very determined and started to say they didn't see what was wrong with people in lumps and clusters. They'd been there themselves after all. If the vanguard stopped being quite so snooty and stuck up perhaps the lumps and clusters would be a bit more helpful.

After a top cadre meeting at the highest point of the vanguard the following statement was issued.

'A threat to the top cadres is a threat to the whole vanguard. The whole existence of the vanguard has been challenged by adventurist, centrist agents of the swamp. Now at a time of crisis for the whole movement of lumps and clusters certain cynical elements are playing on the political immaturity of the bottom cadres to get them to say they no longer should be bossed around by us. Comrade cadres the struggle intensifies, the swamp gets wetter. The time has come for the vanguard to cease being merely a poker and become the puller. We must change from propaganda to active intervention. We have a long haul ahead. But you are fortunate, comrade cadres, in having our leadership. Those lumps and clusters are useless without us. We the vanguard are going to drag them off on the correct path.'

This shut the bottom cadres up for a bit. It sounded like hard work but it was something new. Anyway how could they argue with the top cadres? They had no-one who knew what to do at the highest point of the vanguard. They also felt rather important having to drag the lumps and clusters out of the swamp — even if they weren't as important as the top cadres if they kept their mouths shut and stopped asking awkward questions they might become correct enough to get promoted.

And so the vanguard turned to the lumps and clusters and started to tug and pull. 'Ow,' said the lumps. 'Leggo,' said the clusters. 'Bugger off you snobby lot,' shouted the lumps and clusters. 'It's for your own good,' said the cadres, 'You're an ignorant lot too brainwashed to know your own interest. We're raising you to a higher level.'

'Look here,' said a group from the lumps. 'We don't want to make trouble. We let you poke us about. But we're not going to be dragged off by you without knowing why or where we're going and without having any control over what happens. Keep an eye on your vanguard we say. Vanguards can get out of hand.'

'Economism,' barked the top cadres. 'Lumpism.' 'They're right,' chirped up a commune of clusters. 'We groove with the lumps. We've had our disagreements in the past and we don't dig their life style but we don't want a vanguard.'

'Petty bourgeois anarchism,' hissed the top cadres quivering with rage at the highest point of the vanguard, top heavy with correction.

More communes of clusters spoke up. 'We're not as solid as the lumps. But we're more mobile. We can get out of the swamp with a little help from the lumps, we're willing to accept that even the most hardened cadres can become people again. We're willing to work together but not with top cadres bossing us around.'

So the lumps and cluster entered an alliance. 'Opportunism,' bellowed the top cadres. 'Lumps and clusters are useless without a vanguard. The way through the swamp is dangerous and wet. In order to get anywhere you have to be hard like us. Without a vanguard to lead you, you're bound to come to a sticky end. Clusters and lumps easily sink into the swamp.'

'But if you're our leader and we don't know what to do we'd be in a worse mess than ever stuck out in the middle of the swamp. Very exposed,' said the lumps.' 'Quite so,' said the clusters.

Some of the bottom cadres started to mutter again. 'They've got a point there, you know. If we all got together we needn't be so hard and poky all the time. We could be a bit squelchy and squashy sometimes. More human altogether. After all, when there's a movement of lumps and clusters the vanguard can always become people and join in like anyone else.'

WILL THE TOP CADRES INJECT THE RIGHT IDEAS INTO THE BOTTOM CADRES? WILL THE BOTTOM CADRES BE ABSORBED BY THE LUMPS AND CLUSTERS? WILL THE LUMPS AND CLUSTERS MAINTAIN THEIR UNPRINCIPLED ALLIANCE? WILL THE TOP CADRES DIVE INTO THE SWAMP? WILL THE LUMPS AND CLUSTERS GAIN THE RIGHT TO MAKE THEIR OWN MISTAKES AND LEARN FROM HISTORY? WILL THEY GET OUT OF THE SWAMP? WHAT KIND OF LIFE WILL THEY MAKE OUTSIDE THE SWAMP?

THERE IS NO QUICK ANSWER TO THESE QUESTIONS. THE TAIL OF THE LITTLE VANGUARD IS VERY LONG INDEED.

THIS IS A SHAGGY VANGUARD STORY. GET ORGANISED AND WORK OUT THE END FOR YOURSELF.

OH AND KEEP AN EYE ON THOSE VANGUARDS. VANGUARDS GET OUT OF HAND.

6. The Sad Tale of Nobody Me

'The Sad Tale of Nobody Me'. Poem written in the winter of 1969 to ease sadness. It was published in *Cutlasses and Earrings*, ed. Michelene Wandor and Michele Roberts, Playbooks 2, 1977, and later in *One Foot on the Mountain, an Anthology of British Feminist Poetry, 1969–1979*, ed. Lilian Mohin, Onlywomen Press, 1979.

who told me to paddle my own canoe
into the sewer

of once begun
who told me too many cocks collide
into the pantry
and make some jam

who told me the gift horse
spits in your face
who told me his cock
chops into my head
in for a sheep and in for a lamb
grab the penny and grab the pound
make a ring and all go round

nobody's world is falling down
and nobody told
so nobody knew
while nobody paddled her own canoe.

7. Woman's Rights

◆◆◆◆◆◆

'Woman's Rights' − an account of the Equal Pay Now Demonstration organised by the National Joint Action Campaign Committee for Women's Equal Rights. It appeared in the socialist paper, *Black Dwarf*, 1 June 1969. The action of working-class women was part of the inspiration of the women's movement in Britain, something that is in danger of being forgotten. Even though the women who joined women's liberation groups were mainly middle class, they were preceded by the mobilisation of trade union women, just as black liberation in the US influenced the emergence of the women's movement in that country.

◆◆◆◆◆◆

There was a march from Temple tube to Trafalgar Square. The sight of this far from typical demonstration aroused considerable interest amongst on-lookers not only because it was headed by a pipe-band but because of the pre-dominance of women. In Trafalgar Square drenched figures stood resolutely under a canopy of umbrellas listening to the speakers, who included Agnes McLean, AEF shop steward from Glasgow, Rose Boland from Fords. Christine Page, Audrey Wise from USDAW, Ernie Roberts and Fred Blake from the AEF and NUUB were there too to extend solidarity to the women in the struggle for equal pay. AEF, USDAW, SOGAT, NUUB banners were on the plinth. The speakers stressed how half of the women employed are getting less than 5s an hour, how there are 4 million women getting less than £10 a week.

Agnes McLean made the important point for socialists on equal pay when she stated that it should not be defined as equal pay at the expense of male workers. She said, 'We're not asking for a share in the exploitation of the men. We are asking for it from the shareholders.'

Some of the slogans women had improvised on the official NJACC pla-cards put it more bluntly.

BARBARA GETS HERS WHY NOT US? and
GONE IS THE VICTORIAN AGE
WHEN WOMEN USED TO PLAY
NOW WE'RE WORKING BLOODY HARD
SO GIVE US EQUAL PAY.

A woman from the Post Office Engineers in Enfield held up

WE WANT A CHANCE TO PROVE WE CAN DO THE WORK
OF ANY MAN.

'All my own work,' she commented as I scribbled it down.

Pottery workers from Stoke on Trent carried

EQUAL PAY NOW

WE MAKE MUGS. BUT WE ARE NOT MUGS.

They told us it was the first demonstration they'd ever been on. They thought more women would have come but they were a bit nervous demonstrating. 'You hear such funny things about what goes on at them.' They'd been to conferences before. If it was possible to get enough women involved, and the men saw they had a strong movement, they felt sure they'd stand by them. Part of the problem was that women often found it difficult to speak up at union meetings. They'd formed women's advisory groups in their lodge which met as well as general lodge meetings within the National Society of Pottery Workers. This helped women to work out their problems at work and put a strong case to the men in the union. Transport workers stressed the importance of the men's support and referred to the hostility of some of their men over the issue of women drivers.

Rose Greenford said they were now putting the demand of equal sick pay. For a man this is granted after he's worked for a year. Women have to wait five years. They thought they'd be able to get this through.

The odd hostile man popped up but was instantly denounced and upbraided from all sides. One scornful bespectacled man suddenly became the centre of an angry group of very small young women, who prodded him indignantly and were supported by a great mountain of a man with a red face and black beret. The bespectacled man became most embarrassed and obviously regretted having created the confrontation. 'WE WORK FOR YOU. YOU LIVE OFF US,' shouted the girls. His knees were visibly knocking. 'Sock it to him,' said a young policeman watching with delight.

A policewoman, asked whether she had equal pay, refused to comment. But two policemen said policewomen worked less hours. They did a different kind of work which couldn't be compared. Policemen should get danger money. Dwarfs offered solidarity for police demo.

Everyone I talked to felt this was only the beginning. The movement for EQUAL PAY NOW is going to get bigger, noisier and more determined. And it's not just about equal pay. You can't challenge the economic subordination of women without immediately highlighting the total secondary social position.

Something is stirring.

Something which has been silent for a long time.

8. Problems of Organisation and Strategy

'Problems of Organisation and Strategy' was written in 1972 and never published.

Women, Resistance and Revolution and *Woman's Consciousness, Man's World* were conceived together. I set out to examine the problems women had faced in earlier revolutionary movements. I believed that the changes which had occurred in capitalist society made for significantly different circumstances and consciousness. I intended including descriptions of how individual women came into the movement, descriptions of particular towns and of specific activity. The individual accounts came out as rather superficial and the details of activity dated too quickly. So they were stored in a drawer.

The revolutionary optimism looks a little quaint after a decade in these grimmer times. There is less talk of the spectacle — for better or worse. But at least there are now more places to go for advice and support. Women's groups have gained in knowledge and expertise, though some of the problems of class and political intervention in people's lives are still there though less honestly admitted.

Yet it is evident that the general political problems raised have not been resolved. How do we move from defending ourselves in the world as it is to conceiving how life could be different? How do we proceed with our feet on the ground, our head in the air and our eyes fixed upon the stars?

This article has been cut for reasons of overall book length.

New areas of political resistance

Though it is difficult to see what is happening, it is even more difficult to see how we can intervene to change things. There are so many phrases, 'adventurism', 'voluntarism', 'economism', 'single-issue opportunism', 'substitutionism', 'tailism', 'infantile disorders', 'Stalinism', 'revisionism', 'reformism', 'centrism', 'Bonapartism', 'Blanquism', 'degenerate workers whatsit', 'lumpen Guevarism', 'state capitalism', 'bureaucratic collectivism', 'Pabloism'. Definitions covered in the cobwebs of acrimony, signposts in a language which is heavy with the past. Even the trusty familiar word 'comrade' has a certain ice in it. It is hard to keep a balance between the old ways and the new definitions which the changing shape of capitalism keeps forcing upon us.

The weakness of those who set out on a revolutionary journey without history is evident: no maps, no inherited tracks, little effective communication, little experience, little skill, little theory, lack of an overall picture of the terrain, a tendency to rush down new outlets as they appear, terrible disillusionment over dead ends, but enthusiasm, trust, new-found confidence, surprise, determination, inquisitiveness, an elusive quality of thinking together separately, and the pressing necessity to keep on because the retreat has been cut off.

The apparent spontaneous inclination of women's-liberation consciousness towards areas of human experience which were not previously seen as 'political', the capacity to communicate through the personal details of everyday living, the understanding of the way capitalism communicates itself not only through explicit ideology but through symbols, images, fantasy and desire, has come in response to the manner in which capitalism has started to penetrate the private world of the family, sexuality and the female self-image in new ways. It has given rise to particular forms of resistance against the family, against the prevailing norms of sexual culture, and against the most fundamental tenets of male-dominated capitalism, brutality, hardness, competition, achievement, success, the cash valuing of human beings seeing work as an end of human living and working to produce things rather than producing things to live.

Now to claim that such realisations were unique to women would be to produce a new and curious kind of biological determinism. The particular emphases of women's liberation have been floating about for some time in a disconnected way as ideas. In the past, they have erupted in a spasmodic manner in revolutionary feminist thought and in female action in revolutionary movements. More recently they have developed especially amongst socialists who are concerned with how society at large communicates to individuals, particularly through psychoanalysis and theories about art. Similar thoughts have been coming through in the music of the underground. However, when ideas are crystallised in a popular movement, they assume new proportions – the boundaries and spaces between them are rearranged. They become practical and obvious. The particular sequences in which disembodied and fragmented ideas bump against the specific social experiences of individuals who begin to discover a resistance in common, are necessarily elusive, half-forgotten and only partially intelligible. Ideas pop up in new colours and nobody troubles them about their origins and antecedents.

The particular crystallisation of women's liberation has not simply indicated new areas of political resistance but new ways of resisting. The particular organisational biases of women's liberation have come from this. We have a notion of political experience which is not a 'theoretical', sloganising one-upmanship but comes out of a constant relating of experience from action to ideas. We try to keep working out the direction at particular stages of a political action, to create an atmosphere in which people can admit to being wrong and plod off again along another route. By concentrating on the personal mechanisms of political commitment we are trying to make a movement in which new people can play a part without anyone patronising them. The recognition that discussion of personal problems is a vital source of strength, implies an idea of consciousness which is not the transmission of some already established higher body of knowledge but of learning by discovering yourself in relation to others. Because all women in women's liberation are struggling against a long-conditioned and evident passivity, there is the conception of a movement in which individuals move continually between a changing perception of themselves and the effort to communicate a collective experience outwards – between self-consciousness and activity. Because we were all isolated, helpless and divided, women's liberation persistently presumes that the isolated, helpless and divided are to organise. Women's liberation includes people previously regarded as unorganisable: the housewife, the woman working in small industrial units, the unsupported mother. It has to be a movement which provides continual support and protection, both practical and psychological, not as luxuries but as necessities. Again, it can't simply reproduce the state of affairs outside, because in those terms we can't encounter each other at all, only certain projected cultural images of femininity, shadows of our undeveloped selves. Suspicion of leaders, spokeswomen and any women who possess skills acquired in the world as it is, is a reasonable recognition that they continually take away our flickering, faintly discernible notion of alternatives, and allow us to sit back and leave them to it as substitute men.

Our strengths and weaknesses are inextricably interwoven. They appear in the loosely connected autonomy of the small groups. The small group is the living cellular organism which gives us the kind of gentle toughness to survive and grow, amoeba-like. But it means, again amoeba-like, that we find it hard to steer any concerted course and can drift into the line of least resistance. Our stress on experience can re-emphasise our terrible awe of theory as something we can never make our own; our opposition to achievement and competition can make us complacent about small advances; our self-consciousness can turn inwards and disintegrate, borne down by its own intensity; we can be so preoccupied with maintaining ourselves that we neglect the ways in which we can be effective. Our emphasis on personal and individual change can harden into an impossible stereotype, an 'ought' which women feel compelled to live up to; we can strain ourselves beyond endurance in trying to live a utopian women's liberation now.

I don't think that a movement like women's liberation can conceivably solve all the questions it raises, or pursue alone the new openings it reveals. It's only when the new questions come into contact with older ones, when new openings meet others, that patterns of organisation can emerge clearly. By relating our particular collective experience to others we can find out whether our own emphases are quite specific and momentary, or whether they carry something which relates to change beyond the boundaries of our own needs. It is by discovering in theory and in practice what in women's liberation is generalisable that we can further develop and organise ourselves. As yet our own indications are only tentative and incomplete. We have barely begun to communicate our experience even to each other. Women's liberation is too narrow in social composition to comprehend the differences between middle class and working class, black and white, young and old, married and unmarried, country- and townswomen. Nor are there massed revolutionary forces beyond us. On the contrary, besides our amoeba-like shape there is one largish husk with some life left inside it but much dead matter, and several little arrow-shaped things of varying intensity and consistency, shooting off in various directions in search of capitalism's weak links, in anticipation of 'the coming crisis'. Capitalism, meanwhile, is very much there, all around us and everywhere, with a resilient tendency to re-establish itself on its own ruins. Every connection we make, every fear we overcome, every suspicion we dissolve, is *despite* the way things are and in direct contradiction to the grain of common sense which accepts as real only what we already know to exist. The revolutionary journey is obvious as soon as it is evident, but very blocked and invisible before.

The most obvious block to us is the difficulty men have, no matter of whatever revolutionary persuasion, in learning anything from women. Perhaps this is reproduced in the feeling they have acquired that not to know how to do something is to be a failure, whereas nothing much in the way of achievement has ever been expected of us. Women's liberation arose as a separate movement because it was impossible for women to define and articulate what was obvious to them from their own lives and thus to assert needs which differed socially from those of men, in the context of male-dominated movements. The problem is now how we can share what we have worked out so far with men so that it can become obvious from a different point of view. The stiffness, arrogance and inhospitality of some of the men on the left has blocking consequences. Either it produces a counter-stiffness in ourselves, or we compromise and go humbly before a hostile tribunal of textual pomposity, or we just scream and scream and go and hide. What tends to happen too is an implicit demarcation line in revolutionary activity, they get on with the 'serious' stuff and we handle sex, children, culture, education and whatnot. It's not really possible for women's liberation to keep trying to turn outwards without an explicit, conscious and open commitment from men in the socialist movement to the need to try and learn from people they presume to 'educate' − not just women. We also need to try and struggle against continually reproducing within our movement the state of affairs without. Our refusal to resist these tendencies consciously means that the hierarchical division of labour, authoritarianism, brutality, self-conceit and paranoia invade all efforts to organise against capitalism. In a capitalist society there can be no absolute, finite solution to this, but there can be conscious effort.

But I think that in the near future as we get bigger we are going to find the block between men and women small in comparison to that between people who see capitalism as a unified and coherent system, in which structures of oppression hinge on one another, and those who want to make a small clearing for themselves without making such connections. Equally, within women's liberation we will make and are making our own blocks by emphasising very strongly particular aspects of the total situation of women. I think that sectarianism in movements comes not because they have 'traditional' Marxist politics or particular organisational structures, but because they possess theories which cannot become practical, either because of the circumstances outside, or because of the barrenness inside which makes thought in opposition dry and arid. Our present situation is not one in which capitalism's defences are strong against any possibility of resistance, but one in which our understanding of how to resist effectively is inadequate. This creates a particular kind of sectarianism, in which some people retreat for certainty into models designed for a long-vanished reality, and the rest exhaust themselves in rhetorical vituperation against this, which only drives the others further into retreat. The resulting bitterness, antagonism and paranoia are amongst the most effective weapons the ruling class have to contain us. The only way out of the deadlock is a very conscious opposition to the growth and survival of these tendencies in the very forms of organising, not only practically but theoretically. We have to apply our theory to the workings of our own movement in new ways.

Immediately, though, the dilemma often presents itself in a personal manner, as a stereotyped polarity between sinister, manipulative, Marxist, political women versus innocent, manipulated, apolitical women, or conversely man-hating, middle-class consciousness, freak feminists versus innocent conscientious comrades who are toiling away to build an outgoing, broadly based movement. Both stereotypes are caricatures but possess enough reality to present very considerable blocks within the movement. Again I think such blocks come through an under-development in Marxist feminist theory, not only in relation to women, but as a weapon which can effectively challenge modern capitalism. Because at the moment certain connections are completely invisible in practice, we are still fumbling around with our ideas. This means that there are many women like me who are divided, in some degree, in two. Part of us sees through the eyes of women's liberation and part of us talks in a highly developed separate language, mumbo jumbo to the majority of men as well as women. Sometimes we go one way, sometimes the other.

The personal experience of middle-class women can easily appear as trivial even to other women. In contrast to the traditions of revolution, it seems limited, protected, incoherent, timid and parochial. The repetition of personal complaints assumes the quality of religious exorcism, we are impatient because other women don't think like us, and are terrifyingly slow to move. An impatience grows within us and develops into contempt. It is particularly hard for a woman in existing revolutionary organisations, because all the certainty of 'theory' reinforces this impatience and contempt and she is under continual pressure to justify her adherence to women's liberation by 'politicising', and 'raising the level' of the other women. In desperation she starts to harangue the women's group, her words falling off her tongue into incommunication. There is nothing so quickly sensed and so absolutely destructive as contempt. All the words like 'exploitation' and 'capitalism' distance her from the others, even though they are precious to her.

Even if we are secure enough in our own political ideas not to see the 'politicisation' of other people as dragging them by the ears into revolutionary acquiescence, the fundamental dilemma remains. Firstly, because there is a disproportion of power, and secondly, because there are two completely contradictory understandings, one stressing past theory and another present experience, and we are unable yet to relate either adequately or clearly. The disproportion in power is most immediately obvious. A woman who is already left-wing regardless of whether she is in a group or not, has a ready-made coherent picture of the world, an alternative information network and access to technical equipment which makes it much easier for her to mobilise within women's liberation. Personally she can feel the strange mixture of suspicion, resentment and dependence which focuses upon her.

To non-revolutionary women it is as if revolutionaries were continually hiding behind their words. Instead of saying honestly what she feels, like anyone else must, the revolutionary woman appears to be using an alien phraseology in order to appear superior, just as men often do. She is covering herself in a language which appears to bear no relationship either to her life or theirs. She just goes on and on, lecturing and dictating. She intrudes upon the trust they have painfully established amongst each other. They listen to her because she is a woman, they extend sisterhood to her, but suspect her within themselves of acting not from inside herself but as her men instruct her. She seems a kind of traitor who is half ashamed of a women's movement. Or they suspect her for lifting already arranged connections out of movements which are often hostile and patronising to women's liberation, and not working through the specific experience of women with a genuine and honest openness. There is a revolutionary male shadow army always somewhere behind her, apparently ready to take over and make their own the first tentative steps we make towards our own identity. Neither of these roles are fixed and immutable. The same person can be both in different contexts.

In fact, the strong emphasis against leaders and against ideas as authority in women's liberation is a very valuable strength against becoming an organisation which is real on paper only, which parrots already existing formulas to increase its feeling of self-importance. By consciously trying always to spread responsibility and initiative we make it difficult for any revolutionary tendency which is short-sighted enough to try and take over. Equally, because women who are Marxists share exactly the same problems which the non-political women feel towards them, and have to struggle continually in the left as a whole against the attitudes of many men who consider themselves revolutionary, it creates a greater awareness of the importance of respecting other women's ideas and experience. Very often, too, women's liberation helps us women who were already left-wing to begin to rediscover the Marxism we acquired passively. By questioning more and more you start to make your own answers. Similarly, the growth of women's liberation means that some men also start to argue within the left as a whole – not only that the women must organise separately – but that men must learn from the women who are doing this.

But all this is painfully slow and we are all still at the stage of stumbling along. However, a certain difficulty remains and I am unable to see any means through or round it. Once you start to conceive of yourself as a revolutionary you decide you know some of the answers to some of the questions, so if people disagree with you, you are bound to feel that they're wrong. As soon as you define other people as wrong and yourself as right, you are making a judgement about the inadequacy of their position. There's an obvious contradiction between feeling you're right and believing in the validity of every woman's experience in women's liberation. And if you feel Marxism and the ideas and experience it carries is a valuable weapon, you are bound to try and make it available to all women in women's liberation. It seems there's no simple, single answer but to respect one another, without muffling your own opinions, to be strong enough to need to stay together even though you don't see the same way.

Problems of consciousness and strategy

The organisational dilemmas which confront us are not peculiar to women's liberation. We need to discover how to act effectively against a society which takes away from us all confidence in our capacity for effective action. We have to struggle continuously against an inhuman system and remain human. We need to find ways of snatching happiness from the future so as not to be consumed by our own bitterness against how things are in the present. We must combine the means of getting things done with developing the creative capacity of every person to act according to their own initiative. Such problems have bedevilled all popular movements attempting to extend the notion of democracy and we need to learn from them and make their history our own. However, the specific context of women's liberation differs from theirs, and we are now raising old questions in new ways, as well as coming up with completely new dilemmas.

Discussion in the organised left in Britain before women's liberation was predominantly around either how to survive and maintain youself as an organisation within capitalism faced with widespread apathy about revolution, or how to take power in the event of revolution, and how to prevent distortion and deformation appearing in the post-revolutionary society. These problems were posed in terms of the consciousness of the male working class – how capitalism had duped them into acquiescence, or in terms of the experience of the Russian revolution. So the task of a revolutionary was to provide workers with an alternative to prevailing notions, whether these were straightforward Toryism or the Labour party's acceptance of capitalism and a muted gradual road to socialism. This was seen in terms of building a revolutionary organisation according to a received historical model.

However, the movement of students, blacks, women and gays along with the cultural emphasis of the underground has forced a recognition that modern capitalism has thrown up contradictions which have brought groups into opposition on a non-class basis. It remains unclear how these groups relate to the traditional struggle of the working class organised at the point of production, or to traditional Marxist concepts of revolutionary organisation. Nonetheless, the emergence of these movements has shifted the abstract question of how a tiny minority of conscious revolutionaries can intervene to change the mentality of the mass of the working class, to a more immediate and concrete question of how particular groups can move themselves out of passivity and silence into self-recognition. Ultimately this must raise how they connect to each other, and how their emergence interacts upon the emergence of other groups. However, for the time being it has served to make many more people see the need for social change, not because they have learned a particular political script, but because they bring the experience of their own lives into their own movement. The possibility of change has been moved both from the far-distant future, or the incomprehensible total apocalypse, into now and everyday living.

One of the besetting problems of revolutionaries in the past has been that the day-to-day economic struggle of workers, guided by common sense and long-accumulated practical experience, only spasmodically goes beyond itself and is necessarily within the terms that capitalism imposes. Thus quantitative trade union demands tend to benefit certain sections of the working class at the expense of others, or make gains in terms of cash, which are passed on by the employers in price rises. Consequently, Marxists have seen the need to bring a revolutionary consciousness from outside the workers' own organisations. The interaction between the workers' experience, and the revolutionary intellectuals' grasp of society as a whole, has been regarded as the means of making an offensive attack on capitalism. The need to take the offensive in theory and practice has always been most evident when the working class is under attack and forced to defend itself. When the workers have enjoyed a period of bargaining strength, the need for an offensive has been less clear. When traditional defensive operations are failing, the idea that the best, indeed the only means of defence, is attack, has gained support.

However, sections of capitalist society have increasingly moved out into an intellectual awareness of the operation of capitalism as a total system, but have found themselves threatened by new kinds of impingements on what they regard as their own basic rights, and have begun to organise to defend themselves not just at work but in all spheres of life. In doing this they have opened up new points of attack, although they have not formulated an alternative strategy for fighting capitalism effectively.

They have, in the process, called into question certain assumptions about how we organise. Marxists have tended to assume that revolutionary struggle will have for its spearhead working-class militants – generally male – organised into a revolutionary party on the Leninist model. Its militants are not only located at the point of production, and hence of economic and social power, but have achieved a consciousness which extends beyond their economic position as workers, and have comprehended the consciousness of people in quite different social spheres, women, students, etc. Thus the task of the revolutionary party must be to provide the element of conscious direction, by intervening not only in day-to-day struggles at work, but in every area of life, in order to generalise particular movements, and to extend the implications of each agitation beyond the boundaries of common sense towards the revolutionary future. In the process of continually relating theory to practice, the revolutionary is engaged in the development of self-activity and democratic experience, as well as in the establishing of the craft skills of propaganda and agitation.

In reality, of course, such an ideal doesn't exist. Marxists who accept such a model of revolutionary organisation would stress that we possess only approximations towards this. However, though the new movements have not produced any general alternative strategy they have made the awkwardness inherent within this ideal more evident. Firstly, while it is true that it is possible to learn from others as to how they experience capitalism, this does not mean that you can in fact share that experience and understand it as if it was your own. Workers have had an understandable suspicion of intellectuals who talk about alienation but who don't actually feel the life and hope being drawn out of them in every part of their body and mind. All those hours, days, months and years which are not your own and in which fulfilment is unrealisable, before the final insult of a pension which barely allows you to survive. There is nothing more irritating than people who have particular skills based on the privilege of their economic social position coming along and knowing some other person's experience better than them because they have words and theory as weapons. Thus, with the best of intentions, revolutionary intellectuals can seem like the Salvation Army with a new kind of jargon and a fancy kind of personnel manager approach. All this applies equally to women.

The problem of revolutionaries combining everybody's experience in a higher synthesis in practice is even more absurd when the state of revolutionary organisation is weak. Because, rather than people learning from each other, you have what often appears as a small band of fanatical know-alls trotting about raising other people up to their 'level' of consciousness, the very notion of which is necessarily elitist and invulnerable.

Secondly, the acceptance that consciousness can be conceived in levels is essentially hierarchical. At the top of the pyramid sit the leaders of the revolutionary party. In the absence of *the* revolutionary party, the leaders of revolutionary groups are substituted. The leaders have to carry a great load of responsibility, and can't help but sustain themselves with a certain sense of their own self-importance. With the 'levels' of consciousness go gradations of cadres. It's all rather like streaming in a comprehensive, and it tends to be self-fulfilling in the same way.

Within women's liberation there is a different idea of consciousness which implies that though you can learn partially from others what it feels like to suffer from particular kinds of oppression, your own experience cannot be adequately comprehended by a general blanket of revolutionary consciousness. In order to guarantee that your specific experience is not simply annexed by the prevailing definition of revolutionary consciousness, you have to create a separate locus of power. The organisation of distinct women's groups within the revolutionary movement is the only convincing method of securing that women's views and interests are represented and articulated. Secondly, within women's liberation a hierarchical notion of consciousness is impossible because the criteria applied to consciousness are much more diversified. You can't take a measuring rod and tick off an ascending order of notches in female consciousness. Consciousness in women's liberation can't be a simple point to be attained. It's true that some women will have particular skills, ideas and experience, but that doesn't mean that they are necessarily equipped to understand the experience of other women or what to do in women's liberation, or in their own relationship with men, nor will other women necessarily expect them to. In fact, it's more likely that people will look rather to new members, who have come in simply because their own lives as women have brought them along, because however long you are in women's liberation every woman's reasons for joining enable you to learn more. Consciousness in this sense is an indeterminate shape, now expanding, now retreating, now intense, now shallow, now exploring, now covering itself. Indeed a jelly fish of a thing, seeping about the place, or flopping down and not moving, creeping into the most incongruous crevices.

But how can such a curious creature move? Why isn't it completely inert and helpless, forced into whatever current within capitalism will carry it along? In fact, it does move, though not in a concerted or linear fashion. For connected to our peculiarly inchoate but resilient consciousness, we have produced a notion of political education which differs both from the study circle for mutual education, which was a feature of the Puritan movement and later of the British socialist movement, and the Bolshevik concept of propaganda, which Deutscher describes as 'the modest and earnest discussion of principles . . . a traffic in ideas rather than slogans'.[1] Although women's liberation groups are educational and propagandist in this sense, they also provide a means not only of discussing ideas but of seeing your own life in a different light. I think 'consciousness-raising' is the wrong phrase for this because it still implies levels and degrees of consciousness. 'Consciousness moving' or 'consciousness forming' are better. When you bring your individual experience of what has happened to you as a woman to a women's liberation meeting, you are doing explicitly what you did implicitly in little pockets of female defensiveness before, over pregnancy, over housework, in the launderette, in the 'ladies'. The explicit action of combining means that you are brought to see yourself as a woman self-consciously. And once in a group you see yourself in relation to other women. You discover a common condition. Then you begin to try and understand the source of that condition, you start to examine how it is maintained in capitalism. So your own perception is continually being shifted by how the other women perceive what has happened to them. You are not only learning a new picture of how things are together, you are creating your own very important strength. You are trusting other women. You are consciousness moving.

The main difficulty, still, is that while the social composition of women's liberation remains narrow it isn't possible to move naturally beyond certain limitations in perspective. It seems also very difficult to translate this consciousness-moving experience out of our own peculiar definition of propaganda into agitational work. As soon as we become involved in agitation for nurseries, within claimants unions, to unionise, to try and secure wage rises or job security, the strength and trust and equality possible in the small group dissolves and we are back in all the distancing rituals of traditional left agitational work. This doesn't seem to me to be a problem which can be easily solved, except by learning through our own practice, even though that is still very limited, and by the movement becoming much broader so that women's liberation groups start to appear not only in colleges, schools and the homes of housewives, within left-wing political organisations, but also in factories, shops, offices, cafés, amongst girls who work on chicken farms, amongst outworkers, lavatory attendants, hospital, office, school and factory cleaners, in trade union branches, amongst nurses, doctors, teachers, prostitutes, striptease girls, pensioners, pop singers, and every other section of the great unorganisable. Meanwhile, we have to try and learn from what we can do at present.

When we do go and try and agitate for something in particular we are still floundering around because we have no commonly accepted end. A revolutionary organisation has a shared end, even though there is no simple blueprint for translating the everyday possibility within capitalism into the future possibility of socialism. In women's liberation it is different because we are together in our discontent but not in our notion of what we are striving towards. Rather than attempting to impose such a unified end from outside, I think we should work through what we have in common as our beginning. We are all resisting certain aspects of the way in which capitalism penetrates our everyday life as women. Very few of us are located at the highly developed points of capitalism, nor are most of us concentrated in large numbers together. We consequently have to seek forms of resisting appropriate to our present condition. Women haven't achieved the organisational strength and work discipline of male workers in industry. We have to overcome millennia of induced passivity before we can even begin.

However, we do possess certain unexpected strengths. Firstly, although we tend not to be all together in large groups, there are a lot of us and we are in the most unexpected places. We are inside more or less everywhere. We don't need to infiltrate – we're there already. It has been so inconceivable that women would cause trouble for so long that we have access to many places where we can collect information, and start to turn our old invisibility to our own favour. These places are infinitely varied, so the way we can struggle resembles small-group guerrilla attacks rather than a large cohesive army with specific objectives. Secondly, despite the disadvantages attached to our underdevelopment there are a few things on our side. We haven't been forced to learn the rules of the game and accept that we have to struggle only within capitalism's terms. We have been contained in our subordination but as we begin to challenge the nature of our false protection we also bring quite contradictory assumptions about what a human being should be able to expect from the world. Thirdly, if events proceeded by means of some orderly linear scheme we would have a long trek indeed. But things move along in leaps and bounds, one bit clashes against the next and produces a new combination as both dissolve. So it doesn't follow that we have to lug ourselves up to men's position in capitalism. It would be absurd, anyway, because we would have to pretend we didn't have children, which is impossible. Instead, we have to work out through our movement what women want. We have to be strong enough to include all kinds of women, every colour, class, age, straight and gay, and we have to be able to keep together despite all our differences and insist that no one group sees women's liberation as getting privileges for one section without, and thus at the expense of, the rest.

I think we have to recognise at this stage that we are fighting against what capitalism does to us. We have not yet developed enough to decide that we are going to do what we want to capitalism. We have first to defend ourselves. Without a strong general revolutionary organisation, if separate groups attempt an explicit offensive they get smashed. Alone, whatever power we have would be lost and reduced, and we'd be forced back on our own underdeveloped isolation.

We have to define what is necessary for our own defence. Within the labour movement the notion of defence has always been looking after your own and sticking together against the daily inroads of the capitalist class on your bargaining power, and against very clear repression, the sacking of a shop steward or the arrest of pickets. But the protection of the union is confined to the world of work. Occasionally it penetrates beyond, help for the sick, for the old, for widows, for people who are threatened with eviction. The class war in its everyday manifestation is ceaseless and exhausting. Merely maintaining existing strongholds can take up your whole life. Now the union exists within capitalism and is concerned to protect its own members in an immediate sense. Very often there is a contradiction between this kind of defence and the need which continually appears to stretch this defensive consciousness into an alternative. In fact, there are parts of the union which go beyond defence and carry an implicit alternative. The union is an extension of bourgeois democracy actually growing within capitalism. The idea and practice of solidarity and brotherhood are the opposite of capitalist competition and every man for himself.

However, any alternative is continually being deferred to an impossible future, because not only does the union have its own vast bureaucratic structure to keep going in capitalism, but it has become partly incorporated into modern capitalism's mixed economy. Because of this, groups of workers have organised actually at work in order to force the union to defend them and socialists within unions have always tried to make solidarity, brotherhood and the notion of collective democracy explicit. The problem has always been the demarcations of privilege actually within the working class. These have shifted and reshuffled ever since capitalism began, now based on this skill, now on that. As craft skill gives way to technology the pattern of segmentation changes. The organisation of the people at the bottom has always been particularly explosive because it puts more pressure on the capitalist structure than it can take comfortably. Women and immigrant workers have always been dominant amongst the low paid and unskilled. Their organising consequently serves to erode the refining of difference and distinction which keeps people in their place. Skilled white male workers can always find someone else beneath and behind them. Somebody else's back goes to the wall before theirs. Women, like blacks, have been told not to force their own demands, not to split the movement, to be patient, to be satisfied with 'brotherhood'. But in fact the only way to challenge segmentation in the working class is for the weak to organise until they are strong.

One of the limitations of unions is their inability to operate out of work. Everyone has to go home at night, after all, and many wives don't go to work at all. As women's liberation groups start in places of work, within union branches, or in the homes of women who don't work, these could help to break down the gap between home and work which has been with us since the industrial revolution. They could also help by democratising unions, and enabling a section of workers predominantly amongst the lower paid to make their own claims recognised. The defence of women at work is a vast task. Many 'rights' men take for granted aren't even conceived as applicable to women. Much of this has to take place over the most basic issues, like the 'right' to unionise itself, and the 'right' to equal payment and job security. Although this presents particular organising problems and requires its own specific strategy, it contains a potential strength. Out of our 'underdevelopment' comes contrary expectations about 'jobs' because we have been conditioned to see our main function as caring for human beings, although with capitalism this has been restricted to looking after our own – the family.

Because the work situation of women is bound up with the family and sexuality, the defence of women is bound to extend into quite different areas. It can't remain convincingly as an economic struggle at the point of production. The defensive needs of women are very varied. There are the particular moments when people are especially exposed: on strike, trying to get an abortion, getting old, left by a man, immigrant girls inspected at ports to see if they're virgins, rape. A movement like women's liberation has to be prepared to provide practical help for women when they need it. It has to become a natural place to turn to – a cultural nucleus. But there is a more continuous state of affairs, not of crisis but of a nagging humdrum stupidity in capitalism's inability to provide for the most elementary needs of women.

Unequal education and training, lousy jobs, lower pensions, lack of nursery facilities, school milk stopped, nowhere to put children when you shop, not enough lavatories for mothers with children, difficulty still in finding out about sex and getting contraception and abortion, long waits in prenatal clinics, the problems of unsupported mothers. Agitation for all these details of inequality is necessary as a straightforward defence of women against our particular subordination. Implicit within such a defence is the idea of equality, the idea that children are the responsibility of the society as a whole, and the assertion of the right of every individual regardless of sex to sexual happiness without fear. It is important in any agitation, if we are to be effective in securing change, to understand how these specific defensive improvements are connected to the general structure of capitalist society. We have to develop the idea of equality in education through to a criticism of the present system of general class inequality which pervades education, and the authoritarianism of the existing system. Genuine equality for women can only be built within a completely different notion of learning and teaching. Similarly at work, you can't expect production to be organised on the basis of consideration for women's needs when its present basis is the need to extract profit. You can't expect an adequate system of abortion without socialised medicine, and transformation of the medical hierarchy and the relation between doctors as well as nurses and patients. Equally, the eradication of the sexual double standard without simply reversing roles would have to mean profound changes in society as we know it, penetrating every area of culture. Modern capitalism's alternative is to reduce both women *and* men to objects of gratification. The genuine social security of the unsupported mother demands extensive changes at work, in the family, and in the communities we live in.

But the deepest and least tangible change of all has to be the transformation of our whole orientation towards the world and ourselves. The onslaught on our consciousness is all-pervasive and profoundly internalised. Our defence necessitates a movement which can cope with the subterranean inclinations of the psyche, the inner as well as the outer bondages. Ultimately this defence requires the creation of a new culture in every aspect of human life, from pop music to the past, from the assumptions of psychology to the assumptions of the medical textbook, from the cowboy film to the revolutionary group, from the beauty contest to tractor design, from the orgasm to the poem. All this implies the birth of completely different ideas of femininity, of beauty, of equality, of human potential. The new woman inevitably demands a new man.

The disparate nature of our defence and the questions raised produce, not surprisingly, great confusion. We find it very different to move around between what we can hope for in the short term and what we can glimpse in the long term. When we grasp the enormity of our task we become paralysed. Instead we should disentangle our strengths and weaknesses.

The small group is our most vital weapon of cultural defence, it not only provides us with the confidence to begin and continue but is the means of going beyond ourselves. Within the idea of sisterhood there is also not just protection but the possibility of a new relationship of women with one another. However, we have not yet developed means of carrying the strength of the small group into agitation. The weakness too in defensive organising is that there is the constant danger of seeing defence as an end in itself rather than a means to an end. This turns us inwards rather than drawing us outwards. Once we turn inwards we capsize with our own weight and start to contract. We are faced with the immediate task of maintaining our defences and carrying within these an implicit offensive alternative. At the moment there are two organisational poles. There is the idea of making practical demands which are apparently realisable within the terms of the system as it is but in fact probably won't be granted, and there is the idea of acting out the totality now. The first has the disadvantage of being unable to move the notion of saying we want more into wanting a different state of affairs altogether. It never touches the tremendous power of thwarted imagination which goes into resistance against capitalism. In practice you find yourself reducing and compressing your much deeper sense of disaffiliation into a tidy package of a 'demand' which can sit comfortably in a newspaper column so they can say, 'They want this', while you know you want vastly more but can't put a shape to it in their terms. But the second is all fantasy and imagination and thus loses its grip on the actual shape and boundaries of other people's lives. Ultimately it fails as much as the former to challenge the terms within which people accept their own lives and the lives of people around them. This dilemma is very well illustrated within women's liberation in the discussion and agitation for preschool education. Either you can start a playgroup, which is inadequate but means the way the children are treated remains in your control. Or you can join the other pressure groups for nurseries which provide a much wider need and are an important weapon of defence for women. Both these are sensible things to do so long as we have no illusions about their limitations. The playgroup doesn't affect enough children for long enough to be anything more than a brief alleviation of the problem of the relationship between mothers and young children. It is also more likely to cater for middle-class children. But even a nursery in its present form doesn't in fact question the roles of men and women or the relation between parents, teachers and children, or between school and community. It could mean that children are subjected to discipline which will help them to accept the discipline of the school and work later without resistance. It could mean that the nursery is simply a means of extracting more labour out of the family unit. Though both playgroup and nursery school are needed in vastly greater numbers than at present and no efforts to secure them are wasted, we must also search for other means of at once partly solving and illuminating the contradictions within the nuclear family. *Kinderladen* and *crèches sauvages* present a more total educational answer, but tend to involve only revolutionary parents – particularly women full time – and exclude almost inevitably, working-class parents because of their work and general attitudes. I think we should move towards more clearly transitional solutions, for example, the Camden houses. In this scheme small nurseries would be set up in houses funded by the local council but controlled and run by parents, with one paid worker. The idea actually originated in the first community nursery, Dartmouth Park Hill. This kind of project can realistically be obtained, doesn't absorb too much labour, is small enough to be based on personal contact, provides a way of learning through practice about how involvement with women's liberation connects with our children, and also sets up places where women's liberation can establish itself naturally and meet the practical and psychological needs of the women in the area. There is also the possibility of developing the idea of involving children as equals with adults. The weapons we use should not be fetishised. We have to struggle now one way, now another.

Our immediate need is to develop through our movement our own accounts of what we have done and gradually accumulate a shared culture of agitation, rather than laying down the line about what we should each be doing.

If we don't wish to be cheated we have to try continually to develop, through our agitation for particular improvements, the implications each carries for a society in which we could develop and grow more completely. For it is clear that most of the isolated gains we can make can be twisted against women and that many partial gains are often a means of silencing one group at the expense of another. Equally, we can't expect to be left in peace. Even the most apparently minimal improvements in women's position carry a very real and material threat to the people in power. For example, it would seem that the right to a week's notice, to a holiday, to full cover money, to a living wage, and to unionise are the most basic of workers' rights in the second half of the twentieth century. But when the night office cleaners tried to secure these they met a response from the cleaning contractors, with soaring profits and little capital outlay, that was as petty, mean and vicious as the most tightfisted Victorian employer. The need to make defensive structures which carry within themselves implicit alternatives, does not come in a vacuum but within a particular balance of social power. Every time we move towards a more conscious position of defence we open up the possibility of new kinds of attack, new forms of repression or absorption. We have to be realistic about our weaknesses and defend ourselves, but at the same time strain towards defining the struggle in our terms. We have to know both what our real position is and what we are doing about it. As long as we react spontaneously to what they do to us without understanding why they do it we can be continually taken unawares. Our problem is to see what it is about our defence as a group in capitalism that carries an implicit threat to the way capitalist society hangs together, and how we can intervene in the interstices. It is clear that what they do to us is not a matter of chance or coincidence, but is bound up with particular interests and a particular kind of society. The first step towards initiating change as an explicit alternative is through learning about the nature and workings of capitalist society. As we do this our implicit notions of how things could be different – learnt from our new relationships with one another, our sisterhood, and the experience we gain through agitation – will assume an explicit intelligibility. Such an intelligibility would be a theory of socialist feminism. It would understand the workings of capitalism in relation to women, it would also see how the subordination of women is connected to the subordination of most men. The making of such a theory is an essential weapon, it is also a vast and profound cultural creation.

PART TWO

MAKING TRACKS:
WOMEN'S LIBERATION
1972–1982

INTRODUCTION

Are we to begin with the particular biography? What is to be told? What constitutes evidence for history when the personal is political. Is the answer everything? How do we put down everything about the lives of every feminist or even about ourselves? We would be in perpetual collective confessional and the world pass us by. And there is always some devastating revelation lurking in the shadows. 'Fancy you missing that,' 'I got the impression from what you said.' The soul evades honesty. We go naked into politics and are revealed in a flash of light which casts only more darkness. So I think it better not to pretend to absolute honesty because this disguises how screens are silently shuffled into place. It is more important to be wary about our own taboos and silences. Some things taken out. Certain things not to be said. Until the scope of feminist thought narrows to a point of purity so small only the most keen-sighted and zealous can spot it.

It is better to opt for earnest intimations towards honesty and a few whistles, dust bin lids and rattles to sound out the alarm. We need to blow, bang and shake them whenever we discover new boundaries, boulders, screening appearing in the name of feminism. The yearning to transform the very pith of politics is to be tempered with respect, cherishing what cannot be in its own sweet time channelled or translated.

Nonetheless, we meander our individual ways through movements so even for those of us with broadly similar politics the specific differences of private life and work, the placing and timing of our doings make for a different combination of emphases.

So sketchy notes about my individual life between 1972 and 1982 might serve as a guide to some of the activities and ideas described in this section. Hopefully this will aid the process of making recognition and contrasting experience and views more explicit.

I earned my living from part-time teaching in a school in Islington and in the Workers' Education Association. From the late seventies I lived off my writing – royalties and reviews mainly. This has become increasingly pre-carious and I have been able to work on this book and another for Penguin on ideas in the women's movement because in 1982 for a year I became Visiting Professor at the University of Amsterdam in the women's studies department.

In the early 1970s I was active in the campaign to recruit night cleaners and improve pay and conditions. I was in Arsenal Women's Liberation group between 1971 and 1978 and involved in the women's centres at Essex Road, Islington in the mid-seventies.

Throughout this period I lived in Hackney, a working-class borough in northeast London with a group of friends. Loving relationships with two men (mainly two I mean) spanned several years.

I have never been able to write about passionate sexual love. I have difficulty finding words to meet the intensities and some reluctance to splatter the lives and feelings of others over paper. Even though I am a notorious gossip, it seems somewhat unreasonable that through the mischance of association with writers privacy is invaded. On the other hand it would be a false picture to say that time passed only with work, meetings and leafletting and to omit to mention that physical and emotional desire brought pain and ecstasy or pretend I did not learn and dwell in happiness as well as conflict with men lovers and men friends.

Feminism has brought very deep political friendships with women. It has also given a more complex dimension to erotic love between women. It has contributed as well to shifting the relation between the sexes in most complicated ways which have hardly yet been charted. There are tussles and intrusions, problems of space and identity. But there is also lust, delight, connection and discovery. We mention it to feminist friends, smile, telephone, exchange letters.

I am not sure how we make political patterns of all this. I think we must try to understand, make some cultural sense beyond the immediate intimacies of desire and friendship. There is a living dialectic between the bedroom and the public platform. But how does this work out in practice? Are we to wheel our beds into the conference chambers? There is a time and a place for everything after all. The personal is political cannot mean quite this.

I dislike most attempts to combine political and clinical language and descriptions of sexual desire. Partly because I am a closet romantic who believes clouds have silver linings and smoke in the eyes is fetching. But also a contrary puritan seeking the exact means of communicating to the utmost of endeavour. And thus repelled by the blundering arrogance of clever categories which colonise the fragile feelings and contradict the longings of the human heart. Nonetheless a politics which disdains passionate sexual love, which cannot melt nor ride the breakers nor merge nor take the tug of pleasure turns to a rasping harshness, empty mouthing echoing round dismal half-filled rooms. I have no solution, simply a reminder that there is a dilemma.

In 1977 my son was born. I discovered a new (new for me, well known to a large part of the world of course) and sensuous kind of passion in his baby-hood. More exhausting this than any sexual love. As I blinked my way out of chaos and exhaustion I learned about the politics of childcare. There is nothing like experience for making theory come alive – howls in the night. What philosophers we all would be if we were only less tired.

But the topics covered in these articles are not simply indications of my own experience. They are sources for a wider interpretation, accounts of local meetings, discussions of political problems which have preoccupied many other feminists and some consideration of how women's liberation relates to a wider context of social change.

With some relief the feminist historian might turn from the consuming and untidy biography to the local account of a small group, or to the chronicle of activities in a particular area or town. Let's forget for a moment who was loving who, having a baby, getting the sack, screaming in the park, seeing visions, paying the bills. Let's focus on the market leafletting, the conference social, the article in the journal, the trades council women's sub-committee, the meeting in the town hall. The experience of every group and locality differ but at least the outer forms are tangible, remain fixed for a moment. Also every description of the particular meeting or place goes beyond itself. Every action taken leads outwards, has wider repercussions. For instance, those members of consciousness-raising groups live in families, belong to unions or political parties, talk to the neighbours, take children to school, post letters, ring up friends. Ideas get around.

But how do these individual lives and relationships, the personal and political comings and goings in all these groups and localities intertwine into a national movement?

At this point the historian of women's liberation is hurtling along on the big dipper. When the ride ends the world settles down a little. Things broaden out geographically. We can consider the campaign. Get out our notebooks and jot down a few problems. There is for instance the tension documented between the small women's liberation group and the more public forms of organising. There is the discontinuity of experience. How shall we pass on what has been learned without a formal structure of 'political education'? How are we to overcome those barriers which informal networks set up? Hidden forms of knowledge and power can be as daunting as the ritualised procedures we rebelled against. How do we go beyond the confines of class, race and sex, without rushing pellmell down the dead-end rhetoric of guilt?

Political disagreements have grown labels, anarchist feminists, radical feminists, revolutionary feminists, socialist feminists. People can never be quite summed up by the labels and there is change. There are also differences which can hardly find names and these are perhaps the most paralysing. For example, under the heading 'socialist feminism' there are differing conceptions of socialism and feminism and contrary understandings of the relationship between the two.

The women's liberation movement has not dwelt in splendid isolation. Our history is inseparable from the course of other movements, among ethnic minorities, trade unionists, gay people, the spread of community organising. It requires historical assessment in relation also to changes in capitalist society. For example the industrial militancy of the early seventies, the changes in local government, the more overtly coercive role of the state, unemployment, racism, the shift to the left in the Labour party, new patterns of class, family and culture, the attack on welfare. Moreover, women's liberation is an international affair and this means a world which is not bounded by Europe and North America. The global greed of the multinationals, the new imperiousness of imperialism and the military might of the rich capitalist countries affect the lives of women as well as men. All these have exerted a pull on feminism.

Because we face an intricate web of power relationships, not simply the oppressive aspects of women's power, socialist feminists in many countries have been increasingly drawn towards tackling not only women's questions but developing our politics in a wider sense. How do we regard the family, law, sexuality, the state, welfare, local government, imperialism, economic strategy, political parties, for instance? But this vital extension has raised an unresolved dilemma, is socialist feminism a current within women's liberation or an approach towards politics in general? In Britain the economic crisis and the political acceleration to the right since 1979 has meant that this has found expression not in leisurely debates but in a fracturing of the loose sense of connection which socialist feminists developed within the women's movement from discussions and activity in local and national campaigns and conferences.

It has become evident that we can no longer confine ourselves to what is happening to women because more than ever women are being swept up in the general debacle. The fates of men and women are more clearly linked. For example, there are differences in the nature of the impact of welfare cuts and unemployment on women and men but they are striking at both sexes. As a consequence there has been a move of socialist feminists outside the structures of the women's liberation movement and the socialist feminist network. Considerable energy is going into trades councils, employment projects, health groups, youth work, coops, non-violent resistance to nuclear weapons. In reaching outwards we avoid the danger in a period when the right is taking the offensive of closing into a sect. But we do not clear up differences in our definition of what kind of socialism and what kind of feminism we ask and the relation between the two. We face now in a new context the problem of defining what we mean by autonomy and on what terms we are to connect and link to the socialist movement. This puts greater pressure on us to resolve what has always been difficult for socialist feminists – how to challenge capitalism *and* resist both the forms of men's power and the acts of male domination as we encounter them?

Separatism of course has no such headache. The crisis polarises political responses. Separatism in its various forms has the advantage of clarity. The enemy are easy to distinguish with their distinctive physical markings. They are to be bundled out of our consciousness.

Separatists can point to a certain fuzziness within socialist feminism. 'The system' is attacked but the relationship of particular men to particular women is obscured. Socialist feminism can let men off the hook by dealing in abstract categories of production, reproduction and the rest. Separatism has the moral advantage here. Indeed in a backhanded way it restores a certain dignity to human beings by endowing them with choice and responsibility. But separatism with its radical-liberal heritage does not stretch much beyond the individual. It does not place the individual in specific relationships and show how the situations in which we find ourselves help to shape our consciousness and our will even as we act upon them. This intractability in separatist forms of feminism makes it possible to isolate one relationship of oppression. Moreover, it means that they can end up by denying the optimism of their radical-liberal origins and predestine us to a ping-pong match between oppressor and victim. This is a dead end.

What of strategy and outcome? If we maintain that men in a lump are just bad, if men are the enemy full stop, what are we going to do about them? Do we take prisoners or skin them alive? Banish them? Won't they come creeping back in anti-sexist camouflage? They are the worst – the very worst of course. Not the chairgentlemen of the multinationals, the bankers, the generals, the presidents and prime ministers (let Margaret be unsexed for a moment not to confuse the argument). These are just some mirage conjured up by the male left.

But who is the real enemy for separatism? The really, real enemy. That is from a woman-centred sisterly, matriarchly, pure, proper, feminist perspective. Who lurks behind those dreadful men who do crêches and share childcare – even more dreadful because they should know better – but women. Women who like men.

This is another dead end in which thought seizes up in guilt and panic. This is primarily why it should be opposed. For men being still advantaged, if somewhat assailed, will contrive the means of their own defence. But consideration and reflection are driven out of the women's movement by this seizure of thought. It devours complexity and nuance and reinforces the deprivation of the oppressed.

It is still important to make a basic distinction between saying feminism means we are against men and saying that feminists oppose the differing forms and historically specific manifestations of the power men hold over women in particular societies. It is one thing to be hostile to the actions and words of specific men, another to condemn men as a group as inherently oppressive and thus define all thoughts, words and deeds of men as part of domination.

However, the negative focus restricts even when this distinction is made clear. The mainspring of women's liberation in my view was not a generalised antagonism to men but the positive assertion and creation of new relationships between women, sisterhood. The strength of this search for a new connection among women gave the hope that new relationships between men and women might also be possible. Both hopes found only a fragile realisation. Also there have been and still are many visions of how to anticipate less oppressive relations and even disagreement about what is or is not oppressive. We can at least acknowledge these difficulties and differences.

But increasingly the space for debate is filled instead with moral anger. This has separatist and socialist feminist manifestations. Rage strikes a spark of consciousness but when it is relit over and over again it becomes all-consuming and destructive. It burns out the generosity of spirit necessary to sustain creative rebellion.

There is a danger now that the definition of feminism becomes again confined simply as hostility towards men. Those of us who think there is more to it than that have not contested this appropriation of feminism effectively. The clarification of difference is painful when you yearn for union. But if we do not begin to unravel some of the over-hasty simplifications which are being taken for granted as 'what the women's movement thinks', there is a danger that a new generation of women and many women who do not remember all those anxious, self-critical discussions, the tentative formulation of concepts and the sharing of discoveries, will recoil from bewildering, rhetorical rage and dismiss feminism as a restricting and dogmatic idiom of thought rather than a source of liberation.

1. Outer Hebrides

◆◆◆◆◆◆

'Outer Hebrides' (September 1973) and 'When You Flinch From Me' (summer 1974) were originally published in *Cutlasses and Earrings*, ed. Michelene Wandor and Michele Roberts, Playbooks 2, 1977. Two poems about the pain of rejecting and being rejected, instead of a long address on the problem of connection and autonomy, the balance of being with others and remaining with oneself, identity and merging, freedom and ecstatic communion, reason and romance and a thousand and one other things a feminist needs to know. After which a still, small voice rises from the philosophical deep, 'Can I have my cake and eat it please?'

◆◆◆◆◆◆

Loving and hurting
have become for us
inextricable,
like the unspoken words
we persistently share
until I can no longer
settle in my own space
without the pang
of your desire.

There is so much of me
in you
nestling, easy, playing, caressing
A slow deep passion with belongings.

Now you are strangely vulnerable
No longer proudly covered
You have willed yourself
beyond
the western extremities
of our island

I've watched your face
over months
drawn in the effort of curing

The commitment tight
A mask melting in the shambling, trembling release
timed between bleeps,
to set again
cut by the black rage against exhaustion
pressing me into isolation.

Part of me had crept quietly away
Before my desertion.

2. When You Flinch From Me

A love
fitted in
between
outposts
spilt strong
over margins.
Its unworded
sureness
prising
the hub
of me.

Until I left you
and returned
to find
a dark stranger
loath and uneasy
in my arms.

When you flinch
from me,
my love
turns inward
and consumes
me.

3. Women . . . How Far Have We Come?

'Women . . . How Far Have We Come?', *Hackney People's Press*, November 1979.

This article indicates how a survey of one small women's group active in the Islington-Hackney area for nearly a decade reaches out to many issues of local and national politics.

It was written after a meeting of socialist feminists in Hackney had made me realise that even in one part of London the memory of what had been done in the women's movement just a few years before had been lost.

It is partial because my own knowledge was limited. But once assembled it is there to be added to or changed. I think we should break the paralysis of thinking we have to tell the whole truth or remain silent. We need to collect, compare and consider the stories of the development and struggles of women's liberation in other areas and other towns. After all, the people, the memories, the local community newspapers, the coverage in *Spare Rib* and women's newsletters are still around.

By examining the particular, even when much is left out, and another member of a group would have another version, we can also see how intention and practice do not always meet. This is a good safeguard against complacency or glibness when we recollect that the personal was not quite political or the collective work was two feminists stranded in a bad temper. We can grimace and remember that in making the world anew we can make no promises that it will be a rose garden.

●●●●●●

The first women's liberation group in Hackney began in the autumn of 1970. We were a continuation of one of the earliest groups in London which had met in Islington since 1969. We had to move because the house we met in was sold. So we called ourselves 'Islington-Hackney Women's Liberation Workshop Group'. At this time, there were seven groups in the London workshop network. The word 'workshop', which had been used in the American and British new left in the sixties carried the idea of working together equally and of organisation as a process.

Our group produced one of the early issues of *Shrew* in October 1970. Each group took turns to do *Shrew* so everyone's views could be expressed. Our issue included a lot of discussion about playgroups and nurseries because we had tried that summer to find out what kind of facilities for small children were needed in Islington by knocking on people's doors and asking them. We felt even then that we did not just need *more*, we needed different kinds of provision in which people had a say.

A single mother in Gingerbread and a woman with two young children were the main influences behind this and there was a long article about being housebound. There was also an interview with a West Indian woman from Hackney about nurseries, abortions, racism and relationships with men.

Next we produced a 'love' story as propaganda for birth control based on a true story a schoolgirl told one of us and a short pamphlet about women's liberation for schools with good cartoons drawn by Jenny Fortune in *The Women's Newspaper*. We thought up all the critical questions people said and each woman took one home and wrote her answer. Then we put it together. These were very basic and very clear – but I found in teaching that the story was always more popular than the pamphlet, though the cartoons were a hit.

In March 1971, there was the first big women's liberation International Women's Day march. After this, the movement in London grew very fast. By the end of 1971, there were fifty-six workshop groups and a men's liberation group listed in *Shrew*. This expansion was exciting but it overwhelmed our old network structure. We could no longer have our general meetings in someone's room! Now even at our local Dalston meetings, 40 women would be crowding into one room. People's faces changed from week to week. We no longer even knew one another's names. Some women never spoke. So we decided to split up into two consciousness-raising groups.

I went into the study group which met at Arsenal though about half of us lived in Hackney. We began by talking about Engels, Reich and Simone de Beauvoir and we organised a meeting open to men and women on Bernard Shaw's, Edward Carpenter's and Havelock Ellis's views on women's position. Reading these writers led us on to thinking about the family. We talked about our relationships with our parents and children, about the family as a place of work for women and tried to see how the family fitted into a capitalist society.

In 1971, a few of us became involved in the night cleaners' campaign, concentrating on leafletting in the City where many women from Hackney and East London were working. We held meetings in the City and in Hackney with the cleaners. The problem we encountered in this attempt to unionise women cleaners, not only with the contract system and the employers but also with the union officials, combined with a pamphlet written by Selma James, on women, the trade unions and work, to raise the whole issue of our approach to women, employment and trade unions.

Some women in the London workshop began to argue that it was a mistake for socialists and feminists to fight for women to work or to struggle in mixed unions. Women already worked in the home and should be paid wages. There was also talk of separate women's unions. In Arsenal, we did not see work as the single answer to women's liberation. But we were against wages for housework as we thought this would not change the existing division of work between men and women. In October 1972, we produced an issue of *Shrew* on work. This included a summary of women's strikes since 1968, articles on black women's position in the labour market, on teachers, secretaries, trade unions, equal pay, housework, motherhood, relationships with children. We wanted a shorter working week for men and women with full pay so both could care for children, tax concessions, not only for biological parents but for groups of people involved in childcare as well as a wide range of other childcare facilities.

By this time there was neither a workshop, a consciousness-raising group nor a study group in Hackney. But there was a network of libertarian women, some of whom had helped to produce *The Women's Newspaper* and the 'Miss World' pamphlet. They had felt the workshop did not take up local community issues which affected most women in their everyday life. They were involved in the claimants' union and in squatting. They were already interested in women's health, both in terms of the National Health Service and self-examination groups. There was also a *Women's Voice* group which emphasised women's situation as workers.

The issue of family allowances (now Child Benefit) was forced on the women's movement by the Tory tax credit plan. Like Essex Road Women's Centre, Arsenal believed the money should go to the person who was mainly responsible for caring for the child. This would usually be women but we did not want to exclude single fathers. With Walthamstow, Stratford and Ilford we formed the North East London Women's Family Allowance Campaign. We also tried to link up with Communist Party women in Tower Hamlets, Women's Voice in Hackney and with libertarian women.

Arsenal helped to call a meeting in Conway Hall, leafletted Ridley Road and gave out a thousand leaflets which we followed up on the estate on Queensbridge Road and neighbouring streets. We mainly got a good response to our petition, though one woman said, 'I'm not going to sign so all those unemployed men can have more babies. Dirty buggers.' I tried to get her to support free contraception which we'd helped Walthamstow group campaign for!

But after all this work, only one woman came to our meeting. She wanted to talk about her divorce, and not about family allowances! I had been involved in many non-starters like this in Hackney before and was inclined to shrug it off. But most women in Arsenal were very upset at our failure. As a result, it was felt that we had not the resources to embark seriously on local organising. Many of us were working full time, had other women's movement commitments and some also had children. Other women in Hackney were moreover getting more deeply involved in housing struggles and defending Rose Ingleby when she was evicted. They even occupied Hackney Town Hall in protest.

The first community nurseries in Hackney were starting around this time as well, while in Islington the women's centre was growing. So in Arsenal we tried to discuss some of the issues which had been raised by the family allowance campaign, wages for housework, the state, reforms and class. We got into rather deep water but we did prepare a paper for the second Socialist Feminist Conference in London in the autumn of 1973.

We were searching for something which related to our outside working lives and which could be of use to other people. Because many of us did or had worked in further education we decided to do a pamphlet about girls' training and women's studies. We did a short paper for a conference of trade unionists organised by the National Council for Civil Liberties in February 1974 and repeated it at the Women and Socialism conference in Oxford the following autumn.

By 1974, the political strains upon the structure of the London workshop were very severe. Behind the arguments about structure were big differences between women who were separatists and those of us who were not. Also new structures like Working Women's Charter, outside the workshop network, were appearing. On 14 September 1974, through the women's sub-committee of the trades council, there was a meeting on women's work in Hackney. I went to this as a representative from Arsenal. Everyone else went to an angry women's liberation workshop meeting. The two events were poles apart.

We began to shift away from the London workshop towards national women and socialism conferences and towards making local links with women in Hackney and Islington. With Essex Road women's centre we called a meeting of socialist feminists in London to report on what we were doing. We were amazed when women from sixty groups came. We set up regular monthly meetings to introduce new members to groups and to try and keep in touch with what all the diverse women's groups in Hackney and Islington were doing. These meetings continued for nearly two years and we did bring together women from health groups, consciousness-raising groups, the Abortion Campaign, the Working Women's Charter, Women in Manual Trades. But Islington groups came more than those from Hackney. Also, we never managed to be really comprehensive. There were such a variety of groups by this time in Hackney and Islington which ranged from Women's Aid for battered women, Gingerbread for single parents, and Under Fives, community nursery groups. I think partly because some of these were not simply women's groups their connection to the women's movement was now more complicated. Also they tended to include people who were very deeply committed and had very little time to spare. The meetings were also only partially successful in involving new members. After these collapsed Arsenal did try and hold other meetings for women who were not in groups, but as at Essex Road, there was a high turnover and we never felt we had found a solution to the continuing problem in the women's movement of creating a trusting personal small group atmosphere without discouraging new women by appearing to be small cliques and networks which no one could find, join or connect with.

We had run into serious difficulty when we tried to write up our pamphlet on girls and further education. We had worked collectively on shorter projects before, but this took so long that everyone became stale and we could not divide the work equally in a continuing way. It also raised a lot of political questions to which we did not have answers and got partially buried in the effort to finish. What were the political implications of trying to get more women into the skilled section of the working class? How did women's attitudes to skilled work relate to other aspects of their consciousness of themselves? The traditional approach of 'women's rights' to training which dealt with teachers, careers officers, trade union officials and employers did not really connect with the feminist emphasis upon changing women's and girls' consciousness. As feminist teachers how did we cope with the clash between what many girls wanted and what we thought as feminists they should want? We never resolved these problems. Though we wrote our pamphlet, it was not published, and none of us felt really happy with it. We did do an article, however, for a radical teachers' paper.

The next Women and Socialism Conference at Mile End was a disaster because of very sectarian interventions by a few women from tiny Trotskyist groups for which no-one was prepared. Arsenal did a workshop and a large part of the conference came as we were the only independent women's group who had any alternative paper ready on organisation. For a while after this there were no more national conferences and we had London socialist feminist educationals for about a year.

There was no longer a network of consciousness-raising and study groups in East London. But the National Abortion Campaign became very active. We had big meetings with left-wing Labour MPs. These marked quite a political change in the women's movement from the early direct action tactics, self-help or consciousness-raising groups. It was strengthening to realise we could hold large public meetings and campaign with loudspeaker vans like a formal political organisation. But we found it difficult to carry over the experience of the women's movement in discussing abortion in relation to our personal experience of our sexuality, our relationships, our attitudes to having children or childcare. There had been other local attempts consciously to combine personal exploration with public political action, for example a food coop on an estate in East London and a women's group at Lesney's toy factory. We could not make these connections in relation to the national campaign for abortion.

On a smaller scale, this was a problem in the Arsenal group as well. From the outside, we appeared to be a successful and productive women's group with a long history. But we never managed to overcome many tensions which had been there from the start. The personal never did become quite the political even in our small group. There was an unevenness in friendship patterns outside meetings. Sometimes, we ignored people's feelings in our efforts to complete projects. Or people felt let down because the others did not turn up to leaflet or give talks. Awkward silences appeared as people felt unwilling to take the initiative in case it was dominating. There were also differences which could be enriching in the good periods and cause conflicts in the bad times. Some women worked full time or part time, some had children others did not, some had a background of socialist activity before the women's movement, others became socialists through feminism. Our class backgrounds ranged from lower middle class to upper middle class. Some came from intellectual, liberal or left-wing families, others from right-wing backgrounds in which we were the first to go into higher education.

In autumn 1975 I wanted to talk about the clash between feminism and organising on the left. This was partly because of NAC and partly a result of the Mile End conference. But another woman opposed this for it would further exclude personal experience and create an unequal power situation between women with a knowledge of left group theory and practice and those without. So we returned to the sources of our feminism as a consciousness-raising group. We chose subjects individually important to us, our work, our families, growing old, women's songs and writing.

This increasingly personal emphasis became more vital for an older member became ill with cancer. We were part of a network helping her with cooking, cleaning and travelling through a long illness and attended her funeral with many others to pay tribute to her life and her work with women.

After this we closed together in a personal way and in 1977–8 became really a social group who enjoyed seeing one another. We were all involved in many different aspects of the women's movement and found we had less energy for Arsenal. Some of us joined socialist feminist groups or other consciousness-raising or study groups. We had a new phase of energy for a time in discussing recent Marxist theory and trying to see how it related to feminism but the impetus had gone and rather unsatisfyingly we dwindled to a halt in the autumn of 1978. It was like the end of a huge collective relationship because the women's centre in Islington had also collapsed.

In the late 1970s, the growth of socialist feminist and *Women's Voice* groups marked a more explicitly socialist phase of women organising. Community groups in which women work with men are much stronger now than in 1970. Practical campaigns to defend abortion rights and resist the devastating cuts are obvious priorities. There are also many informal support networks all over Hackney among women in which feminists are involved. Sometimes these can become the basis for more public action. For instance, in the Sandringham Road Housing Action area an Under-Fives group has been formed to try and get a toddlers' drop-in centre.

But the communication of the collective experience of women organising locally, which has been a much deeper process than a single personal account can express, remains piecemeal and haphazard. I still wonder uneasily about how women can become involved who do not see themselves as socialists or who do not bump into a friendship network. I also feel again that there is an urgency to learn what groups exist in Hackney and what they are doing. There have been moves in Islington for women to get together. Is there any chance of us doing this in Hackney this winter?

4. Storefront Day Care Centres, the Radical Berlin Experiment

(Edited by an authors' collective (German text 1970) by Catherine Lord and Renée Neu Watkins, Beacon Press, 1973.)

'Storefront Day Care Centres', *Women Speaking*, January-March 1974.

This review deals with practical efforts to solve particular needs for childcare in the German anti-authoritarian student movement of the late 1960s and the British women's movement of the early 1970s.

I have included it because these two attempts to develop forms of childcare did not simply meet a practical need. They raised the possibility of developing new relationships and consciousness, and, in the case of the North London Children's Centre, Dartmouth Park Hill, laboriously established an important precedent of the right to resources from the state while insisting on direct control by users and workers.

These were two important political realisations. They need to be affirmed and reassessed in full awareness of all the snags which have come up in trying to put them into practice, not only in relation to childcare but in education, health and the rest.

When I wrote this I had no idea that for two years my own material survival and the chance to write and think would be made possible by a nursery on the lines of Dartmouth Park Hill. And that I would be granted peace of mind because my son groaned when it was the weekend and he could not go to the nursery.

Much more goes into a book than meets the eye.

The right has mounted an enormous offensive on radical education from the nursery to the university. They have not only been able to make cuts, they have assailed the whole concept of democratic education. We need to assert an alternative tradition and persist in involving parents, children and people from the wider community in education. Teachers have skills but also need to be learning while they teach. This is an old adage well known in workers' education movements. Learning is not only reading, writing and arithmetic. In the early 1970s I watched the schoolchildren march along the embankment in the school strike singing, 'we shall over-come,' and learned a lesson I will never forget.

The storefront day care centres or children's shops in West Berlin came out of the practical needs of women who became active in the student movement of the late sixties and were part of their expression of discontent. They found that empty shops were cheap to rent – hence the name.

In the German student movement there was a great deal of discussion about education, culture, sexuality, authority relations. In the words of one male student leader, Krahl,

> To fight this society, we must begin, in the very way we conduct the political struggle, to sow the first seeds. To provide the first models for an alternative approach to human relationships, one freed from the duality of oppressor and oppressed. . . . To deny this society and catalyze another pattern of relationships we must be able, as individuals, to renounce our own egoism for the sake of the freedom of others and, at least partially, to repress ourselves to ensure that freedom for each individual coincides with freedom for others.

However, the reality was somewhat different. The student movement, committed to a strategy of large-scale and violent confrontations with the police, not only took its psychological toll on the participants, it left the women to 'push their carriages alongside the march or behind the front ranks. . . . The alternative was to stay home as passive sympathisers in the movement and to admire, or nurse the heroes on their return. This hit hardest the wives or girlfriends of men in the movement.'

The Women's Liberation Action Council was formed in the S.D.S. (Students for a Democratic Society) in January 1968. In the summer of '68 the groups which had already formed came together as the Central Council of Socialist Day Care Centres. They used as starting points the works of Reich and A.S. Neill's book about Summerhill. A pamphlet by Vera Schmidt 'Education without Repression' was also important but sadly is still not translated into English. Vera Schmidt's anti-authoritarian nursery in the Soviet Union is described by Reich in *The Sexual Revolution*. It was closed down in the early 1920s because of her refusal to repress infantile sexuality. However, the Germans came to feel there was a basic contra-diction in these earlier anti-authoritarian models because children were being educated to be free in an unfree society. In a speech to the students' conference in Frankfurt in the summer of '68 Helke Sander put this very clearly. The women's concern for day care was 'a necessary precondition for us to resolve our problems. Our hardest job is to avoid creating sheltered refuges for our children. We want to encourage them as they strive for freedom and so to give them the strength to face reality in a way that is committed to change.' Her speech was a very important moment in the emergence of women's liberation in Germany. Its intensity still comes through.

> The separation between private and public life always forces the woman into lonely endurance of the problems of her role. . . . Women can only find their identity if the problems previously hidden in the private sphere are articulated and made into the focus for women's political solidarity and struggle. Most women are apolitical because the one-sided political parties have always ignored their needs.

The Children's Shops were seen not only as a practical solution to the parents' needs but as a political means of breaking down this division. They were not just to be places where children were dumped but places where both parents and children could develop comradeship. Helke Sander struck home when she spoke of the effect of a long period of militant activity and the separation between public and personal life. 'Why don't you admit that you are exhausted by this last year, that you don't know how you can stand the strain of dedicating yourselves physically and mentally to a cause that gives you no direct reward. . . . Why do you all buy Wilhelm Reich? Why do you discuss the class struggle here and discuss at home what's lacking in your sex life?'

During 1969 other groups began to take up the ideas of non-authoritarian education in rather different contexts. Teachers and social workers started to struggle within state institutions. In West Berlin they formed the Socialist Teachers' League and the Workshop of Critical Social Workers. They agitated for sex education among young people. In the summer, exposure of conditions in a reform school led to investigation by a legislative committee and revolt among the young prisoners. As this spread to other reform schools and orphanages student houses and communes started to overflow with runaways. A strike of West Berlin kindergarten teachers was followed by one in Kreuzeberg in the autumn.

Although initiative for educational change was now coming from several different points the connections between them remained tenuous. The teachers' strike was defeated and there was growing uneasiness among the organisers of the Children's Shops. Some people felt they were being used by the state and that the non-authoritarian education of the children of left academics presented no challenge to the educational system as a whole. They feared they were becoming incorporated within an umbrella of liberal middle-class self-help.

The same dilemma has come up again and again in discussions about nurseries within women's liberation, not just in Germany but elsewhere. Indeed, in a recent article in *Red Rag*, Val Charlton argues it was one of the reasons why the campaign for nursery education never got off the ground in the British movement. It is very difficult for working-class parents to participate in a nursery where parents are in control but on the other hand a state nursery is unlikely to educate children in a radical way. 'Women in women's liberation were confused, suspicious, uncertain. They didn't want nurseries for everyone if the nurseries remained hot-beds of sexist ideology and authoritarian organisation.'

But on the other hand a refusal to campaign for nurseries which were financed out of rates and taxes meant you were letting the state and the local authority 'off the economic hook' (Valerie Charlton, 'The Patter of Tiny Contradictions', *Red Rag*, no. 5). In North London members of Women's Liberation have created an important new form of nursery. This is a house which is paid for by the council but controlled by the parents. The organisers see it as significant only if it spreads, for, like the Berliners, they don't want to make 'sheltered refuges'.

The similarities and differences between the North London Children's Centre and those in West Berlin are instructive. Both stress parent participation and the need for meetings to discuss ideas, organisation and to learn through the relationship with the children. Both see the children's learning to relate to one another as an essential aspect of education. They both mention the use of play materials which allow the children to improvise and create for themselves and emphasise real things, rather than toys, so that the child is not enclosed within a false fantasy of childhood. However, the West Berliners seem surprisingly unconcerned about the perpetuation of distinct sex roles and much more interested in the general question of not repressing infantile sexuality. This latter, in turn, does not seem to be a matter of concern in North London. The Germans too had a more directly socialist approach to educating small children. They point out that children in modern society are not really invulnerable and protected from social and political forces. In this century they have been the victims of war and starvation, they are assailed by right-wing propaganda in the form of patriotism and commercial values in advertising. The Berlin Children's Shops did not indoctrinate children in a passive or authoritarian manner, instead they trusted small children enough to give them the means of thinking and struggling for themselves.

> Political slogans coming out of children's mouths cause subliminal recall of horrible episodes in German history. The crucial error lies in fearfully avoiding any political education for children and swallowing the myth of an idyllic childhood in the bosom of the family, a myth which just favours reactionary indoctrination. . . . There is a difference between children carrying flags because a leader told them to and children carrying a flag that relates to their existence, one that means resistance to known oppression, e.g. in school.

The conviction that the creation of a new society requires a new and non-authoritarian type of education has a long tradition. In the mid-nineteenth century in Britain followers of the Cooperator, Robert Owen, organised nurseries and cooperative Sunday Schools while the socialist movement later started Socialist Sunday Schools. The Russian Revolution produced many experimental schools, though of a less radical kind than Vera Schmidt's. In Britain Dora Russell ran a free school in the 1920s and 30s. More recently the 'creches sauvages' appeared in France after May '68 resembling the West Berlin experiments in many ways. It is very important to chronicle the experience which has been gained from these to learn from past mistakes and successes and for this reason the account in *Storefront Day Care Centres* is extremely valuable.

5. Women Workers and Class Struggle

'Women Workers and Class Struggle', with Beatrix Campbell, *Radical America*, September-October 1974, vol. 8, no. 5. Since this was written, many studies of women's work and women and the trade union movement have been written by feminists going into the problems raised in this article more deeply, though a detailed study of women's industrial militancy in the 1970s remains unwritten.

Women's liberation ideas are now discussed more commonly in the trade union movement. Motions have been passed, campaigns mounted, conferences held, speakers invited and thousands of trade unionists have marched for the right of women to abortion. These are important changes. However, they are not enough — inequality remains and arrogance and contempt still bluster from the chair.

Having said this, we do well to remember that differences of class and race among women, differences in the nature of the work done by women with and without children, for example, make for a variety of needs. A movement for the liberation of women is about listening as well as demanding.

We have to hear not only what fills the public halls. Attention to personal life has always been the strength of our politics. Behind the weekend school there are arguments about housework. Behind the study of women and unemployment in the potteries there is a working-class man learning a new responsibility in relation to children. Behind a mother getting a lie-in on Saturday morning there is the shop steward taking a four-year-old to a meeting of car workers.

Working-class women have been saying in many ways over the last decade to men in the labour movement, 'We're *not* behind you, we're with you.' Unfortunately, in order to work as equals, there has had to be argument and conflict. This is likely to continue. The point is not to celebrate it, or dwell only on disagreement and fragmentation, but to seek ways of overcoming them and to remember that they have not been and are not the whole story. For unity and solidarity are our strengths and they are founded upon cornerstones of mutual respect.

Women now make up forty per cent of the workforce in Britain and over half of all women go out to work.[1] This means that the older pattern of spasmodic work outside the home with a long period spent in child-bearing is being replaced by a more continuous relation to the wages system. The effects of this change on women's consciousness are complex but extremely significant. They are complicated by the fact that the increase in the number of women workers is largely among married women with young children forced to do part-time unskilled work. Also the conditioning of little girls in the family to be submissive – to attend, serve, complement, and defer – continues when women go out to work. Feminine conditioning and job prospects reinforce each other.

Moreover, women are still mainly responsible for housework, so for women with families, work for wages is only one aspect of the total pattern of labour. Housework and caring for children and men is hidden labour, but essential for the continuing of work in the wages labour system. This double shift means that for the woman who goes out to work her work really is never done. Women are not just physically exhausted but also have trouble concentrating. Thus although women's lives span the community and industry – domestic production in the family and commodity production for capital – the perception of most women remains fragmented. A woman shop steward describes this fragmentation: 'A woman makes up her politics from bits and pieces. She only half listens to a programme on TV whilst she's doing the ironing or some other household job. She hasn't got the time to sit down and listen to something all the way through.'[2]

The male orientation of industrial relations and trade union bargaining reinforces this fragmentation by ignoring the specific situation of women as a sex. Women workers are thus presented as unorganisable and 'backward', a view which is unfortunately reinforced by many socialists. Within the women's movement in Britain in the last few years there has been a growing recognition of the need to understand how class exploitation and female oppression intertwine, and how some aspects of women's consciousness could, if recognised, have a positive and radical potential in questioning bureaucracy in the unions and the economistic concentration of much wage bargaining.[3]

This article reviews the various forms women's action at work has taken in the last few years in an effort to distinguish similarities to and differences from men's action. We will discuss both the struggles women have had to fight like men workers, and agitation against the specific inequalities of women, like strikes for equal pay.

Women at work are obviously subjected to the same pressures of the economic decline of British capitalism as men: unemployment, inflation, the determination of employers to resist wage demands, and the increasing tendency for the state to intervene directly to control pay. Unemployment, though, has probably affected women as a group less than men, because the immediate effect of redundancy has been in industry rather than in the service sector where women predominate.[4] On the other hand, women in manufacturing which is hit by unemployment have been affected rather more than men in the same industries, and have been involved in several struggles against redundancy. Much female employment is always hidden, because of the use of women by capital as a reserve of cheap and casual labour.

Women are concentrated in the low-paid jobs – in which immigrant women constitute a lower level even among women workers. Therefore the effects of inflation and wage freeze on women are especially harshly felt, particularly by women who have to be the sole supporter of a family. Job insecurity and a low level of union organisation often go with poor pay. Only just over a quarter of women workers are in unions, as opposed to half of the male labour force. Even among women who are union members, their role is often a passive one of paying dues but having little influence on policy making with their specific grievances frequently overruled.

Groups of workers who are badly paid, many of them in the public sector where the government can directly impose wage restraints, have been propelled into an unaccustomed militancy in the last few years. Perhaps another factor besides rising prices has been the determined intervention of employers and the state in the traditional mechanisms of trade union understandings of a fair wage and of accepted inequities between various sections of the working class. Thus productivity deals, incomes policy, and the rhetoric of economic planners about the plight of the lowly paid have ironically thrown long-standing implicit acceptances of differences open to examination.[5] This has strengthened the continuing tendency within capitalism to break down old craft skills and confuse the distinction between skilled and unskilled. Demands for parity and equal pay extend the range of what is comparable.

Influences upon consciousness are difficult to chart and prove without very deep and detailed studies of particular disputes which we lack at present. While the existence of women's liberation has had some directly traceable effects on particular disputes in which women have been involved recently, its impact has been more as an external symbol of defiance. Simply hearing about the action of other women at work can be important too. The Fords sewing machinists who went on strike for the right of women to be accepted on the higher pay grades in summer 1968 and closed down Fords undoubtedly encouraged other women.[6] In 1972 a shop steward, June Marriner, involved in a dispute in Goodmans loudspeaker factory in Havant, Hampshire which had not been previously unionised, said the women workers read about and discussed women's liberation and were encouraged by the action of other working-class women who resisted redundancy by occupying a shoe factory in Fakenham, Norfolk.[7]

New rank and file militancy

Whatever the precise causes, there have been several upsurges of rank and file militancy in industries where either there has not been action for a long time or militant action has not been taken before. Women have played a significant part in both these developments. Early in 1970, 14,570 workers in the Leeds clothing industry, many of them women, erupted after about thirty years of quiescence. They stopped work in protest against an agreement signed by their union officials which had productivity strings attached. The unofficial strike spread to South Yorkshire and the Northeast of England.

Like many strikes in which women are involved, it had an element of released exultation and celebration. In Leeds, a hard and dour manufacturing city, the women poured out onto the grass verges, walking from factory to factory to get other workers out, howling down the union official who came up to get them back to work and setting up a rank and file committee which brought the fusty trades council to life. During the dispute the question of equal pay was raised. The final compromise, though, left the women deflated and disillusioned.

A continuing and problematic feature of much of the rank and file militancy in the last few years has been the difficulty of connecting and sustaining the offensive. This was certainly true of the Leeds clothing strike, though the women did pass on the use of the mass picket which was to be crucial in winning the miners' strike in 1972.[8] The pattern of short unofficial strikes in the early sixties began to change in the beginning of the seventies when the number of long official strikes went up. Large numbers of workers have been involved, many of whom have not taken action for a long time, if ever. Many of these workers are in the public sector, nationalised industries or government service. 6,000 post office workers went on strike between January and March 1971. Women played an active part demonstrating and chanting in London, though the press highlighted women who broke the strike. There was no strike pay in the post office strike. Young girls who moved to London for work paying weekly rent in bed sitters (one-room apartments) without savings were in a difficult position. The Post Office workers did not get the fifteen per cent they asked for; instead they were given nine per cent. The official strike of workers unaccustomed to militancy has proved as vulnerable as rank and file upsurges unless help comes from other trade unionists.[9]

There have been other strikes in the public sector which have included large numbers of women. In hospitals, ancillary workers in 1972–3, and more recently radiographers and nurses in the summer of 1974, have taken action. It has always been difficult for these workers to act because a strike affects people who are the patients, not profits. It is particularly hard for women in hospitals, especially nurses, where the emphasis is on the altruistic caring aspect of the job. Teachers, where women predominate in the lower-paid sectors, are in a similar predicament. So are social workers, who, with other local government employees, went on strike this year.

It is interesting that in these disputes the rejection of professionalism and the growth of trade union militancy have been accompanied by a questioning of the manner in which capitalist society shapes and distorts the public and social services. Thus hospital workers have started a ban on private practice and are insisting that patients come within the National Health Service. Socialist teachers have been struggling for anti-authoritarian relations with pupils in the schools as well as more pay. Teachers in the women's move-ment have been contesting the sexist values which are still dominant in the education system. Similarly, social workers in the radical grouping Case Con have exposed the aspect of class control and the particular containment of women both within the workforce and as clients.[10]

These official strikes in the public sector have involved large numbers of workers; but there have also been pockets of militancy among low-paid workers – including women – in the private sector. The numbers involved have probably been less but they have nonetheless occurred with a persistent and significant frequency. Their importance has not been so much in the extent of their immediate gains, but in the effects on people's consciousness of trade union struggle in areas which are often geographically remote and in factories and work places where trade unionism is far from automatic.

One example of such action is the long-drawn-out strike in a thermometer factory in a small town called Cleator Moor in Cumberland. The strike was quite simply for the right of workers to join a union and keep their jobs. The employer, Brannon, had been given a grant by the government to take his business to Cleator Moor, where there was little alternative employment. He was not only paying low wages but was negligent over safety, and cases of mercury poisoning occurred. The strike divided the small town very deeply, causing conflict not only between friends but within families. Despite this the strikers, mainly women, showed great determination and tenacity. In such circumstances the struggle for unionisation becomes a question not just of economic gain, but also of political commitment.

The occupation at Fakenham in Norfolk was an indication of the speed with which new trade union tactics, like the work-in to avoid redundancy, can be taken up by workers who have no background of trade union militancy and are initially politically conservative in their views. The Fakenham occupation transformed the outlook of the women. They started to break down craft privilege, teaching everyone closely guarded skills. They started to make leather goods in a creative way instead of just repeating the same shoes. Like the Cleator Moor strikers they met all kinds of people, ranging from socialists from Norwich to Dutch members of women's liberation. But these new trade union tactics are still limited by the continuation of capitalism. The Fakenham women successfully established a cooperative but found they had difficulty in selling in the open market.

There have been various other occupations in which women have participated. For instance, men and women at Briants' colour printing occupied their factory in South London. The women had to fight an attempt of one of the older male stewards to send them home at night. They insisted on an equal part. 'We're not behind the men, we're with them.' In September 1973, after a five-week strike for union recognition, men and women at a Seiko watch repair centre in Kilburn, London, barricaded themselves into the manager's office for twenty-four hours. They took in sleeping bags and food. TV and hot and cold water were already there – courtesy of the management, who were unable to do much to harass the occupiers without potential damage to thousands of pounds worth of watches. Their demands were all met, the union recognised, back pay given for the weeks on strike. However, and this is another example of the limitations on new militant tactics, three months later they got dismissal notices two days before Christmas. Another, and this time rather more successful occupation which included women, occurred at Tillotsons, Liverpool, a print and packaging factory.

Employers respond

Employers in unorganised and semi-organised jobs respond to the most basic demands, like the manufacturers in the period of early industrialisation, by trying to crush workers with severity rather than coopt them by accommodation. A particularly blatant case of this was the women's liberation campaign to unionise night cleaners working in offices between ten at night and six in the morning.[11] The women work in small groups. They are already exhausted by housework, caring for small children and husbands when they go to the buildings. Many of them are immigrants, and few have had any previous experience with unions. The employers responded to their joining the union by moving the women from building to building, by racist insults, victimisation, refusing to negotiate with the union officials and not recognising the union. Despite this onslaught, some gains were made by cleaners in London and other towns where the campaign was taken up. But even when a particular contractor was forced to give way, if the contract was given to another company the agreement with the union ceased to be valid! The harsh brutality of life in capitalism's bargain basement is a frequent experience of women workers.

In November 1973 seventy women in a Biro-Bic factory in Reading sent in a petition complaining because they were working from 7:15 A.M. to 4:15 P.M. with a thirty-minute lunch break, taking home £15 a week with a fine of £1.75 on top of a loss in wages if they missed a day. After two half-day walkouts they joined the engineering union, AUEW, and elected stewards, only to have to then fight for union recognition. It is important to remember that for many women workers simply joining a union can be an exhausting, consuming struggle. While modern capitalists devise complicated mechanisms to control well-organised workers, old-style straightforward repression also still operates for the unorganised.

The economic situation and the government measures to control workers make this even harder. With the failure of industrial legislation the Tory government tried to limit the rights of workers to picket, and police were not over concerned if workers picketing were hurt by management. Very recently unionised women workers thus found themselves in quite violent pickets. At General Electric (GEC) Salford Electrical Instruments in Eccles and Heywood, Lancashire, ninety women and men who were only recently unionised went on strike because their wages were being held back under phase 2. Management drove through the Eccles picket line and used a dog to intimidate pickets, biting one. A woman who was in women's liberation and an International Socialist member were arrested supporting the picket.

At both Eccles and Heywood the women transformed the whole activity of picketing by literally inhabiting the picket line. South Wales miners donated a little yellow fibreglass hut which the Eccles women sat in outside the factory gates. They installed cooking facilities to make tea, and chairs and tables. One day the management, so incensed by its presence, hoisted the hut and lifted it over the factory fence, leaving behind it the perplexed women who'd been sitting under it. The strikers at Eccles drifted back to work, but those at Heywood stayed completely solid and got backing from workers on the shop floor. They made themselves a picketing base by occupying an empty house owned by the firm just opposite the factory, putting in carpets and cooking apparatus and even decorating the mantlepiece with flowers.

There are several examples of women opposing other government measures. Jean Jepson, a convenor at Armstrong Patents, was sacked for refusing to accept the three-day week in Beverley, Yorkshire, in January of this year.[12] Also in January, 1,200 workers, mainly women, in Camborne, Cornwall, threatened to strike when management arranged the three-day week to include working on New Year's Day.

There have also been strikes against redundancy and attempts by management to break up work patterns to gain more control over workers. In March 1974 2,000 production workers at Birmingham's Lucas factory walked out in protest against redundancy. Ninety per cent of these workers were women. In publishing in May 1974 Claire Walsh was made redundant at Allen Lane, Penguin Books. She was reinstated after forty-one workers, including women on the switchboard, occupied Penguin's and 250 printers refused to print hard-back Allen Lane books. 200 women at GEC Raglan Street in Coventry went on strike to defend their jobs because management intended to move the work over to another factory in Swansea. This was seen as an attempt to break the union militancy of the Coventry factory.

Support from male workers

In these struggles of women to unionise, to get more pay, and to fight against particular aspects of the current crisis, in both the private and public sectors, support from other workers has proved vital. This has taken several forms. Women workers have been helped by men in picketing. When the night cleaners at the Admiralty building in Fulham went on strike in the summer of 1972 the refusal of delivery men to take in milk, food, and perhaps most vital beer, was an important means of pressure. Similarly, at Barbour's rainwear factory in South Shields in the same year, sixty women earning £10.60 for a forty-hour week went on strike for union recognition and a £2 rise. Men in the Transport and General Workers Union and fifty sheet-metal workers from the neighbouring factory helped them to picket after police brought in reinforcements. There have also been occasions when not only has the potential division between men and women workers been overcome, but also the old suspicion between manual and non-manual workers. In April 1974 six typists in East Kilbride Scotland working in a subsidiary of Bunch oil won increases of £4–£5 after engineering workers on the shop floor blacked deliveries. Nurses in June were supported by other trade unionists with one-day strikes or demonstrations in Nottingham, Carmarthen, Manchester, Doncaster, Darlington, Leamington, Norwich, Edinburgh and Sunderland. The workers involved included dockers, miners, dustbin men and market workers. A particularly impressive example of support occurred in 1969 in the British Sound Recording dispute, where 1,000 workers, mainly women, went on strike for four months for union recognition. The local council of East Kilbride in Scotland supported them. There were also short stoppages in solidarity throughout the central belt of Scotland which involved a total of 200,000 people and were successful.

Despite these instances of support there have also been cases of opposition and apathy from male workers.[13] In July 1973 at GEC Spon Street, Coventry, women workers earning a basic rate of £13 a week found that the introduction of new materials would bring their piece rates down even more. They decided to go on strike despite the opposition of the convenor in their union, the Amalgamated Union of Engineering Workers. Albert Beardmore told drivers to please themselves about crossing the picket lines and set them a militant example by crossing it himself saying, 'I'm not going to have my men laid off by a bunch of silly girls.' One picket was knocked over trying to persuade someone not to enter. Beardmore then tried to take away his deputy Elsie Noles's AUEW union card because she supported the women. By September the factory had been completely closed down. Beardmore was overruled by a mass meeting but remained intransigently chauvinist. He organised a kangaroo court of other stewards which voted to expel Elsie Noles. This was hastily changed by the AUEW district committee which reinstated her.

Black and Asian women

Even more wrinkled and complex struggles have faced black and Asian women in several disputes which have had a racial as well as an industrial component. In some of the big public service strikes black women have presented a new and dynamic presence, not surprising since thousands of black women are employed in this sector, particularly as hospital workers.

However, there have been a number of disputes in recent years with distinct racial overtones in which sometimes the strikers have found themselves pitted not only against the employer but against the union too. Most recently, about half the 600 or so Asian workers who walked out of the Imperial Typewriters factory in Leicester were women. The strike was sparked by a bonus dispute, in which the management had cheated the assembly line workers out of their bonus. During the strike the strikers, particularly the women, spilled much accumulated resentment against their treatment at the hands of white racist foremen. The local union leadership was positively hostile to the dispute and uttered many a bitter word against it, supporting the 500 or so workers who had remained inside the gates. However, the strikers appealed to the national leadership of the Transport and General Workers Union, and after many weeks a settlement was reached involving a return to work without victimisation. Significantly, the women decided to organise a women's group within the union in the factory through which they can air specifically their own grievances.

Despite the continuation of racist attitudes, despite the survival of men like Beardmore in the trade union movement, and despite cases of official trade union half-heartedness about the organisation of women workers, a very important shift has occurred since the Fords women's strike in 1968. Men like Beardmore are now being increasingly forced onto the defensive. This change in the climate of assumption towards women workers has not only forced through legislation about equal pay, it has meant that several unions have taken important initiatives in these areas of special female inequality.

At the end of the sixties, a commitment which had existed formally in the Labour movement since 1888 on equal pay was expressed in legislation when the Labour government's employment minister, Barbara Castle, drew up a long-awaited bill to introduce equal pay by 1975. The bill appeared in the wake of sporadic outbreaks of quite dynamic industrial action, notably the Fords women's strike and the British Sound Recording dispute in Scotland, and escalating pressure from industrial spheres in which there was strong union organisation involving women. The legislation, however, long awaited as it had been, arrived thin and flimsy, fraught with loopholes and without the crucial back-up of anti-discrimination legislation. Barbara

Castle's Tory counterpart, Robert Carr, the shadow minister in opposition, had suggested including a discrimination clause in Castle's bill, but was defeated on the ground that a special anti-discrimination bill was not required. When the Tories took power in 1970, they were first resolutely unconvinced by the years of arguments and wave of pressure for a bill, and spent the next four years filibustering and prevaricating, only to come up with proposals so limited and limp as to be useless.

It must be said that the arrival of the act was soured too by the memory of Barbara Castle's patronising and defusing intervention in the Fords women's strike, symbolised by her 'talking it over' with the ladies over a cup of tea. Out of the coincidence of industrial action and the need to mobilise quickly for the implementation of the Equal Pay Act grew the National Joint Action Campaign for Women's Equal Rights (NJACWER), which attempted to span both the incipient women's liberation movement, the incipient organisations of the left and the trade union movement. But despite some initial effects and public pressure, this frail body was extinguished, more by internecine tug of war than of anything else.

Women's liberation and working women

Since the demise of NJACWER there has been no nationally coordinated women's movement around work and industrial struggle, and in practice the women's movement has neither had the confidence nor the contact with industrial workers to directly penetrate the labour movement.

Having said that, the very existence of the women's movement has generated a degree of consciousness which has percolated through many spheres and institutions, no less the trade unions than anywhere else, and the past two or three years particularly have seen a little more potent commitment to equal pay than hitherto. One of the four points of the engineering workers' struggle in 1972 was equal pay, a demand which all too quickly evaporated in many areas because in general the struggle had falled to really take off – thus the women's demand was the first to go. Nevertheless, the union had made some form of commitment to equal pay.

A tougher line has been taken by the Engineers' technical and administrative section (TASS), which has both encouraged and backed industrial action by women consistently. It was one of the first unions to smash through the counter-inflation barricade to win very substantial pay rises for women clerical workers in the Nuswift fire extinguisher factory in a small, hard-bitten Yorkshire industrial town called Elland. Here the women went on strike over the Easter holiday, staying out for over two months, after having been union members for only a couple of months. They were immediately supported by the male production workers, who walked out and stayed out. When the strike ended successfully, the men marched into the factory behind their union banner, through a corridor of cheering, clapping women.[14] Now this union is appointing a women's organiser.

Similarly, another administrative workers' union, APEX, unlike TASS not known for its militancy, has committed itself to taking industrial action in support of progress toward equal pay, and has insisted that all pay settlements include improvements in women's relative earnings. However, this has been strictly within the financial limits set by the Tory government's counter-inflation curbs, which permitted initially a one-third and later a one-half reduction in the pay differentials between men and women. Hundreds of factories were affected by this union's decision and scores were hit by industrial action. As mentioned earlier, the most bitter struggle was at a subsidiary of Arnold Weinstock's massive GEC empire, which had clearly pitted itself against any equal pay breakthrough. For the union GEC was the hardest employer to crack.

Another white-collar union, Clive Jenkins's scientific, technical and supervisory staffs' ASTMS, has taken specific action to mobilise women. Within the Pilkington's glass complex the union got the management to agree to regular meetings of women's representatives from each Pilkington site in Britain. The same union is having regular meetings of women in the Northwest of England, and in the South women members are getting together. Clearly, in terms of union initiatives, the most consistent progress around equal pay has arisen where the union involved already had some real commitment and sensitivity both to women's situation and to women's demands. According to an official in the Sheffield-based small tools engineering industry, much of the movement generated around women's demands there at the end of the sixties and early seventies was precisely because the union had set up a women's advisory committee regionally to alert the union to women's demands.

Despite the tenuousness of the links between trade unions and women's liberation, it is certainly true that union consciousness has been informed by the feminist movement, and in some unions progress has been the result of pressure by feminist women. Of course, more generally important has been the percolation of ideas and experience from the women's movement into the trade unions. Although women's liberation has not been able to organise particularly effectively among working women, it has always been ready to give support, and is now beginning to initiate and participate in a new broad movement based on women wage-earners' demands.

Out of the official trade union movement this year came the 'Working Women's Charter', a compendium of points covering pay, opportunity, training, maternity leave and childcare. It emerged initially from the London Trades Council, which comprised representatives from scores of trades councils throughout the capital. At an initial meeting in London the charter and possibilities of organising around it immediately became the focus for sectarian wrangles. However, in other parts of the country it has become the pivot of equal rights campaigns based on work and indeed involving men, and of significant attempts to breach the gap between the feminist movement and women workers. Certainly although the charter came out of an official trade union context it is likely to be taken up most enthusiastically by the rank and file movement and by the women's movement, and indeed this is already the case.

At the same time the struggle for anti-discrimination legislation has been supported by women's liberation, the labour movement and other agencies, not the least of them the National Council for Civil Liberties. The NCCL this year has made a considerable intervention in the struggle of women, both by organising working women's conferences, which for once really do draw together shop stewards, union members, and women's liberation activists, and by launching a model bill which is both more comprehensive than any of the half dozen which stumbled vainly through the House of Commons and the Lords, and more effective.[15]

The special position of women workers

Women's position at work cannot be understood in class terms alone. The ideas and feelings women have about themselves, the attitudes of men, the material circumstances of women's producing life are part of the particular predicament of women as a sex. Although there are differences between the circumstances of women of different classes, there are also important similarities. The sex divisions have a real basis in the actual situation of women, and form a crucial element in women's consciousness of themselves as workers. Women share all the difficulties of men at work. They have to struggle against employers and sometimes against apathetic officials in their own unions who see union work as a job like any other and regard militancy as an irritating interruption to their routine. But there are the added problems of being female: internalised passivity so you feel incapable inside your deepest self, the external reality of inequality at work, the double shift of housework, and the arrogant inability of some male officials and workers to recognise the specific oppression of women workers and learn from them. Sylvia Greenwood, a shop steward, describes this: 'It's a hard job for a woman trade unionist. You're not just battling against management, you're battling against the sex problem, and it's one of the most difficult there is.'[16] In the case of West Indian and Asian women there is the added problem of racism, as the dispute at Imperial Typewriters showed.

Some of these difficulties take an explicit form. Men organise meetings when women have to put children to bed and then complain that the women are backward when they don't turn up. Others are less explicit and harder to confront, such as the overwhelmingly masculine atmosphere of many trade union meetings, so women feel pinned down and cornered by the force of male assumptions. There is also language. Audrey Wise, a trade unionist in the shop workers union USDAW expresses this: 'there's . . . the deep-rooted male terminology. . . . At one meeting I was at the chairman used the term "old women of both sexes" and when I objected . . . I knew I'd be told I had a trivial mind . . . and sure enough up got the other speaker and said, "I'm very surprised at Comrade Wise bringing us down to this trivial level." But you see it isn't trivial and you have to take a very deep breath to stand up for women as a sex, as people.'[17] Too often, too, far from really confronting specifically women's problems, discussion is steered into the same spheres as any other trade union gathering, without either the seriousness or effectiveness of the mixed congress.

Each instance of male contempt is invariably seen as trivial. The effect of innumerable instances smothers and stifles women's dignity as a sex. It saps the courage from us. The challenge which has been made to this internationally by the growth of the new feminism is a source of great strength to women, but the direct application of this consciousness and organisation in the work situation of working-class women is still tentative. New forms of organising can't be constructed artificially. They grow out of changing combinations of circumstances. But the recognition and sifting of their initial appearances can nonetheless have a crucial influence on their chance of survival. Within women's liberation in Britain there has been a good deal of discussion of the questions of separatism and autonomy. There has also been an attempt by a working woman in Lancashire to start a separate women's union, and this was discussed though rejected by some of the women in the Fakenham occupation.

Separatism and autonomy

The initial appeal of clearing off and getting on with it on your own is powerful. The problem is the real world goes on without you. As far as women's separate unions go there are strong practical disadvantages. The separate union cannot overcome the real vulnerability of many women workers, either because they work in small units of production or in labour-intensive sectors where they can be replaced, or because of lack of strong unionisation and the responsibilities of women's double shift. Also separate women's unions share the dilemmas of small breakaway unions, of not having large enough funds to pay strike money, and therefore being doomed to militant rhetoric and the practice of a friendly society. There were even problems with women's separate organisations within trade unions. The Women's Trade Union Congress meeting is always in danger of becoming a kind of ghetto where women's talk is contained and safely ignored by men. This is an old argument in the trade union movement and the reason for the hostility of many women trade unionists to separate organisation.

On the other hand, the women's TUC does provide a place where women who would otherwise be squashed out can express and develop proposals. The experience of the women's movement has been that there is a world of difference between being segregated to keep you quiet and dividing to organise autonomously off your own bat. Autonomous organisation means you are in control of your own organisation, it does not mean that you are cut off from connections with men at every point. When women meet together they create a confidence and trust which is vital in overcoming centuries of conditioning into suspicion and rivalry. Moreover it is only by meeting together as women that we can bring out and delineate the contours and extent of our specific oppression as a sex. Without this exposure oppression festers and consumes us.

Autonomous women's groups at the work place, within an industry or in a trade union branch, could be an important means of preventing male-dominated trade unions from dismissing women. There have, it is true, been spasmodic and temporary groups which have formed in the past, but not on a conscious basis of fighting sexism at work and in the unions, and not with any connection to one another. The women's movement forms a means of at least indicating such a consciousness and such connections.

There are a few tentative signs that this is happening among women who are in or affected by women's liberation. This parallels the growth in trade union militancy of white-collar workers, many of whom are women, in teaching, the civil service and local government, including social workers, and the publishing industry. Local government employees, non-manual as well as manual, accountants, planners, architects, clerical workers in town halls and social service workers have been on strike for several months in London for an all-London allowance for extra cost of living and working in the capital. There has also developed a group of women social workers who are members of the National Association of Local Government Officers union to discuss and work out the connections between their position as women working in the family and conditioned into femininity in relation to their work which produces within the welfare state many features of the female caring role in the family. There have been similar developments among school teachers.

It would be misleading to exaggerate the extent to which these connections are being made. Nonetheless, there are definite stirrings among women at work and a determination to resist on several fronts. An important strand in the way in which feminism is informing an understanding of class exploitation is the theoretical debate about the reproduction of labour power by the woman in the home. The discussions of the women social workers in the radical Case Con grouping are making this more concrete. The emphasis within the women's movement on culture and language in defining women's consciousness has been taken up by Audrey Wise and given a specific application in relation to trade unions. She has also criticised the dismissal of aspects of women workers' demands by male-dominated trade unions. Women are often seen as backward because they insist on the improvement of conditions, whereas unions are geared to translating grievances into money. Audrey Wise argues that women's attitude towards work reflects a determination to stay human in dehumanising circumstances, a refusal to give themselves over totally to the wage bargain with capital, which comes from women's peculiar situation in capitalism, at once in the wage labour system and yet also responsible for another form of work which is not valued in cash.[18]

Finally the implications of feminism are not of relevance only to women. They force a re-examination of the distorted manner in which men can be men in capitalism. Men are changed by women changing – even if the process is a long and painful one. The autonomous organisation of women within the trade unions and at work would inevitably affect the consciousness of male workers. It could be of great significance in breaking down the splits between work and home, between economic and personal life, and could extend the concept of workers' control to cover the whole range of human activity.

6. Women in Islington

'Women in Islington', *Islington Gutter Press*, June-July 1975, no. 21.

This article captures the mood of the women's movement in the mid 1970s. The small groups had taken root locally. Women's centres were being set up and taking on the wider problems in the community. The abortion campaign, health education in schools, defence of hospitals, legal advice, women's trade union organisation, links and struggles with trades councils, the militancy of workers in the service industries which involved battles not only with private employers but with the state, with local councils, Labour as well as Conservative, were all part of this process of activity and political education. The Working Women's Charter and local women's centres helped to develop links in some areas, while the women's sub-committees on trades councils in other places were beginning to have a real life. The process of connection was always somewhat haphazard and incomplete but it was not in fact being done by the established parties and groups or even by any one strand in the women's movement like the socialist feminist 'current'.

This activity of the mid-seventies deserves examining. At the time it could organise meetings of several hundred people locally and mount national campaigns and abortion demonstrations involving thousands of people. When Renée Short spoke in Hackney Town Hall at a meeting on abortion in this period she expressed surprise at the spontaneous movement which had sprung up. With a smile I reflected upon the concept of spontaneity. As Trotsky said in his *History of the Russian Revolution*, for every tram driver who refuses to drive any further there is a long process of political thought and struggle. Spontaneity requires a lot of organising. It is necessary to be dishonest in order to tell the truth.

The Cooperative Hall, Islington, was very full on Wednesday June 18th. People were packed in at the back and sitting on the bookstall. Some of the speakers still hadn't arrived at 7.30 when the Working Women's Charter meeting was due to begin, so the Broadside Mobile Workers' Theatre started things off with a performance of the 'International Women's Year Show'.

They took up the demands of the Working Women's Charter and made them come alive with sketches and songs. What does International Women's Year really mean for women behind all the politicians' dinner parties with celebrities and nods to women at official meetings?

It could mean employers dodging the equal pay act by regrading women's work.

It has already meant the law lords deciding a rapist can be acquitted if he honestly, scouts honour, or something, believes consent has been given no matter how unreasonable that belief might be.

'What do you mean, she led you on?'

'She was on her own at a bus stop, wearing a skirt.'

The audience laughed at this sketch, but behind the women's laughter was a recognition of the bias in the laws against women, and especially against working-class women.

The performance presented issues like this as a kind of live news and captured moments behind the bland information you get in newspapers.

They showed women fighting back too, demanding safe legal abortions, the right to decide whether to have a child, campaigning for nurseries, equal pay, for well-paid work. They sang Peggy Seeger's 'I wanna be an engineer' which expresses the difficulty women face in trying to get skilled work. The girl in the song who wants to be an engineer is discouraged by her mother, her husband, and then employed at a lower rate than the men as cheap labour by the boss. Another song, by Sandra Kerr, 'I'm just a maintenance engineer' described the unrecognised labour women do in the home caring for men and children.

These songs are both ironic. They make you smile, but in the smiling they bring the everyday ways in which women are kept down out onto the surface. Songs can make you realise things that talking cannot.

The most moving song was from Germany in the 1930s and was written by Bertolt Brecht, the socialist poet and playwright, in protest against the change in the abortion laws. The song has an obvious meaning for us. There is James White's bill before Parliament now. If it were to become an act it would mean that most women who became pregnant by mistake would not be able to get an abortion. The campaign against this bill is not just to defend the law which made it illegal to get an abortion. Behind this decision was the Fascist attitude to women. The Nazis were against women having independence and choice. They wanted to turn women into passive breeding machines who could not think and decide things for themselves. And they wanted a lot of babies born to grow into soldiers and factory hands. They were not concerned about either the children of the mothers as individuals, but only about the power of the state.

In the song a working-class woman goes to a male doctor for an abortion and is sent away with a smug lecture about her duty to breed. She explains her poverty and desperation, but he brushes that aside. He could never face such problems. How can she bring up another child? What kind of future will the child have? Is the mother's life to be one of unending struggle until she is old?

It reminds us that our struggle is not only for the 1967 Act which is by no means perfect, nor is it even for abortion on demand alone. It is part of a wider struggle for control over our lives part of which involves being able to express our sexual feelings without guilt or fear. In Brecht's song the contempt of the doctor for his working-class patient, his control over her future, is a symbol of the power of the state over us in a society based on class, sex, and race inequalities.

After the theatre group, Pamela Ditton, a solicitor from Islington Community Law Centre, described the gaps in the bill which is trying to make sex discrimination illegal.

Linda Smith talked about the effect of inflation, redundancies, and the crisis on women and stressed the importance of women's resistance to James White's bill.

Sue Oppenheimer, a member of Islington Working Women's Charter, said what the group had been doing in Islington. Women in Islington were working in sweatshops completely unorganised, or at home for very low rates. Even in large and established firms like Marks and Spencers the union was still banned. Some of these conditions were so familiar that people took them for granted. The women's charter group was trying to change that. She went on to describe the activities of the campaign to save Liverpool Road Hospital, the campaign against White's bill, and the nursery campaign.

Brenda Newman and Cathy O'Brien who were both made redundant from Crosfield's Electronics factory when it was taken over by de la Rue, a holding company, told the meeting about their experiences in the eight-week occupation. Brenda Newman said that she had really learned from the occupation and stressed that the women were completely equal with the men workers. Cathy O'Brien has found out since about how things are stacked against women. She is a trainee electronics inspector but can't find work as a woman. She's been told to return for a job as a receptionist.

Finally, Jane Maple rushed in straight from a union meeting of Hackney Nursery Workers who have been involved in a long struggle with the council. She spoke with great determination of the solidarity of the women and their anger at the council's refusal to grant them the same conditions as other local government employees.

7. Leninism in the Lurch

'Leninism in the Lurch', *Red Rag*, no. 12, spring 1977. The ideas in this article were formulated in the course of Workers' Education Association classes I gave on the recent history of the left in Britain and on ideas in the women's movement. The students included feminists, trade unionists, people in left groups, local government and community workers. It developed into my section in *Beyond the Fragments* via talks at meetings organised by socialist societies, the International Marxist Group and discussions in a women's group which prepared a paper for a socialist feminist conference.

There was an eigthteen-month pause, however, between the *Red Rag* article and starting to write *Beyond the Fragments*. Leninism was left to stew in its own juice. The reasons were not philosophical but material. I went into labour a few days after doing this article.

Bea Campbell replied to it in the following issue of *Red Rag*, with critical support of Leninism.

It's often hard to pinpoint when you first understood the ideas which have grown around and out of us in the women's movement over the last few years. This makes it hard to realise and express their significance because we have all been participators. Learning has been a living experience, not a collection of detachable theories we can move around easily. The ideas are so close that they loom obvious until it becomes impossible to distinguish how much we have innovated.

It is perhaps this difficulty of living in a movement and detaching ourselves enough to disentangle what is generalisable in our politics which has contributed to the split many of us who are socialists and feminists know. We sit with our feminism amidst all those intense and close debates on domestic labour and sexuality in small groups, then we pass to a more external and formal context as socialists to trade unionism, the vanguard party and points of order. The existence of this split is perhaps historically understandable as the women's movement has grown up largely despite the leadership of the socialist organisations, with a good deal of guerrilla burrowing by individual women on the left. We are not rabbits, however, and continually burrowing between the two divides has begun to make it hard to move now. Many of us are forced to opt either for forms of organising which ignore the issues and ways of seeing we have developed as feminists, or to absent ourselves from left politics outside the women's movement. I know many socialist feminists feel uneasy with the false option of theoretical deference or emotional rejection of the whole heritage of revolutionary debate on organisation. I believe the option on this particular burrow to be a dead end. In order to get out of it I think we need to be more explicit about how we are changing Marxism and of the implications of these changes in relation to the traditions of organising on the left.

We have spent a lot of time examining the economic significance of housework. Despite the technical and political disagreements which have come out, most socialist feminists would insist on the need for a socialism which would transform the total sexual division of labour. It is necessary to find ways of changing both how work is organised between the sexes at home, and at the point of production. They are in fact crucially linked, because work for wages depends on the work in the family, and domestic labour influences women's waged working life. In terms of an effective strategy for now, it is important to analyse the points of interdependence and to try and understand how these have changed historically.

Socialists have been concerned with the transformation of ownership and control at the point of production. They have ignored the significance of reproduction in an economic sense in the family, or have assumed that it would change after the transfer of control over production along with the other forms of social existence. The preoccupation with the work place has been most marked within the revolutionary syndicalist tradition, but it has also always been present within Leninist practice. More recently, the new left and libertarian Marxists have asserted the idea of community control which is beginning to connect with a longstanding socialist practice of activity in tenants movements and local campaigns. But this local activity can easily become an isolated activity which absorbs lonely groups of leftists. There is no connecting theory on the left which can relate all aspects of this struggle around the reproduction of social existence, even though the intervention of the capitalist state and the cuts in welfare are making these personal areas of life so evidently public politics. It has been the women's movement which has asserted the inner relationship between production and the reproduction of social existence, because in most women's lives the separation of the two is so evidently artificial.

The division of work between the sexes within the working class and among the growing body of non-manual wage-earners has not been explored much by socialists. Differentiation within the working class touches an awkward nerve in the history of revolutionary organisation, for despite a rhetoric against craft elitism the male skilled worker has often been predominant on the organised left. Not surprisingly his values, assumptions and interests have tended to be equated with advanced political consciousness. This has not only excluded women but also unskilled men. Again changes in the organisation of work are forcing some socialists to re-examine the narrow political and economic criteria with which Leninists have measured consciousness. But this analysis of work often remains locked in the sphere of production.

The women's movement has emphasised the importance of control over procreation. Although this was present as an idea and demand in some strands of nineteenth-century utopianism, among some anarchists and a small group of socialist feminists in this century, it has never been seen by Marxists as a central political question. Again it has been assumed that change in the sphere of procreation and sexual relations follows automatically from the workers controlling production. The specific situation of women as a sex has thus been folded into class exploitation. Following

Engels, Marxists have seen the division of labour between the sexes as only assuming oppressive qualities with the development of private property. Although this may have been attractive as a historical myth of a golden age, in the context of late-nineteenth-century thought, it has had a fatal consequence in the dogmatic dismissal of sex oppression. Sexual relationships between men and women or between people of the same sex have been seen by Marxists as either decadent and diversionary or as personal questions outside politics. At best, they have been treated as something lumped under the general heading of 'the family' or perhaps 'culture' rather low on the agenda. As the extreme right has been less blinkered about the significance of sexuality, the left has been continually placed on the defensive.

The feminist movement in demanding control for women over procreation has thus broken with the refusal to recognise the material and social circumstances which contribute to the oppression of women as a sex.

The ramifications are extensive: agitation for contraception and abortion, criticism of how decisions are made about scientific research, of state policy in which methods are devised and made available, and of the ideology of the medical profession. It also raises the question of choice in the conditions of our own maternity, in the circumstances of child rearing and living arrangements. Feminists have challenged men's power to define women's sexuality in terms of economic and legal power, in sexual practice and in the hold over ideas. Feminism and the gay movement have opened up these areas of personal life as political.

The struggle to control sexual reproduction carries the possibility of extending the concept of socialist transformation into all aspects of everyday life and consciousness. It does not mean that we seek private sexual utopias, but that we learn through the experience of seeking new forms of life, just as we learn through particular industrial or community struggles. Feminists have insisted that how we live, now, has a practical significance for how we can organise.

It has become evident in even the relatively few years of the movement's existence that we are opposing not only an oppression which is carried by individual men, which could be solved simply by avoiding men or by making men behave differently towards us, but even deeper patterns of relationship based on authority and submission, within such relationships both men and women are trapped from our first encounters in the family, through school and during the rest of our life. The discussions of how we acquired femininity, in consciousness-raising groups have now widened into study groups on psychoanalysis, or therapy groups and the emergence of men's groups. I think the emergence of these forms of organising represents a recognition that the ways in which we feel and perceive the world from our innermost selves, needs to be brought out into the light of day and that this applies to men just as much as to women.

Such an assertion of subjectivity and of the need to find organisational means to unlock structures of feeling as part of a political practice is quite alien from the traditions of Leninism. Indeed Leninism was explicitly opposed to the earlier socialist preoccupation with ethical questions and new forms of life. I think the old controversy of means versus ends needs rephrasing, because the struggle against advanced capitalist society is of such complexity and we are so tenaciously held down, that subjective forms of struggle have become vital.

Implicitly within the women's movement we have tried to find ways of organising which do not simply reproduce the division of labour and hier-archies of family, school, work. We have also challenged the Leninist grading of consciousness by asserting personal experience which does not yield to the classification of advanced or backward. I think that we have come up against the same stumbling block as those sections of the libertarian left which have emphasised objective changes in consciousness. The danger has been to see these changes as ends in themselves rather than as ways of helping us to act more effectively against capitalism. When subjective transformation is removed from other kinds of socialist practice, it becomes an intolerable external morality which isolates, terrorises and destroys. We need consciously to find organisational forms which do not exhaust us in the pursuit of liberated stereotypes, but which enable us to learn ourselves anew. Only such a process of continuing renewal can give us the resilience to survive, pitted against every aspect of capitalist society, and yet still open to the majority of other people who do not see as we do.

It is not just a matter of adding new forms to existing political structures. I think it is a fundamental challenge to the Leninist idea of a revolutionary party. Within Leninism there is no conscious commitment to struggling against the forms of relationship, which are created by the division of labour under capitalism, as part of the effort to make socialism. It is assumed that the existence of the revolutionary party itself, can transcend the particular interests of sections within the working class. The actual conflicts between skilled and unskilled workers, between white and immigrant workers and between men and women for example, are thus obscured by sleight of hand. Any attempt to solve the problem of the subordination of the subordinate within the revolutionary organisation is then deferred until after the creation of socialism and packed off with denunciations of utopianism, exhortations to unite and the ace card of democratic centralism. Such a theory of organisation has made it impossible for women to even begin to express what is specific to our oppression as a sex. Vanguard organisations seem never to have taken the initiative. Again and again it has been pressure from an autonomous feminist movement or the militancy of working-class women which has forced some grudging response from the leadership of Leninist organisations.

I can see the arguments which socialist feminists bring to working within the main organisations of the left which are based on versions of Leninism. They have more coherent notions of organising, there is a framework for relating theory and practice, they work after a fashion, above all they *exist* in the real world and historical creations are not to be lightly dismissed. The alternative appears to be nothing but an inchoate rumble of theoretical dissidence within modern Marxism, mere talk about struggle around everyday life, of personal politics and authoritarian relationships and as for practice a few isolated failures groping for a theory. It is worth remembering that Marxism itself must have seemed a delicate growth in the 1840s, that new theories of how to transform the world do not arrive ready-made out of the sky. I believe that the women's movement is playing an important part in earthing ideas about a new form of socialist organisation which will make it necessary to break with the Leninist tradition. Though the manner in which this would be created remains unclear.

8. My Friend

◆◆◆◆◆◆

'My Friend', *One Foot on the Mountain*, An Anthology of British Feminist Poetry 1969–1979, ed. Lilian Mohin, Onlywomen Press, 1979. This was written for Sue with whom I have lived for many years. It is easy to take people you know well for granted and to forget that the sweetness of long friendships sustains us. Written for Sue, it is a way of saying thank you to many other friends.

◆◆◆◆◆◆

My friend
cooks sweet
apples
far into
the night.

A gift
of gentleness
through time,
country kitchens
in the sun
perfume
the dark
still.

Their fragrance
lingers
until
light.

9. 'Who's Holding the Baby?'

◆◆◆◆◆◆

'Who's Holding the Baby?' *Leveller*, no. 29, August 1979.

◆◆◆◆◆◆

June 18th. Will, me, Will's pushchair and a big bag of 'in cases' (a mac, in case it rains; nappies, in case Will wets the one he has on; trousers, in case it goes through) set off to the photo exhibition and demonstration, *Who's Holding the Baby?* at the Hayward Gallery, London. We are too late for the bus so it's puff, puff on the tube. Watch the escalator. Someone told me a horror story of a child's wellington getting stuck down the side. Puff, puff up all those steps and down to the South Bank.

Will makes a dash for some swings down a temporary bridge. I heave him in the direction of the Hayward. Perhaps they will have all gone. It's getting very hot. We spot two runaway children. Relief. Turning the corner there they are still. Banners, children, anxious and bewildered adults. 'I've just joined,' says someone from the Southwark Childcare Campaign, 'Will you sign my petition?' I sign thinking a mobile demonstration with floats might have been better. The problem with demonstrating outside the Hayward is that you are not really seen by many people and it's hard to watch the kids.

A worried man is wondering where to take the kids to next. A small group sets off in the direction of some gardens near Parliament. There are large contingents from several nurseries including two Hackney Community Nurseries, Market and Beatty Road. One of the Hackney Flashers [a group of women photographers] who took some of the photos in the exhibition, looks cheerful despite the problem of how to take photos while holding a toddler at the same time. She tells me to go inside and she'll keep an eye on Will who by this time has met the dog from Beatty Road.

I zoom round, spending most time on the Hackney Flashers work. I had already seen the exhibition on nurseries in a local community bookshop, Centerprise. There are collages about the politics of childcare, photos of demonstrations. They look a bit entombed in the Hayward, their immediacy distanced by the atmosphere of a large gallery. But the pictures of the children and nursery workers in a Hackney Community Nursery are still direct. They are moving because they are not only protesting the injustice and disregard of capitalism, but asserting the intensity of people's ability to love and communicate, even despite these.

The London Nursery Campaign were demonstrating against inadequate provision for young children in the widest sense: not only the lack of nurseries but the problem of travel on public transport, lack of crêches in shops, the banning of pushchairs in some museums and galleries – the whole question of priority in the design of communities. They have informal links with nursery campaigns in other places, for example, Sheffield, Leeds, Birmingham, Oxford and, rather surprisingly, Bournemouth where the council did not know what had hit them! Myra Garrett, a member of the campaign who has been particularly involved in the trade union side, told me they act as an umbrella for a large number of varied groups; 'Under Fives', local childcare campaigns and trade union branches. They have produced a booklet, 'The Do It Yourself Nursery Campaign' (50p including postage), and have a copy of the cartoon film about nurseries, *Who Needs Nurseries? We Do*.

A group exists which is concerned with the training of nursery nurses. They try to counter the ideology behind many of the courses. There is not only the issue of differing approach to girls and boys which has been most thoroughly discussed in the women's movement, but the emphasis upon the individual interaction between adult teacher and the child rather than upon interaction as a group and cooperative learning among children.

Myra thought it would be useful if some discussion of feminist and socialist attitudes towards psychology could be directed to these problems which have such practical implications for helping us develop an alternative vision of childcare. At the moment there is a lack of much theoretical connection between the women's movement demand for nurseries, much muttering and some practice over the years of men and women sharing childcare more equally in couples or in groups, and the growth of new forms of community childcare and trade union supported nurseries at work. It also occurred to me that while discussions about the personal experience of being with children is an obvious subject for women's groups and men's groups, it is less customary for a socialist group to talk about this.

Community Nurseries are a fascinating growth. They assume several shapes and forms. Some are partly operated by parents with the assistance of paid helpers, one in Hackney is funded by the Equal Opportunities Commission, others by various council grants. They have often arisen out of playgroups and nationally their existence is patchy. Hackney is really an exceptional case. The current waiting list for council day nurseries stands at over 800 top priority children. Eight council day nurseries provide only 400 or so places and there are now seven voluntary nurseries which have come into being on an ad hoc basis.

The council grudgingly gave them the nod because they were a cheaper form of childcare. But this meant nursery workers were being forced to claim social security as they were under the poverty line. However last year in Hackney they joined NUPE and demanded parity with council-run nurseries. They won much better pay, conditions and holidays.

This is not to imply that council nurseries are some kind of utopia. Pay is still relatively low. Socialist and feminist nursery workers are full of stories of struggles against sexist and authoritarian attitudes. One Islington worker said to me that after work she was so tired she just wanted to switch off completely from the kids. In community nurseries, though, this is never possible. These nurseries have to argy bargy their way through the Kafkaesque world of council funding.

In Hackney, for example, they are becoming increasingly involved in the 'Under Fives', which links all aspects of activity in the area. They have managed to convince the councillors of their case even though many of the council workers remain suspicious. The argument is not only about cash but about control. The Hoxton group for instance, which includes two child minders, has fiercely impressed upon Hoxton councillors that they want a community nursery run by themselves. So the emergence of community nurseries has created a group of people who have become increasingly aware of the lack of provision, of bureaucratic red tape, of the dismissal of the needs of the under-fives, and are beginning to work out what kind of education they want for their children.

But this kind of development appears at present to be peculiar to certain boroughs in London. None of the people I spoke to knew of community nurseries in other towns. They suggested it might be even more difficult to get money elsewhere. They are very keen for ideas and information to be communicated. The 'Do It Yourself Nursery' was written with this intention.

My journey home was a mobile object lesson in what we had been demonstrating about. I attached myself to the Beatty Road contingent. We decided to go by boat down the river.

That was great until we landed. No bus home so we trekked on foot like the Children's Crusade to Aldgate, twenty children, five adults and a dog. 'Hold hands. Do you want to go now? We'll soon be home.' Summer had decided to arrive that afternoon. My mac was redundant and heavy. The children were swathed in woolly coats. I staggered home shattered with no comforting notes. It had never seemed quite the right moment and I had a shortage of hands and quiet.

Two thoughts began to form hazily in my head. One was that in demanding childcare, we are not only asking for a thing or for money, we are contesting for the use, control and distribution of social resources. This involves a concept of how we want to work, care for children and play and indeed to love. It means an argument about how life-time is apportioned between the sexes and between classes. In the present economic crisis, with the Tories on the offensive, this is going to be a very desperate struggle. This strategic vision is therefore particularly vital now. Otherwise isolated struggles will sink into exhaustion and despair.

Despite these problems there really is a strength in the wide range of community projects which have developed, particularly in the last decade. Not only those for under-fives but everything from community arts groups to law centres.

My second thought was that while some of these are implicitly contesting the dominant values of a profit-based society, how do we go about communicating our understanding of socialism more explicitly to children? How do they involve one another? Most of the energy seems to have concentrated on children's literature. Radical groups exist which try to develop cooperation and democracy like the Woodcraft Folk (who are helped by the Coop Educational Fund), Forest School and Flysheet Camps. They all believe very much in education through doing. Woodcraft Folk from six-year-old elfins onwards elect leaders. Forest School Camps also have leaders but the Flysheet Camps, an offshoot of the late sixties and more explicitly non-hierarchical, have daily camp coordinators.

But there is not much *socialist* organising for children. There are occasional events planned with imagination like the crêches at the Communist University, the Socialist Workers Party Skegness Rallies, or the Conference of Socialist Economists and the Men's Week with kids at Laurieston in Scotland. But now the Socialist Sunday School movement has dwindled there seems little for everyday life. I wonder whether socialist children's groups would still be popular today?

10. Sally on Saturday

◆◆◆◆◆◆

'Sally on Saturday', unpublished, written summer 1981.

◆◆◆◆◆◆

Two friends
sit on a Saturday
at the crossroads
with sons
playing with trains.

'I think it's our age,'
you said.
I'd thought
it was rather the times
we live in,
colliding my psyche
with the state
of the nation.

We chat
of this one and that one
sketching quick outlines
of what can be known
amidst interruptions.

You go out shopping
and return,
We search for tea –
and when you leave
anxious
because Daniel's cold
is making it hard for him to breathe,
I feel a loving sadness.
A Saturday spent
at the crossroads
without time
to journey between outlines.

11. Mother, Child and State

◆◆◆◆◆◆

'Mother, Child and State', a shorter version appeared in *New Society*, 1 October 1981. The question of feminism and children was present as an abstract idea before I had a child. Living tied up in the mother-knot restrains the effusion of excessive intellectual adventuring, but it also concentrates resolve. It makes it impossible to see things through and makes you unable to neglect necessity. It enables you to start off saying one thing and end up asserting the opposite. 'I want to be alone. I really miss them when I'm alone.'

All these are salutary considerations to be taken into account by those who seek to make the world anew, along with the attempt to understand what sharing childcare means in practice at home and in the neighbourhood.

By the time I had a child, the isolated community nursery and the vain attempts to get a childcare campaign established had been extended. A few more community nurseries had been formed, nursery workers had experienced not only trade union militancy but joined with parents, children and other trade unionists to defend nurseries. Local networks like 'Under Fives' had taken up the whole range of childcare needs. First a London Nursery campaign grew up. It developed alternative schemes for the training of nursery workers. Then a National Childcare Campaign was formed. It is committed to gaining access to resources controlled by the state for childcare and to creating forms of democratic community control over how our children are cared for. It is an advance. It also needs support. (Write to NCCC, 17 Victoria Park Square, London E2 with cash or at least stamps.)

◆◆◆◆◆◆

As I sat listening to talks on 'Child Care and the State', at a conference organised in Loughborough by the National Child Care Campaign and the Cooperative Union Education Department, I began to muse on my own schizophrenia in relation to the state.

I am firmly convinced that demands must be made upon the state. Clearly welfare resources of cash and labour need to be divided more equitably. To force the issue on to voluntary effort intensifies inequality.

But in my everyday life, if the state comes anywhere near me, I feel very uncomfortable indeed. If it appears in the shape of a form, I bury it and hope superstitiously that by hiding it from view I have removed myself from the eye of the state. If the state arrives in the shape of a person, I leap towards the teapot with a gripped enthusiasm to dissolve the state back into a human being who drinks tea rather than an official wielding a file.

Now this twitchiness is partly an illusion. I have even been a bit of the state myself when I worked as a teacher. In one of my Workers' Education Association classes, I taught the manager of a social security office history. In another, my class secretary sent out telephone bills. They were no more fearsome than other mortals.

On the other hand, there are some grounds for my unease. Hackney midwives, for instance, declared the house I lived in unfit for me to return to from hospital with a two day old baby. The grounds for this were that the bathroom was shared with other adults. I ignored the ruling of the state on this occasion, and returned after forty-eight hours in hospital. I was exceedingly relieved to be home, and not too interested in discussions about the role of the state at the time.

But it is not an easy relationship – this triangle of state, children and parents. It becomes loaded with even greater ambiguity when other adults are involved. Take child minding, for example. If a child is hurt while in the care of a child minder, it is very difficult to establish legally who is responsible.

The registration of child minders is a move towards regulating a service which has long been a private transaction. There are many bad features in this transaction for both children and minders. Minders are not only low-paid but also sometimes have difficulty in actually getting the money owed to them. The Child minders' Association favour registration because they see this as a way of improving the conditions of care and thus raising the status of child minders. Some local authorities have developed services to help minders meet in groups – an important step both practically and emotionally. Evidently in France all nurseries have a room which minders can use.

Nonetheless, there is a certain tension between child minders and the people who administer them. In addition to assistance there is also authority and judgement. Moreover, the judges do not share the predicament of many minders. They are on the outside, looking in at chaos and overcrowding.

There are material problems. A large part of the unsuitable care which child minders provide is due to bad housing, especially in the inner city areas.

This touches upon the awkward fact that many women are caring for their *own* children in bad conditions. And the minders' situation is comparable to other kinds of women's work like home working and office cleaning, which are labour-intensive and relatively isolated, and where the need for flexibility and cash in hand overrides the need to improve conditions in the long term.

Historically, trade unionists, socialists and feminists concerned about the oppression of women in this kind of work, have shifted between attempting to organise them, and seeking state legislation. The first is difficult and laborious, the second can go against the immediate interests of women involved.

At Loughborough, however, the discussion of the dilemma made me uncomfortably aware how much easier it is to accept the principle of state supervision for someone else rather than for yourself. Those to be regulated can very easily coagulate into a sticky mass in the minds of both conservative and radical planners of a social policy.

Plans are one thing and people another. Which is not to say we do not need plans but that the whole process of planning requires careful political scrutiny. For planners of all persuasions, there is a danger that individual faces, names and actions dissolve into masses to be pummelled or steered.

There is a long and bitter tradition of administering with a crude psychology of carrot-and-stick; and also with an insulting frugality which dates from the days of Bentham's bright ideas for pauper bedding which could be pegged in (to save the cloth which tucks you in). 'Masses' have not been allowed human beings' complexity of requirements and longings because this would clog up the machine of government with too large a dose of sentiment.

There is, of course, an equally long tradition of protest about this since the days of William Cobbett, Charles Dickens and William Morris. And there are innumerable state workers who, despite the pressure upon them in nurseries, schools, hospitals and social services, do try and see the people for whom they care both as individuals *and* as people caught by social circumstances outside their control.

The contradictions of welfare work are even more obvious at the present time because of the cuts. There is enormous confusion about whether welfare workers in general are carers or workers. The two notions inhabit different zones, which partially correspond to women's activity and men's activity.

For the child minders there are clearly advantages in moving away from the shadowy ambiguity in which they are neither properly carers or workers. The enthusiasm for minders as mother substitutes seeks to raise their status as carers. But it is over simple, because it assumes that mothers have a clear status. In fact, mothers are doormats as well as Madonnas. Turning workers into mothers helps neither mothers nor workers.

We must question why we can only measure the value of care in terms of the relationship of mothers and children. Surely the point is to extend, rather than narrow, our concept of care. The Child minders' Association want to assert the role of minders as caring workers. The energetic efforts to organise nursery workers and other childcare workers in the last decade indicate that carers still need more money. But the expenditure of creative energy is also enormous. I would like to see the day when nursery workers and school teachers sail off on sabbaticals, and do not work every day.

It is difficult in this kind of work to balance the interests of workers (many of whom are women brought up to put caring for others above cash), while making sure the children do not lose out. Even in the best of worlds, this would be a problem. In the actual world of the cuts, it is made more acute.

The slogan, 'workers' control', is clearly inadequate to meet this dilemma. Instead, the National Child Care Campaign demand 'community control'. It was this which led to the creation of community nurseries. Originally they were formed on a self-help basis; but the groups involved have also bargained for resources from the state, and they are now run with various combinations of money from local authorities and the labour of parents and supporters. Community nurseries are modern examples of an older relationship between self-help and the welfare state. During the first world war, self-help mother-and-baby clinics like Sylvia Pankhurst's refurbished pub in east London, The Mother's Arms, helped to give shape to the idea of state welfare centres. But in the process, the crucial issue of control became lost.

The problem which has dogged the whole development of welfare services is the power to decide what is *someone else's welfare*. There is the Fabian tradition of social policy in which enlightened administrators do the deciding. This has never been too popular with large sections of the recipients of welfare. The Labour Party has always combined respect for the efficiency, and uneasiness with some of its effects, rather awkwardly. The Fabian tradition is impressive in its assembling of the great mass of necessary detail, its capacity to take an overview, and to grapple with the civil service to get things done. On the other hand, it shares with its utilitarian forbears an impersonality and disregard for the complexity of human sentiments and passions.

In the last decade, there has been an important challenge to the definition of social needs from on top. We now understand the politics in determining welfare needs better than we did.

The experience of putting this criticism into practice can help us to understand more closely a further problem, that needs within the community can also conflict. For instance, many of the projects inspired by feminism have had two aims: to reach outwards and to challenge authoritarianism and sexism. But they have often found these aims to be contradictory because some parents do not share their approach.

Even more knotty, is the acknowledgement that human beings can have contradictory needs – especially human beings caring for children in a world in which the value of cherishing and nourishing is subordinated to the value of making money. In the women's movement the interconnectedness of women's life in the home and at work has meant that childcare has been seen in relation to women's control over fertility and access to jobs. It has been seen to require a transformation in the design and construction of our houses, our transport and cities as well as divisions and reorganisation of the work between the sexes. The exclusive involvement of mothers with small children has been criticised as oppressive to both. The aim has been to involve both fathers and other adults in childcare not only through state provision but in the home. This has acknowledged the need to bargain for time as well as money. For it is hard work combining care for children with both parents working full time. Shift work makes this combination even more difficult.

Nonetheless, many of us could also accept the point that these big changes undermine the sensitive area of defensive power women have as mothers. This is apparent in the extra pain in legal conflicts for custody between husband and wife when husbands have participated in childcare. There is moreover an emotional knot in the uneasiness which can emerge between mothers and child minders and nursery workers. Our ideas of adult womanhood are so bound up with our mothering. It is not just that our children need us. We often need to be needed. And then we feel an intense irritation that we keep being needed so much. At the Childcare Conference we were all committed to various ways of either supplementing or replacing the mother's exclusive involvement with children. But the account of a society in Southern Africa where the biological mothers (called 'little mothers') do not look after their own children who are cared for by older women ('big' mothers) and other women who the children choose to relate to while the men are away working in the mines sent a gasp and a wince around the room as well as fascination and amazement.

All these dilemmas rumbled through the weekend surfacing occasionally in perplexed disagreements because we came with many different assumptions. But the strength of the childcare campaign is in bringing together people who grapple with the different elements of childcare, child minders, social administrators and researchers, nursery and community workers, mothers and fathers, and the Woodcraft Folk. There were a few gaps, for example the Lollypop People who would be well placed to tell of the battle between children's needs and the motor car. But still enough diversity to see that the strategy for childcare not only involves questioning the organisation and dominant values of our society but also our own feelings and attitudes. A campaign which demands both the liberation of women and the liberation of children reveals not only the immediate tensions between the two, but an even deeper challenge to capitalism than the assertion simply of rights. It requires a society based on cooperation and free association.

12. Women, Power and Consciousness: Discussions in the Women's Liberation Movement in Britain 1969–1981

'Women, Power and Consciousness. Discussions in the Women's Liberation Movement in Britain 1969–1981'. An unpublished talk. Versions were given at the University of Toronto Women's Studies Conference on Women and Power, October 1981; Barnard College, New York, November 1981; Goldsmiths College, London, March 1982; The University of Amsterdam Women's Studies Department, May 1982; The Politics Seminar, York University, June 1982.

The geographical span of the above list is an example of how the economic crisis and Tory offensive has got me out and about.

This talk brings together scattered ideas and observations made by feminists about how to develop alternative forms of power. It raises the dilemma – how do we tackle the already existing hold of the powerful? It does not provide a neat solution, I'm afraid, and my Trotskyist friends will probably point this out. This is not because I do not recognise it as a serious problem but because I would argue it requires a collective solution in the conscious commitment of women and men all over the world to a renewal of socialism. As the Polish workers in Solidarity discovered tragically, this can be a struggle to the death within socialism itself.

135

The early 1980s have pushed many of the discussions which during the 1970s took place in tiny groups, local meetings and single-issue campaigns in the women's movement out into a wider political arena. What kind of society do we want to make? Where do we start? What are our needs? What happens when they are not shared by other people? Or when they conflict and change? What do we do when we meet opposition within our own ranks, or the tank in the street or the disembodied echo in the corridors of power telling us we have to phrase the yearning for liberation according to already existing procedure or it cannot come before the right committee?

We have to meet these challenges and rise to the responsibility while remembering still to 'wonder', in the words of Eve Fitzpatrick, how our 'love can beat the pattern back'.

In a very general sense it is clear that the women's movement internationally has contested the power relationship between men and women. Socialist feminists have generally argued that these are linked to other forms of power and oppression and that it is necessary to challenge all aspects of inequality and hierarchy. I do not think we can analyse power in capitalism in terms of a single root cause, sexism, imperialism or class, for example. I believe that we are born into a web of relationships of varying kinds of authority and inequality and that the forms of resistance to these and hence the alliances between the subordinated will differ and change historically.

I want to look at the following senses in which feminists in Britain have come up against the problem of power. They overlap but these are my divisions.

1) Taking power.

2) Creating alternative sources of power, in terms of consciousness and practical defensive forms of resistance.

3) Breaking down the concentration of power and redistributing power by developing autonomous organising in which everyone can participate.

4) Creating anticipatory forms which negate authoritarianism.

5) Redefining power and the sources of power.

I have put taking power at the top of the list for this is the activity which has been customarily seen as the business of political organising. How do we take power — by degrees through gradual reforms or in a clear confrontation and historical moment of insurrection? However, until very recently this has not been the aspect of power which has preoccupied feminists in Britain, for reasons which I think will emerge from my account of the other contexts in which power has been resisted. In the early stages of the movement we had to fend off criticism from socialists who said it was reformist to campaign for nurseries or that consciousness raising was not the way to challenge the armed power of the state. We reacted to these onslaughts defensively at first and accepted the terms in which they were set. It has taken time for feminists to develop alternative approaches and for a more sophisticated understanding of strategy to emerge in the socialist movement in Britain, or in parts of it at least.

This does indicate that in thinking about power and women's liberation we are considering a most unorthodox species of politics. I think this is partly because it is a movement for women's liberation and that the rebellion of women as a sex potentially calls into question power itself. The historical expression of this in feminist movements is never so clear cut – real movements being more murky affairs than concepts of liberatory potential. However, at this point in British society there is also a very strong suspicion of power of which the women's movement is only one aspect. This has radical and conservative implications. There is a joke going around that the social democrats are the party who have taken the politics out of politics. Among many socialists, though, there is also considerable ambivalence about power politics. The women's movement has tended to develop in the same milieu. There has been a mutual interaction. Feminism has grown considerably in influence over the last decade without seeing the *taking* of power as being a main aim. This is clearly changing the pattern in which politics is conceived.

The women's movement has, on the other hand, been extremely preoccupied with an aspect of power which other grass-roots and radical movements *have* seen as their concern – namely, the creation of alternative sources of power, both as a means of defensive resistance and as a means of developing the capacity for self-organisation among oppressed people.

This understanding has been behind the support which feminists have given to women's struggles which are not explicitly feminist or around simply women's oppression as a sex but also raise class and race. There have been countless instances: the right to unionise, strikes against low pay, unequal pay and the sweated conditions in which many women work, especially women from oppressed ethnic groups. Feminists have picketed, held meetings, reported, researched, helping both to unionise women and becoming active in their own unions.

Most persistent has been the argument that women's double workload of home and wage labour have to be tackled together. For these are women's real lives and consciousness.

A woman clothing worker involved in a clothing strike in Leeds evoked this.

> You see, a man's job is to be a bread winner, isn't it? To earn a wage to keep his family. And he wants what is due to him by hook or by crook. . . . Now a woman has a lot more things to think about. Families and pressures at home and owt like that. A man can stick up for his rights and all stick together but a woman has a lot more things on her mind. Feeding her family you know . . . and you think to yourself (on strike) the first hour you think to yourself, you're militant, you know, and then by the second hour, you're thinking 'Oh, I could be doing my washing . . . I could be at home, doing my shopping.' And that's the whole difference.[1]

A woman shop steward described this in relation to domestic work. 'A woman makes up her politics from bits and pieces. She only half listens to a programme on TV whilst she's doing the ironing or some other household job. She hasn't got the time to sit down and listen to something all the way through.'[2]

The interconnection of work and home life is thus inescapable for women. Feminists have taken these arguments into the trade union movement and have found increasing support in the women's conference of the Trades Union Congress. Ideas about working-class power which stress only the control over the work place developed in relation to male workers are thus beginning to be questioned. It means extending our concept of work to include unpaid labour, revealing the social power present in the definition of skill, seeking to overcome inequality within the working class and moving towards a concept of creative activity which incorporates the rearing of children and is no longer confined predominantly to women.

Within the women's movement resistance against material conditions and the transformation of relationships and consciousness have been implicitly assumed. This has been in contrast to the prevailing terms in which Marxism has been discussed on the left. This has created a regrettable division in which something called 'theory' floats around above the everyday. The women's movement has not completely avoided this but there has been a lot of attention given to descriptions of how struggles against material conditions enable people to see the connections between power relationships of different kinds.

For example, Maria O'Reilly, an organiser of a flat dwellers' action group at Netherley Flats, Liverpool, described in *Spare Rib* how resistance developed after a child was nearly fatally hurt in 1973. Resentment which had been smouldering on the council estate as lifts broke and roofs leaked and the council neglected repairs focused initially on the rehousing of the family whose child had fallen from the balcony. She explained that the council were 'reluctant to set a precedent, a precedent in humanity'. From this the tenants group began to take on the issue of repairs and how people were allocated houses. Maria O' Reilly says this meant facing power in several ways.

> I have faced male chauvinism I failed to see existed before. As a representative of the other women I always tried to press our case forcefully. The councillors had their salaries to rely on; I only had the other women's trust. Sometimes our faith failed us. Four years is a long time when progress is slow. . . .
>
> We have met interesting people over these years, people we wouldn't have met otherwise, people with strange ideals none of us were used to. We learned to accept people as they really were, not by what they had on or whether they were dirty or poor. We came to understand politics, usually thought of as a man's world and expected more of ourselves — knew more about what we could and couldn't do for ourselves. People now call us women's libbers. I never realised but we must have become just that, though we're not all aware of it. Of course some of the men around regard us suspiciously and think that we hold ritual bra-burning sessions to which we might invite their wives.[3]

In 1977 five women from near Pontypridd, South Wales, chained themselves to the local town hall railings for twenty-four hours. They were from a new estate of terraced houses with central heating. The electric central heating was too expensive for most of the tenants to heat. Either they turned it off which caused condensation or they fell behind on their rent. At first women tenants asked themselves what they could do as women for the tenants' struggle. But then they began to reflect upon what it had done for them as women. The following quotes are from a book about women and community struggles. The section on Pontypridd is by Barbara Castle.

> When we started the Action Group I was really nervous meeting people. And he used to tell me I was like a mouse and ask me why I didn't stand up for myself. Now he tells me I'm dictatorial and bossy, so you can't win. . . .
>
> I can't imagine going back to my life before we started this. What did I used to do. . . . I question is it completely satisfying for a woman just to do housework and look after children, and grow old and die? I mean that's what I see a lot of women seem to do. Especially in South Wales.[4]

I am not suggesting that the interconnection between various relationships of authority and inequality can only be grasped by women. But the particular character of the subordination of women as a sex certainly makes them more difficult to bypass.

The tenants' struggles to which I have referred are part of a wider spectrum of community resistance which has developed against what Cynthia Cockburn has called the 'local state'.[5] Not only tenants but claimants, the blind, the old and many other groups with little power because they are dependent upon welfare have challenged the remote bureaucratic authoritarian aspects of the welfare state during the 1970s. Women who are caring for children alone are dependent on welfare. They have played an important role in claimants unions and childcare groups. Similarly, many women have been involved in radical self-help health and therapy groups, as well as campaigns to keep hospitals open.

The implications of this piecemeal, often painful process of everyday resistance to the supposedly benign face of the state are drawn together in the book *In and Against the State*. The authors, who work for the welfare state and include a group of socialist feminists, challenge the notion of welfare as something we simply need to defend from the cuts. They contest the relationships of authority which they are expected to maintain in their jobs and say we must extend the idea of welfare to mean democratic participation and control over social resources.[6] There are now various cooperative forms of community-controlled welfare not just a single polarisation between self-help and the welfare state. The defence and extension of these community self-help organisations has become an area of acute political conflict under the Thatcherite attack on welfare.

There is now quite a body of experience of such resistance. From this has developed an awareness of the strengths and constraints of local community politics. Recently there have been some interesting attempts to form links between trade unions and community groups. Examples of this are Newcastle, through the socialist centre, and Hackney, where a recent conference brought together community activists and people from the local trades council. Socialist feminists have been involved in both cases.[7]

The defence of living conditions has thus meant that women have found themselves confronting both their specific situation as women and the shared problem of how to develop alternative forms of power through trade unionism, tenants groups, claimants unions, community groups and campaigns. Consciousness of the interconnections between different kinds of power and the authority vested in the welfare state have emerged.

Equally, the defence of women against the physical assertion of men's power has created new understandings of the links between sexual control, violence and the fear of violence and new forms of defence, aid and refuge – for example Women's Aid and the Rape Crisis Centres which are intended not only to help but to enable us to see ourselves not as victims – 'to become aware that we do not have to accept the identity given to us by this society'.[8] Again resistance to material oppression is inseparably bound up with consciousness.

This is a woman from the Dundee Women's Aid Centre quoted in *Spare Rib* in 1976.

> The refuge gives you time to think and get organised. My husband wanted to dominate me completely. He was very fussy about the house, always criticising my housekeeping.
>
> He gave me a black eye and a burst lip when I was expecting my first baby and when I went into labour he went on about the ironing needing doing.
>
> He was never in, always at the pub. He thought if you had a roof over your head and food to eat that was all you needed. I felt trapped, didn't know who to talk to.[9]

In a paper at the London Women's Liberation Conference in 1977 Women's Aid commented on the extremes of control and passivity which many battered women have experienced.

> All the women had been kept in the place which was decided for them by their husbands. They were held back from trying anything. The first time they took any initiative was when they got themselves out of their dreadful situations into the refuges. And this required a very great deal of initiative. . . . They couldn't think of their own needs when every thought and action had to be watched so as not to provoke a beating. They now have the opportunity to realise they are not odd, ill or deviant women. They can question the institution of marriage, where before they would have been faced with a total lack of approval and support from a society which upholds marriage as the ideal state in the face of many, many instances of its blatant failure.[10]

Without idealising the women's aid refuges which are often over-crowded and fraught with the tensions of unhappiness and poverty, they are still an important example of an organisational form developing to resist one aspect of women's dependence and powerlessness in a male-dominated capitalist society. However, the problem of dependence is not only a matter of these dramatic and extreme confrontations. It is an everyday pattern which women have chronicled in countless accounts in feminist magazines. Some women have sought relationships with women, or non-monogamous relationships or celibacy. Others have simply struggled within their relationships with men against the loss of identity, the feelings of inadequacy.

Other aspects of feminism, Why Be a Wife?, the Right to Choose, Reclaim the Night, are all asserting a kind of counter-power. There has been an enormous emphasis upon feeling and realising our own power as women. It is not just that the interconnecting power relationships are so evident but because women face physical coercion as an ever-present danger. There was a very extreme example of this during the series of murders committed over a period of years by the 'Yorkshire Ripper' when women simply were terrified to go out alone in northern cities. Although there were large and angry marches and although prostitutes developed some forms of self-defence, taking down car numbers, for example, the isolated savage attacks made effective resistance from women impossible.

But ingenious tactics have been developed to resist more everyday forms of sexual harassment: 'In Islington women got tired of being kerb-crawled, of having men cruise behind them in their cars. So they decided to take down the number plates of the cars involved and publish them in the *Islington Gutter Press* (the local community paper). Some women's groups have talked of having an aerosol of non-removable bright paint which would be sprayed on the bumper. Women in Birmingham made stickers to put on the cars of kerb crawlers.'[11] (I can imagine though fumbling around in your bag for your aerosol can and your stickers.)

In Hackney some women have been descending on kerb crawlers with banners and have forced them away. The difficult problem is that they have aroused the antagonism of the local prostitutes by thus driving off trade.

Conflict of interest between women can make the concept of a unified counterpower of women against men problematic. For we also have inequalities among ourselves. These cannot be overcome by an effort of will alone, any more than real divisions in the working class. Amrit Wilson, in her study of Asian women in Britain, *Finding a Voice*, says for instance that 'Asian women are very reluctant to talk to white women about their inner feelings . . . they think white women wouldn't understand because they don't come from the same background. Asian women are aware of living in a very racist society and this casts a shadow over their relationships with white people unless they know these white people very well.'[12]

However, the problem of women's counterpower is also a political argument about whether men's power is the root and source from which all other oppressive relations develop. This leads to disagreements about what should be done. In Britain these disagreements have become so severe that we have had no national women's liberation conferences since the late 1970s when the last one exploded in considerable acrimony with one group of women advocating castration. (A curious demand to make upon a male-dominated state.) The slogan 'kill men' has appeared on a wall near where I live. Wittier versions have appeared in graffiti on adverts.

'Renew his interest in carpentry.'
'*Saw his head off.*'

'If it were a lady, it would get its bottom pinched.'
'*If this lady was a car she'd run you down.*'[13]

While there is a general acceptance among feminists of women's right to find 'effective' forms of resisting physical coercion, this is usually seen as being checked by not letting 'the desire for self-preservation turn into oppression of others'.[14] I believe this is a vital proviso. Rhetorical calls for castration and extermination simply reproduce the most authoritarian aspects of power and hierarchy. The condemnation of human beings simply because of their membership of a sex is an aspect of militant feminism which has very right-wing implications.

The exclusion of boy children from crèches and meetings merely confirms the notion of power as biological destiny which feminists have opposed.

The main preoccupation of the women's movement has not been to excel in physical coercion. Nor have we been satisfied with developing an equivalent political power to that of dominant groups in capitalism. There has been instead a very determined attempt to break down concentrated forms of power wherever they are encountered and to redistribute power among the powerless. What is most remarkable has been that this concern has appeared in many countries. (I owe this point, for instance, to an Indian socialist feminist friend, Radha Kumer.)

I do not feel able to say why this should have been an implicit understanding in women's liberation in so many places at once. I can say a bit about the desire not to reproduce power relations within our own movement which I believe is a vitally important element of modern feminism, and which many radical and socialist feminists have in common. From the early days of the movement we have not only seen democracy in terms of the outer forms of life – industrial democracy, community control – but we have wanted our own meetings to be situations in which everyone can participate.

This following quote comes from a London women's liberation news-letter, *Shrew*, in October 1969. At this time there were a few small groups of us scattered throughout Britain. The first national conference was held in February 1970. The group which produced the newsletter printed a con-versation under the heading, 'Why do we emphasise small-group dis-cussions?' The conversation went like this . . .

> 'Traditional forms of reaching people, like large meetings where someone gives you a speech and then there is a discussion are counter-productive. These meetings repress almost everyone who is there because people who are certain, or who think they are certain stand up and make a speech, and it deters others from making their own tentative questions, so you never get around to the basic issues and the discussion remains on talking about the level of appearances.'
>
> 'Surely the first essential is to get over information, and the most practical way of doing this is to have a good speaker and a large meeting.'
>
> 'No, our first priority isn't to get over information, but to know what every-one in the room thinks. We believe in getting people to interact, not to listen to experts. We want them to *themselves* make an analysis of their situation. I think the way of doing this is not in big meetings, is not in having men dominate us through various organisations which already exist and which use old and ineffec-tual methods.'[15]

In a sense the argument has remained unresolved, though the commitment to the small group was to prove the particular strength of the new move-ment. It became evident that simply changing the forms was not an *automatic* guarantee of democracy. There are quite undemocratic ways of manipulating small groups and this is a political skill which can be acquired like any other. Equally, it can be more difficult to challenge an implicit consensus than a speaker. Power relationships can go underground. The small consciousness groups could of course be supportive and open enabling many women to get involved. But where were they to go then? The small-is-good approach did not provide a solution for what to do when large numbers of women gathered together at women's conferences. The final plenaries at our conferences in Britain have often been fraught affairs only remotely democratic and not at all supportive. In challenging the offputting formality of the established left and the unstructured aggression of the male-dominated student movement we have only been able to spasmodically develop a more open, harmonious alternative.

There has however been an important breakthrough in understanding consciousness. Already in the *Shrew* article in 1969 it was recognised that we were not discussing in consciousness-raising groups subjects to be learned in the way education was seen by the left at the time. 'It's how people perceive their lives and how they change their lives. We couldn't have an expert come and talk about people's fears about abortion. I don't mean physical fears, I mean emotional fears which an expert can't allay, because it's a question of our own values and experiences.'[16]

On the other hand, it was to prove difficult to combine this emphasis on the collective workshop and the need to communicate, pass on and thus redistribute specialised knowledge and skills. A constrained collectivity can be paralysing and result in awkward silences in which no-one wants to speak in case they appear dominating.

These ideas about organising – the inheritance of the women's movement in its early days – developed in a particular political context. The first work-shop groups in Britain had close links with the American new left. I know this was also the case in Paris and Rome. Some of the women who got involved had also been active in the student movement in the late 1960s in which the concept of specialised knowledge as a form of power had been important.

However, this form of organising made sense to many other women with no idea of its political roots. So it has survived not as the answer to all problems of democracy but as an important means of sharing experience and developing new understandings. Through the informal closeness a more intimate and personal association has developed in sisterhood than is possible in the idea of solidarity. During the 1970s, the concern to make the forms of relating inwardly democratic and cooperative did not prevail in the left organisations. It was mainly carried by the women's movement. Now ironically a new generation see it as a characteristic of feminism rather than as a radical rejection of bureaucracy and hierarchy in every sense.

Its survival in the women's movement does indicate, however, a deeper more probing concern to anticipate the future in the present among feminists than within the male-dominated left. We have as women such an intense struggle with our own passivity – not only with an external oppressor –

that we have had to tackle the question of why we consent from the start or we would never have overcome the distrust which makes women eye one another as competitors. Seeing pomp and circumstance with their pants down we have also become impatient with a platform rhetoric of equality which is not taken home. We need immediate changes in order to begin doing anything at all.

Slowly and sometimes painfully thousands and thousands of women have embarked on this journey in many countries. The search to develop less oppressive relationships in everyday life is very different from the notion of women's rights which demands equality but does not carry the notion of transformation. Access into the male world as it is is not enough. Nor do the politics of rights express the attempt to change sexual and family life. In an article in the socialist feminist paper, *Red Rag*, four women – Nell Myers, Annie Mitchell, Adah Kay and Val Charlton – say,

> We examined our life histories and became increasingly aware of pressures on us to reproduce relationships. . . .
> We need to know more about the alternatives in practical terms to the blood-tie family, possible now.
> But such explorations need to be grounded not in moralising but in the awareness of the problems of transforming our lives now, under capitalism as feminists in a variety of ways, with men, alone, with children, with other women. A tolerance of the different struggles we are all engaged in and an understanding of the gap between the present theory and its implications is what we need.[17]

In practice, what happened for many socialist feminists in Britain in the seventies was a rather uncomfortable split in which women found themselves organising in one way on the left and another in the women's movement. Well, I consider myself to be part of the left and so of course do many socialist and probably anarchist feminists. But it was exceedingly depressing to realise that we had created a ghetto. We could go into socialist meetings and it was as if all that energy and creativity had never been. I don't want to be too rosy. This can still happen. But in the last few years I think a shift has occurred amidst the seismic shock of Thatcherism. There is a new phase of trying to develop combinations of organisational forms to fit differing purposes. There is too a wider commitment among some socialists to what Raymond Williams has called 'starting as we mean to go on'.[18]

In a curious way quite diverse political experiences echo one another. For example, a group which formed one of the first lesbian clubs in Britain describe how the personal is inescapably political for lesbian women: 'To be openly gay is to risk losing your job, especially if you work with children, to risk losing your children if you are fighting a custody in divorce courts. To walk into a pub unescorted by men, or arm in arm with a lover is often to face hostility, even violence.'[19]

And Lech Walesa, the Polish workers' leader, who is unlikely to have read their statement in *Spare Rib*, said recently in an interview, 'There isn't a catalogue which lists what's political and what's not. I was taken to court for laughing politically, walking politically, you can't divide things into political and non-political so easily.'[20]

The personal is political means that political power cannot be conceived just as a matter of running for office or even about seizing power. It is about power as it manifests itself in society. Resistance within these relationships cannot then be postponed until our candidate wins or until after the revolution. Our consciousness cannot be parcelled out neatly, with parts handed over to a trade union and parts to a party. We cannot be given the line by experts. Our fears and passivity go with us to work and come back home. In order to overcome them we need forms of association which can help us develop courage and confidence in our ability to act and think. We need to find ways of living and relating which begin to to develop alternative possibilities. I don't mean that we try and pickle a utopian future in the present. And I don't mean that we lift ready-made answers from an idealised version of feminism. Simply that we recognise that there has been this very strong theme of anticipating the future recurring persistently in the women's movement in Britain and elsewhere. I do not believe that political forms of organising are biologically determined so the 'we' now is referring to socialists and feminists.

Socialism is not writ on stone tablets. As the Dutch left communist Anton Pannekoek said, 'Socialism is not a fixed, unchanging doctrine. As the world develops, people's insight increases and as new relations come into being, there arise new methods for achieving our goal.'[21]

I am labouring the point. I usually assume that it is taken for granted. Unfortunately it is not.

These ideas have become very obvious to socialist feminists. They have begun to be implicit in the practice of socialists in Britain. They were the theme of *Beyond the Fragments*.[22] Lynne Segal and Hilary Wainwright and I hoped that other groups, for example, tenants and shop stewards would start to write down their experiences of organising. We were not trying to say that the women's movement was the only place where anyone had been learning things. I believe that a renewal of our understanding of socialism will have to be based on the concrete experience of all these attempts to create new forms of resistance. The experiences of the past are also important but not when they are presented as dogmatic models. Without this renewal and the conscious development of new strategies we will be always on the defensive against modern capitalism. The resistance of the Polish workers reminds us yet again that existing socialist societies have for whatever reasons been based on an authoritarian and undemocratic version of socialism in which Marx's concept of free association has been lost. There are very grim examples of the consequences of putting the need to increase productivity and a national *Realpolitik* before the transformation of relationships. Whatever the immediate gains, the long-term losses have been enormous. This grimness is now ingrained into people's very conception of socialism.

For several reasons the whole issue of democracy has come to the fore in Britain because of increasingly authoritarian forms of state control, because of the debates about democracy in the Labour Party, and because of growing opposition to nuclear weapons. Thatcherite Toryism has rejected the notion of any bargain with the working class and so some trade unionists have begun to move away from the idea of simply going for a larger piece of the cake or in hard times just defending the gains of the past. The new militant right has mounted an ideological offensive against welfare, against the unemployed in the name of taking-your-medicine, competitive efficiency. As the economy crumbles, Mrs Thatcher's response has been 'There is no alternative.' This has forced us on the left to begin to work out where our alternatives might be.

From the Labour left, the Trades Union Congress and the Communist Party have come in response a series of proposals to reflate the economy and begin to recreate employment – the 'Alternative Economic Strategy'. There have been several criticisms of the underlying assumptions. The terms in which they have been discussed do not envisage a qualitative transformation. A group of trades councils and combine committees have got together and produced a declaration called 'Popular Planning for Social Need' which is being discussed at present in the labour movement. This document is concerned with power in the sense of creating alternative sources, breaking down concentrated forms of power and developing anticipatory forms.

Having watched professional politicians devastate our lives, rank and file workers are developing their own plans. These take the idea of control beyond the work place and into society. They are saying we need a fundamentally different society. They believe we have to reject 'the idea of competitive success as the objective of industrial reconstruction'. Instead we should 'start by linking the social needs still unmet as a result of the rundown of public services with the resources (particularly human resources) of the manufacturing, energy and construction industries'.[23]

Discussion has begun in a fragmented way about how workers' plans could be developed to relate to service industries which employ large numbers of women workers and how local communities could make use of people's skills and also extend and coordinate the activities of innumerable local groups. Some Labour local authorities, for example in Sheffield and the left of the Greater London Council, are beginning to respond to this planning from below.

A socialist feminist challenge to the Alternative Economic Strategy is developing. It is not clear yet whether we can amend, insert, add on a feminist perspective. However, the debate has focused the general approaches which have been developing into a more coherent sense of presenting a long-term strategy for socialism which will include changing the distribution of work and pay between men and women as well as between classes. Anna Coote, a socialist feminist who works on the *New Statesman*, has recently argued that we cannot enter the terms set up by the emphasis on economic recovery as a priority in the Alternative Economic Strategy. She, like the authors of 'Popular Planning for Social Need', believes we must start from the need to change how we organise life. She says we should ask what kind of ways we want to care for our children and then work out the economic requirements of this. For when competitive production is put first, the needs of people, especially those without organised forms of asserting their power, get put aside as fringe luxuries.[24]

Socialist environmentalists are also arguing against a socialism based on existing ideas of growth.[25]

So what is beginning to emerge is a notion of planning for social need from below which anticipates a different kind of society. We could not have imagined all this when we wrote *Beyond the Fragments* in the very different political climate before the Tories were in power. Without inflating these tentative and fragile developments, I think they are extremely significant.

What remains unclear from these disparate discussions of needs, though, is how conflicting needs are to be resolved, or how we tackle the problem of our needs being often deeply rooted in defending existing conditions of life. Our perception of our needs does not automatically move from defence of what we have to the anticipation of a new culture.

For instance, women caring for small children alone could find that inflation means they 'need' work. If they manage to find a job they will need someone to look after their children. This will most likely be a child minder forced to reproduce through necessity and scarcity the conditions of the mother alone at home. The women's movement has not only asserted the need for somewhere to leave children but the conscious desire for a new relationship between parents, non-parents, childcare workers and children and a vision of non-authoritarian, non-sexist childcare. Both need and vision have to interact. We have the experience of a rather faltering practice in childcare. This has now been encouraged by the growth of a loosely coordinated childcare campaign which includes trade unionist and childcare workers and parents.[26] But there are many snags, for example non-authoritarian and non-sexist can be somewhat contradictory. 'I want to be nurse', 'No, you want to be a doctor', 'Oh no I don't', 'Oh yes you do', etc.

This leads on to my fifth point – the problem of redefining power and the sources of power. This has been a most persistent preoccupation in the feminist movement internationally. It is not enough to create more democratic forms of power. Feminists keep tussling with the very notion of power itself.

For some feminists there is no problem. Either power is simply men's power and thus no concern of women, something that is to be avoided or that will hopefully wither away along with the penis from prolonged disuse. Or women's power is simply everything which is not male. The first view implies that men are biologically inclined to power and would appear to be doomed. I hope this is not true for either their elimination or severe physical restraint seems to be the gloomy prognosis of this strand of feminism. How this is to be done without women falling into evil male ways appears unclear. The second position conceives the separate creation of a women's culture. I think its influence is much more pervasive. It is an obvious and attractive response when women first begin to think about women's music and art, for instance, or of women's studies.

However, a positive does not sit in a negative. The negative itself has to be transformed in order to create the positive. How is this to be done? I think the honest answer is that nobody quite knows. From my knowledge of the British women's movement I'd say we've revealed the problem but we only have very rough guidelines about how to proceed. These guidelines are pretty shaky and have tended to emerge as realisations about how we cannot simply identify a separate sphere of women's power. Nor can we eliminate all individual problems by calling them political. Or avoid the question of executive power by revealing power relations in everyday life. We do not solve the problem of taking power by rightly asserting that there are other forms of power. The multinationals and governments go on despite separatist communes or indeed despite community struggles and workers' plans.

What follows is necessarily tentative. I want to draw out some of the implications of a range of quite diverse debate among socialist feminists.

When the women's movement began in Britain we socialists who were involved were severely criticised by people with a very economic and industrially orientated version of socialism which stressed the industrial power of workers. In the early 1970s there were very dramatic instances of militancy among miners, dockers and power workers which we feminists who were also socialists supported.

However, we also were intent on challenging the idea that the only kind of power consisted in halting production. We looked instead towards the power to reproduce life in three senses; the area of service work, including the unpaid labour of women in the home, biological procreation, and the generation of concepts about women's identity and their communication through the media through images and through the family. This has enormous ramifications, so I will focus on housework and motherhood.

This was the context of what is now referred to as the domestic labour debate. We started off reading Margaret Benston and Peggy Morton and then the reading list got longer and longer. Well, the women's movement in many countries did establish the fact (long known to housewives but not it seems to economists and sociologists) that housework was indeed work. We also revealed that this domestic labour was necessary, along with procreation and childcare, if society was to carry on. But that from women's point of view it was not necessary that we should be exclusively responsible for all three. Feminists do not agree about whether capitalism benefits or whether men benefit from the existing social arrangement or both. Though there is agreement that many women are fed up with the existing state of affairs there is not a simple way in which power can be simply switched on. It is not easy to organise resistance from this recognition of the vital necessity of women's position in the family. For domestic work and childcare are material activities but also involve relationships between people which cannot be adequately understood in terms of work on the cash nexus. Also it would be children and the dependent old who would really suffer.

One strategy has been to argue that we should somehow seek to make housework equivalent to other kinds of work. There have been various suggestions, payment to housewives, or houseworkers or mothers or people looking after children. Thus money has been seen as the means of creating an alternative source of power. The mainstream response of the women's movement in Britain has been that payment for housework would fix rather than transform the existing division of labour. Most feminists however support increased child benefit.

It is generally recognised now that we need to distinguish between housework and childcare. The first can be reduced and reorganised. The second involves a relationship with people. Women in capitalist society become most dependent upon men when children arrive. One response has been for many feminists to decide not to have children. The independence of the woman without children can be inspiring but it does not provide a solution of how to create a more equitable balance for society between independence and responsibility in which to be dependent does not imply powerlessness. I think this is necessary for mothers and needed by society in general.

The mythic symbol of the independent woman is the Amazon. In an interesting study of the use of this symbol Mandy Merck makes the point that the Amazonian myth confirms dimorphism and the sexual division of labour. Emancipation which avoids women's biological difference and the social circumstances which surround this difference can be a source for imagining ourselves in a different way. But fictional resistance is not enough. 'Nothing of the real oppression of their sex is challenged by these mythic heroines, it is merely transcended.'[27]

The initial emphasis of feminist anthropology was to argue that women were politically subordinate to men in all known societies. But that this did not mean that women were without any other forms of social power. This approach also suggested differing forms of male dominance. Subsequently, however, there has been a revival of interest in theories of matriarchy.

The strong emphasis upon women controlling fertility has meant that while women's sexuality has been seen as a potential thwarted and frustrated by male dominance, reproductive power has been a less popular candidate. Though Sandra McNeill argued in the socialist feminist newsletter, *Scarlet Women*, in 1978, 'Our enemy, whether you consider them as men, or the ruling class, or the state or all three, are aware of our power of reproduction and are seeking to take it from us.'[28] Well, this does not avoid biological difference. It falls into the opposite danger of reducing the human potential of women. It confines us.

Motherhood as a basis for a feminist redefinition of power is as problematic as the Amazonian symbol of independence. In feminist poetry this ambiguity is apparent. The yearning to find a new relationship with mothers combines with anger. Mothers are the ones who restrain the aspirations of daughters, who prepare them not to expect too much. In Betty McArdle's words,

> No way mother am I going up for auction
> Tapping out a foxtrot with my silver-plated toes
> Papering the walls while the dance-hall johnnies
> Trip around ripping my best silk hose.[29]

Mary Kelly comments on the attempt to make a female culture from what she calls metaphorically,

> . . . 'mother art', identification with the woman who tends; i.e. the mother who feeds you. She produces milk and therefore all 'good things', patchwork quilts, candles, bread and assorted magic rituals. She is the phallic mother, the uncastrated 'parthenogenator' of the pre-oedipal instance. But there is also the castrated and (unconsciously) despised mother of the Oedipus complex. Her labour of love is signified as 'womens work' a kind of iconography of victimisation . . . obsessive activities like scrubbing, ironing and above all preparing food.[30]

An important element in the feminist redefinition of power is about overcoming the inadequacy of all existing symbols of female power and changing the material and social circumstances of women's sexuality and fertility. For women's existence as child-bearers has been a source of both pride and dignity and of subjection and dependence.

I did a rapid survey of the attitudes of the men who live in the same house as me. I asked them which they found most frightening, Amazons or matriarchs. One said he'd prefer to be speared by an Amazon and get it over with as matriarchs would play with you like a cat, torturing you for a lifetime. The other said Amazons sounded much worse and opted for the matriarch. He thought while there was life there was hope.

I incline to the view that both these symbols of women's power tend to express more about men's fears of women than about women's aspirations towards independence. I acknowledge that even inadequate symbols can help us glimpse how reality might be transformed as long as we remember that they are representations of human existence which came from other people's imaginations to capture a historical relationship. These images of female power have been passed on to us. They thus have a certain internal resonance because they have become elements in how we conceive ourselves as women. But this does not mean that they must determine the scope of transformation.

The solution is not to fix upon material reproduction in the sense of procreation. Feminists are now aware that this reinforces the separate spheres of men and women. Three socialist feminist anthropologists, Felicity Edholm, Olivia Harris and Kate Young, have proposed that instead of seeking for a single determining cause for women's subordination we should examine the specific relationship between the conditions of biological reproduction and production historically.[31]

Joan Kelly, in a survey of debates among American feminists of the problem of spheres, has concluded that women need to find 'a position within social existence generally'.[32]

Thus a redefinition of power would involve a transformation in the social conditions surrounding women's fertility. It would also involve not only a redistribution of tasks and activities between men and women but also a change in the balance of power involved in the significance given to how we organise the care of children and dependents and how we produce wherewithal and wealth. Whether and how these changes in social existence would begin to shift the symbolic representation of power seems to me to remain an unresolved problem. Perhaps phalluses, dragons, Saturn and the high priestess would take on new meanings. For the Marxist approach to social transformation does appear to be inadequate to explain their persistence. However, for feminists the existence of universal and ahistorical psychic patterns clearly has to be contested because these confirm and legitimate male power.[33] Perhaps they will be transformed but even more slowly than material circumstances and more conscious elements in our consciousness.

Having said the personal is political it has never been clear how we establish what changes we can make simply by willing ourselves into different relationships. Nor is there any agreement about whether biological differences between the sexes are the basis of the subordination of women or whether it is the social meanings which have been given to physical differences. A third contender would be a dialectical relationship between nature and social life in which both can be seen as transforming the other historically.

There are quite bitter divisions now among feminists in Britain on these issues. They tend to fester rather than be argued out.

After more than a decade too I think there is a greater wariness about our capacity to create personal alternatives. The existence even of a movement which declares the personal to be political is not a sufficient guarantee for individual strength, happiness and peace of mind. Personal vulnerability is not necessarily overcome because we can analyse its social basis. I would suggest that these recognitions have contributed to the growth in interest in various forms of psychoanalysis and self-help therapy and a more speculative less overtly propagandist approach to feminist culture expressed in theatre and in the current enthusiasm for feminist poetry readings. This is partly coming from feminists but also from women involved in worker writer groups. This may not at first sight seem to be part of a redefinition of power. I think it does indicate an implicit understanding among feminists that if we are to recreate human society, in Margaret Walters' words, 'dream must interact with analysis'.[34]

It must be said, however, that the times are not particularly favourable for such a project. A quite opposite movement of feminists outwards is observable. The economic crisis has forced connections which were theoretical to become practical. There is a new convergence apparent between industrial, social and political areas of struggle. The new militant right are breaking down the boundaries which arose in less severe times.

Many socialist feminists are no longer in women's groups but defending the community resources gained in the 1970s: bookshops, literacy schemes, law centres, community-controlled nurseries. They are doing battle in the trade unions. For, as Anna Coote and Peter Kellner point out in *Hear this Brother*, while women's membership of the unions has doubled in the last twenty years, women have very little power in most unions.[35] This is doubly true of Asian and West-Indian women.

In this context socialist feminists have begun to argue for a more coherent sense of strategy which would combine working conditions, power in the trade unions, increased child benefit, changes in the distribution of jobs between the sexes. We are no longer simply developing these among ourselves but taking these into the labour movement and consciously seeking to affect the social policies of the Labour Party and the TUC.

This is a new development and impossible to assess yet. Its prospect for success must be in my view its ability to touch the imagination and desires of working-class women in large numbers. For a real transformation of the labour movement must be the creation of women themselves.

I think it is important for us to bear in mind the reasons why many women fear and resent feminism more than they resent their subordination to men – better the devil you know.

In order to want change we need to be confident of an alternative. The inspiration for Workers Plans, for instance, came from the plans Lucas Aerospace workers developed for alternative uses for their skills. Instead of making weapons to destroy life the same skills could help disabled children to be mobile, save energy, increase production in the Third World. Knowing that you could do something else means that you can see arms cuts not as just losing your job but as changing what you produce.

The women attracted to feminism have on the whole been women for whom capitalism has partially but inadequately opened up alternatives to women's customary lot. Strategies which seek to redefine women's power in society thus need to present ways in which these inadequate alternatives could be improved. We have to make sure that the redefinition of power is accompanied by the conscious development of new sources of strength. Otherwise women can perceive radical change as a threat and will thus hang on desperately to the traditional sources of female identity.

Anna Coote and Jean Coussins in a recent pamphlet, 'Family in the Firing Line', have shown how the Tories have hypocritically made real life difficult for women with children while exalting an ideal of motherhood.[36] In another pamphlet, 'Breeders for Race and Nation', an anti-fascist women's group examined the right-wing rituals of women's power through sacrifice as widows and the mothers of soldiers.[37]

Feminist strategies also need to take into account the uneven effect of capitalist society upon the lives of women from different classes and ethnic groups. For example, feminists in Britain have tended to argue that the welfare state has served to strengthen the family. But this has not been the case for black women. Immigration law divides Asian and and West-Indian families. The family is a dispensable luxury for imperialism.

The authoritarian political offensive which has partly created the crisis has meant that for more and more women struggle against power relationships in daily life is inseparable from state power.

The first black women's conference in Britain was held in 1979. Increasingly repressive immigration policies and harassment of women by immigration officials and hostility among the police to young black people means that they are facing not only fascist attacks but the official face of racism. This became clear in the arrests which followed the riots this summer when West-Indian parents who would not be previously involved in radical protest, far less riots, have begun to form defence committees. In Ireland and Britain many feminists who would not support the IRA have supported the H-block campaigns. Imperialism has thus become a living issue for the women's movement in Britain, not simply in terms of solidarity but because of the need to prevent our government's actions.

The very real danger of annihilation has brought women in large numbers into the anti-nuclear movement. This has meant for feminists like Mary Kaldor who is in the Labour Defence Group tackling the international arms industry and the complex political and technological machinery which sustains it. Women have also come up against male dominance in the anti-nuclear movement and have formed women's groups. Some of these women argue that it is all a matter of male power. Others are resisting nuclear weapons as mothers. This polarises the issue between women as carers and nurturers of life and men as destroyers. It also conveniently muffles the support women have given to right-wing militaristic regimes.

I can see there are real reasons why women as the carers in our society should resist annihilation and that this carries a radical hope for human survival and cooperation. I feel since I had a child a more direct and passionate desire to safeguard the future. On the other hand, I steadfastly believe in the need to extend this care and passion beyond the confines of biological motherhood. I also think it is oversimple to assume that all men have equal power over the state. This assumption would leave no scope for alliances between groups of people against differing forms of power.

Within the anti-nuclear movement it is possible to grasp that ambiguity about power which is so evident in the history of feminism. Some feminists are echoing Virginia Woolf, 'We can prevent war not by repeating your words and following your methods but by finding new words and creating new methods.'[38]

But others are deciding that this amounts to an evasion and moving into the more traditional areas of political power like the Labour Party in considerable numbers. There are also many of us caught in between seeking a new language and new methods without denying the significance of established forms of organisation and resistance.

There is no likelihood of feminists, or revolutionary socialists 'taking power' in the sense of an insurrectionary moment. There have been enormous shifts in the Labour Party despite Benn's defeat. The Labour left also badly needs the support of the left outside its own ranks. But this would not be sufficient to guarantee a transition to socialism, even if a left Labour government were to be elected because such a government would face the devastation caused by Thatcherism, the hostility of the media, international capital, the US government, and possibly the armed forces in Britain. To withstand these pressures even a government of moderate reform would require popular and active support on a scale far beyond the existing scope of the left, the women's movement and the labour movement.

It is in this context then that the polarisation of revolutionary versus reformist strategies which have been with us since the Russian Revolution are being re-examined. It is not clear whether resistance to capitalism will take the form of an outright confrontation in which state power will be wrested from the dominant class. It seems more likely that there will be a prolonged contest for power the outcome of which will be affected by our ability to start making practical alternative strategies which do not only serve the needs of the existing working-class movement, which is predominantly white and male, but also make sense to women and people in oppressed ethnic groups. Lenin was a great pragmatist. He seized the time, as they say. But times change. I do not think the model of the Russian Revolution an adequate guide for the conditions we face in advanced capitalism. How we can develop a new kind of socialist movement in which the gains and strengths of autonomous movements can be safeguarded, while we also understand the necessary connections between the different groups, remains unclear.

The women's movement has and will make crucial contributions to how power can be conceived and resisted. But I do not mean by this women as a group taking power, because I do not believe the conflict between women and men is the only form of power relationship.

I believe the subordination of women to men as a sex is not the same as class oppression. Men are in an oppressive relationship to women, they can behave oppressively to women but there are elements in the relations between men and women in which mutual aid, interdependence, affection and love are also realities. I believe we must challenge the oppressive aspects of these connections without denying the positive feelings which people value and which contribute to an everyday understanding of cooperation and community. For an understanding of the social restraints distorting what we already value is a powerful impetus to seek new, less oppressive relationships.

Eve Fitzpatrick's poem, 'To My Father', expresses this better than I can.[39]

> Since you do not know
> what you know,
> how much are you culpable?
>
> That is an old question;
> and your answer is that
> lack of knowledge is always a reason for lack of knowledge.
>
> In your unreason you
> crippled your momma through me:
>
> she could not know
> you would not know,
>
> I must know.
>
> Some say I show my scars bravely,
> Others despise me for them.
>
> You taught me the vices men dream of;
> You bared the fangs of the brute wolf,
> the crush of the great bar,
> the bolt of the bull who will not wait,
> the vanity of peacocks,
> the greed of the prize ram,
>
> until, in terror, I turned to women.
> And that, you spat with contempt, was that.
>
> With women I have what I know I need,
> but the learning has been bitter;
> never for me the careful arms of a husband,
> the safety of the marriage lock,
> the to and fro of unlike needs they tell me of.
>
> The love I've fought for has its special bliss,

but not without the special hell of
mind from tortures moulded dull and fearful,
flesh from ignorance found unfaithful,
self, turned inward, racked with fantasy.

My me unwillingly apologises every day.

I turn to my son, got so deliberately,
and wonder if my love can beat the pattern back,
can teach him to admire equally
the grace of women, the good gifts of men.

Or must my shame be his shame
and my needs his helpless pain?

And you, my father, in your ceaseless rage,
blessed with such great unknowing,
how, now, do you see your line,
your patronage, your name?

PART THREE

HOLDING TRANSIENCE: MARXISM, FEMINISM AND HISTORY

INTRODUCTION

'In its rational form,' Marx maintained, dialectic 'includes in its comprehension and affirmative recognition of the existing state of things, at the same time, also the recognition of the negation of that state, of its inevitable breaking up; because it regards every historically developed social form as in fluid movement, and therefore takes into account its transient nature no less than its momentary; because it lets nothing impose upon it and is in its essence critical and revolutionary.'[1]

This would be a fine quotation for a socialist feminist historian to live up to.

I sigh and imagine the affirmative recognition and the breaking up, the making and unmaking in my mind's eye. But how to hold what moves? To even fold back tiny corners and watch transience flicker through one's touch? Especially as we are part of movement and required not only to record but to change the world. We historians are expected to join hands with our own history and elbow our way between the moment and the transformation of the moment. It has always been a tight squeeze.

And then there are always livings to earn and two new fish to feed. One came for its holidays, the other appears to have moved in.

To mention the inconvenience of daily life is not to reduce the strenuous excitement of the dialectic. You eat your dinner only to face the washing up. Even as we munch, delight turns into a dirty plate.

Nor is it just awkwardness to mention that Marx's approach to history is, like all knowing, an approximation – full, resonant and magnificent, but still approximation. He does not come clean about this. A fighter and polemicist, he omits to apply the dialectic to his own subjectivity, even though he was able to see the educator should be educated. He thus takes too little account of faith, morality and vision. In grasping the inadequacy of an ahistorical utopia he didn't make explicit enough his own beliefs in human creativity. In attacking his opponents he squeezed too hard and some of the political assumptions he shared with them were squandered.

There is, after all, always someone doing the comprehension and recognition. Where is the thinker in all this, modern feminism has asked, and remained sceptical, putting its finger on the blind spot of the dialectic.

It is a good question. But where do you go after pointing out bias? Feminism has pre-Marxist roots. These have their own problems. The political origins of feminism have been stronger on rights and utopia than transience and moment. Rights and utopia are important but they tend towards a rigidity which confuses what ought to be with the existing state of things. Feminism's political traditions do not incline towards historical locations. They do allow more space for subjectivity than Marxism. 'I believe', 'I want', 'I need', 'I desire' are more clearly present. So we can at least exchange starting points, democratise the means of communication, open identity to scrutiny, shift meanings and arouse imagination.

This opening to subjectivity has had very radical implications in the here and now. It has also inspired feminist historians to include daily life and personal experience as evidence of past happenings.

But there is a problem of repetition. If I feel this and I feel that and he believes and she believes and you might want what I don't want, who decides? And the world goes on the same.

Dissatisfied with repetitive assertions of subjective needs and desires which do not reflect upon their own relation to history, some feminists have extracted from Marxism the distanced critical analysis. The existing state of things is pinned down, held in place and deconstructed. And the self? The self fragments into its social and psychic components. Such detachment may bring peace of mind, new space for speculation, but still the world goes on the same.

Surely we require more from Marx than this? For potentially he left us the means to fashion thought in movement. This was his great gift. To read his writing is to experience the *instance* of analysis, shaped by the contours of past and present, pushing us into a new reality which opens understanding. Marxism asserts the coincidence of changing circumstances and human activity. So there is never simply repetition. The 'I' who affirms can be understood as both there and changing. The search to understand historical transformation, to know the tremulous circumstances of others, must then also be the search to understand ourselves, our own.

Both are difficult and bring headaches for historians and politicians. It is true that they are not the same. They must be distinguished but they are still together and mutually influential.

The intrusion of our own person washing up may make Marxism inspire less confidence. But surely we have to rely on our own endeavour and understanding, as feminism with its sturdy pioneer origins, building a community with bare hands, reminds us. For what kind of phoney fantasy is it to lean on hollow structures, an echo in a ghost town? Is the last fight to be a repeat of Startrek reliving the mythologised West of Wyatt Earp on streets where the houses are just fronts?

We pry into the lives and times of others partly because we are nosy – but also because we do not want the world to go on the same . . . that is if we seek an approach to history which is at once critical and revolutionary.

1. History

◆◆◆◆◆◆

'History', early 1970s, unpublished. This poem is the confession of a nosy parker who takes on too many things at once, has difficulty in getting to the point and aspires to be a historian – among other things.

◆◆◆◆◆◆

I cannot quite get hold of history
I take it around with me,
bags and parcels
I never quite explore
One day I'll go right through.
One day I'll really know
exactly what
I lug about.
But somehow I never find the time
to settle down
and search.
I often want to fling the lot
out
into time
jump
on a moving bus
and steam into the future
driving a red double-decker
Instead I stand
sniffing the dust
my parcels wrapped around me
bolstering the night.

2. Search and Subject, Threading Circumstance

◆◆◆◆◆◆

'Search and Subject, Threading Circumstance', introduction to the American edition of *Hidden from History*, Pantheon, 1974, unpublished in Britain.

This introduction to *Hidden from History* went well beyond the scope of the book. It is easier to pronounce on history than to do it.

I tried to make the context in which I came to write about women's history more explicit for an American audience. After a decade this has some relevance for British readers. It can no longer be assumed. I also suggest some directions which a socialist feminist approach to history might take.

◆◆◆◆◆◆

Part 1

My earliest memories are a ragbag of stories and pictures: King Alfred burning the cakes and Robert Bruce of Scotland learning to 'try, try and try again' from a spider making its web after he had been defeated and driven into hiding. Boadicea, with flaming red hair, driving her chariot in battle against the Romans or Queen Elizabeth dancing and rather vainly pretending not to see a foreign courtier watching her from the gallery. Young Queen Victoria comes down the stairs, demure, pure and gracious in her nightdress and shawl to learn that she has succeeded to the throne. It was mainly kings and queens, this childhood history; the common people hardly figured at all. There was Nell Gwynn though, the mistress of King Charles II. Her picture was on the jar of a particular brand of marmalade. I found out as much as I could by asking grownups about this beautiful marmalade person with her orange haircap and ringlets and her tray of oranges under her bosom. Behind her picture there was darkness. I imagined dim, winding streets and adventure. The stories the grownups told about her could never illuminate those streets. I think I hankered even then for a history that would enable me to follow her down them, to find out where she came from. But my first conscious memory of having an idea about what history was came as an abrupt blink of excitement. We read a story in school about the Phoenicians discovering how to make purple dye. I realised quite suddenly a world without the obvious, a world in which everyday things were absent, in which nothing was purple.

I was lucky at school between eleven and fourteen for, though history became less exciting, it was never completely killed for me. It was still more than just space on the timetable. Wars and explorations left me cold. I was interested only in how extraordinary events penetrated the lives of ordinary people. I was quite happy to imagine being a peasant in the Peasants' Revolt or the Wars of the Roses, a young lady at Bath in the eighteenth century in a family with Jacobite connections or a revolutionary 'agitator' skirting English villages during the Napoleonic Wars.

As I grew older, history began to run more strictly along examination routes. I took 'O' level exams when I was fifteen and 'A' levels before I left school at seventeen. I was exceptionally lucky in my history teacher, Olga Wilkinson, who saw exams as hurdles to be surmounted with history growing undeterred over and around them. Her own background and views were closely bound up with the kind of history she felt at home with. She came from a farming family in East Yorkshire, and was a Methodist and a liberal, who disliked enthusiasm and fanaticism and liked baroque architecture and classically tailored clothes.

The history she taught belonged to the present, not history textbooks. For example, in 1956 she poked fun at Eden for going into Suez as she described Palmerston bringing out gunboats to protect British prestige. The Nation and Empire, hitherto unquestioned and sacred, began to stagger before my eyes. The Union Jack, the Dambusters, Winston Churchill, the Royal Family, Gracie Fields began to crumble and disintegrate. Jimmy Porter in John Osborne's play *Look Back in Anger* was to give them their final prod. I doubt if Olga realised at the time how subversive one historical irony could be. Now it seems almost inconceivable how outrageous it still was to someone from a conservative, small business background like mine simply to laugh at patriotic trappings and symbols.

The school I was at was Methodist and we were exposed to the popular history of Methodism, Wesley's life and the splits with the Primitives. Through Olga, a sociological dimension to the history of religion opened up. It was not simply a matter of God, faith, grace and redemption. The church and the various doctrinal strands and their historical fortunes emerged as part of the more general development of society.

She also had a radical view of the kind of sources we could learn to use. She put us to work in the country archives at Beverly with enclosure maps and accounts of local misdemeanours; she taught us to see buildings as historical records, steering us around Norman churches and stately homes and land-scape gardening as well as into deserted villages and Dominican sewers. I always wanted to be more adept at this digging-up kind of history. I envy people now who can make sense of the countryside, who can spot ridge and furrow and the structure and shift of settlement. I was rather dim and slow at it, however much I tried. But at least I glimpsed that this tramping and plodding in Army Surplus anorak or late 1950s plastic mac over field and moor in the English rain was part of the historical craft. It was an unusual glimpse at the time and by no means the normal stuff of historical schoolteaching.

My rebellion came at first sporadically and only gradually acquired coherence. Olga Wilkinson's beginnings were very different from mine. She had been reared in the reaction against the first generation of radical English social and economic historians like Tawney and the Hammonds. It was not the task of the historian to moralise or to judge. Red lines scarred my essays in a continuing war against sentimentalism and purple passages. I discovered *Religion and the Rise of Capitalism* when I was about seventeen and devoured it enthusiastically to her resigned dismay. But her inoculation against the Hammonds was more successful. Several years later when I finally came to read *The Village Labourer* I felt that she had cheated me of good history by mocking their indignation against enclosure. She would have been the first to tease me for accepting her views so unquestioningly, and it is true that they could not have had such an effect if they were not confirmed elsewhere. In her insistence against judgement and sentiment she reflected assumptions which were very much part of the idiom of much economic and social history in the 1950s. It was considered naïve to be critical of the actions of people in the past, though significantly this was always seen as applying to the upholders of the status quo, not those who were trying to change things. One consequence was that poverty and suffering appeared inevitable if vaguely regrettable.

I went to Oxford, which little social and economic history seemed to have reached even by 1961. It was very bewildering. We had to read Gibbon, Macaulay, de Tocqueville and Bede the first term, after which we launched into the Romans and Anglo-Saxons and European diplomatic intrigue in the nineteenth century. The syllabus changes slowly at Oxford, and I suppose we were still being prepared to serve in the early twentieth-century Indian Civil Service or the foreign office, or perhaps for nothing in particular. So far as I know, people who go to Oxford still suffer under this bizarre syllabus.

I was fortunate, however, to bump into bits of history along the way which did interest me. The education which has been manufactured to prepare such an imaginative ruling class as the British is sufficiently oiled to allow for odd accidents. I thrived on these accidents. There was, for instance, quite a shuffling of tutors as we were farmed out to other colleges for tutorials as well as within our own. What you were taught for your weekly essays thus depended on the luck of the draw and the draw varied. Glimmers of light came through in my second year with the Peasants' Revolt, religious heresy and the Puritans.

I sought my own history too as I met people who were socialists who argued with me. I tried to find my bearings by reading about socialist ideas and movements in the past, mainly in nineteenth-century Europe. I learned how different ideas had arisen, the crosscurrents of argument, schisms and heresy. I entered an echo chamber of contested orthodoxies and tragic conflicts. Familiar and fascinating stuff for someone reared on biblical criticism and Wesley's theological doctrines, or the proud and bitter feuding between orthodox Methodism and the dwindling remnants of the Primitive persuasion.

When I read Marx, I found something more than descriptions of arguments. The arguments sprang from the real world. The early political economists presented their vision of the world as it was then and claimed that this was as it must always be. But even within their growing world its impatient opposite was also developing in the creation of the working class and the assertion of labour as a source of value. There was such a density of detail combined with great sweeps of contempt, a playful irony and the continuing slow accumulation of the structure of Marx's theory. I was interested in the significance he gave to class conflict and the way in which he exposed the arrogant and preposterous swindle which had been perpetrated against the sellers of labour power − to sell your whole capacity to make and then be bound by religion, law and morality to be grateful and respectful to Mr Moneybags and his henchmen.

His view of history was inseparable from his view of the present. It was possible because of Marx to begin to see a pattern behind the way I myself had come to see the past and the present. He seemed to share my lack of interest in purely political events like Lord North's period in office or the diplomatic manoeuvring of Austria and Prussia.

The difficulty with Marx was one of scale. On one side you had his kind of history, like a gigantic organ with all the stops out; on the other you had your weekly essays, tiny little things dealing with short periods in detail. It was like trying to stop the organ for a minute to find out the right moment in its accumulative crescendos to ping the triangle in the school band.

I often found myself puzzling over some controversy which appeared to have originated many issues back in the *Economic History Review*. The arguments presented themselves in their own chronology. Each article had to be remembered intact. It took me years to know what so-and-so was saying or why. The sources of these controversies were mysterious. Quite often they seemed to have originated in something Marx had said or that someone had decided he had said somewhere. But since in those days it was not the thing to put Marx in your footnotes even if he had started the whole thing off in the first place, the terms of argument were not always explicit. The trouble was that many more historians seemed to have been produced who were eager to show you how wrong Marx was. The ones who agreed with him were sparse indeed. You were left in your half week or so with a mountain of empirical evidence showing how this or that could or could not be said. Capitalism had always existed or it had never existed at all; things always went from bad to worse or progress was built in so why waste time fretting about a few handloom weavers drinking nettle soup in hard times? E.H. Carr's *What Is History?* was the only criticism I came across in the early 1960s contesting these views. They were never presented as methods of looking at history explicitly, but as objective, unbiased common sense.

It was very difficult to study history which was not about Parliament and the growth of the treasury or about cabinets, treaties and coalitions, partly because we barely questioned how we should be taught and partly because a different kind of history was still in the making. It was before the days of student militancy – all sheepish and meek we were, no alternative syllabuses or shares in decision-making for us. We had to make our own individual solutions, so that any questioning could evaporate into guilt and an overwhelming sense of personal inadequacy. This was particularly true of us women, who were a tiny minority in a male stronghold and subtly taught our place by being told how privileged we were to be there at all.

Much labour history has accepted a strictly political definition of what history is about too, merely substituting working-class leaders and institutions for those of the dominant class. This bias towards the people at the centre or the history of organisations has affected both social-democratic historians, who look towards the creation of working-class institutions as part of the gradual accretion of reforms, and Marxist historians, who have studied the party as representing the most conscious among the working class. It is reinforced by the accessibility of sources. Formal organisations leave records. This kind of source produces a particular kind of history, which excludes people who have not been prominent in formal labour organisation. From this point of view, women's role has invariably been supportive and secondary. While consciousness is seen in a pyramid of levels, women are always seen as on the bottom and in need of being hitched up.

Another kind of history was shaping, though, and I learned it awkwardly, half from books and half from people I met. In the early sixties, ideas from France about the kinds of sources which could be used and a different type of historical question were having a belated influence in England. Historians of the 1789 Revolution and of the later revolutions in France were enquiring about the composition of the revolutionary crowd, the organisation of the sans-culottes, the movement of population, the incidence of cholera and revolt. This kind of history appeared for me in the person of the historian of the revolutionary army, Richard Cobb. One of my tutors sent me off to him for tutorials. Strange and exciting events they were as he leapt over the sofa saying, 'The Spanish people will rise again,' with me wondering momentarily quite how he was going to land. Richard Cobb hunted down food hoarders and police informers gleefully, sided with risings of the left and right, arbitrarily sauntered down a prostitute's beat or probed a sans-culottes' anti-Semitism or dislike of homosexuals. About the same time a few historians working on the British labour movement were moving away from the strictly political history of labour and the history of official institutions. They were beginning to explore the relation between religious heresy and dissent and early political protest. They wrote about class consciousness as it was expressed in action and in the records of local meetings, or as it was reported by informers. They described not inevitable and impersonal forces, but real men and women acting in specific situations.

Their appearance was not accidental, though at the time it appeared so to me. Edward Thompson's *The Making of the English Working Class* was the most massive single work and exerted a tremendous influence, not only in its particular theme, but in making the undergrowth of consciousness and organisation a subject for enquiry. Both Edward and Dorothy Thompson's history, like that of other Marxist historians of their generation, was nurtured by the Communist Party historians group. This combined in their case with contact with their students in the Workers Education Association and with the radical political tradition of the area round Halifax in the West Riding of Yorkshire, where they lived in the 1950s and early 1960s.

The existence of historical work which was using Marxist ideas in a non-dogmatic fashion meant that there was a context in which to learn an alternative kind of history. These historians formed a very loose grouping who by the early sixties were more likely to be without than within the Communist Party and to have political roots in the New Left. The meetings of the Labour History Society were a means of communicating the work which was being done. As the decade rolled on the Society became increasingly august and the study of labour history itself began to be respectable. In the late sixties more informal gatherings at Ruskin College, the trade union college in Oxford, where worker students read papers which related to their own lives and work experience, became important to younger people who had been radicalised by the student movement and the Vietnam Solidarity movement and were searching for some way of locating their own politics. The Ruskin History Workshops grew larger and larger, becoming half political gathering, half celebration – hundreds packed on the cold floor with a diet of bread and cheese and a sleeping bag at night.

Implicit within this history, which in various ways focused on work and community struggles, popular action and the submerged consciousness of people without power, was the possibility of studying the position and action of women, but the contours of the female historical experience were still only glanced at.

Interest in women's position in the past has grown as women's liberation has grown, partly because women within the movement have started to study women in the past and partly because the existence of a new feminist movement has stimulated enquiry among other historians. When the women's movement began in Britain in 1969 it was so small and there was so much to be done that interest in the detailed study of the past was necessarily limited to just a few of us, though the idea of calling the first conference, which was held at Oxford in February 1970, came out of a meeting of women at one of the Ruskin History Workshops and included two papers on women and history.[1]

When I turned to women's past I realised how unconscious I had been of how the history I had studied before women's liberation had neglected women. We were always led to believe that women were not around because they had done so little. But the more I read, the more I discovered how much women had in fact done. Because I was a socialist I started by trying to find out what role women had played in socialist movements in the past, and *Women, Resistance and Revolution* came out of this. I wanted particularly to learn whether women had questioned their role as women as well as trying to make a new society. It was difficult to know where to start. Alice Clark's *The Working Life of Women in the Seventeenth Century,* Edith Thomas' *The Women Incendiaries* and Wilhelm Reich's *The Sexual Revolution* and the references to Alexandra Kollontai which I followed up from Reich's book were invaluable. They provided starting points which gave me some inkling of the vastness of the silence about women in the past. As I discovered more, I became more and more excited. It was apparent that women had used forms of opposition which did not come within a strictly political definition – hence the word 'Resistance' in the title. Yet even by 1972–1973, when I wrote *Hidden from History*, I was unable to follow up these less political forms of resistance because I was still writing a general study based mainly on secondary sources.

Since *Hidden from History* was published, there have been several meetings of people studying women in the past in Britain and it is evident that the rediscovery of our history is an essential aspect of the creation of a feminist critique of male culture. I think that in America you are ahead of us in terms of the amount of work done, circulated and published. But I do not think that the question of a feminist approach to the past is an easy one or that any of us have produced an adequate definition of what such an approach would be.

I know that my own urgency towards the past is not an isolated eccentricity, but is shared by other women in Britain and in the women's movement internationally. We are privileged to be able to think, write and communicate in such a context, which, though limited, is still *there*.

Some of our difficulties come from the newness and closeness of the subject of women in the past. We are, after all, young as a political movement, scarcely born as a critique of the whole of existing male culture. Our existence is flimsy. There is the danger that by overdefining a tenuous reality you produce dogma. An existing culture, asserting the world as it is, is rich in ambiguity, fertile in contradictions, moist, malleable, elastic. A critical culture, which springs from people without control in the world, is, on the contrary, fragile, brittle, taut with the effort which has gone into its creation. There is the closeness, too, between search and subject. The search for what happened is out there, but we are the subject in here. We ourselves are there even as we look at them, the others, in the past.

There is a tension between any conscious radical commitment to the creation of new social relations and the writing of the history of an oppressed group. It is possible for such a political commitment merely to force history into its own mould, to manufacture a past to fit its own present. The idea that the writing of history is a utilitarian process, that its only purpose is to produce neatly capsulated lessons for political dilemmas in the present, is destructive of anything more than exhortation. The opposing reaction to this tension is to say that we should bury our heads in documents and just do more work. It is important to do more work and particularly important to do more work about women in the past because our knowledge is so meagre. But it is an illusion that the collection of facts alone will change the orientation of our views of the past, for there is no such thing as an empirical study which does not come from a particular vision of the world. 'Unbiased' history simply makes no declaration of its bias, which is deeply rooted in existing society, reflecting the views of the people of influence. A radical critical history has to be clear about the distinctness of the assumptions with which it begins. It does not imply a dismissal of the craft skills of historical work. It does not know all the answers. It requires a continuing movement between conscious criticism and evidence, a living relationship between questions coming from a radical political movement and the discovery of aspects of the past which would have been ignored within the dominant framework.

Feminism — the assertion of the need to improve the position of women — has had various political strands appearing historically in different forms. Just as there are several feminisms there are several feminist approaches to history, which it would be interesting to try to unravel, for this would show the impact of political ideas on the writing of women's history. In the feminist movement of the late nineteenth century, for instance, there was a popular myth of the universal, total subjugation of women in the past. This undifferentiated view of women as completely weak and helpless was a projection backwards of the contemporary lot of middle-class women. It was not recognised that women could be aggressive and take part in production even though they were subordinate to men. As the study of economic history developed, the participation of women in the guilds and their part in agricultural production in precapitalist society were described by the first generation of economic and social historians, who were themselves challenging the scope of history.

A great deal of what was accepted then and now as history excludes most people. It has really been only since the working class became a force to be reckoned with in capitalism that the confines of this narrow definition of history could be challenged. In the nineteenth century, Carlyle criticised history which was only about kings and queens. He wanted a history of people who had made a name for themselves – Let us now praise famous men. In 1924, Eileen Power remarked in *Medieval People* that he should have gone further:

> He did not care to probe the obscure lives and activities of the great mass of humanity upon whose slow toil has built up the prosperity of the world, and who were the hidden foundations of the political and constitutional edifice reared by the famous men he praised. To speak of ordinary people would have been beneath the dignity of history.[2]

For Eileen Power, the history of ordinary people included women along with men. The work she and other historians did was important in showing that women were not always excluded from labour as the women of the Victorian middle class were.

The feminist movement in the early part of this century thus coincided with a period of substantial historical questioning. In the case of Alice Clark's *The Working Life of Women in the Seventeenth Century,* published in 1919, this resulted in an examination of the nature of women's productive activity during the period when the capitalist division of labour was just beginning. Alice Clark was a Fabian socialist who begins her work with an admission of feminist partiality.

> It is perhaps impossible to divest historical enquiry from all personal bias, but in this case the bias has simply consisted in a conviction that the conditions under which the obscure mass of women live and fulfil their duties as human beings have a vital influence upon the destinies of the human race.[3]

Among the people she thanked was the feminist Olive Schreiner and her book *Woman and Labour*, which Alice Clark says 'first drew the attention of many workers in the emancipation of women to the difference between reality and the commonly received generalisations as to woman's productive capacity'.[4]

By enquiring into the effect of capitalism upon the economic position of women, Alice Clark questioned women's relationship to the state in capitalist society, 'which regards the purpose of life solely from the male standpoint'.[5] Though she does not seem to have been able to pursue this idea in her writing of history, her book does show very clearly how the developing division of labour in capitalism removed the productive role of women and fragmented productive activity. She contrasts the lot of the woman in family industry with that of the wage-earning poor. Perhaps her assumption that family industry was so widespread in the late Middle Ages exaggerates, for it is possible that in certain regions the number of wage-earning poor people was larger than has been thought. It was not a straightforward transition from family industry to landless labourer, but greatly modified by the region and type of agriculture. But the central point remains – a challenge to the view that women had been universally subordinated without seeing that subordination can assume different forms depending upon how particular societies organise production.

Mary Beard, an American, is another example of a historian whose interest in women's position in the past made her question the emphasis implied by some histories that women had been silent and suppressed before the struggle for the vote in the nineteenth century. Her *Woman as a Force in History* is, she says, a 'study of the tradition that women were members of a subject sex throughout history'.[6] She locates the source of this tradition in diverse places, including the feminist movement influenced by Mill and the socialists who followed Bebel, though she adds that the Marxist socialists did qualify this by accepting the idea of mother right. Because she is studying a 'tradition', she darts around the centuries, from ancient times to German fascism and American women in the Second World War. Her case that women have always been a force in history is confused by the fact that she does not distinguish between women of different classes. She approaches medieval history through the history of law, literary evidence, education and organisation of the guilds. But these sources mainly throw light on the lives of upper-class women or those of a middling status. Nor does she disentangle the differing nature of women's influence. Economic activity and education are not synonymous with political power. Thus, while it is true that women have been a force in history and that the notion of universal passivity and subordination is ahistorical, there are also differences between classes, and in the particular cultural shape of subordination.

However, both Alice Clark and Mary Beard provide interesting examples of how contemporary assumptions which came out of political movements, in this case feminism, can contribute towards a history which asks large questions.

The modern women's movement has produced an immense popular enthusiasm about women's history as part of the challenge to masculine cultural hegemony. History is part of the way in which we have been defined by men. There are two channels in the course of this feminist history at the moment. One is to identify romantically with women in the past. The strength of this impulse is that it is defiantly popular. It refuses to address itself to a limited audience. Its enthusiasm is important because it insists that history belongs to an oppressed group and is an essential aspect in the cultural pride of that group, just as the working-class and black movements celebrated their past and as gay people are beginning to discover themselves. The dangers in this identification are that we become impatient with the time it takes to do careful research and substitute present assumptions for the unravelling of what happened. The other channel consists in the quiet burrowing, yet to see the light of day, of innumerable lonely women making meaning of remote academic credentials by studying women in the past. Here the perils are reversed. The pursuit of the past can become a substitute for trying to change the present. It can become divorced from its original radical impulse and we might find ourselves creating just another academic subject. We need somehow to avoid letting this divergence become too extreme. We need to combine popular enthusiasm and directness of style with painstaking research, even though present-day society, with its pressures of work, money and political activity, makes it difficult for one person to supply both.

Within both channels of this new feminist history there are the implicit assumptions that women's history will be done by women and be about women. I think that these assumptions are disorienting and can actually restrict the radical implications of a feminist approach to the past when they are presented as unchanging principles. I think that we should distinguish between a principled definition of feminist history in these terms and a tactical choice we make at this point. There are tactical reasons for demanding that at particular times women should be employed rather than men as teachers of history because we have been so discriminated against. This is different, though, from a general principled commitment to women writing our own history. This commitment can misfire because it is possible to find women who are anti-feminists and because it restricts human consciousness to biology in a deterministic manner, forgetting that a man writing history can be transformed by the existence of a feminist movement. The criticism of a male historian who does not inform his history by an understanding of the questions raised by the women's movement would be the same as the insistence that historians who are middle-class must learn from the action of workers if they are to interpret the history of the working class. Equally, simply studying women in the past does not necessarily question the whole scope of history. It could mean that we study exceptional women or that we study only the political aspects of the women's movement in the past or that we simply stick women onto the study of the labour movement. There is also a chance, if we interpret feminist history in this way, that we pursue an abstract category called 'Woman' through history and isolate women from social relations in the family and at work.

But just as we need tactically to insist in certain cases that a woman rather than a man be set to work, we need to focus particularly now upon the role of women in the past because of the overwhelming neglect and ignorance which exists. The manner in which we go about these immediate and tactical moves, though, is crucial to their outcome. In saying that a woman should be employed to teach women's history we also have to question the mode of teaching, not try to create a female equivalent to a professional elite whose academic knowledge has no relation to the social needs of most people. Similarly, in saying that we choose to study woman's past we should not perpetuate a notion of 'Woman' as an isolated, frozen category, an unchanging historical entity. Instead, we should begin to transform our approach to the past by starting from the different material conditions of women, recognising that these have not been the same under all systems of production and have varied also according to class. The social relations of women have altered over time, just like those of men, but most history looks at women through the situation of men. A primary focusing on women is tactically necessary in order to disentangle ourselves from this all-pervading identification of the norm with the specific predicament of men. A conscious feminist commitment, thus, is crucial if this identification is to be challenged.

But feminism alone is not enough to encompass theoretically the forms of oppression women have shared with men. Class exploitation and the cultural indignities which have accompanied it have affected both men and women in the working class. The fate of all women has not been the same. If we start from the material circumstances of women's lives and try to work out how they maintained and reproduced the means of continuing life, how they saw themselves and the world, how they resisted or acquiesced in their fate, how the movements of women differed from those of men, it does not mean that we can ignore class or race. Nor does it mean that we do not look at the social relations between men and women. But it does mean that our understanding of men as well as women in the past gains a new perspective. If we are to begin to integrate the study of the social relations of men and women we need this conscious commitment to what is specific and what is shared. At present we not only lack such a perspective, we barely know what has happened in the lives of the great mass of women.

What follow are suggestions of some ways of looking and some means we could use as starting points for enquiry. None of these are trouble-free, they all have their snags. By using them the snags will become more evident and we can change or discard them.

Part 2

Marx's thinking about history and his understanding of the significance of class conflict as a crucial factor in historical transformation have exerted a continuing influence on all people who have pitted their humiliation in the world as it is against the hope of the world as it could be. His particular comments about what happened in the past have provoked voluminous controversy among historians. These are worth studying and unravelling, but more immediately relevant are where he thought historical enquiry should begin and how he saw it proceeding. In *The German Ideology* in 1845–6, he says that it starts with 'the real individuals, their activity and the material conditions under which they live, both those which they find already existing and those produced by their activity'.[7]

His view of history was inseparable from his view of human social existence:

> . . . men must be in a position to live in order to make 'history'. But life involves before everything else eating and drinking, a habitation, clothing and many other things. The first historical act is thus the production of the means to satisfy these needs, the production of material life itself.[8]

The production of needs is a social action, their satisfaction making new needs possible. This production of life, both of one's own labour and of new life through procreation, decides how production is organised and how men and women are bound to one another within a system of production. History is, thus, the study of this everyday human activity:

> In each stage . . . there is . . . a sum of productive forces, a historically created relation of individuals to nature and to one another, which is handed down to each generation from its predecessor; a mass of productive forces, capital funds and conditions which on the one hand is indeed modified by the new generation, but also on the other prescribes for it its condition of life and gives it a definite development, a special character. It shows that circumstances make men just as much as men make circumstances.[9]

Here the emphasis is on objective social change, but he also believed that the action of human beings changed the course of history. In *Capital,* for instance, he said that force was the midwife of every new society pregnant with a new one. Men and women make history, but not always in conditions which are under their control. There is a continual tension within his thinking about history between material circumstances and the action of human beings. The emphasis varied depending on the problem he was considering and the purpose for which he was writing. Thus, in *The Communist Manifesto* in 1848 he stresses the action of the working class and in his 'Preface to a Contribution to the Critique of Political Economy' in 1859 he says that the dissolution of a social order can only occur when all the productive forces which can be contained within it have been developed.

He did not see human consciousness as removed from this material movement of society. Historical consciousness arises from the totality of the social relations of production. The dominant class creates the world in its image. It owns and controls language and culture as well as the means of material production. The struggle of the oppressed is thus material and ideological. Material existence, the particular mode of production and the relations between human beings are inseparable from specific visions of the world.

Marx's view of history opens up the possibility of including the mass of women within its scope and provides a means of understanding how women have only sporadically been able to challenge the dominance of men in all culture. Women's subordination is not only material but is expressed in a subordinated consciousness. But the specific oppression of women remains implicit. Marx was primarily concerned with the social consequences of class antagonism, not conflict between men and women. By the time he wrote *Capital* he concentrated on the exploitation and alienation of the worker who sells his or her capacity to labour to the owner of capital, who gives only part back in the form of wages. Though this covers the situation of the working-class woman as a wage earner, it does not explore the position of the woman working in the family, the sexual relations between men and women, women and women and men and men or our relationship to our bodies. In *Capital* Marx takes for granted the necessity of women's labour in maintaining and reproducing wage earners, but he does not examine this in any detail or discuss its implications for women's consciousness.[10]

Although there have been repeated attempts to relate class exploitation and alienation as Marx described them to other aspects of human life and experience and although it is apparent that we can have only a partial view even of class consciousness if we neglect childhood, these questions remain in considerable confusion and obscurity. Marxism has only sporadically illuminated those areas of women's activity which are outside the point of production and are only indirectly linked to class-conscious organising. Consequently, Marxists have shared the neglect of other historians of sexuality, maternity, production and reproduction in the household and the family.

While some social historians have very recently begun to examine these aspects of life, they have been for a considerable time integral to the subject matter of studies of precapitalist societies, perhaps because the separation of these human activities from politics and production is less pronounced than in capitalism and because the anthropologist does not look towards written records. Some of the questions an anthropologist would ask are obviously relevant to the study of the position of women in the past. For instance, what do beliefs and practices of witchcraft or the ritual pollution of menstruating, pregnant or nursing mothers or ideas about the mystical strength of women, the voracious ferocity of the vagina, reveal about men's view of women and the social relations between men and women in precapitalist societies?

Anthropology, however, is not neutral or ahistorical. It bears the marks of its Western colonial origins. It developed as a subject which assumed the superiority of Western capitalism. Even when this was challenged, it remained a means of understanding and thus controlling the colonised. Also, because the oppression of women is not just a product of capitalism, the societies studied are themselves male-dominated. It requires a specifically feminist commitment to uncover this, for much of the work has been done by men and seen through their eyes.[11]

It has been difficult to make a Marxist critique of this Western capitalist orientation because Marxism itself was so much a product of nineteenth-century capitalism and because in its subsequent development it tended to remain isolated from non-Marxist empirical work in anthropology. Marxism has been stunted in the areas in which anthropology has grown and developed. Marx's preoccupation in *Capital* is with capitalist society, a society in which labour power is sold to the owner of capital as a commodity. He is only peripherally interested in other forms of production within capitalism, such as housework, and in precapitalism. Subsequently, Marxists tended to concentrate on the wages system. This orientation was reinforced by a schematic interpretation of Marxism which took Marx's analysis of capitalism as providing generalisations which could be applied willy-nilly to every form of society, projecting laws of development specific to capitalism backwards. It also contributed to a dogmatic isolation in anthropology. Marxist anthropology for so long meant a fundamentalist faith in Engels' categories about the evolution of primitive society in *Origin of the Family*[12] that Marxists have only recently begun to engage critically with the main currents in anthropology and to question the assumptions that anthropologists should bring to a society. Instead of asking how does it function, how does it continue, or only looking at the ideas of the dominant people in a community, they have also begun to look at the conflicting views of people who are not responsible for maintaining the status quo. The impulse behind this challenge has been the disintegration effected by imperialism and the rebirth of non-dogmatic Marxism. The penetration of capital has made a static, functional approach unable to explain social changes, whereas Marxism provides a means of understanding transformation and its effects on people's consciousness. It has been Marx's writing in the *Grundrisse* on precapitalist economic formations, not Engels', which have influenced this anthropology.[13]

Anthropologists have devised ways of understanding consciousness which is not explicitly stated through political organising. This has a particular relevance to women, for our consciousness has dwelt hidden in a twilight world. The notion that people who do not have a coherent intellectual philosophy can still have a picture of the world has begun also to influence historians working on the sixteenth and seventeenth centuries. Their work opens up new ways of looking at women in the past. Lawrence Stone, for instance, in a review of recent studies of witchcraft including Keith Thomas' *Religion and the Decline of Magic* and Alan McFarlane's *Witchcraft in Tudor and*

Stuart England, suggests that magic and witchcraft can be seen as part of an underground view of the world held by the common people. He sees this search for *'mentalités collectives'* as an essential part of social history.[14]

Similarly, in *The World Turned Upside Down*, Christopher Hill describes the extreme democratic views of the sects during the English Civil War. He also discovered from writing this book that these ideas could be traced back into the Middle Ages, a continuing subversive vision of how things should be.[15]

By seeking the kind of clues and signs of consciousness which anthropologists have struggled to decode, it is possible to find out about women's resistance and about relations between the sexes. For instance, witchcraft and magic provide a means of understanding how people conceived their relationship to nature. They indicate how far they felt they could placate or control the external world. Similarly, various forms of community ritual and folk beliefs were a way of regulating social and sexual relations and of defusing conflicts.

The problem of uncovering this hidden experience can be approached in more recent periods simply by talking to older people. It is true that there is always the problem that time passing will affect how people remember, but this is also a disadvantage with written sources like evidence to Royal or other commissions of enquiry or biographies. Oral history could be an important means of discovering what women thought and felt in the immediate past. It could also restore aspects of experience which are seen as too trivial and everyday to be recorded elsewhere. Menstruation, pregnancy, and menopause, for instance, are rarely the subject of history as it is taught in schools and universities. This concealed dimension of living has an obvious bearing on women's history. The women's liberation movement has insisted that all aspects of female experience be recognised, considered and redefined. Once stated, many of these neglected areas appear as quite obviously important. They have always been important to the women who experienced them, but because the ideas in society of what is significant and what is trivial exist within a male-dominated context, it has been easy to ignore these kinds of female experiences. Oral history can cut right through this, especially when one woman is talking to another woman, because this could make it easier to talk about things that a man would not always notice.

It is not just the commitment to personal testimony but the theories about the economic and social position of women within the new feminism which affect what we recognise as important in the past. For instance, the women's movement has shown that housework is economically essential to capitalist society, though it is rarely seen as part of production. Because of the relation between man and woman, mother and child, the work women do in the home is seen as a purely personal rather than an economic activity. The extent to which the nature of the work has changed even in this century is often forgotten too. A woman who comes to a morning class I teach on social history for the Workers' Education Association in London interviewed her mother-in-law about her childhood in a respectable working-class family during the period around and immediately after World War I. Her mother-in-law's memories of washing are so vivid that they communicate much more than any general statement about the change in household technology.

> Washing and cleaning in the home really were heavy chores. To do the washing you first had to save everything that would burn to stoke up the stone copper or stone and cast-iron copper. My mother-in-law remembered that her mother was friendly with the owners of the corner shop who would give her wood in the shape of boxes. Once you had your fuel, you had to fill your copper by hand and when the water was hot you ladled it out into a tin bath where you would use a rubbing board and blocks of soap.
>
> Once all the washing had been rubbed it went back into the refilled copper together with bleaching soda and ordinary soda and would be left to boil for twenty minutes. It was a steaming job pushing down every so often with a copper stick. As the children went out to work and there was a little more money, her mother would use Hudson's Soap Powder instead of the two sorts of soda.
>
> When the wash had finished boiling it would be lifted out into a bath of clean water to be rinsed and 'whites' would be 'blued' with Reckitt's blue bag or starched and finally it would all be wrung out through a hand-operated mangle.
>
> After the wash had been dried it would be ironed on the kitchen table on an old piece of blanket with a sheet or piece of cotton over that. The irons would be hot irons heated by the fire and the only sure way to see if they were hot enough would be to spit on them.
>
> In 1923, her mother had to have an operation for breast cancer and a neighbour, whose husband was a dock worker and more often than not was not chosen to work, came in and did all the washing, not the ironing, for 2s.6d. The neighbour came at 8 A.M. and left at 1 P.M. and would only stop for a glass of beer and bread and cheese half-way through the morning.[16]

When you focus on the woman's role in production in the family, all this hidden labour comes to light. Alice Clark's study of seventeenth-century household production revealed women doing a wide variety of tasks because more things were produced in the home. In her introduction to *The House-hold Account Book of Sarah Fell*[17] she showed how an account book could be used to retrace the actual extent of this labour. Statements of its effect on consciousness are relatively rare. Lucy Larcom, who went to work in the Lowell mills at the age of eleven, described a period of domesticity in her life: 'I felt myself slipping into an inward apathy from which it was hard to rouse myself.'[18]

If the first step is to discover and reveal aspects of woman's life in the past which have been ignored, we need also a means of understanding how this has related to the lives and activity of men and to children. Woman's production in the home has a double character. It maintains the other members of the family and makes it possible for them to reproduce the means of life through labour. It also involves reproduction in the sense of procreation. The relationship between this form of labour and other forms of production and reproduction is not usually made without a feminist orientation and commitment. Although this double character of women's productive capacity is implicit within the Marxist view of the social relations of production, the sexual sphere is often subsumed within economics.

This affects consideration both of the question of women's social contribution through the reproduction of the species and of the relationship between procreation and the reproduction of the means of life through labour. It has left Marxist historians particularly vulnerable to the criticism of those non-Marxist historians who tend to abstract population from other factors in production. When population is detached it can be presented as the sole determinant of historical change and the complex interaction between human action and the social and natural world is reduced to a model of stimulus and response. Demography becomes a separate school of study. While an understanding of demography as a technique is vital in the development of any history which includes the family and woman's reproductive activity, this does not mean that history can be streamlined into a technical or statistical process.

In asserting the need to see reproduction in the family as part of material production and reproduction as a whole it is important not to reduce relationships within the family to a purely economic activity. For the woman's position within the family is not simply an affair of either economic or sexual production. To see it only in those terms would be to impose a materialist determinism which falsely excludes the personal and social relations within families.

But here again there is a theoretical absence within Marxism which raises several problems if this aspect of women's lives in the past is not to be ignored. Relationships within the family have been neglected by Marxist historians and seen by non-Marxists in isolation from the society outside. There are very few precedents which could help us to study family relationships interacting with other forms of social relationships in various historical periods. This is an obvious difficulty not only for women's history but for the history of childhood.

The existence of women's liberation can help to make this kind of connection, though this is still one-sided and we would need to know about men's relations to women as well as women's relations to men and the relationships between fathers and sons as well as between mothers and daughters. Women's groups have begun to integrate the personal experience of childhood and motherhood with the collective social experience of what it means to be a woman in a particular society. This could have important implications for how we look at history. After all, if our memories of our own mothers' lives and even their mothers' are part of how we became women, it is not such a step from this to regard our own and other women's memories as a source for women's history in the recent past.

There are many examples which could be given in illustration, but one account by an American black woman writer, Alice Walker, describes it very clearly.

In the late 1920s my mother ran away from home to marry my father. Marriage, if not running away, was expected of seventeen-year-old girls. By the time she was twenty, she had two children and was pregnant with a third. Five children later I was born. And this is how I came to know my mother, she seemed a large soft, loving-eyed woman who was rarely impatient in our home. Her quick violent temper was on view only a few times a year, when she battled with the white landlord who had the misfortune to suggest to her that her children did not need to go to to school.

She made all the clothes we wore, even my brothers' overalls. She made all the towels and sheets we used. She spent the summers canning vegetables and fruits. She spent the winter evenings making quilts enough to cover our beds.

During the 'working' day, she laboured beside — not behind — my father in the fields before sun up, and did not end until late at night. There was never a moment for her to sit down, undisturbed, to unravel her own private thought, never a time free from interruption by work or the noisy inquiries of her many children. . . .

Yet so many of the stories that I write are my mother's stories. Only recently did I fully realize this; that through years of listening to my mother's stories of her life, I have absorbed not only the stories themselves but something of the manner in which she spoke, something of the knowledge that her stories — like her life — must be recorded.

Alice Walker says that her mother's own artistry was expressed even within the tight confines of her life, through gardening:

> Before she left home for the fields she watered her flowers, chopped up the grass and laid out new beds. When she returned from the fields she might divide clumps of bulbs, dig a cold pit, uproot and replant roses, or prune branches from her taller bushes or trees — until night came and it was too dark to see.[19]

The women's movement also has begun to question the tendency in our society to divorce sexual emotion from culture, to see sex as somehow outside history. Sexual love continues to be seen as an unchanging, natural factor in human existence, not a social creation. This is deceptive, for in reality sexuality and the feelings generated by the particular sexual relationship come out of the totality of human social relations. The women's movement has concentrated on the distortion which the social dominance of men over women has had upon sexual relationships and upon our affections. This emphasis can lead us to consider how we would begin to think about the kinds of feelings of people in societies where the working relationship was often synonymous with the sexual relationship. It was only with the development of capitalist society, in which the capacity to labour is exchanged on the market like any other commodity, that personal emotion for the mass of the people can appear as separate from work and production and as inhabiting an ideal sphere outside society. What appears to us as normal and obvious would be quite strange to a medieval peasant. Marx and Engels noted the historical appearance of the idea of romantic love. But we have to dig deeper than conscious systems of ideas. Our very sexual responses and ways of relating are not removed from society or history; they are learned as part of our sexual culture and are thus open to change.

> It is not just the ideology of the age which is produced within the mode of production; the type of feeling is specific and bounded too. It is not just bourgeois ideology about love and sex, or bourgeois morality and conventions that sustain bourgeois sexual practice; it is the very structure of our most intimate and powerful perceptions, emotions and ways of acting.
>
> Imagine how differently sex must be felt to connect with emotional and other attachments to people in a kinship society where sex is a matter for public initia-

tion, deflowering an occasion for solemn communal rejoicing, a *social* act on behalf of the collective hope for fertility, not a private act of emotional commitment or sensual pleasure between two individuals.[20]

The women's movement has made the need to uncover every aspect of women's experience an immediate political issue and in doing so has started to redefine what is personal and what is political, questioning the present scope of what is defined as politics. This new feminism has made enquiries which have not been made so persistently before, enquiries which can initiate new historical questions. Women are hidden from most history in the same way as the lives of men of the poor are obscured, because of class. But we are also hidden as a sex, and it takes a specifically feminist consciousness to come to terms with the full extent of this.

History which includes women will mean that we study the role of women in movements which are usually described from the point of view of men, for example, the part women have played in revolutions, in political organisations, in trade unions, as well as women's own movements for suffrage or for peace. Similarly, we need to know how periods of change and upheaval have affected women, war, revolution, the growth of capitalism, imperialism. But more than this, we have to go outside the scope of what history usually is. We need to look at folk beliefs, at magic, at the means by which people sought control over sexuality, fertility and birth. The personal testimony of any woman who can remember – not just women who have witnessed major political events – is a source for this history. It is also a source which can enlarge our concept of what we're looking for. Our definition of women's work will include not only production paid in wages, but the unpaid labour of women in the home which makes work outside possible. We have to understand the relationship in different historical periods between procreation, the production of new life which will make existence possible in the future, housework, the labour in the home which enables workers to go out and continue to labour in the wages system in capitalism, child rearing, making the survival of the future makers of new life possible, and women's work outside the home for wages, which in modern capitalism is becoming more and more general. We can only understand women's part in production when we can trace changes and grasp the interactions between these various aspects of women's labour.

Women's history, though, is not just about production in a material sense, for human beings create and re-create themselves in the effort to control, to bring the material world within the grasp of consciousness. Here too we inherit what we seek to go beyond and what defines our limits. We are the daughters of the tales our mother told us and drop easily back into the same way of seeing and telling even if the tales are changed by our transformed circumstances. We learn how to relate through our families and with children who themselves come from families. These relationships affect us not as external ideas but from the innermost self – feelings in our bones. They are nonetheless part of the movement of society. Our views about love between men and women, women and women, men and men, parents and children are historically shaped as much as our views about government, poverty, the organisation of production. Moreover, not just our conscious ideas of love but our unconscious experience of loving relationships, the manner in which we express sensual feelings, are also socially learned and as such are the proper if buried subject matter of history.

Much of this is such an uncharted province that to ignore any maps and compasses which exist, however imperfect, would be feckless. My own suggestions of how to begin are necessarily bounded by my own ignorance, the contours of my own history: the writing of earlier feminists, Marx's theories about history and class consciousness, anthropological studies of production and reproduction in precapitalist societies, new work in social history which seeks to uncover the everyday perceptions of the poor, demographic history, oral history. It is one thing to announce that all these could be useful. However, it is quite another thing to *use* them, and beyond my present knowledge. The writing of our history is not just an individual venture but a continuing social communication. Our history strengthens us in the present by connecting us to the lives of countless women. Threads and strands of long-lost experience weave into the present. In rediscovering the dimensions of female social existence lost in the tangled half memories of myth and dream, we are uncovering and articulating a cultural sense of what it is to be a woman in a world defined by men. We are tracing the boundaries of oppression and the perpetual assertion of self against their confines, the erosion and encirclement, the shifts and tremors of new forms of resistance. We are heaving ourselves into history, clumsy with the newness of creation, stubborn and persistent in pursuit of our lost selves, fortunate to be living in such transforming times.

3. Women and Radical Politics in Britain, 1820–1914

'Women and Radical Politics in Britain, 1820–1914', *Radical History Review*, winter 1978–9, no. 19. The impetus of the women's liberation movement has contributed to a realisation that the scope of history and the questions considered worthy of consideration have been too narrowly defined in terms of the world of men. It has also challenged many cut-and-dried tracks, for example, in the history of the labour movement, trade unions, the suffrage movement, socialist organising.

It is not simply a matter of writing women in or only writing about women. The focus on women should be a means of opening up new perspectives. Among these is the recognition that the history of men and women, even in radical movements which have accumulated an impressive scholarship, requires continuing reinterpretation.

Barbara Taylor, 'The Woman – Power, Religious Heresy and Feminism in Early English Socialism', in Susan Lipshitz, ed., *Tearing the Veil: Essays in Femininity*, Routledge and Kegan Paul, 1978
Dorothy Thompson, 'Women and Nineteenth-Century Radical Politics: A Lost Dimension', in Ann Oakley and Juliet Mitchell, eds., *The Rights and Wrongs of Women*, Penguin, 1976
Jill Norris and Jill Liddington, *One Hand Tied Behind Us: The Rise of the Women's Suffrage Movement*, Virago, 1978

If women's history has raised a vast range of new areas of study, it has also made it necessary to reexamine thoroughly well-trodden ground, including the history of past radicalism by their exploration of the interconnections between male movements, social ideology, personal and family life, and the position of women at the time.

Barbara Taylor in 'The Woman – Power' looks at the relationship between the followers of a female messiah, Joanna Southcott, and radical and Owenite cooperators in the early 1830s. Joanna Southcott prophesied a new dawn of love which would release women as Christ had saved men,

> Then see ye plain, ye sons of
> men,

the way I've led all on.
It was to Woman, not to Man,
I in this power did come.[1]

The enormous upheavals of the industrial revolution created a radical movement for a new moral world. The milieu of religious and political unorthodoxy was fluid and there was a widely shared conviction that the old world was about to fall apart. The Owenites placed great stress on changing values and were consequently able to imagine how personal relationships between people could be transformed. Their politics implied an attempt to live something of the future in the here and now. Barbara Taylor's work shows them discussing cooperative housekeeping in communities, men's privileges in marriage, the role of women in religion and in radical politics, and the creation of alternative rituals surrounding birth, marriage and death. An Owenite tailoress argues that, 'God made Eve out of Adam's rib to show not that she was inferior, but that she was essential to his existence, was his equal'.[2] Emma Martin, an Owenite speaker, stressed a communitarian vision of socialism which included cooperative housework, well-fed children, faithful husbands and a life of personal dignity and intellectual enlightenment.[3] By the late 1830s, Owenites were challenging the right of Church and State to sanction marriage. A woman from a cooperative wrote:

> Of what utility is the mummery of priest or lawyer? Why should sexual connections be more fettered than hunger or thirst? . . . If we cannot love as we like, why attempt to bind parties together who do not love? . . . A time is fast approaching when this important subject may be fairly met . . . [W]oman, abused, ill-treated woman must ere long be placed upon an equality with man, and love of the most disinterested nature be experienced by both sexes.[4]

The Owenite socialist feminists do not seem to have resolved the contradictory problem of 'faithful husbands' and unfettered love between men and women. It was a debate which was to appear again within radical movements.

They began to search for ways of imagining not only how men and women could live differently together, but new ways of being men and women. In 1841 the Owenite paper *The New Moral World* published an article by Goodwyn Barmby, called 'the Man-Power, the Woman-Power, and the Woman-Man-Power'. This was a secularised version of the Southcottian prophecy of the rule of love. But Barmby believed the feminine principle, love, was the basis of libertarian social organisation and necessitated communism. He thought Southcott's mistake had been to equate the ascendancy of the feminine principle with the actual rule of women. '. . . [S]he saw the might of gentleness in woman, but knew not that her natures were really common with those of man, although the better natures of man were actually dormant.'[5] Barbara Taylor points out the problems in arguing for a female mission.

> Love, which the communists wished to see 'socialise our planet' was rhetorically roped back into the bedroom and the kitchen, and for both working-class and middle-class women 'female influence' became a synonym for the reality of social powerlessness.[6]

This appropriation and primping of love was bound up with the establishment of the bourgeoisie as the ascendant class, the changing context of the romantic movement, as well as with a new version of womanhood. It left a socialist movement which acquired a closer but narrower focus. Perhaps the experience of living in capitalism wore down some of the very sources of imagination which awakened resistance. Socialism developed a more sophisticated analysis with greater historical depth, as exemplified by Marx's work, but love and the inner life were pushed to the sidelines. At best they frame the picture. This was to become more and more marked in our own century. As Barbara Taylor notes,

> The fading of the Owenite heretical imagination which had envisaged workers' power and women's liberation as morally and politically inseparable had important consequences for the struggle of working-class women; for them it meant not only the loss of their tentative strategical base of the 1830s and 1840s, but also the decline of a radical culture and language rich in the symbols of emancipation.[7]

In 'Women and Nineteenth-Century Radical Politics: A Lost Dimension', Dorothy Thompson looks at the participation of working-class women in the radical movement, concentrating on Chartism, from the early 1830s to the early 1850s. Within Chartism the spectrum of thought ranged from an Owenite vision of a new moral world breaking off clearly from the old, to a passionate defensive radicalism firmly within the values of the 'older domestic-industry communities'.[8] Part of the strength of the Chartist movement came from people having *lived* an alternative to the factories and new industrial towns. A memory, even a crushed and distorted memory, has a force to convince which is stronger than a theorised utopia. The combination of memory and utopia is even more powerful.

Dorothy Thompson examines the forms of action which involved or excluded women. This was a transitional period in which traditional forms of political activity – such as mass demonstrations and other acts which involved entire families and communities – coexisted with 'early versions of the more sophisticated organizational forms which were to be the pattern of later nineteenth-century politics'.[9] Women, as Dorothy Thompson shows, had previously been involved in food riots and demonstrations, early female friendly societies and trade unions. In the 1830s and early 1840s women continued to be actively involved. They organised food boycotts and occupied churches. They were particularly active in the demonstrations against the new Poor Law of 1834 and in the 1842 Plug Riots. Women were also active in the internal organisation of the Chartist movement, attending meetings, decorating halls and speakers' wagons, and they were important in the social side of the movement, creating, for example, alternative schools for children.

Although the demand for the vote for women did arise, it was not accepted as a national demand. Chartist men might support the rights of single women, but they tended to assume that on marriage, women's interests merged with those of the family. Yet while the women themselves commonly deferred on this point, female Chartists had a strong sense of their more general rights as women, and claimed their standing both as a sex and as members of the working class. Their sense of dignity was bound up with the assertion of a better family life which the industrial revolution had torn from them. We need to know much more about the circumstances of family life among different groups of workers before the nineteenth century in order to understand what this really meant, but what is significant is that the Chartists, although less self-consciously than the Owenites, did begin to recreate an alternative even while defending what was lost. Radical families passed on 'traditions, beliefs and radical folklore'.[10] By the 1830s, radical women had their own stories of demonstrations and of the struggle to sell the uncensored radical papers. The experience of having been brought up as Chartists must have had an important effect on children. Radicals made their own rituals which adjusted to new political situations. As a contemporary observer notes in *The Morning Chronicle* in 1849, '. . . a generation or so back, Henry Hunts were as common as blacksmiths, a crop of Fergus O'Connors replaced them, and latterly there has been a few green sprouts labelled Ernest Jones'.[11] It would be interesting to know after whom the girls were named.

In the early days of Chartism, a great variety of forms of political involvement were related to women's everyday life. Ceremony was made with what came to hand. Dorothy Thompson quotes a Chartist, William Aiken, who came from the radical community of Ashton-under-Lyme. He remembered the importance of gatherings in the late 1830s at 'owd Nancy Clayton's' to 'drink in solemn silence' in memory of the attack on the radical demonstration at 'Peterloo'.[12] The black petticoat Nancy Clayton had worn there was made into a flag with a green cap of liberty and hung out on the anniversary of 'Peterloo'. Every year on August 16th, radicals met to drink home-brewed ale and eat potato pie under these emblems of liberty and class memory.

In the later period of the Chartist movement, however, women were only occasionally involved. Ernest Jones wrote in his *Notes to the People, 1851–1852*, that women were ignored in social institutions but made to bear the greatest share of suffering.[13] He received a letter from the corresponding secretary of the Women's Rights Association in Sheffield, Abadiah Higgenbotham, in which she agreed with him, but brought the criticism closer to home, commenting on the radical movement itself:

> Did our brothers but admit our rights to the enjoyment of those political privileges they are striving for, they would find an accession of advocates in the female sex . . . not only by exercising their influence out of doors, but by teaching their children a good sound political education. This, sir, will never be done while men continue to advocate or meet in pot-houses, spending their money, and debarring us from a share in their political freedom.[14]

This reference to 'pot houses' reflects a change in attitude towards women drinking with men between the 1830s and the early 1850s. Women and men no longer shared many of the previous activities which had served to cement their common political opposition. This split, Dorothy Thompson suggests, was part of a wide change. Chartism gave birth to the modern, formal organisation of the working class which enabled skilled male workers to defend their conditions in trade unions, cooperatives and pressure groups.

> In a variety of ways they were able to find means of protecting their position within an increasingly stable system. They left behind the mass politics of the earlier part of the century, which represented more of a direct challenge to the whole system of industrial capitalism at a stage when it was far less secure and

established. In doing so, the skilled workers also left behind the unskilled workers and the women, whose way of life did not allow their participation in the more structured political forms. These forms required both regularity of working times and regularity of income for participation to be possible.[15]

The growth of these new organisational structures was concurrent with a change in the position of women and in attitudes to women's roles among this skilled section of the working class. In one sense this reflected a real improvement in women's conditions over the days of factory work, but it also involved an image of women as passive and home-centred. 'Women and Nineteenth-Century Radical Politics' presents a complex process of gain and loss in the development of the working-class movement.

Many questions still need to be asked about how radical men and women narrowed down their demands after 1850, about the later participation of women in the socialist movement and the upsurge of 'new unionism' in the late 1880s and early 1890s. Problems arise not only from a lack of knowledge, but from the political orientation of the questions asked. Some of the blind-spots of labour history are bound up with the theoretical neglect of the inter-connections of sex and class conflict within the socialist movement. This perhaps explains the curious acquiescence in a picture of suffrage history which focuses on the role of the London leaders, emphasises a simple polarising moment in Sylvia Pankhurst's expulsion from the Women's Social and Political Union, and reduces the working-class women involved to passivity. The valiant exception was Marian Ramelson's *The Petticoat Rebellion*, which was published by Lawrence and Wishart in Britain in 1967.

Now, in *One Hand Tied Behind Us*, Jill Norris and Jill Liddington provide an alternative perspective by describing the movement for the vote among Lancashire working-class women. Their book dissolves the arbitrary organi-sational categories of 'suffrage', 'labour', 'social', and 'political' history, so that the complicated relationships between socialism and feminism and between working-class and middle-class feminists begin to emerge.

The explicit disagreement between the WSPU and the Labour Party was over the demand for votes for women in the same terms as for men, which meant a property qualification and excluded many working-class voters. The WSPU argued that the limited measure was tactically more likely to succeed and could be extended. Supporters of universal adult suffrage pointed to the class privilege, but were not very active in asserting the rights of women. Behind this dispute was a wider disagreement about class differences and the dismissal by many socialists of women's oppression as a sex. The lines were never clearly drawn. Keir Hardie argued passionately within the Independent Labour Party for 'Votes for Women'. Some working-class women like Hannah Mitchell joined the WSPU, exasperated by the socialists' lack of real commitment to women's suffrage. However, the radical suffragists disliked the manipulative politics and lack of internal democracy in the WSPU, and later they were opposed to its militant tactics. They demanded 'universal womanhood suffrage' without a property qualification. This would not have been granted without including voteless working-class men, but it put more emphasis on women's franchise than adult suffrage. *One Hand Tied Behind Us* shows that it was a difficult choice and that individuals moved between different positions. It also shows that the relationship between suffrage organisations and the socialist movement involved not only national issues but local and personal loyalties.

Jill Liddington and Jill Norris also explore other influences on working-class women's consciousness. They look at the work process in detail, examining particular experiences, for example, in dressmaking and tailoring and the cotton industry. They show the radical suffragists serving their political apprenticeships in trade union meetings, socialist groups and administering poor relief. Ada Nield Chew, a tailoress, was active in the ILP and the Clarion movement, which emphasised socialist propaganda and culture, before becoming a radical suffragist. Her daughter Doris Chew had heard her parents talk about how her mother had gone off speaking in the Clarion van while her future husband George Chew had gone along to look after the horses. She added, 'I think he must have been very much in love because nothing else would have persuaded him to look after a horse.'[16]

Jill Liddington and Jill Norris were able to talk to daughters of radical women and to bring their story to life with detailed observations. Hannah Mitchell's account in *The Hard Way Up* had also alerted them to the importance of work and relationships in the family for an understanding of working-class women's involvement in politics. Hannah Mitchell wrote, 'No cause can be won between dinner and tea, and most of us who were married had to work with one hand tied behind us.'[17]

Hands were bound by both lack of time and the opposition of men in the family. 'My wife,' exploded one member of a cooperative who was married to a suffragist, 'what does she want with meetings? Let her stay at home and wash my moleskin trousers.'[18]

It was not only unsympathetic attitudes which made it hard. Selina Cooper, a winder in the cotton industry, was often away from home campaigning for the vote. Her daughter Mary Cooper remembered 'My mother'd fetch me a frock back or something like that when she'd been away. You know, she used to go looking in her bags to see what she could fetch me back. But I pined for her.'[19] Ada Nield Chew solved the problem by taking Doris with her.

Both Selina Cooper and Ada Nield Chew had socialist husbands who supported their ideas. Robert Cooper was in the Men's League for Women's Suffrage. And both had only one child. For women with hostile husbands and large families it was hard to sustain political activity. At trade union meetings women became restless if speakers went on too long; meetings had to be at convenient times; and local participation was easier than national activity. The jail sentences which were the consequence of the WSPU's policy of militancy effectively excluded most working-class women. *One Hand Tied Behind Us* shows the importance of *forms* of political action which could involve women as part of their everyday lives. The Women's Cooperative Guild, for example, was a mass organisation of working-class women which organised picnics for the children, provided a play space in the local Coop Hall when it was wet and gave practical help and information to its members.

So although it was never a simple opposition between working-class and middle-class women, working-class suffragists could not detach the demand for the vote from the cause of labour any more than they could be active in the socialist movement without confronting the attitudes of men in their own families to women. Thus, their politics could not create the dramatic moments of militancy of the Pankhursts, but were instead rooted in relationships with a living community. As Selina Cooper put it when asked by a middle-class suffragist to abandon labour for a purely suffrage programme, 'I may have a good voice, but my power would finish if I came over.'[20]

It is, of course, remarkable that the debates among the Owenites about the family, marriage, the relationship of men and women, have been relatively ignored by historians and that the voluminous scholarship on the Chartist movement has only contained odd references to women's participation. Even within the history of the suffrage campaign, the activity of working-class and lower-middle-class women on a local level has been obscured by the preoccupation with London leaders. The issues of sexual politics and the experience of family life, of the circumstances which made it possible or impossible for working women to participate in social and political movements, the relation of sex and class consciousness, all need to be pursued further.

All three studies have important implications for the interpretation of our radical past. Barbara Taylor's work challenges the assumption of a continuous progress in socialist thought. At particular moments within the development of capitalism the possibility of transforming different forms of relationships appears more clearly than at others. Some of the utopian socialists were able to make connections which were impossible for the later Chartists movement or indeed for Marx and Engels. They could envisage changing both the existing form of the sexual division of labour and the pattern of feeling associated with masculinity and femininity. Dorothy Thompson also questions the notion of a smoothly maturing working-class movement. It was rather that particular sections of the working class found new kinds of effective resistance while older forms, expressing a militant community which included women and the unskilled, were shed. Both 'Women and Nineteenth-Century Radical Politics' and *One Hand Tied Behind Us* indicate the need for a wide-ranging cultural and social dimension to radical politics which overcomes the separation between work and the family, street life and trade union politics, the women's sphere of the house and shop and the men's world of political meetings and the pub. They also show that it is not only a question of extending the forms of entry into the left but of understanding how the sources of politics come not only from work and public meetings, but from personal life and relationships in the family.

In these three studies we begin to see how radicals, socialists and feminists did housework, named and cared for their children, and passed on their ideas. Their vision of marriage, the family and their own masculinity and femininity comes clearly into view. These are important lost dimensions in understanding our past which come from a focus on the participation of women in radical politics. This interior life of working-class organisations was not, of course, experienced by only one sex, but it rarely appears in the history of socialism. An open approach to 'women's history' enables us to illuminate relations between men and women. It can contribute towards a wider comprehension of the socialist past which touches all forms of human relationships.

4. When Adam Delved, and Eve Span . . .

'When Adam Delved, and Eve Span . . .', *New Society*, 4 January 1979. Why are women oppressed? Why does oppression of any kind exist in the world? They have to be asked, these questions, but they do not have final solutions. In order to hazard approximate answers we can most usefully proceed by breaking the questions into historically specific shapes. Why is this group or that group subordinate at a particular time in a certain place?

The biological difference between the sexes makes the conundrum appear timeless and natural. But the variety in the forms of subordination suggests that biological differences have assumed many social meanings.

The relationships between people in other times and places are always hard to encounter. For very early times we can only speculate. But we can at least be clear about the assumptions we take to the past, just as Marxist feminist anthropologists have warned of the danger of Western feminism presuming to colonise women in other cultures.

* * * * * *

. . . who was then oppressor and oppressed?

There is not one debate about the origin of social differences and inequality between the sexes, there are several.

The arguments are inseparable from our picture of early times. Do we assume a barbarism of tooth and claw, or an egalitarian Golden Age? There are some strange line-ups. Some feminists and anti-feminists believe men have always dominated. Other feminists maintain an early supremacy of women. The egalitarians, who include Engels, go for the idea of complementary power between the sexes.

The perilous and uncertain quest into How It All Began would hardly be worthwhile if theories about the origin of oppression did not bear closely on ideas about the causes of inequality. Our analysis of causes affects strategies for change. Ideas about how things came about are constantly intervening in discussions of the manner in which society could be made less sexually oppressive.

My own interest in these argy-bargies about origins has spluttered out of such immediate debates. It has become one of those urges to sort and unravel which belongs to impossible attics in the spring. The point of dusting down and disentangling these old controversies is not an illusory expectation that we will find the origin of everything or anything, nestling there. It is to make clear what can and cannot be found, and what we might or might not imagine.

The purpose of this is not to achieve a floating scepticism, but to distinguish the surfaces of reality from shadows. We can begin to touch the complexity of the forms in which relations between the sexes have appeared. Seen in this way, the intricacies of argument about the causes of sexual inequality assume a new fascination.

It used to be customary to go back to Adam and Eve. When all discussion of separation, alienation, authority and scarcity could be expressed in terms of the myth of the Fall, it was important to produce your own interpretation of what happened in the beginning. The authors of a pamphlet published in 1640, called 'The Woman's Sharpe Revenge', maintained that God had intended woman to be man's equal because he had made her from Adam's side not his foot. Mary Tattle-well and Joan-hit-home believed that this proved God had meant Eve to be Adam's 'fellow-feeler, equal and companion'. Stirrings of this argument appear again two centuries later among the radical Owenites, in the 1830s.

Even today, concern with Adam and Eve has not been completely laid to rest. At least one recent feminist writer, Merlin Stone, in *Paradise Papers* (published by Virago in 1976), felt it important to reinterpret the myth of the Fall. But from the mid-nineteenth century, the main debate shifted away from the bible towards historical attempts to reconstruct the forms of the family and the position of women. Myths from antiquity, early archeological discoveries, examples from contemporary ethnography, and arguments from the study of animal behaviour – all were used by theorists preoccupied with establishing a universal pattern of human evolution. In 1861, the German historian, J.J. Bachofen, interpreting myths literally, developed the idea that there had once been a matriarchy which evolved after a military defeat of the men. But the rule of women was tied to the physical world of fertility, Bachofen believed. It was followed, he thought, by the ascendancy of the 'divine father' – which was necessary for the development of spiritual faculties.

Within the evolutionary framework, the past was seen as moving towards the present as a goal. Dissidents produced their own rival versions. Feminists, searching for proof that women should be spiritually respected and intellectually elevated, stressed both the responsibility of mothers for the moral and cultural future of the whole society and the idea of a militant patriotic sisterhood. The one emphasis asserted and idealised woman's biological differences; the other approach minimised and dismissed them.

Engels developed a material explanation for male ascendancy in *The Origin of the Family, Private Property and the State* (1884). The anarchist, Kropotkin, in *Mutual Aid* (1902), argued against 'natural' competition, and gave examples of animals surviving through cooperation. Echoes of these controversies continued long after academic prehistory and anthropology had discarded both the method and the preoccupations of the evolutionists.

Simone de Beauvoir, in one of the formative books of the modern women's movement, *The Second Sex* (1949), broke decisively with the notion of a matriarchy, set in the distant past. She regarded the Golden Age of Woman as itself a cultural creation of male power. The Goddess Mother was a conception 'of the male world'.

This was the starting point for an emerging feminist anthropology, which has based itself mainly on studies of women in known contemporary societies, rather than on the search of origins. Like de Beauvoir, these anthropologists wonder why 'the world has always belonged to the men'. Margaret Mead's view was that while societies may divide activities between the sexes in quite different ways, men's occupations are always highly valued whereas women's are seen as less significant. This has contributed to the assumption that men have always been dominant.

But these anthropological approaches contain a certain political awkwardness. Feminists who rejected women's biological inferiority were elaborately documenting an apparently universal social secondariness to men. They were sewing up the possibility of an alternative, not only for every known society, but right from the beginning of time.

At one level it made sense to say that the complexity of the division of labour in other societies enabled us to see that our own arrangements were historical, rather than natural. Even if male dominance had always existed, and even if it was still universal, this did not make it either desirable nor inevitable. But it was perhaps naïve to presume to bury dead ages so briskly, especially when proposing to uproot demarcations of gender. There was a gap between anthropological theory and the enormous effort of legitimating the feminist onslaught on the fortress of 'It has always been so.'

Paula Webster describes the effect of this on American women anthropologists in the early 1970s in *Towards an Anthropology of Women*, a collection edited by Rayna R. Reiter in 1975:

'Women in the movement were asking us why women had never been politically powerful, why men had always had higher status, and why a matriarchy was impossible. They insinuated that we had been brainwashed by the male academic establishment, and the more we thought about it, the more we began to wonder if they were not right.'

This yearning towards a past potential remains. A frozen idealised alternative is projected into vaguely defined distant times. Women's lack of possibilities in the here and now are inverted, and opposed to an abstract state of power which was mysteriously lost.

Of course, the problems of *proving* whether an original matriarchy existed, or whether men have always been dominant, are enormous. To start with there is considerable vagueness about when it occurred (if it occurred); and the very term 'matriarchy' is unclear. Does it mean the rule of women, as Elizabeth Gould Davis argues in *The First Sex* (1971), or that women held an 'esteemed place', as Evelyn Reed maintains in *Woman's Evolution* (1975)? Matrilinear kinship arrangements, matrilocal patterns of family settlement, and worship of a female goddess, are still sometimes confused with 'matriarchy'.

Archeological 'facts' have to be put in their historical and social context. Red ochre in graves, temples with carved female breasts, anthropomorphic figurines, for example, cannot be collected like butterflies, and then pressed together willy-nilly to prove matriarchy. Boadicea rode a chariot. Princess Anne is often to be seen on a horse. But there have been a few changes since Roman Britain. The presence of the same symbol even does not necessarily indicate that the values attached to it are unchanging. The symbol of the Virgin Mary has had different historical interpretations.

The assumption that men have always been dominant is, in fact, as problematic as a universal stage of female supremacy. It has a more realistic air to it, because it fits in with our observation of known societies. But the need to distinguish between guess and actuality remains. Simone de Beauvoir's assertion that 'women's lot was a very hard one in the primitive horde' is as much a hunch as Evelyn Reed's claim that women were the first potters.

A response to these problems among some feminists, has been to dismiss the whole attempt to be historical. Women's experience is denied by male culture. Our perception of historical reality is too immersed within male definitions of knowledge. Women need only assert an imaginary fictional past. The purity of a matriarchal myth is marred by evidence.

But you do not need to deny the possibility of enquiry to concede that the borderline between myth and history can be hazy. The most cautious prehistorians can slip out of scepticism when they come to the origin of the sexual division of labour. For example, Grahame Clark and Stuart Piggott rush over the relations of the sexes and the problem of biology and culture in their chapter on 'Man's place in nature' in their *Prehistoric Societies* (1965): 'Since hunting puts a premium on masculine qualities, this activity became the special province of males, and a sexual division of labour was instituted under which women continued to gather plants, insects and comparable foods while men developed the skills required for tracking down and killing game.'

They surmise that the earliest man was monogamous, because his absence as a hunter would make it impossible to keep a harem or obtain enough meat for a polygamous family.

Sally Slocum writes, in Rayna Reiter's book, on 'Woman the gatherer: male bias in anthropology.' She points out that 'this reconstruction . . . gives the decided impression that only half the species – the male half – did any evolving'. It also underestimates the importance of gathering. Even in the marginal environments of modern hunter-gatherers, women's contribution to the food supply is crucial. Exclusively male, long-term hunts supplement the diet. But the major part comes from gathering and the hunting of small animals. Sally Slocum argues that if we think in terms of cultural inventions, rather than tools and weapons, containers for food gathered and some kind of sling or net to carry babies, must have been extremely important: 'Too much attention has been given to the skills required by hunting, and too little to the skills required for gathering and the raising of dependent young.' She also notes that 'monogamy is a fairly rare pattern, even among modern humans'. The assumption that it was the custom among proto-humans is an enormous leap into the unknown.

Feminist anthropologists have used understandings from the investigation of contemporary societies to question other theories of the origins of the sexual division of labour. One corollary of the 'Man the Hunter' approach assumes conflict, rather than the harmonious distribution of tasks. This is the proposition that women were raped and battered into submission at some questionable evolutionary stage, and then forever held their peace. Anthropological enquiries reveal complex and ingenious systems of resistance and negotiation, and suggest that this, too, is an over-simplified view of relations between the sexes.

A more sophisticated stimulus has been provided by the theories of Engels and Lévi-Strauss. Engels argued that men and women's relationship was one of mutual dependence until men came to dominate with the domestication of animals and the expansion of trade. They overthrew mother-right in order to pass on wealth to their own children. Lévi-Strauss – who influenced de Beauvoir – accepts the exchange of women by men as a fact which is located not within a particular historical social relation but within the conceptualising capacity of the human psyche.

Feminists revisiting Engels's evolutionary ideas and clambering amid Lévi-Strauss's structures, have collected valuable insights into the interrelationship between biological reproduction and production, kinship and 'marrying out' as a means for forming social bonds. They have also emerged with criticisms. For example, Engels's assumption that men were always the collectors or producers of subsistence is questioned by evidence from modern hunter-gathering and horticultural societies. Recent research has shown that cultivation and pastoralism developed around the same time, as different adaptions.

Engels assumes a period of non-oppressive division of labour before the existence of private property. Though he recognises the importance of biological reproduction, he equates it with economic production. He emphasises ownership, and the reproduction of the capacity to labour, rather than social relationships around sex, child-bearing and child-rearing.

Lévi-Strauss's concept of the exchange of women as a pre-cultural phenomenon has given rise to exploration of what we mean by nature and culture. Feminists have begun to dismantle his idea as a universal structure, and reconstitute it as a social phenomenon which can be understood only with reference to specific material circumstances.

These criticisms reveal forms of male bias which are not consciously anti-feminist, but nonetheless touch points where scholarly vigilance settles comfortably into male-oriented assumptions of what can be taken for granted. The ensuing ambushes seem to me to indicate the real political consequences of the debate about the position of women in non-capitalist society better than abstract speculations on a matriarchal takeover or a continuing patriarchy.

In a recent article, Felicity Edholm, Olivia Harris and Kate Young question the whole attempt to theorise about women's position in terms of a 'universal explanation of what is perceived – rightly or wrongly – to be a universal subordination of women'. Instead of a biological definition of the category 'women' they distinguish between the diverse *activities* of women, child-bearing, rearing, household labour, and participation in production for the community. Biology is not an eternal definition, but a material condition which finds a differing meaning within a variety of historical relationships.

Feminist critiques have developed within the context of anthropology, rather than engaging directly with the recent findings of prehistory. But they have been paralleled by a major upheaval in the whole framework of prehistory. Since the 1920s, British prehistorians have been largely dominated by theories of the cultural diffusion and emigration of people. The ancient civilisations of Egypt, Mesopotamia and Greece were seen as the influences on prehistoric Europe. But new techniques in both radiocarbon and tree-ring dating have dissolved the assumption of the gradual dissemination of culture and technology from the Near East. They show that the megalithic chamber tombs of Western Europe, the temples of Malta, and Stonehenge, all developed much earlier than was previously thought. It now appears that people who did not live in cities or keep written records could erect complex stone monuments, smelt copper and set up astronomical observatories. This has forced archeologists to question their definitions of civilisation and barbarism, and search for new explanations of how societies change.

Colin Renfrew, in *Before Civilisation* (1973), summarises this new approach as a 'shift . . . from talk of artifacts to talk of societies and from objects to relationships among different classes of data'. Questions about environment, subsistence, technology, social organisations, housing patterns and population density, are being asked by archeologists with soil samples, splinters of bones and shells and estimates of population capacity for slash-and-burn agriculture.

These raise, with a new complexity, all the problems of how we avoid foisting twentieth-century values on societies vastly different from our own. Marshall Sahlins, for example, in *Stone Age Economics* (1972), argues that gloomy assumptions made about the hard life of subsistence hunting societies express our own preconceptions of the good life. We cannot directly compare the marginalised existence of groups like the Australian aborigines with the richer environments of Stone Age people.

The emphasis on the internal development of prehistoric societies, rather than on the spread of culture and technology, has reopened the debate about the relationship of anthropology and prehistory. Peter Ucko has argued for anthropology as a means of widening 'the horizons of the interpreter' because prehistorians will inevitably bring unconscious assumptions from their own lives and times to the past.

His own study, *Anthropomorphic Figurines* (1968), illustrates this. In contemporary societies there are examples of figurines being used in sympathetic magic ceremonies against miscarriage, to cure sickness, harm an enemy, for teaching about sexuality at puberty and initiation rites, or as dolls. They can be buried to commemorate chiefs, or with dead husbands and wives to mediate with the spirits. They can be used to express disapproval within a community. Ucko cites an instance of clay figurines being left in the garden of a man who had left his wife and children to live with another woman.

Knowledge of these contemporary uses does not in itself provide proof of figurines' prehistoric significance. But it could lead to a few pauses and deep breaths between digs, to query the assumption made by late nineteenth-century scholars with a background in classical archeology that the discovery of figurines necessarily showed worship of a female deity.

Ucko points out that a single explanation of all anthropomorphic figurines from one area or from one site is likely to camouflage the different uses they may have had. The type of material they are made out of, whether they are human or animal, male or female, with or without sexual charac-teristics − all have to be taken into account. The context of their discovery is important, too. A figurine in a tomb could have a very different social meaning from one found in household debris or outside a building.

The picture which seems to be emerging from recent prehistory is of diverse and localised patterns of worship, rather than a takeover of a male religious system from a female.

Colin Renfrew heralded a new social archeology in his inaugural lecture at Southampton University in 1973. It is good to hear that 'archeology no longer despises the short and simple annals of the poor'. His picture of archeologists grubbing for carbonised grape pips, and not dismissing the 'poor man's rubbish', is in accord with the approaches of anthropology and recent social history. But it would be unfortunate if women were forgotten again amidst this 'undramatic debris', and the insights of feminist anthro-pology ignored.

Indeed, I must come clean, and confess to a vision more mischievous and less worthy than the dusting of attics in the spring, which has been luring me back to beginnings. This is of a new television series of *Animal, Vegetable and Mineral*, set in a prehistoric rubbish tip, somewhere between *Paradise Lost* and *The Origin of Species*. I am listening while a raging chimera, part lion and serpent, confronts an expert on radiocarbon dating, and a group of mother goddesses hold forth on the problem of the appropriation of surplus labour. While controversy rises, I will make my escape and slope off over the bleak and heathlike margins into modern times.

5. The Trouble With 'Patriarchy'

◆◆◆◆◆◆

'The Trouble With "Patriarchy" ', *New Statesman*, 21–28 December 1979. In criticising the use of the term 'patriarchy' in the women's movement I was trying to warm up a few theoretical jellies that had got stuck in the fridge before the lumps melted properly. Since then socialist feminists internationally have become more wary of the world and cautious about its implications as a concept.

But the argument about how women are both in opposition and in connection with men makes us feminists like cats on hot bricks. I believe we have to live dangerously, hold onto antagonism and mutuality. This means we risk getting burnt but learn our way around town.

There are other arguments behind 'the trouble with patriarchy'. When we opt for socialist feminism what kind of philosophical traditions do we seek out? There have been many visions of socialism. There are many intellectual emphases in Marxism. There are great chunks of thought which Marx could not imagine. Feminism too has many political and intellectual strands.

Initially we could take some assumptions for granted. But this only takes us so far. I think we need to argue more explicitly in relation to past philosophical traditions in our search to combine socialism and feminism and reach a new starting point.

Sally Alexander and Barbara Taylor pointed out in reply to this article that I was ignorant of psychoanalysis, of the contribution of structuralist Marxism and too soft on men. They reminded me that, 'The ropes which bind women are the hardest to cut, because they are woven with so many of our own desires.' I know full well that this is true.

I admit to much ignorance. I think the alternative term I used, sex-gender relations, is ungainly. But I do not accept that Marxism and feminism are modes of analysis which we can retire calmly to consider apart in peace and quiet. Are we not living within their combination in the very choice to consider them as separate approaches? For we, the real individuals, are there doing the analysing and we act within the hurly-burly by of history. Consciousness and action do not sit still. The theory which holds the moment of human experience in the light gives rise to new insights. It is then itself shifted by the action of people in time.

It may be that other people's testimony of what they think and feel is problematic. But we'd better give them at least the benefit of the doubt. For really after our feminist readings of structural anthropology, our awareness of the inscription on our psyches of many a trauma, we still resort to quite inadequate and unrigorous notions of I, you, they, we, him, her. We have our own opinions of our experience and we bring them to the task of analysis. We, the individuals, are present when we shape the experience of others. This does not mean that we abandon shaping or ignore the ideas which help. But we can concede that if we are present so are others and it could be that if what they tell us does not fit or accept the terms of our analysis this might help to refashion analysis and question our own situation as analysers. There is a democracy in the making of theories which set out to rid the world of hierarchy, oppression and domination. The act of analysis requires more than concepts of sex and class, more than a theory of the subject, it demands that in the very process of thinking we transform the relation between thinker and thought about, theory and experience. So theory is part of experience and experience carries theory. This is how I understand the implication of Marxism, and much of my understanding has been learned through feminism. I hope that others with greater inclination to philosophy will develop these arguments. Meanwhile turn to Sally Alexander and Barbara Taylor, 'In Defence of Patriarchy' in *People's History and Socialist Theory*, ed. Raphael Samuel, Routledge and Kegan Paul, 1981.

When contemporary feminists began to examine the world from a new perspective, bringing their own experience to bear on their understanding of history and modern society, they found it was necessary to distinguish women's subordination as a sex from class oppression. Inequality between men and women was not just a creation of capitalism: it was a feature of all societies for which we had reliable evidence. It was a separate phenomenon, which needed to be observed in connection with, rather than simply as a response to, changes that occurred in the organisation and control of production. So the term 'patriarchy' was pressed into service – as an analytical tool which might help to describe this vital distinction.

The term has been used in a great variety of ways. 'Patriarchy' has been discussed as an ideology which arose out of men's power to exchange women between kinship groups; as a symbolic male principle; and as the power of the father (its literal meaning). It has been used to express men's control over women's sexuality and fertility; and to describe the institutional structure of male domination. Recently the phrase 'capitalist patriarchy' has suggested a form peculiar to capitalism. Zillah Eisenstein, who has edited an anthology of writings under that heading, defines patriarchy as providing 'the sexual hierarchical ordering of society for political control'.[1]

There was felt to be a need (not confined to feminists) for a wider understanding of power relationships and hierarchy than was offered by current Marxist ideas. And with that came the realisation that we needed to resist not only the outer folds of power structures but their inner coils. For their hold over our lives through symbol, myth and archetype would not dissolve automatically with the other bondages even in the fierce heat of revolution. There had to be an inner psychological and spiritual contest, along with the confrontation and transformation of external power.

However, the word 'patriarchy' presents problems of its own. It implies a universal and historical form of oppression which returns us to biology – and thus it obscures the need to recognise not only biological difference, but also the multiplicity of ways in which societies have defined gender. By focusing upon the bearing and rearing of children ('patriarchy' = the power of the father) it suggests there is a single determining cause of women's subordination. This either produces a kind of feminist base-superstructure model to contend with the more blinkered versions of Marxism, or it rushes us off on the misty quest for the original moment of male supremacy. Moreover, the word leaves us with two separate systems in which a new male/female split is implied. We have patriarchy oppressing women and capitalism oppressing male workers. We have biological reproduction on the one hand and work on the other. We have the ideology of 'patriarchy' opposed to the mode of production, which is seen as a purely economic matter.

'Patriarchy' implies a structure which is fixed, rather than the kaleidoscope of forms within which women and men have encountered one another. It does not carry any notion of how women might act to transform their situation as a sex. Nor does it even convey a sense of how women have resolutely manoeuvred for a better position within the general context of subordination – by shifting for themselves, turning the tables, ruling the roost, wearing the trousers, hen-pecking, gossiping, hustling, or (in the words of a woman I once overheard) just 'going drip, drip at him'. 'Patriarchy' suggests a fatalistic submission which allows no space for the complexities of women's defiance.

It is worth remembering every time we use words like 'class' and 'gender' that they are only being labelled as structures for our convenience, because human relationships move with such complexity and speed that our descriptions freeze them at the point of understanding. Nancy Hartsock[2] recalls Marx's insistence that we should regard 'every historically developed social form as in fluid movement'; thus we must take into account its 'transient nature not less than its momentary existence'. Within Marxism there is at least a possibility of a dialectical unity of transience and moment. But it seems to me that the concept of 'patriarchy' offers no such prospect. We have stretched its meaning in umpteen different ways, but there is no transience in it at all. It simply refuses to budge.

A word which fails to convey movement is not much help when it comes to examining the differences between the subordination of women, and class. The capitalist is defined by his or her ownership of capital. This is not the same kettle of fish at all as a biological male person. Despite the protestations of employers, their activities could be organised quite differently and, in this sense, the working class carries the possibility of doing without the capitalist and thus of abolishing the hierarchies of class. But a biological male person is a more delicate matter altogether and is not to be abolished (by socialist feminists at least).

It is not sexual difference which is the problem, but the social inequalities of gender – the different kinds of power societies have given to sexual differences, and the hierarchical forms these have imposed on human relationships. Some aspects of male-female relationships are evidently not simply oppressive, but include varying degrees of mutual aid. The concept of 'patriarchy' has no room for such subtleties, however.

Unless we have a sense of these reciprocities and the ways they have changed among different classes, along with the inequalities between men and women, we cannot explain why women have perceived different aspects of their relationship to men to be oppressive at different times. We cannot explain why genuine feelings of love and friendship are possible between men and women, and boys and girls, or why people have acted together in popular movements. In times of revolution (such as the Paris Commune, the early days of Russian communism, or more recent liberation struggles in developing countries), women's public political action has often challenged not only the ruling class, the invader or the coloniser, but also the men's idea of women's role. Less dramatically in everyday life, men's dependence on women in the family, in the community and at work, is as evident as women's subordination – and the two often seem to be inextricably bound together. Some feminists regard this as an elaborate trick, but I think it is precisely within these shifting interstices that women have manoeuvred and resisted. We thus need an approach which can encompass both the conflict and the complementary association between the sexes.

If we could develop an historical concept of sex-gender relationships, this would encompass changing patterns of male control and its congruence or incongruence with various aspects of women's power. It would enable us to delineate the specific shapes of sex-gender relationships within different social relationship, without submerging the experiences of women in those of men, or vice versa. If we stopped viewing patriarchy and capitalism as two separate interlocking systems, and looked instead at how sex-gender as well as class and race relations have developed historically, we could avoid a simple category 'woman' – who must either be a matriarchal stereotype or a hopelessly down-trodden victim, and whose fortunes rise and fall at the same time as all her sisters. We could begin to see women and men born into relationships within families which are not of their making. We could see how their ideas of themselves and other people, their work, habits and sexuality, their participation in organisation, their responses to authority, religion and the state, and the expression of their creativity in art and culture – how all these things are affected by relations in the family as well as by class and race. But sex-gender relationships are clearly not confined to the family (we are not just sex-beings in the family and class-beings in the community, the state and at work): like class relations, they permeate all aspects of life.

Equally, we inherit the historical actions and experience of people in the past through institutions and culture – and the balance of sex-gender relations is as much a part of this inheritance as is class. The changes which men and women make within these prevailing limitations need not be regarded simply as a response to the reorganisation of production, nor even as a reflection of class struggle. Indeed, we could see these shifts in sex-gender relationships as *contributing* historically towards the creation of suitable conditions for people to make things differently and perceive the world in new ways.

Rosalind Petchesky has argued that

> . . . if we understand that patriarchal kinship relations are not static, but like class relations, are characterised by antagonism and struggle, then we begin to

speculate that women's consciousness and their periodic attempts to resist or change the dominant kinship structures will themselves affect class relations.[3]

Relations between men and women are also characterised by certain reciprocities, so we cannot assume the antagonism is a constant factor. There are times when class or race solidarity are much stronger than sex-gender conflict and times when relations within the family are a source of mutual resistance to class power. Nonetheless, the approach suggested by Petchesky opens up an exciting way of thinking about women's and men's position in the past, through which we can locate sex-gender relations in the family and see how they are present within all other relationships between men and women in society.

However, we need to be cautious about the assumptions we bring to the past. For instance, women have seen the defining features of oppression very differently at different times. Large numbers of children, for example, could be regarded as a sign of value and status, whereas most Western women now would insist on their right to restrict the numbers of children they have, or to remain childless. Feminist anthropologists are particularly aware of the dangers of imposing the values of Western capitalism on women of other cultures. But we can colonise women in the past, too, by imposing modern values.

We also need to be clear about which groups we are comparing in any given society, and to search for a sense of movement within each period. For instance, the possibilities for women among the richer peasantry in the Middle Ages were clearly quite different from those of poor peasants without land. And presumably these were not the same before and after the Black Death. Change – whether for better or worse – does not necessarily go all one way between the classes, nor even between their various sub-strata, and the same is true of changes which varying modes of production have brought to sex-gender relationships. The growth of domestic industry, for example, is usually associated with the control of the father over the family. But it could also alter the domestic division of labour, because women's particular work skills were vital to the family economy at certain times in the production process. This might have made it easier for women in domestic industry to question sexual hierarchy than for peasant women.

Similarly, nineteenth-century capitalism exploited poor women's labour in the factories, isolated middle-class women in the home, and forced a growing body of impecunious gentlewomen on to the labour market. Yet at the same time it brought working-class women into large-scale popular movements at work and in the community, in the course of which some of them demanded their rights as a sex while resisting class oppression. Out of domestic isolation, the extreme control of middle-class men over their wives and daughters, and the impoverished dependence of unmarried women, came the first movement of feminists.

An historical approach to sex-gender relations could help us to understand why women radicalised by contemporary feminism have found the present division of domestic labour and men's continued hold over women's bodies and minds to be particularly oppressive. These were not really the emphases of nineteenth-century feminism. What then are the specific antagonisms we have encountered within sex-gender relationships? And what possibilities do they imply for change?

It has often been said that as women we have come to know that the personal is 'political' because we have been isolated in the personal sphere. I think this is only half the story. We *were* isolated in the personal sphere, but some of us were hurtled dramatically out of it by the expansion of education and the growth of administrative and welfare work, while some (working-class and black women) were never so luxuriously confined. What is more, modern capitalism has created forms of political control and social care, and has produced new technologies and methods of mass communication, which have disturbed and shifted the early nineteenth-century division of private and public spheres. As a result, the direct and immediate forms through which men have controlled women have been *both* reinforced *and* undermined. Kinship relations have increasingly become the province of the state (we have to obey certain rules about the way we arrange our private lives in order to qualify for welfare benefits, for example). Contraceptive technology has enabled women to separate sexual pleasure from procreation. And the scope for sexual objectification has grown apace with the development of the visual media. Men are being sold more strenuously than ever the fantasy of controlling the ultimate feminine, just as their hold over real women is being resisted. Women are meanwhile being delivered the possibility of acting out male-defined fantasy of ultimate femininity in order to compete with other women for men. All the oppressive features of male culture have been thrown into relief and have served to radicalise women: who does the housework, unequal pay and access to jobs, violence in the home, rape, the denial of abortion rights, prostitution, lack of nursery provision, and male-dominated and exclusively heterosexual attitudes towards sex and love.

This convoluted state of affairs has created a new kind of political consciousness in socialist feminism. In tussling with the specifics of sex-gender relations in modern capitalism, feminists have challenged the way we see our identities and experience our bodies, the way we organise work and childcare, and the way we express love and develop thoughts. In other words, they have challenged the basic components of hierarchy to create a vision of society in which sexual difference does not imply subordination and oppression.

Just as the abolition of class power would release people outside the working class and thus requires their support and involvement, so the movement against hierarchy which is carried in feminism goes beyond the liberation of a sex. It contains the possibility of equal relations not only between women and men but also between men and men, and women and women, and even between adults and children.

PART FOUR

MEMORY AND
CONSCIOUSNESS

INTRODUCTION

I can still see the cloud of faces and remember my terror as I gabbled nervously into the microphone at the first Women's Liberation Conference in the spring of 1970 at Oxford. The subject, the action of women in the French Revolutionary movements of the nineteenth century, might appear nowadays to be a rather remote topic for a feminist conference, especially one that was to mark the beginning of a new movement.

But it indicates the close involvement between the search for a past and the reawakening of feminism. In Britain this has been particularly intense and found expression not only in books but in talks, articles, weekend schools, courses in adult education, schools and universities, films, posters, plays, exhibitions and songs. Feminists have had to contest men's power to say what was, is and should be, from a woman's point of view. This can alert us to wider political problems of selection and interpretation in the historical assessment of what was tried, thought and done. Organisations act like colanders, quite a few lumps never get through.

What about those who were left at the washtub, or who acted without belonging to formal organisations, or joined everything and evaded the spot light, who dreamed, thought, met, picketed, marched, tub-thumped, plotted, died without trace or echo?

They might have a few words with history.

And what about the history of our own movement? Goodness knows what young feminists will be saying in the 2080s.

One of the curious and disturbing aspects of being an historian and a participant in a popular movement is the experience of how memory dissolves. Even as we scan the past our own beginnings slip away. Already records have been lost.

It is always the assumptions which seem too obvious to state that are the most elusive. When I met and interviewed Florence Exten-Hann, a socialist feminist who had been active in the trade union movement, the suffrage cause and peace organisations, she was keen to help in the new women's movement, although in her eighties and unable to get about much. 'Of course,' she said, a little sadly, 'you're not interested in the trade unions like we were.' We stared at each other over sixty years. I had assumed in the heady arrogance of youth that it was *us* who connected women's liberation to class struggle. They were the bourgeois feminists – the mistakes of whom we would of course avoid.

As another socialist feminist veteran from Glasgow remarked to Susie Fleming and Gloden Dallas in 1975, 'Truly you need seven-league boots to keep up with an untruth.'[1]

The cherishing of memory is partly a means of breaking the silence of subordination. The extraordinary resilience of the memory of rebellion can in certain circumstances endure coercion, hardship, ridicule, betrayal, even the sophisticated onslaught of the modern media.

In Barcelona after Franco died I asked socialist feminist friends who had been active in the anti-fascist underground, 'How did you become socialists under fascism?' They looked at me incredulously. 'The historical memory,' one replied patiently.

It is not all heroic stuff. A friend who worked at Fords, Dagenham, talking about the Civil War in the seventeenth century, steered through heavy traffic and reflected, 'Cromwell? He was one of our bastards.'

Once we start remembering we have to hear home truths and be prepared to take the rough with the smooth. How else could we ever come to bear the compromise of power?

Memories are precious and the power to hold, share and inherit memory are crucial elements in the emergence of a critical consciousness which denies that things have to be because they have always been.

But certain memories only find resonance at certain times. The present works upon memory and draws out stories. For example, the questions which feminist historians, this time around, ask about the relationship of feminism and socialism, feminism and anarchism, are clearly affected by our experiences of acting within a movement which has had the gump and strength to 'frontiers-trespass'. Also the crucial insight, 'the personal is political', has brought all sorts of stuff into history out of fusty cellars and forlorn attics, converting old warehouses and halls of science, and swelling the crowd setting off from washtubs to Westminster.

It has not only been a matter of remembering who was doing the washing but also reinterpreting the publicly seen aspects of the rebellions of the past. We have marked out the shape of informal local networks, paid attention to how women have combined personal life and public action, explored the interconnecting thread of consciousness between family, work and trade union meetings, sought out the interior existence of political organisation.

We have left much undone. But we have tried not deceitfully to cover our traces but to explain and include our own journeys backwards. Time waits for no woman and many hands make light work, as the sayings go.

But all insights and illuminations carry their own blind spots and the slogan, the personal is political, is no exception. It does not mean that *all* individual experience is equivalent to politics. We will all probably die with a few dirty secrets. Tension and difference remain.

Nor can we put all our trust in the capacity to remember. Rebellion springs from the moment and this is just as well for memory can be wrenched away and people become too downtrodden to recognise themselves. Or perhaps the mirror becomes cracked and blurred with unrequited hope. Or perhaps there is no reflection, no sound or echo, no voice to articulate time passing.

In her study of the Owenite socialist feminists, Barbara Taylor quotes a nineteenth-century radical George Jacob Holyoake, recounting opposition to women's struggles for their rights. He said the 'public tongue of women' was supposed to be 'in the mouth of men'.[2] Such a graft makes it impossible to speak clearly. But even this difficulty in oppression can be turned to advantage.

Knowing inhibitions upon one's own communicating and understanding makes it possible to enter other people's silences.

But there is a terrible gap between immediate grumbling complaint, mute sympathy and a critical consciousness which can grasp a whole context of subordination, analyse and act. It is a painful terrain which political organisations of the left have struggled within. Analysis is not enough alone, for we enter the beings and worlds of other people through imagination, and it is through imagination that we glimpse how these might change.

The problem of combining a vision of how life could be completely transformed so that nobody was oppressed and the development of a practical strategy which met existing discontents has long been a puzzler for socialists. Even before Marx, political radicals campaigning for the vote as a means of securing further change took the cooperator Robert Owen to task. His schemes, they maintained, threatened no-one because they were too visionary.

Marx and Engels criticised Owen's ideas, which they called 'utopian socialism'. Since then most socialists have been wary of ideal alternatives which ignore how change can be carried out. Marxism has stressed the need to assess the odds and relate action to the existing balance of historical forces.

Lenin astutely developed this into a pragmatic system of political strategy which was geared to the exigencies of underground struggle against auto-cratic power. This has tended to demote the creation of different forms of association as a means of changing consciousness and give priority to organisation to secure a particular end.

It became popularly assumed among both revolutionary and reformist socialists that utopianism was bad but science was good. It has taken some disastrous effects of science like valium and the bomb to upset this conviction.

However, there is another tradition of socialism which while moving away from the model-building utopias has still emphasised the need to nurture new expectations. This recognition that action and and organisation have to achieve specific ends and serve as springboards for the imagination to make a utopian leap never completely dies, appearing for example in the Independent Labour Party and among anarchists most noticeably. But it has been overlaid by the more serious attention paid to science, strategy, ration-ality, and realism. These are valuable but they are not enough.

In his biography of William Morris E.P. Thompson writes, '. . . "desire" uneducated except in the bitter praxis of class struggle, was likely, as Morris often warned, to go its own way, sometimes for well, and some-times for ill, but falling back again and again into the "common-sense" or habitual values of the host society.'[3] He points to, 'the whole problem of the subordination of the imaginative utopian faculties within the later Marxist tradition: its lack of moral self-consciousness or even a vocabulary of desire, its inability to project any images of the future, or even its tendency to fall back in lieu of these upon the Utilitarian's earthly paradise – the maximisa-tion of economic growth'.[4]

The women's movement in the last decade has revived this questioning of everyday habits, respected the releasing of imagination, tussled with inner desires and tried to make living alternatives in the here and now. Recently a widespread dissatisfaction with existing definitions of socialism and approaches to organising has emerged on the left. There is a search for indica-tions rather than absolute assumptions that we can live any way we decide regardless of existing conditions. The renewal of the utopian element in socialism does not mean pretending that we can opt out of capitalism. It means tracing choices between differing directions and clearly asserting moral preferences. This makes us give *equal* balance to assessing the odds, achieving an end and transforming expectations in devising strategies. The most valuable source for developing such a strategy is the great wealth of our experiences of what has been tried and done in practice – in our own lives and in the past a consciousness about how and what we remember is thus vital for a new vision of socialism.

1. The Years Before Eleven

◆◆◆◆◆◆

'The Years Before Eleven' was originally published in *Cutlasses and Earrings*, Playbooks 2, 1977. Until I was seven I lived in Harehills, Leeds. The area was 'going down' and the demand for mining equipment presumably going up as my father, an engineering salesman, could afford to buy a house in a middle-class suburb, Roundhay, by 1950. Well, Roundhay was recognised as 'nicer' than Harehills. But I missed my friends and the logs in Potter Newton Park and my den and the gang warfare.

In Harehills my mother had intimated that I was somehow better than the other children I played with. So I learned class arrogance. But in Roundhay the mothers of neighbouring girls banned them from seeing me. My mother had to explain that it was because I was too rough and shouted a lot and was considered to be common. I remember loneliness and resentment and a confused inclination to anyone else called 'common'. But they thought I was posh.

Being neither one thing or the other made me wonder about myself and dislike what appeared to be stupid ways of fencing people off. My mother encouraged me in this, for while observing the formalities she took people as she found them. My father hammered away at my improvement and was furiously resisted by a thankless daughter. Nonetheless he imparted the conviction that I was as good as anybody else, when it came down to it, and only a snob would deny it.

Neither of them had any idea that this was how you breed a socialist feminist historian.

◆◆◆◆◆◆

Looking at a marigold
My mind goes back
To early summers on the lawn
There is a lost fragrance
A texture I can't touch again.
The taste of tomatoes in the sun
Cream, soft grass
The darkening shadow of his wrath
Broken glass
My screams at night
Her knotted string
And reassuring light.
Earlier walled dens in roses.

In between two churches
Large boys attack
Without your gang
Blushing once with one.
The kids with runny noses
The mystery of crab apples
The journey to allotments.
Whispers as the blacks move in.

The game on logs
Between the gaps
Slippery surfaces
Slithering in socks
Mud-pies,
Dusty book lots
Of the Egyptian dead
You could have used those
After they'd gone
He said.

Some kind of differentness
Taught, on rote, built in
A certain bewilderment.
Some children wore white plimsolls
In the snow.
Stayed by pubs
At night,
Played with toads
In gutter streams.
Some houses had bare boards
And holes.
It was explained
Their parents
Didn't care about them
Not like you.
But when you moved
The neighbours tried
To keep their children

Safe.
Said you were common
Said you screamed
Made them dirty
And afraid.

You listened to the wind
Alone.
And learned to sense the rain.
You played
Your stories in your head
A boy
Until breasts
Came
With blood
And pain.

2. Florence Exten-Hann –
Socialist and Feminist

'Florence Exten-Hann – Socialist and Feminist', *Red Rag*, no. 5, 1973.

Florence Exten-Hann died in the spring of 1973. What follows is based on notes she wrote for a Workers' Education class in 1968 and on an interview with her in 1973. I have kept her story in her words wherever possible and have included background information only to make it more easily understandable.

I wrote the article both as a personal tribute to her life and work and as a contribution to the discovery of socialist feminism in the past. Since it was published much more has come to light about the interconnection between socialism and feminism and the impact of feminism upon trade union and working-class women. But there is a great deal more that needs to be said.

Florence Exten was born into a socialist family and grew up in the climate of agitation in the late 1890s and early 1900s. Her father was one of the first socialists to be elected to Southampton council. She became conscious of class when she was still a young girl while 'helping my father in elections and visiting the back streets of Southampton's dockland'. He was a member of the Social Democratic Federation, a Marxist grouping dominated by the rather dogmatic and sectarian Hyndmann. Though the local branches were less dogmatic, the central figures in the SDF saw Marxism as a doctrine which had to be kept pure from grass roots organising with people who did not agree with them. This meant they dismissed trade union work and it is perhaps because of this policy in the group that Mr Exten had to resign when he appeared on the same platform as a member of the Clarion cycling club. It must have caused some furore in the Exten household because Florence remembered it particularly. The Clarion cycling clubs played an important social and cultural role in the early socialist movement, organising camps and outings and bringing socialists of varying views together. The Clarion itself was a paper edited by the journalist Robert Blatchford. He was a brilliant propagandist but his socialism was both nationalistic and imperialist. Clarion cyclers though were unlikely to be troubled by doctrinal debate as they pedalled off into the countryside. For the young worker or clerk the bicycle was the means of escaping from the daily humdrum of working, for the young woman it symbolised the new freedom of the advanced and emancipated 'boots and spurs'. Some even wore clothes which made pedalling easier but which were regarded as shocking by most people. 'Mother and I rode bicycles and wore bloomers, but had to carry a skirt to put on when riding in a town for fear of being mobbed.'

Florence's family was not very well off but the atmosphere was one in which political activity and ideas were part of everyday life. As Florence put it, 'We were born into the socialist movement.' There was, though, a gap between theories of equality and existing practical restraints on that equality which presented young girls who were growing up with an unevenness which made questioning if not rebellion against the old ideas of feminine behaviour very likely indeed. It must have posed dilemmas for socialist parents too which they solved by responding in contradictory ways. Florence was thus brought up as an intellectual equal to her brothers. But at the same time her father was a man who believed very strongly in his own opinions and in his role as head of the family. He also did not take his daughter's desire to 'break out into a career' very seriously, though it was assumed that Florence would earn her living for the Extens did not belong to the class which could afford leisurely daughters. So instead of becoming a teacher which she would have liked Florence went out to work as a clerk.

In the early 1900s shop and clerical workers were organising for better pay and trying to get their very long hours of work reduced. The conditions of their work and the control employers could exert over their life out of work are vividly described in H.G. Wells' novel *Kipps* and in Hannah Mitchell's autobiography *The Hard Way Up*. Here Florence's socialist background was important for her father encouraged her to join the union, which she did, aged seventeen. In order to be active in a union a young girl had to have sympathetic parents because the personal restraints on what she did were still strong. Florence was allowed much more personal freedom than most 'respectable' young girls of her class.

> It is difficult now to recall that when I was a teenager one could not walk the streets alone (it was not done!). I was considered fast and loose because I used to travel to London alone at this time to attend the Women's Advisory Council of the Shop Assistants Union at least once a month arriving home at 1.30 in the morning. I had an extremely bad reputation among the neighbours and my parents were told how wrong they were to allow it, fortunately my parents were understanding.

Women were not always welcome even when they did become active in the labour movement. 'Once I turned up at a Trades Council but was prevented from attending solely because I was a woman, though an accredited delegate.'

Many trade unions still excluded women who organised in separate unions not from choice but from necessity.

These formal kinds of discrimination and personal cultural attitudes were obviously closely connected and a young woman who was politically active was likely to gain a reputation as a virago. 'I was known locally as a she-devil.' It was not really surprising that when Annie Kenney, a Lancashire mill girl, became full-time organiser for Mrs Pankhurst's 'Women's Social and Political Union' in the Southern region that this 'she-devil' should gravitate towards the suffrage movement. The WSPU had come out of the Independent Labour Party and in 1908 still had quite close links with the socialist movement. The splits in the suffrage movement and between the suffragettes and the socialists were still not so marked. Locally too the London controversies were less important and there appears to have been a close connection between feminism and men and women involved in other forms of radical activity. Florence, still in her teens '. . . spent many early morning hours chalking the pavements of Southampton with slogans among others "Votes for Women" until the local council passed bye-laws prohibiting it'. She also 'did much fly-posting at night' and 'bill-delivering', helping to organise indoor and outdoor meetings. She acted as press secretary – a thankless task because the newspapers would not give the suffragettes publicity in case it brought them more supporters.

'The most nerve-wracking experience was going round the streets ringing a bell and shouting through a loud hailer about the meetings.

'Most meetings were the butt of students who threw stones, eggs or tomatoes, and many an indoor meeting had to be abandoned because of floating pepper thrown by the opposition.'

Besides this local agitating she went on the big demonstration in London in 1908 when half a million people, men as well as women, converged on Hyde Park demanding 'Votes for Women'. Sections marched from every railway terminal and the WSPU had organised cheap rail tickets for the occasion. Florence carried the Southampton banner with great pride from Waterloo. She was seventeen. 'Because of my pigtails the police accompanying the march were highly amused.'

In 1910 the Exten family went to Bristol. Florence was still a member of the WSPU but was 'ceasing to be active for I disapproved of the altered strategy so fundamentally that I broke away at last'. As Emmeline and Christabel moved towards the policy of direct action and the shock tactics of militancy they lost women like Florence who believed it was more effective to struggle within organisations legally. By 1911–12 Florence was joining various bodies which could 'by pressure help the women's movement'. Socialists used similar tactics.

Although Florence had broken with the WSPU, her politics 'continued to be governed by the interests of girls and women'. While still a member she had learned of the low pay of the Cragley chainmakers, the exploitation of home and sweated workers which was exposed by the Anti-Sweating League. Her own experience taught her more.

'. . . one found that a woman is required to be more experienced and better equipped than a man in order to obtain a post; then to work harder and obtain twenty-five per cent less salary . . .

'In 1911 I earned 8s per week at what was grandiloquently described as a "departmental section clerk".'

But she was an aristocrat when compared with the women manual workers at the same place of work. 'In this brush factory girls made miners lamp brushes ½d each but if the stock broke before it was finished, even if it were almost complete she received no pay. To make these brushes women had to sit around some boiling pitch, tie a very small bunch of bristles and dip it in the pitch, then push it in the stock.'

She continued in Bristol with her trade unionism, speaking in 1911 at the Shop Workers Conference against the idea of separate womens unions on the grounds that this treated women as a separate class. But this did not mean that she dismissed the very real prejudice which existed. 'The differences between man's work and woman's is no more than a cherished trade union phantom. This was proved during the two world wars.'

Union meetings were becoming not merely political activity because she met a young trade unionist, a grocery assistant, called Maurice Hann who was to become her husband in 1913 and rather later the General Secretary of the shop workers union. 'I did all my courting in trade union meetings.' Katherine Glasier, a member of the ILP, used to call them 'the doves' because of this combination of courting and trade union branch meeting. Some anarchists and socialists rejected marriage as an institution and lived in free unions on principle despite the prevailing attitudes. Florence said that she and Maurice did discuss this but married in the end.

She had a less happy time in the Women's Mutual Improvement Society, formed by ILP women in Bristol to encourage women to come to discussion classes and hear speakers. 'I got into hot water for telling the women off for knitting. I thought it was rude.' The other members took offence and said they 'weren't going to be dominated by such kids as Miss Exten'.

When the First World War broke out Florence became a pacifist – she was sympathetic to the Quakers. Although Christabel and Emmeline became zealously patriotic, other feminists opposed the war, either like Florence on moral grounds or like Sylvia Pankhurst because they saw it as a capitalist war. But the peace movement was not strong enough to dwell on internal differences for they faced overwhelming opposition and had to work in some secrecy. (Florence met Sylvia through the peace movement and liked her but thought she was always hampered politically 'by her artistic temperament which wouldn't allow her to be calm'. She was less keen on Emmeline, however, 'Her mother was more or less a sergeant major.') Florence became the official organiser for the No Conscription Fellowship in the southern and eastern regions. This work which she did for a very low wage, included visiting conscientious objectors in prison and army camps. While the war lasted the address list for the Fellowship was kept in a biscuit tin, buried in Florence's garden. In 1918 the tin was dug up because it was thought that the danger of a police raid was over. But the police did raid and found the tin which had been left in the bathroom. It was politically useful to them in the insurrectionary atmosphere of 1918–19 to have the names of members who had had the courage to resist the war.

Florence continued to be active in the peace movement. She also remained a socialist and a feminist, though as the years went by the connection between the two became increasingly remote. She turned her organisational energies to innumerable other issues. During World War I she was on a committee to raise money for a statue for Keir Hardie, the ILP member who had championed the women's movement. Her interest in trade unionism continued. She was proud of contributing to the upkeep of the home. When the first war finished she worked for the League of Nations Society, during World War II she was a civil servant in the Marlborough Street Employment Exchange for Women, and after World War II she worked on the *Municipal Journal*. In the last twenty years of her life she became very involved with the WEA in Stanmore and developed an interest in archeology and medieval history. She did a lot of clerical work voluntarily for the branch, addressing envelopes and the general administrative work of a branch secretary. Besides all this she was always taking on small tasks for people and was frequently knitting for somebody's baby.

As the years went by and no new women's movement emerged her feminism became increasingly a matter of personal feeling for which there seemed no political expression and towards which younger women did not seem to incline. It must have seemed to women of Florence's generation that women were content with the limited freedom which had been gained. It is hard to maintain political ideas in isolation and it is some indication of the strength of the early suffrage movement that women like Florence did continue to question when the world appeared to be going against them.

3. Theory and Practice of Early American Feminism

◆◆◆◆◆◆

'Theory and Practice of Early American Feminism', *New Society*, 26 February 1981.

◆◆◆◆◆◆

William Leach, *True Love and Perfect Union: the Feminist Reforms of Sex and Society*, Routledge & Kegan Paul, 1981
Meredith Tax, *The Rising of the Women*, Monthly Review, 1981

William Leach describes in his book the wide range of subjects which pre-occupied American feminists between 1850 and 1880. They criticised established medicine, interested themselves in health reform, birth control, eugenics, coeducation, dress reform, as well as legal and economic changes. While they were quick to point out bias in prevailing scientific theories, they had great faith in science and harmonious social planning. They believed in having no secrets. 'Live in the open air,' declared a feminist doctor, Mary Putman Jacobi. Feminism was to pierce the mask of sham, hypocrisy and grundyism. Caroline Dall said she wanted, above all, the quality of 'eyesight'. There is an interesting link with spiritualism. Feminist clairvoyants revealed physical illnesses and domestic conflict.

Leach reveals some of the tensions within this phase of radical feminism. The rationale of no secrets could come painfully close to the less dignified muck-raking journalism in exposing sexual scandal. Fashion also proved recalcitrant. In the 1850s some feminists adopted a utilitarian approach to clothes. But women in bloomers became such laughing stocks that most feminists compromised and adopted a mixture of rational dress and fashionable attire. Other feminists delighted in clothes, and their conventions rustled with rich silks. The radical feminist, Elizabeth Cady Stanton, not only had seven children; she was also renowned for her coiffure and 'did not pretend to have a soul above point lace'. In the early days cultural rebellion in dress was tolerated. But in 1879 Dr Mary Walker, who always appeared in male evening dress at feminist events, was hustled off the platform.

Leach shows feminists pushing liberal theory to its limits by extending the concept of individuality to woman's self-ownership of her own person.

Radical feminism shared the dilemmas of liberalism in this period. Stanton searched unsuccessfully for a wider social base by helping to form a Working Women's Association with women printers, which attracted single skilled women workers. New York feminists in 1872 sought to unite the labour reformers, members of the First International, prohibitionists and spiritualists. But in this period class divisions, especially among women, were becoming more marked. Radical feminism's emphasis on freedom, truth, self-help and self-ownership had only a limited relevance for workers facing depressions, tenement industries and the militia. Nonetheless Leach's book shows this to have been a most creative period in feminist thought and he compares these women to the later generation of progressives who campaigned for education and social reform in the settlement movement.

It is not clear what happens in between. The leadership of the suffrage movement moved to the right in the late nineteenth century and focused on the vote. However, Meredith Tax's *The Rising of the Women* indicates that this was not the whole story. By the 1880s some feminist women were turning towards settlements and social reform. The Illinois Women's Alliance, for example, was formed in 1888 after shock reports about women's working conditions. It included women's organisations, socialists, trade unionists, spiritualists, dress reformers, anarchists and religious groups. They exposed corruption and sweated industry, and campaigned against child labour and for public education. The Alliance broke up over the issue of a legal eight-hour day.

Both socialists and feminists have over-simplified the question of cross-class alliances among women. Tax's detailed account of the specific encounters carefully balances the contributions middle-class women could make – the effective publicity for the struggles of working women or the provision of settlement rooms for meetings, assistance in setting up a cooperative – against ambiguity about limiting the hours of labour, acceptance of charity and a tendency to shift away from trade union organisation toward legislative lobbying.

She also shows how male trade unionists frequently forced working-class women to accept support from middle-class women by their indifference to women's situation and then grumbled because they were deserting their class. Leonora O'Reilly, for instance, one of the organisers of the Women's Trade Union League, was torn between the condescension of some of her female allies and the indifference of trade union men. Socialist women faced a similar problem – caught between feminists who did not agree with socialism and hostility within left organisations to the liberation of women.

Both books move away from an organisational approach to feminism which examines only the suffrage societies. Leach does this by relying on a great volume of journals, letters and books written by feminist literary luminaries of the day. These sources restrict his outlook. He tells us sometimes how the feminists saw working-class women. It would give some perspective to learn what Troy laundresses in New York or women printers thought of the feminists.

He also confronts us with a bewildering number of names in the quotes with which he illustrates his themes. This leaves us with little sense of what else these people did or thought, or of the shape of middle-class radicalism in particular places. I feel he rather skates over the communitarian links and stresses the individualism in the feminism of this period. Some American feminists carried from the earlier community building the idea of cooperative house-keeping and were sympathetic to producers' cooperatives. These ideas reappear in the later evolutionary socialist feminism of Charlotte Perkins Gilman and the social reforms of the settlements.

Tax's account is based on activity rather than opinion. This makes for a clear and lively narrative, but I wish she had gone more fully into the debates of the late nineteenth century and early twentieth century – for example, the arguments about protective legislation.

Her book makes an important contribution to a contemporary argument. she is critical of the Marxist tradition of seeing the liberation of women as surbordinate to class emancipation. But she also shows the limitations in present-day socialist feminist theories, in which the two struggles are seen as separate but equal. This tends to a static view which 'leaves out the relations between the struggles and the way each affects the other'.

She argues for a dialectical and historical approach which examines particular instances of the meshing of sex and class rather than a reduced formula from which all meaning tends to drop out. This would mean not simply that women are added to the existing history of labour but a change in perspective to include relations at home and in neighbourhoods as well as at work and in public politics. This is easier said than done, and *The Rising of the Women* focuses mainly on women's public action.

It is not just that feminism necessitates a new understanding of women's part in radical politics. It also means thinking about the lives and actions of radical men differently. For instance, the conflicts which have occurred between men and women trade unionists can reveal male assumptions about control over women and children. Recognition that the family shapes consciousness applies to men as well as women. Equally, radical political assumptions about who is backward and who is advanced, or about human dignity, have been entangled with prevailing ideas of what it is to be a man. We cannot assume that there is a history of working-class men which we can take for granted.

Leach quotes the feminist, Antoinette Brown Blackwell's criticism of Darwin for his 'time-honoured assumption that the male is the normal type of his species'. She was irritated that in 1875 the female was seen only as 'a modification to a special end'.

Well, the time-honoured assumption is still pervasive in all aspects of our culture – Marxist labour history not excepted. It cannot be effectively challenged by simply modifying the modification.

4. Optimistic Feminist

'Optimistic Feminist', *On Women and Revolution*, Crystal Eastman, *New Society*, 26 April 1979. The feminist movement's history is international. But the circumstances and political traditions of thought within each country have affected the development of feminism. The United States has an invigorating tradition of radical feminism which developed in the nineteenth century. It was part of an optimistic climate in which it seemed possible to make all human relationships anew. This was partly because great stock was placed on the development of the individual, but also because people set up new forms of community. Utopias were obvious courses of action.

The contemporary women's movement has rediscovered this tradition. It has helped to remind us of old truths which had been forgotten by European socialists.

However, American socialist feminist historians have turned a critical eye upon their own past. They have examined conflicting strands in feminist thought and class and race bias. Their work is thus a good antidote to the assertion of feminism as a moral absolute rather than as a political movement with many strands. It deserves to be better known in Europe.

On Women and Revolution, Crystal Eastman, Oxford University Press, 1979

'Now we can begin,' wrote Crystal Eastman in December 1920 in the American socialist journal, *The Liberator*, which she coedited with her brother, Max Eastman. American women had finally got the vote. So why was this seen as the beginning? Crystal Eastman, who was a socialist feminist, felt that now women could 'say what they are really after . . . freedom'. The feeling was undoubtedly extremely widespread, and yet the real extent and complexity of this wider feminism during and after World War I not only in the United States but internationally, remains obscure.

In editing and introducing Crystal Eastman's writings, Blanche Wiesen Cook provides us with valuable and inaccessible material on socialism and feminism. The only other historian to write about her life and ideas at any length, June Sochin, mistakenly believed that Crystal Eastman 'had no audience of her views' and that her writing remained unpublished. In fact, Crystal Eastman wrote in various contemporary feminist, radical and socialist papers about a whole range of subjects, which included schoolgirl fiction, Lenin, children's toys, birth control, her love for her mother, short skirts, and the shop stewards movement on Clydeside.

Blanche Wiesen Cook says Eastman 'claimed feminism as her birthright'. She gave her first talk on the position of women when she was fifteen. Her mother and father were open, independent-minded Congregational ministers, who supported women's rights. Her father not only encouraged his wife to become a minister, he accepted Crystal's demand that there should be no sex differences between her and her brothers' household tasks. Later he supported her decision to study law and cut off her hair, and he stood by her refusal to wear the customary skirt and stockings for swimming.

Before the war, Crystal Eastman was a labour lawyer and drafted New York State's first workers' compensation law. She worked in settlement houses and became part of the new feminist and radical community which was just then emerging in Greenwich Village. A militant supporter of the suffrage movement, she persuaded her brother Max to work in the Men's League for Women's Suffrage. Against the war, from 1915 she was a member of the Women's Peace Party (now the Women's International League for Peace and Freedom).

The war had split the feminist movement internationally. By 1919 another conflict had developed among liberal pacifists and socialist feminists like Eastman. Not only did she greet the Russian revolution and take the first greetings of American socialists to the short-lived Soviet republic in Hungary but she, and other younger feminists, rejected the sexual respectability important to older suffrage women. 'Feminists are not nuns,' she declared in 1918. Like Margaret Sanger, she believed birth control was a necessity. Women must be free to love and to choose or refuse motherhood.

Though she recognised the problem of women's emotional dependence upon men, she argued that feminists should create the outer circumstances 'in which a free woman's soul can be born and grow'. The prime condition of freedom was economic independence and access to all occupations and trade unions, with equal pay and training. With the characteristic optimism of the early twenties she believed all this was relatively easy. But she wanted not only 'breadwinning wives' but 'homemaking husbands'; and she saw that this meant transforming the upbringing of boys and girls as well as the dominant assumptions of what was male and female. 'It must be manly as well as womanly to know how to cook and sew and take care of yourself.'

This was a remarkable statement in 1920. Most feminists were arguing for women to enter a man's world or for women to have more protection as women. Eastman drew back, however, from her insistence on equality in accepting the demand of 'motherhood endowment'. This was seen by feminists at the time in terms of enough money from the state to keep a mother and her children. They did not argue that whoever was bringing up the child should receive the allowance, which could apply to anyone – male or female. On every other issue, though, she maintained a consistently 'equalitarian' position. She believed feminists should refuse alimony and financial support from men. She also opposed special protective legislation at work for women.

This last question really split the feminist movement in the twenties. It also divided Crystal Eastman from most socialist women, who were for protective legislation. Her later writings give a sense of the process of fragmentation which separated socialism and feminism. The socialism becomes less exuberantly revolutionary and the feminism more preoccupied with inner organisational structures. But the process was barely perceptible to contemporaries when Crystal Eastman died in 1928, aged only forty-six of nephritis – a kidney disease which had never been properly diagnosed or treated. Though she was in pain, she still worried that there was so much to do. Her optimism and gift for happiness remained – 'My heart is warm and life is sweet.'

5. She Lived Her Politics

'She Lived Her Politics', *Wildcat*, no. 6, March 1975. Lilian Wolfe died in 1974 aged ninety-eight. This account of her life indicates interconnections between the suffrage movement, the impact of syndicalism and direct action and anarchism. Even less is known about these than about socialist feminism in the same period.

Like Florence Exten-Hann, Lilian Wolfe was part of the anti-war movement in the First World War. Her account reveals that there was a personally linked underground network which involved anarchists. Socialists and syndicalists were also part of this. It has a shadowy existence behind the anti-war organisations. It is yet another indication that we cannot follow only the records of formal organisations.

Lilian Wolfe was also a vegetarian, believing in healthy food, and she lived in a commune half a century ago.

I met Lilian Wolfe for the first time in September 1973, at a meeting to commemorate the centenary of the birth of Rudolf Rocker, the East End anarchist who organised the Jewish clothing workers in the 1900s. But I had read about her in the Stratford *Shrew* and knew she had been in the suffrage movement, had opposed the First World War and been an active anarchist for many years. I went to interview her at the War Resisters International in Kings Cross a few months later, where she was busy stuffing copies of *Peace News* into envelopes.

She explained her very impressive filing system to me and fed me on vegetarian food from the anarchist community of Whiteways. I left her, frail, tiny and determined, mounting a bus to go to the Chinese exhibition, chuckling about how she could get to the front of the queue as a pensioner. We corresponded for some time after that and then I heard that she had died, in April 1974, aged ninety-eight. This brief account of her life is based on the *Shrew* article, on my interview with her, on a letter in *Peace News*, 24 May 1974, from John Marjoram, and on an article in *Freedom*, 25 May 1974, by Nicolas Walter.

Lilian Wolfe's father was a Jewish jeweller and politically conservative: her mother had been an actress who left the family when Lilian was thirteen to join a touring opera company, leaving Lilian and her three brothers and two sisters 'to think and do as we liked'. Lilian worked as a telegrapher at the Central Telegraph Office in London and 'hated every minute of it'. She had already drifted towards socialism without remembering quite how – 'I found myself thinking that way' – along with her younger brother, despite the conservatism of her background.

At work she joined a group of socialists within the Civil Service, who were called the Civil Service Socialist Society. When she first heard of the suffragettes' militant tactics, she was shocked. 'I thought it was terrible the way they were acting.' Then her supervisor in the Civil Service took her to a meeting and they explained they used tactics like burning letter boxes in order to make it impossible to ignore them. She joined the Women's Freedom League, a breakaway from the Pankhursts' Women's Social and Political Union because she found Christabel and Emmeline too arbitrary and authoritarian. Once while speaking on women's suffrage with a friend in Salisbury Market Place she was pelted with cabbages by hostile onlookers.

There was a strong current within the left before 1914 which rejected working for reforms through Parliament and believed in direct action. The suffragettes were in a funny half-way position. They were using direct action, but in order to influence Parliament. Lilian came to feel increasingly that all the effort to persuade politicians to change their mind was misplaced, and she began to move towards anarcho-syndicalist ideas and direct action. With a group of friends who shared her views she thought of restarting a paper called *Voice of Labour* which had collapsed a few years before.

'When we were going to start the *Voice of Labour* we held a meeting to know how we should go about it. We talked and talked and didn't know how to go about it. We had no experience.' Tom Keell, the compositor and editor of the anarchist paper *Freedom*, came along with 'a watching brief'. After they'd talked in circles for some time, he stood up and explained clearly how they could get started. Lilian was indignant at his silence and the time wasted and demanded, 'Why couldn't that man have spoken before?' That was the first she knew of Tom Keell.

'That man' was to become her companion for many years. An extremely skilled compositor, Tom was renowned for his ability to set type at the same time as having a spirited debate. Lilian remembered him with affection and pride. 'We got friendly and eventually fixed up together. He was the nicest man I ever met. The sort of man you could discuss anything with.' She said the years they spent together were the happiest in her life.

The *Voice of Labour* reappeared in 1914, edited by Fred Dunn helped by Lilian's organisational efficiency. 'I did the hack work.' It was a weekly, becoming a monthly when the First World War began. Apart from Tom Keell and Fred Dunn, Lilian was politically close to two anarchist women, Liz Wilkinson and the feminist Mabel Hope.

In February 1915 an anarchist commune was started in Mecklenburgh Street, London. Domestic work was divided by the people who lived there, who included Lilian and Tom. They held meetings and socials every Saturday night to raise money for *Freedom* and the *Voice of Labour*. They had a piano and youngsters from Rudolf Rocker's anarchist group in the East End used to come and dance — waltzes mainly. 'The older ones used to come and talk and talk.' Lilian didn't remember there being many anarchist groups at that time; apart from the East Enders there was one in Stockport. There were just people around, individuals rather than groups.

The anarchists, like the socialists, split on the question of support for the war. Lilian was in the anti-war tendency and helped to found the anarchist Anti-Conscription League which called on workers to refuse call-up. Fred Dunn, with a few other men including Bert Wills and George Wilkinson, took off to the Scottish Highlands to avoid conscription. The *Voice of Labour* in April 1916 printed a front-page article called 'Defying the Act' by 'one of those outlawed on the Scottish hills', which said: 'A number of comrades from all parts of Great Britain have banded themselves together in the Highlands the better to resist the working of the Military Service Act.'

By May most of the outlaws had been arrested. But Tom had printed 10,000 copies of the article and Lilian with her customary efficiency distributed them, even though when the article was being written she urged restraint. Copies were intercepted by the police, and she and Tom were arrested in May and tried in June under the Defence of the Realm Act for 'conduct prejudicial to recruiting and discipline'. Tom pleaded not guilty and Lilian guilty. He was fined £100, she was fined £25. When they refused to pay they were both imprisoned.

Lilian was pregnant so she spent her sentence in Holloway prison hospital, to the bewilderment of the prison doctor who seemed to have never 'had to deal with a pregnant woman before. He seemed very confused.' Her vegetarianism caused more confusion. She begged to be given the 'water the cabbages were boiled in' because she was afraid that the diet would be harmful to the baby she was carrying.

Psychologically the prison affected her very badly though she was not physically ill-treated. 'I thought I was going mad. My head was going round and round and round. But the only person nasty to me was the clergyman – he shouted at me that I was German. So I lived for some months in terror that they would repatriate me.'

She paid her fine two weeks before she was to be released because she was afraid for her child's safety. She had already resigned from the Civil Service and from the work she had always hated before being imprisoned. 'I wasn't going to wait until they chucked me out.' She applied to go into Queen Charlotte's Hospital to have her baby, but they refused her, not because she wasn't married but because she was an unrepentant sinner who intended to live with the baby's father afterwards. 'I certainly was one of the first single women to have a baby deliberately.' Her son was born when she was forty-one years old and she called him Tom after his father.

Although free unions were discussed in the left at the time, it took considerable courage to act on your principles. The decision to have the child came more from the anarchist rejection of the authority of the state than feminism. Lilian says she was not really interested in feminist ideas, though her friend Mabel Hope who wrote for *Freedom* was.

After the child came Lilian did not become economically dependent on Tom. Indeed, quite the reverse; she worked to keep Tom, young Tom and *Freedom* going by running health-food stores in London and then Gloucestershire. In the 1920s and 1930s they all lived in Whiteway Colony, Gloucestershire, where Sylvia Pankhurst came to stay for a short time. Lilian got to like and admire Sylvia though she had an old animosity to Emmeline and Christabel. Whiteway was a self-governing community which ruled itself according to the Quaker custom of general agreement until conflict between anarchists and Marxists made voting necessary.

Tom died in 1938. Lilian continued her shop in Stroud through the war, despite bread queues and ration cards, until 1943 when she came to London to work for *War Commentary*, as the anarchist paper was called during the war. Her political activity continued – marching on Aldermaston from 1958 onwards, sitting down with Committee of 100 between 1961 and 1964 and getting arrested and fined yet again. She was a great encourager and helper, saving from her pension to give money to anarchist papers, political prisoners and other radical causes. *Freedom* sent her on a holiday to America in 1966 (to celebrate her ninetieth birthday – her first time in an airplane) where she toured around and met old friends.

She worked without expecting any recognition and remained open to new movements and ideas. Thus though she did not agree with some feminist ideas she was surprised and pleased when the interview by the Stratford group appeared in *Shrew* and she was quoted in my book *Hidden from History*. She did not seem to mind that I was not an anarchist but was distressed to find I wasn't a vegetarian and shook her head when I said I didn't like cheese.

But feminist or not, I certainly detected more than a twinkle when she described how she did the 'hack work' on *Voice of Labour*, and I said a lot of women on the left who went into women's liberation when it started had found themselves in that position. Her commitment to living her politics also brings her close to socialist feminism because we are struggling with internal as well as external transformation.

6. In Search of Carpenter

'In Search of Carpenter', *History Workshop Journal*, no. 3, spring 1977.

This search explains itself. It came out of the study I did of Edward Carpenter in *Socialism and the New Life* (with Jeff Weeks, Pluto, 1977).

The pub at Millthorpe near Sheffield was deserted with a 'For Sale' notice outside when I went there with friends on a grey March day in 1976. Just down the road there was 'Carpenter House' where Edward Carpenter had lived from the early 1880s until he moved to Guildford in 1922.

Going to visit Millthorpe, Dronfield and Totley was a geographical locating of a group of radicals, socialists and feminists who had lived in the area or visited while Carpenter was there. I have been and still am struggling with the more complicated social, political and personal placing of this group. They have had a curiously persistent fascination for me ever since I read a review of a biography of Havelock Ellis by Arthur Calder-Marshall when I was in my teens in the late 1950s. Carpenter, socialist and writer on sexual liberation, feminism and homosexuality; Ellis, pioneer sex psychologist; and Olive Schreiner, the South African feminist, author of *Story of an African Farm*, have all become important to me at different times rather like the kind of closeness you have with old friends. There is the waxing and waning of intimacy with the security of knowing they are always around. The friendship is getting on for being a twenty-year relationship which is longer than with any of my real friends. Information has accumulated in a haphazard kind of way as it does with old friends. I've slowly introduced myself to more and more of their circle until it has become like having an address book of the past. So I had to pinch myself as I walked on that foggy March day down the road to Millthorpe to remember I wasn't going to find them sitting there. It is one of the sadnesses of history for me – this loving intimacy with ghosts.

I was attracted first by the picture of Ellis as a medical student which was printed with the review, and then intrigued by the description of his mystical experience when he was a young man, alone in Sparkes Creek in Australia. Ellis had somehow come across James Hinton's *Life in Nature*. Hinton's vision of reconciliation between religious feeling and materialism illuminated Ellis's own spiritual anguish. He said,

> It acted with the swiftness of an electric contact; the dull aching tension was removed; the two opposing psychic tendencies were fused in delicious harmony, and my whole attitude to the universe was changed. It was no longer an attitude of hostility and dread, but of confidence and love.[1]

I was educated at a Methodist school and so accepted the idea of religious grace as part of common experience. Heart-warming, the infusion of light, treading air are described by Methodists as salvation by grace. I was already uneasy about Christianity. Reading Ellis's account of his experience was exciting. It seemed there was a kind of secular grace outside the Methodist Church. The inner witness was not bounded by John Wesley.

'In an instant the universe was changed for me. I trod on air',[2] Ellis had said. I recognised the simplicity of the language. I was tantalised by its familiarity with religious mystical statements. It is as if such experiences are so filled with feeling that there is no space for the detachment of language. Here were moments dissolving time and melting words until there was only light and ecstasy. I was torn by the longing to melt into the light and the longing to touch and shape the moment. I was already itchy with words, watching, describing, filled with nostalgic sadness for moments I could no longer enter. I knew even then the sadness of history, the final recognition that it is already the past. Only ecstasy eases this sadness.

Ellis appeared also to be something to do with sex. Now I was as interested in sex as I was in ecstasy and history, though unsure quite what it was. Perhaps this book would explain. So I pursued Ellis and the business of getting the book about him with great resolve. My mother, already accustomed to strange requests, bought me the biography for my sixteenth birthday. She did not know who Havelock Ellis was, but a friend of hers did, and let out a squeal of horror at my mother's innocence in buying me such a dirty book. My mother was a stubborn and thwarted lover of freedom and gave me Calder-Marshall's *Havelock Ellis* nonetheless. I read it, as I read everything then, searching for a total explanation of me, life, death and the universe.

In considered retrospect it is not a very good biography of Ellis but at the time it was revelatory. There were funny things in it about the relations between mothers and sons, the connections between urination and sexual pleasure, about infant sexuality and about lesbianism. It was the first time I realised that there was a psychological view of the world. Perhaps it seems remarkable that so many years after Freud it was possible to grow up in the English small-business northern middle class innocent of Oedipus. But it was so. Later I found a paperback edition of Ellis's *Psychology of Sex* and laboriously toiled through it in some bewilderment.

The picture of Olive Schreiner when she met Ellis was recognisable. There was a mixture of physical defiance and submission. You can feel her body at once pressing against her formal Victorian clothes, with no choice but to accept this outer confinement. When I read about her I felt close to her. Perhaps it was her loneliness and spiritual travail or her masochism or her idealism, or her vulnerability or her will – I wonder. When I read *Story of an African Farm* I remember feeling those floods of adolescent identification. Out there long ago and far away someone had felt like me and escaped. There must be others. Somewhere over the rainbow I might meet them.

At school a small and serious group formed in the sixth form. We were seekers of truth and higher things – though my friend Lindsay thought I lowered the spiritual tone sometimes and told me off for my earthy enthusiasm. Among other things, we read *Story of an African Farm*. Dressed in black stockings and wearing luminous pink lipstick we gained a reputation for eccentricity which we cultivated with care.

You are fickle at that age and I deserted Ellis and Schreiner for Kerouac, Ginsberg and the beats. I suppose I was rebelling by then rather than escaping because sixteen to seventeen is an eternity of a year and the whole world changed when I left school. Seventeen to nineteen I was too busy to remember Ellis and Schreiner and by my last year at university I was apparently matter of fact, settling the world as a Marxist, shedding the romantic chrysalis of ecstasy, but tending also towards dialectical loops of passion in the midst of order.

Edward Carpenter I had yet to meet really. He hadn't registered at all. But I was beginning to read about the history of the socialist movement. Initially this was the way I could understand Marxism: as a relationship between me and people in the past. I wanted to know how all these people came to their ideas and what happened to them when they acted upon them. It's a terrible way to think; it means you are never satisfied.

Then came a flurry after my finals. What could I do? I drifted half-heartedly off for jobs in Welwyn Garden City. I finally got a research studentship at Chelsea College working on the history of University Extension. University Extension was a movement for adult education which started in the early 1870s with the hope of educating all classes together. It happened that Edward Carpenter went off as an Extension lecturer. So we met again. He has been flitting in and out of my life with a kind of ghostly insistence ever since.

I must have been about twenty-one when Edward Thompson showed me his 'Homage to Tom Maguire', the account he had written of the emergence of socialism in Leeds.[3] Carpenter appears tangentially in this. He was a friend of Maguire's and of Alf Mattison, who helped Maguire organise the gas workers and was a frequent visitor to Millthorpe. Through Dorothy and Edward Thompson there was a living connection to those early days of West Riding socialism. Among others they had met Alf's wife Florence Mattison, still active in the Leeds labour movement. Edward Thompson started to tell me about that northern socialism, how for a time preoccupation with changing all forms of human relationships had been central in a working-class movement. Somehow the connection had broken and people like Carpenter had drifted away, become slightly cranky and inturned. I didn't really understand what he was saying then but could feel from the way he said it that it was somehow important.

In the Thompsons' house I used to explore the collection of books that had been assembled in the writing of *William Morris, Romantic to Revolutionary*. There was Olive Schreiner again and thin hardbacked pamphlets of working-class poetry including Tom Maguire's *Machine Room Chants*. There was a picture of Tom Maguire as a dark-moustached young man. In his poems the touches of humour and affection, especially for women workers, made me imagine the twinkles of understanding he must have shared with them. His death through poverty and alcohol while still young was tragic. I read an illustrated edition of Edward Carpenter's *My Days and Dreams* with the carefully studied photographs of Carpenter dressed in Walt Whitman hats and of his lovers George Hukin and George Merrill.

I went to the Sheffield local history library. I remember arriving at the station, getting lost then tramping up the hill. Little did I realise that I'd still be visiting it over ten years later. I began to pursue Carpenter's acquaintances, not just Ellis and Schreiner but Henry Salt, a vegetarian opponent of vivisection, and his wife Kate Salt who loved Edward Carpenter with a hopeless passion.[4] Carpenter appeared in a new dimension through his friendship with the Salts and Bernard Shaw. I felt I would have liked Kate Salt. She seemed to be even more overwhelmed than Olive Schreiner by the strain and effort of searching for freedom as a woman in the late nineteenth century. I was beginning to know Carpenter a little through his friends. There was a self-conscious grouping at King's College, Cambridge in the 1880s concerned with their love for one another and with the reconciliation of mysticism and social action.[5] The group included Charles Ashbee, who later became an architect, designed art nouveau jewellery and formed a Guild and School of Handicraft under Morris's influence, but hoped that pride in workmanship could be substituted for social revolution. There was his friend Roger Fry, unconvinced even then of the virtues of social commitment. G. Lowes Dickenson was also among this group and E.M. Forster who wrote Dickenson's biography was to become a kind of junior member. They stayed with Carpenter at Millthorpe, met his friends and went to socialist meetings with him. They were to draw back from his politics but continued to feel an identity with his writing about homosexuality and the East. Carpenter seemed to have formed a means of reconciling the outer and inner life. Lowes Dickenson asked him once how he achieved this unity and he replied breezily that 'he liked to hang out his red flag from the ground floor and then go up above to see how it looked'.[6] Also among his friends were the Walt Whitmanites of Bolton who included Charlie Sixsmith. They used to meet to honour Whitman, passing a loving cup between them. Carpenter went over to speak from the 1890s. He had quite a following in Bolton. I was beginning also to know his Sheffield friends in the Socialist Club but they remained a little hazy still.

None of this was very relevant to a thesis on University Extension. Indeed in 1966 and '67 I was wondering quite how it was relevant at all. It did mean that I knew there had once been a strange kind of socialism which had not been like the Bolsheviks. But that was as far as it went. I drew back from the more personal part of Edward Carpenter's life out of a kind of shyness, a restraint I've come to recognise in my own desire to communicate immediately and directly all at once. It is partly a puritan suspicion of whatever most delights me; a fear of my own fascinations. It is also, too, some knowingness about experiences I cannot stretch towards. Whatever the reason, I felt I had no business to be there peeping and prying.

So he floated away again; except not quite, because by this time I had read some of his writing, and liked particularly *Love's Coming of Age*. True his style is waffly and impressionistic but he wrote about ways of behaving that I could still recognise around me. I was absorbing some of his ideas. I learned also the outlines of his extraordinary life.

He came from an upper-middle-class family in Brighton. His father was radical in his politics and Edward Carpenter was brought up within the tolerant tenets of Broad Church Anglicanism. Instead of consenting to a conventional future he left a safe position as a curate in Cambridge to go and teach in University Extension in the early 1870s. Carpenter had already questioned some aspects of Victorian society, while he was still at university. He moved in radical and feminist circles, was influenced by republicanism and troubled by class conflict, by the Commune and the First International. Undoubtedly aware of the pressure for women's colleges at Cambridge, he was a believer in higher education for women on a wider scale. Another of his interests, like other radicals of his day, was in ideas of land nationalisation. But most immediately, Carpenter was unhappy about the social relations of people of his class. As a homosexual he was forced by the restraints of

Victorian society to conceal his feelings. In the writing of Walt Whitman he felt he could find recognition of open loving friendships. Carpenter wanted not just a political democracy but a personal democracy of feeling.

He did not find either through the University Extension Movement. The railway wanderings of the Extension lecturer were exhausting, the land-ladies' cooking indigestible and the structure of the Extension Movement reflected all too often the class hierarchies of the northern towns. By the late 1870s Carpenter was in urgent need of a calmer rhythm to his life. Through two of his students, a scythe-maker called Albert Fearnhough and Charles Fox, a small farmer, he went to live in the countryside at Bradway. He stayed for a time at Totley, at St George's Farm, a communal farming venture backed by John Ruskin which had failed. A friend of Carpenter's, George Pearson, had taken the lease after the communitarian group disintegrated and worked the farm with a Christian socialist, John Furniss. In 1882 Carpenter moved to Millthorpe. Originally a rural retreat the house was to become a centre for dissidents of all varieties.

Carpenter finished with lecturing and wrote a long Whitmanesque poem called *Towards Democracy*. In the early 1880s he moved towards socialism influenced particularly by Hyndman's *England for All*, and it was he who provided the money to launch the Social Democratic Federation paper *Justice*. He also became involved with a group concerned about inner spiritual change as well as with external social relationships – the Fellowship of the New Life. Through the Fellowship he met Havelock Ellis, still under the influence of James Hinton and beginning his empirical studies of sexual behaviour. He also met Olive Schreiner who was involved in a long emotional love for Ellis. Because of his sexual inhibition this love could never be physically fulfilled. When Ellis eventually married another member of the Fellowship, Edith Lees, they lived apart and did not have sexual intercourse because Edith Lees was physically attracted by women. Ellis, Schreiner, Lees, along with the Salts and Shaw, Ashbee, Lowes Dickenson and later Forster, were frequent visitors to Millthorpe. As the socialist movement took roots in the north, working-class visitors came too. Alf Mattison and Tom Maguire came from Leeds, others came from the Midlands and of course from Sheffield.

Carpenter had helped the Socialist Club to form in Sheffield. In the 1880s he spoke at meetings, going out on a bicycle to the small towns nearby. It was a very sociable politics. He used to play the harmonium at socialist meetings and he collected socialist songs together in a book called *Chants of*

Labour. This was characteristic of organisation in this period. The socialist movement created a whole network of cultural forms. There were cafés, meals for schoolchildren, rambles in the countryside. From the 1890s the *Clarion* cycling club and the *Clarion* choir continued this tradition.

There were close personal as well as political connections. One example was Carpenter's love for George Hukin, a razor-grinder who tried to organise a union among workers in the scattered workshops. There was also love between Bob Muirhead and James Brown, a tailor. They had settled near Millthorpe and were from the Glasgow Socialist League.

Carpenter met George Merrill, who was to be his companion for the rest of his life, in the early 1890s. Merrill came from the slums of Sheffield from a poor working-class family. He had led a wandering life and done a variety of jobs. Carpenter's manuscript account of Merrill's life gives a rare and fascinating glimpse into the existence of a working-class homosexual in the nineteenth century.

Early in 1891 the Socialist club had split and an anarchist-communist grouping appeared. Some of the Sheffield anarchists became involved in the Walsall bomb 'plot'. A police spy, Coulon, came to Sheffield, befriended Fred Charles an idealistic young anarchist who was attracted to Coulon's desperate enthusiasm for terrorism. Charles was later to be among those charged and imprisoned for making the plan of a bomb for Russian revolutionaries.

Carpenter was friendly with Charles but critical of his politics. He had become increasingly estranged from the Socialist club and the fights within it partly because of the ascendancy of the anarchist group, partly because of his visit to Ceylon and India in 1890–91 and his growing interest in Eastern religious experience. This, combined with his writing and his relationship with George Merrill, meant that he was no longer so active in local politics though he continued to speak for socialist groups all over the country and after the Independent Labour Party was formed he went again on propaganda outings particularly to mining communities. In the 1900s, he supported the Syndicalists, read the Guild Socialists' *The New Age*, and welcomed the suffrage movement. He continued to wear his sandals, take his sun baths and work in a shed by the brook in the garden.

Carpenter's advocacy of reducing needs by 'simplification of life' was undoubtedly serious and practically worked out. He outlined his ideas in an essay in 1886 published in *England's Ideal* the following year. In this he carefully explained how much it cost to maintain a person and how varnished floors upstairs and stone on the ground floor save housework. In the context of the later Victorian paraphernalia of large households with elaborate rituals and a complete chasm between life upstairs and life downstairs this streamlining of living was startling. 'Simplification of life' was at once a moral pursuit – it signified a better life – and a practical one – it was the means of ensuring some independence from the domestic labour of others. Carpenter's attempt to practise his own message appeared startling to contemporaries. It was after all unusual – in the 1880s and 1890s – to find a middle-class man who wandered the streets in sandals and broad hats copied from the American poet Walt Whitman, who tried to live intimately with people of a lower social station and combine intellectual and manual work.

He was unusual too in the variety of intellectual strands which combined in his person. Influences upon him ranged through Shelley, Whitman, Thoreau, Ruskin, Lewis Morgan, Olive Schreiner, William Morris, Hyndman, Buddha, Havelock Ellis, J.H. Noyes, Ulrichs, to Kraft Ebing and Moll. A motley crew, some of whom would have been disconcerted to find themselves in the same company. Carpenter did not only respond to socialism in the 1880s, he went on to challenge other aspects of Victorian orthodoxy. He queried for example the superior benefit of 'civilisation' over other cultures, the superiority too of Christianity over Eastern religions. He questioned the mechanical basis of scientific thinking and Darwinism. If his conclusions were vague and mystical he was at least conscious of a real problem – how to connect the question of the social control of the external world with the needs of human biology. He was aware that much that was seen as natural in his culture was not 'natural' in other cultures. He pointed out that behaviour regarded as criminal in one context was not seen as criminal in other cultures.

His writing on sexuality which began to appear from the 1890s was consistent with these concerns and with his belief in the virtue of released natural emotion. His main preoccupation, as in his earlier writings, was with the theme of separation. Sin is described as 'the sundering of one's being' in *Love's Coming of Age*.[7] His writings on the position of women were regarded as shocking in the 1890s but he went even further towards unrespectability when he touched upon the subject of homosexuality. The contract for *Love's Coming of Age* was abruptly cancelled by Fisher Unwin because of the publisher's fear that a pamphlet on 'Homogenic Love', Carpenter's term for homosexuality, would be included. Carpenter describes the fortunes of this pamphlet in his autobiography *My Days and Dreams*:

> I . . . had only a comparatively small number of copies struck off which were not sold but sent round pretty freely to those who I thought would be interested in the subject or able to contribute views or information upon it. My object in fact was to get in touch with others and to obtain material for future study or publication. Even in this quiet way the pamphlet created some alarm . . . but it is quite possible the matter would have ended there, if it had not been for the Oscar Wilde troubles. Wilde was arrested in April 1895 and from that moment a sheer panic prevailed over *all* questions of sex and especially of course questions of the 'intermediate sex'.[8]

It was not until the 1906 edition that *Love's Coming of Age* could include a plea for a freer homosexual as well as heterosexual love.

Carpenter believed that the liberation of women required both real economic freedom and a change of women's consciousness. 'Too long have women acted the part of mere appendages to the male, suppressing their own individuality and fostering their self-conceit.' It also necessitated 'her complete freedom as to the disposal of her sex'. The liberation of women was thus economic, social and sexual. He distinguished between the varied predicaments of the middle-class woman brought up to devote and sacrifice herself to a man or to play the hypocrite and pander to male egotism, of the working-class woman who faced exploitation at work and remorseless drudgery in the home, and of the prostitute who had to sell her body. His descriptions of their situations still ring true. Undoubtedly his influence at the time was partly because he was a most passionate describer and his ideas are brought home through these detailed cameos.

> Few men again realise or trouble themselves to realise, what a life this of the working housewife is. They are accustomed to look upon their own employment, whatever it may be, as 'work' (perhaps because it brings with it 'wages'); the woman's they regard as a kind of pastime. They forget what monotonous drudgery it really means, and yet what incessant forethought and care; they forget that the woman has no eight hours a day, that her work is always staring her in the face, and waiting for her, even on into the night; that the body is wearied, and the mind narrowed down 'scratched to death by rats and mice' in a perpetual round of petty cares. For not only does civilisation and multifarious invention (including smoke) make the burden of domestic life immensely complex but the point is that each housewife has to sustain this burden to herself in lonely effort. *ibid.*

He calls upon women to declare themselves free women, 'to insist on her right to speak, dress, think, act and above all to use her sex as she deems best' and on 'every man who really would respect his counterpart' to encourage women to be free. 'Let him never by word or deed tempt her to grant as a bargain what can only be precious as a gift; let him see her with pleasure stand a little aloof, let him help her gain her feet.' *ibid.*

It was consistent with Carpenter's faith in the ideal to appeal to lofty sentiments rather than self-interest. He expected people to have the strength to will themselves into freedom. Conservative contemporaries saw the kind of freedom he wanted as synonymous with sexual and social chaos. Carpenter pointed out that in fact the reality of the existing dual standard of morality was hypocrisy at one side and devastation and degradation at the other. He was confident that the new morality would not be destructive in its effects. His idea of sexuality was not synonymous with freedom for sensuality. His note on 'Preventative Checks to Population' in *Love's Coming of Age* indicates that he saw physical sexuality dwindling as love became more diffused in society. He retained the Christian division of higher and lower love, spiritual and physical just as he saw masculine and feminine characteristics as fixed. His views of the women who became feminists reflected this. In his opinion, among the feminists there were many women whose sexual and maternal 'instincts' were not strong. He said they were 'mannish' in 'temperament', or 'homogenic', that is, 'inclined to attachments to their own, rather than the opposite sex; some are ultra-rationalising and brain-cultured, to many, children are more or less a bore; to others man's sex-passion is a mere impertinence, which they do not understand, and whose place they consequently misjudge.'[9]

These stereotypes of feminism are similar to the fixed ideas he had about women generally. He tended to classify and idealise, presenting the free woman as a kind of spartan goddess striding athletically and asexually to liberation. These rigid definitions of masculinity and femininity affected not only his theories about women but also about homosexuals. He was influenced by Whitman's poetic assertions of homosexual comradeship as well as by the German writer, Karl Heinrich Ulrichs, who defined a male homosexual as a person with a female soul enclosed in a male body and a lesbian as someone with a male soul in a female body. Just as he challenged capitalism and civilisation, he was also critical of male-dominated culture. So by a peculiar combination of scepticism about dominant cultural values and a theory of fixed gender characteristics, he arrived at a theory of 'the intermediate sex' as a superior elite combining the best of both sexes and with a less sensual and more emotional nature than heterosexuals. Here again there were higher and lower types of homosexuals, the lower inclining towards sentimentality.[10] This tendency to stereotype and generalise impressionistically is in direct contrast to his recognition that sexuality took various forms in different societies and that there was an immense potential for individual diversity in human sexual activity. Nonetheless, it was while pursuing this kind of thinking of higher and lower beings that he stumbled upon the significance of the separation between sexual pleasure and sex for procreation. For while disapproving of existing forms of contraception because of their inconvenience for women, he advocated sustained intercourse without male orgasm as a 'preventative check'. He followed here not only Eastern religious ideas but a strand of American sexual radicalism which sought new forms of sexuality rather than contraception. In the 1870s, J.H. Noyes, the leader of a community in the United States had advocated 'male continence', the diversion of sperm through the urethra. Similar techniques were suggested again in Alice B. Stockham's book *Karezza* in the early 1900s.

Edward Carpenter's courage in asserting the rights of the 'intermediate sex' in the 1890s and early 1900s and his interest in sex and society led him into the relatively new fields of anthropology and psychology. In 1911 he published two anthropological studies of homosexuality. His own homosexuality served as a case history anonymously for Havelock Ellis's studies and was frankly acknowledged in Carpenter's autobiography in 1916. He drew on the ideas of Lewis Morgan, and Bebel, characteristically giving the evolutionary anthropological account of the connection between property and power a psychological slant. His theories of psychology were based on Ellis, Ulrichs, Kraft Ebing and Moll, but peppered with his own observations and poetic licence. He retained from his Broad Church Anglicanism a rejection of materialism and an Arminian conviction that truth can be attained by many routes. Eastern religious thought seemed to provide an alternative which avoided materialism and the Christian hierarchical dualism of spirit and matter. In the East they seemed to have found a place for pleasure without shame and a more easy relationship between mystical ecstasy and physical eroticism than the West. His eclectic quest makes his thought something of a lucky dip. It is easier to pull bits out than to understand the connections. But his struggle to make these connections was not merely theoretical, it was his whole life. The way he lived was a demonstration of what he thought and the two are inseparable. His influence, which was considerable, was less a matter of logic than of a cultural stance. He belonged to a radical and socialist milieu unhappy in late-nineteenth-century capitalism not only because things were unequal but because people were cut off from one another and from their own physical natures. His influence was at its height in the period before the First World War. It was international, going far beyond Yorkshire, Lancashire and the Midlands. He continued to be read and discussed in the 1920s, but already in the 1930s, when his friends produced a collection of biographical essays in his memory, his writing and ideas appeared a little dated. In the socialist movement he was remembered certainly until the Second World War and the hymn-like strains of 'England Arise' wafted around labour halls and pubs for some years after. I have not heard it since the mid-1960s when the Young Communist League used to meet in the Dolphin pub at Kings Cross and 'England Arise' could be heard along with the 'Internationale' and folk songs.

I have become more and more curious about the diversity of Carpenter's influence, and also in trying to retrace the process in which it was dissipated. Finding out about Carpenter and what became of his attempt to connect personal and sexual relationships and feelings to the struggle to change the external world is part of a much wider search for a broken revolutionary tradition which is relevant to the feminist movement, to sexual politics and to the evident weaknesses in our understanding of socialism. For instance, I've come across him and Ellis in reading about birth control and feminism; in the early twentieth century Carpenter helped found the British Society for the Study of Sex Psychology and a determined young feminist member called Stella Browne gave a talk in 1915 on women's sexuality. Stella Browne was a campaigner for birth control and abortion in Britain, she was friendly with the American Margaret Sanger, and she tried to connect her demand for women's sexual self-determination to ideas of workers' control. Sanger, under Ellis's influence, broke away from the revolutionary syndicalism in which she had been involved and concentrated on birth control as a single-issue reform. Both Ellis and Carpenter were read by other young radicals in Greenwich Village who were trying to live by a new morality. In the early twentieth century there was – however implicit – a connection between sexual and personal life and socialism. This connection became more remote after the First World War. Carpenter's links both with D.H. Lawrence and

E.M. Forster provide some clues about how this has happened.

There are striking similarities between Carpenter's ideas and Lawrence's and they have been described by Emile Delavenay in his *D.H. Lawrence and Edward Carpenter. A Study in Edwardian Transition*.[11] Both men had a horror of capitalism and of its distortion of all human social relationships. The places where they part company are interesting. The ambiguities in Carpenter's thought between mystical experience and social action, between the loss of individuality and the creation of a new elite of 'uranians', the intermediate sex which he thought would combine the best of 'femininity' and 'masculinity', are resolved by Lawrence in his rejection of the left, of feminism and of politics. Although there is no evidence that they ever met, there was a small group of advanced thinkers in Eastwood in the 1900s, some of whom knew Carpenter, or had read his books or heard him speak and Lawrence was friendly with some of them.

E.M. Forster did meet Carpenter and acknowledged his influence. In his 'Terminal Note' to *Maurice* Forster wrote that the book dated from 1913, and 'It was a direct result of a visit to Edward Carpenter at Millthorpe. Carpenter had a prestige that cannot easily be understood today.' Forster was drawn to him because 'he was a believer in the love of Comrades, whom he sometimes called Uranians. It was this last aspect of him that attracted me in my loneliness.'

He met Carpenter through Lowes Dickenson and saw him briefly as a saviour.

> It must have been on my second or third visit to the shrine that the spark was kindled and he and his comrade George Merrill combined to make a profound impression on me and to touch a creative spring. George Merrill also touched my backside — gently and just above the buttocks. I believe he touched most people's. The sensation was unusual and I still remember it, as I remember the position of a long vanished tooth. It was as much psychological as physical. It seemed to go straight through the small of my back, into my ideas without involving my thoughts. If it really did this it would have acted in strict accordance with Carpenter's yogified mysticism, and would prove that at that precise moment I had conceived.[12]

There are echoes of Carpenter in Forster's other works, particularly in *The Longest Journey*.

So I've slowly and irresistibly been drawn back to Edward Carpenter and his circle over the last few years. I've started to track them down obsessively now with street plans and ordnance survey maps, down Rockingham Street, Sheffield, where the secularists and socialists spoke and distributed their literature in the Hall of Science, down Pinstone Street where the socialists and anarchists held a meeting for the men from the ironworks in 1889, to Fargate where the police attacked one of the Socialist Club's early meetings. In Holly Street and Scotland Street there were radical and socialist cafés. Then off down the Totley Brook Road where the first sinister semidetached houses were noted in 1897. Through Totley railway station where the first intense look passed between George Merrill and Edward Carpenter and Merrill followed him down the footpath to Millthorpe. I did visit St George's farm with my friends in March and we stood in the drizzle talking to George Pearson, grandson of the other George Pearson. He said there is an avenue named after John Furniss nearby but I didn't find it.

I will have to go back and wander down the lanes where Carpenter and his friends strode in their Indian sandals, look at the hills where city-bred Alf Mattison was overwhelmed by the sunset. There are too many names in my address book of the past, unfinished acquaintances I cannot abandon.

It has not been an affair of chance of course this slow reappearance of Edward Carpenter, Havelock Ellis and Olive Schreiner in my life, nor is my fascination with the socialists and anarchists in Sheffield just nostalgia. The women's movement made me realise the significance of Carpenter's writing on feminism and feel other people would be interested in *Love's Coming of Age*. Since then I have found more and more people trying to track down Carpenter, his immediate circle and the ramifications of his influence. Gloden Dallas became interested in Maguire, Mattison and Isabella Ford and began finding and listening to people who could remember the early socialist and feminist movements in Leeds. Slowly the interconnections have emerged for me as I've listened to her talking. Ann Scott and Ruth First are working on Olive Schreiner, looking both at her feminism and her role in South African radical politics. Over in America Linda Gordon has written about Margaret Sanger and sent me copies of letters Sanger wrote to Stella Browne. Jane Lewis, far away in Western Ontario, Canada, has written about the 'new feminism', Keith Nield has written about Carpenter in the *Dictionary of Labour Biography*. The echoes continue. I learn that Havelock Ellis was being read by South Wales members of the Plebs League, by Glasgow workers in the 1920s, and by a Communist Party branch in the 1930s. Carpenter is remembered by a woman in the Labour Party in Glasgow as one of those 'poetic socialists' whose songs she recited at Socialist Sunday School. When you mention Carpenter to people in Sheffield they all say you should go and talk to Rony Robinson. He seems to have been haunted by the same ghost for he wrote a play called *Edward Carpenter Lives*.

But I wouldn't have begun to try and write about him myself if it had not been for friends I met through the Gay Culture Society at the London School of Economics. They printed a short duplicated pamphlet by Graeme Woolaston, now out of print, which discussed his views on homosexuality. He is critical of Carpenter's stereotyping of masculine and feminine, and of his elitist idealisation of the 'intermediate sex'. Nonetheless he shows his significance as a pioneer theorist of homosexuality. So I started a few years ago to write a small pamphlet on Edward Carpenter. The small pamphlet grew and grew. There appears to be no end to it. As I learn more and think more, people begin to show me things I hadn't noticed. Friends in men's groups for instance have made me think about Carpenter's rebellion against the notion of what a man of his time was allowed to be, his love for a man called Beck in Cambridge for example and the influence of Whitman. And talking to people about radical therapy I am beginning to wonder too if all those electric currents, and sensations above the buttocks are not so odd after all. Carpenter makes sense because of sexual politics; not only because he wrote about feminism and homosexuality but because he sought a new way of life in which there would be no longer

> The starving of human hearts, the denial of the human body and its needs, the huddling concealment of the body in clothes, the 'impure hush' on matters of sex, class-division, contempt of manual labour, and the cruel barring of women from every natural and useful expression of their lives.[13]

I want to find out what it was like to be a socialist in the late nineteenth and early twentieth century before the First War, before the Bolsheviks and before the Labour Party. I want to know what became of their concern to transform all aspects of relationships, and the preoccupation with living the new life in the present as well as the future. I want to learn about their emphasis upon a revolutionary culture, that lost practice of socialism which still carried a connection between personal life and external change.

I can see it was an idealist socialism which denied the material reality of class and sex and obscured conflict. It was a romantic socialism which nurtured the dream but had no strategy for its implementation. It was a gullible socialism too ready to believe the capitalist state was a neutral force for welfare and that if you waited long enough the Labour Party would bring you socialism. Where from indeed? It grew complacent in old age and took office or it was forced into bizarre nooks and communes making socialism in one parish. It was fearful of power, so accepted it on the terms of the governors. Or it fled. When anything nasty came along like fascism or Stalinism it did not know how to fight them or what to do. So it died a forgotten archaism, merely the occasion for an easy joke. All those voices raised,

> The long long night is over . . .
> Arise O England for the day is here.[14]

But the day wasn't and isn't, Carpenter would still be complaining we're being a long time about it. He and his friends may have become a little odd as the years went by. When political hopes splinter and part company the fragments appear distorted.

The rediscovery of Carpenter's socialism is nonetheless a reminder that many of our present concerns have a past. There was for example an implicit understanding among them that the kind of society they were after involved not just redistribution of wealth, or a change in the ownership of production, not even just workers' control of production but a transformation of all human relationships. They did not reduce what they wanted to economics because capitalism had forced us all into the cash nexus. They were against not only exploitation but the waste of human creative capacity which is the result of exploitation. So they were not dismissive of artistic endeavour. They wanted not only justice but beauty too. Socialism was to release the creativity and artistry in everyone. It was to heal the breach between the heart, the body and the mind.

So they did not think that economics or politics had a priority over art and culture. They were without a strategy, which makes them utopian; and the absence of a strategy made it easier for them to be absorbed within the gradualist politics of the Labour Party. However it also meant they developed a practice which has an increasingly contemporary relevance as modern capitalism invades more and more the personal, domestic domain. They understood that political commitment is not just a matter of education or even of experience through agitation. They saw socialism as an inner transformation which meant change in the here and now. They sought this new life in the everyday, in their stress on the warmth of fellowship and comradeship, in their clothes and furnishings, in a network of associations from cycling clubs to Socialist Sunday Schools, which could sustain them through isolation, hardship and despair.

Carpenter was not alone in his desire to live more simply and directly, to be more open with others and closer to natural rhythms destroyed by industry and the city. Others shared his hope that

> People should endeavour (more than they do) to express and liberate their *own* real and deeprooted needs and feelings. Then in doing so they will probably liberate and aid the expression of the lives of thousands of others; and so will have the pleasure of helping without the unpleasant sense of laying anyone under an obligation.[15]

We are rediscovering in a faltering way some of the understandings of this broken socialist tradition. It is not nostalgia for a cosy past or an archaism which would lift their politics intact, but because the present movement of capitalist society is pressing hard on our private consciousness, forcing intimacy into politics. Slowly and laboriously I can open my eyes and peer into that intense world of long ago with recognition. Those feelings in the small of the back seem no longer exclusive and private but part of a continuing opposition to capitalism. Even though it remains unclear quite how they fit into the agenda.

7. Mountain Women Blues

'Mountain Women Blues', *Spare Rib*, no. 27, 1975.

The mining districts of East Kentucky, Tennessee, Virginia and West Virginia have a double tradition of union militancy and music. In both these traditions women have had a crucial influence. The people came originally from English, Welsh, Scottish and Irish homes to farm and brought their songs with them. In the early part of this century industry moved south. Wages were low in the coal mines and the textile mills but were still more than could be earned on the farms. Attempts to organise met with bloody resistance from the employers. Many of the organisers were musicians and many were women. Songs like 'Girl of Constant Sorrow' and 'Which Side Are You On' were written by miner's wives who sang of the poverty and rebellion of the mining community. Some of the women were killed by National Guard troops and a textile worker and singer Ella Mae Wiggins murdered by gun thugs in 1929.

Aunt Molly Jackson was an organiser, singer and midwife who was recorded by Alan Lomax in 1939. She was born in 1880, the daughter of a coal miner and preacher and accompanied him to picket lines from the age of five. She married Jim Stewart, a miner, at fourteen, bearing two sons and training to be a midwife in Kentucky before she was seventeen.

Her work meant that she knew not only about union struggles but about women's personal and sexual lives. She delivered babies to live 'on lentil beans and corn bread in log cabins full of cracks so big you could throw big cats and dogs through'. She understood the difficulty of rearing children in such circumstances. She learned about the feuds and conflicts between families and the women's beliefs in witchcraft and charms. On the record she tells how Ol' Aunt Jane was suspected of being a witch and was greatly feared. A neighbour's cow used to stray onto Aunt Jane's corn, trampling it, and she threatened to curse it so it would fall down and never get up. Next time the cow strayed sure enough she waved her hands three times over its back and it fell down. The neighbour was in despair for she depended on its milk. Only when the cow's owner promised to make sure it would never get out onto Ol' Aunt Jane's corn again would she kick it and bring it back to life. The fear of witches produced its own defences. Some people were commonly held to have powers against the witches. These witch doctors could make counter spells to negate the charms of the witches. Aunt Molly says there were still witchdoctors in Kentucky in the thirties though not so many as there had been earlier.

After Jim Stewart died she married Bill Jackson and worked in Harlan County as a nurse and midwife until 1931 when she was crippled by an accident and forced to leave the county because of her unique activities. Writers like John Dos Passos and Theodore Dreiser came to investigate a killing during a strike in Harlan County and took Aunt Molly back to New York with them to raise money and propagandise. She lived on the Lower East Side in the Depression and although she still spoke and sang she felt uprooted and lonely away from Kentucky. She was seen either as a joke country person, hillbilly, or as a folk heroine – of interest not for herself but for what she symbolised politically.

Her songs on the record tell of the conditions in the mine and prisons, urging workers to join the union and resist. She sings too of political repression and how they called her a 'Rooshian red'. One of the saddest describes her poverty and isolation in New York.

> My heart it is breaking, it's Christmas
>   eve night
> I'm in the slums on the East Side without
>   any light
> I've no gas or electric to make myself a cup
>   of tea,
> Oh tell me fellow workers, how can this be?
>
> Tell me fellow workers, how can this be
> A home of the brave and the land of the
>   free
> Starvation and misery is all that is free
> For poor hard working masses like you
>   and me.

She had waited three days for the gas and electricity to be turned on. After she wrote the song it was nine o'clock at night and she went off to the police station to try and put in an emergency call. 'Listen, I'm a very sick person', she told the police captain. But he said they couldn't do anything because it was a holiday. Aunt Molly took a dim view of this. Just because Jesus Christ had decided to be born one thousand nine hundred and thirty-six years before she didn't see why she should sit without a cup of tea or a bite to eat. In Kentucky she had been poor but had friends, in New York this city poverty left you alone, cut off, cold and ignored.

After World War II came depression, not prosperity, for the mining industry was on the decline. The miners and their families lived on the dole or took off for cities like Cleveland, Cincinnati, Detroit, Akron, Baltimore, Minneapolis. The men went to work in the auto plants or the steel mills. They went with high hopes of finding the American dream. But they lived in wooden houses in the poorest part of town, coated in the grime from the great sprawling wasteland of factory plants. Nor was it just that they were poor; like Aunt Molly in New York, they found that city people looked down upon them as hillbillies.

Hazel Dickens and her eleven brothers and sisters went to Baltimore. Hazel worked at the Blue Jay Bar where she met Alice Gerrard, a traditional singer from the West Coast who had been to college in Ohio. Alice came from a different musical tradition, her mother had been a travelling classical singer and her father was also a musician. The friendship between the two women was partly an exchange and merging of these different traditions.

Alice Gerrard wrote 'You Gave Me a Song' thinking of Hazel.

> We used to be a family in our little cabin
> home
> Whose windows they are broken and
> whose chimneys dark and cold,
> But jobs were hard to find back then, it
> wasn't easy to survive
> So one by one we all left home to change
> our way of life.
>
> Got a job in the factory on the old
> assembly line;
> Gonna climb up on the hill and leave my
> past behind;
> But the only climbin' that I did was five
> flights up the stairs,
> And the past I thought I'd left behind
> went with me everywhere.

Hazel describes how important it was for her and the other country people from the south to meet Alice and recognise her respect for their music.

Alice's interest in folk and country music developed during the mid-fifties and increased enormously after settling in the Washington-Baltimore area where lots of southern people were living who had moved north to find work. And some were even playing their music and singing about the hills of home. They were very much in need of friendships and people who would appreciate their music. They found all of this in Alice's living room which became famous for all-night picking parties – where much good music was played and many good friendships were born.

The city people, interested in music found that for Hazel and the other southern exiles singing was not a removed culture but part of their life and the southerners responded to their interest. Alice calls it a 'two-way love affair'.

Hazel and Alice began singing bluegrass music together around 1962 in bars. Their songs continue the tradition of the women like Aunt Molly from the twenties and thirties. They sing like her of hardship and poverty, of men going to prison

> Weepin' like a Willow, mourning like a
> dove,
> There's a man up country that I really
> love

The imagery goes back even further to seventeenth-century English — they sing of exile from 'the green rolling hills of West Virginia . . . the nearest thing to heaven that I know', just as people from Ireland, Scotland and Wales have made songs about leaving places they have been brought up in but forced to leave because they can't find work.

> My daddy said, 'Don't ever be a miner.
> For a miner's grave is all you'll ever own.'
> Oh it's hard times everywhere, I can't find
> a dime to spare,
> These are the worst times I've ever known.
> So I'll move away into some crowded city;
> In some northern factory town you'll find
> me there;
> Though I leave the past behind I will
> never change my mind,
> These troubled times are more than I can
> bear.

The sadness and nostalgia would have the hopelessness of people who can never return. But they have added another verse about going home and changing things for the better.

> But some day I'll go back to West Virginia
> To the green rolling hills I love so well,
> Yes someday I'll go home and I know I'll

> right the wrongs
> And these troubled times will follow me no
> more.

This last verse is strangely prophetic for although there is still poverty and hardship in the Appalachia mining regions the oil crisis has meant that coal has come into its own again – black gold. Mines are being opened and the workers are in a stronger position to bargain with the companies. Some people are going back and they are going back now knowing how people live in the rest of America. They no longer accept that it is inevitable that they should live in wooden shacks with lavatories without flushes, die of black lung or that their sheriffs should be company stooges, their union leaders corrupt and in league with gun thugs. The women too, especially the younger women, have seen there are different ways of being a woman, that you do not need to be worn down with child-bearing by your early thirties and that women can live as equals with men, not as their slaves. One woman who picketed in support of miners on strike in Harlan County last autumn told a *New York Times* reporter, 'We seen all those women's libbers picketing on television and we didn't see why we couldn't too.'

But there is still a great gulf between the kinds of possibilities open to most women in the women's movement and the Appalachian country woman. Hazel and Alice carry both these consciousnesses. Uprooted themselves, they are still close enough to the mining communities to feel the lack of connection between dream and reality. Alice Gerrard thinks about this and describes a woman in a song by another country singer, Loretta Lynn, called 'One's On the Way': 'There she is in Topeka, in her house with the screen door banging. She reads about the modern way to live and hears about what's going on with women's lib. But meanwhile there are the kids, coffee boiling over on the stove, husband unexpectedly bringing a friend to dinner and another baby on the way. What about her?'

The combination of influences, musical and social make what they are doing not just an antiquarian reproduction of the songs of the period before the last war. They express changes as well as continuities for the lives of women who went to the cities and worked like they did in the late fifties and early sixties were still confined and stereotyped but very different from the textile mills in the south or being married to a miner. Here the alternative to marriage was there but it was still being used by men.

> Well there's more to her than powder and
>   paint,
> Than her peroxided, bleached-out hair;
> Well if she acts that way, it's cause you've
>   had your day;
> Don't put her down, you helped put her
>   there

Men have always used women as prostitutes. The difference as Hazel Dickens says is that more and more women – not only those in women's liberation – are challenging the man's right to decide what is moral.

'Why is her "sin" so much worse than his just because she was born a woman? Men can no longer place the burden of shame solely on the shoulders of women!'

It is hard too for women in their thirties and forties who grew up in the fifties trying to conform to the 'feminine' stereotype which was so strong and pervading then to adjust to the new ideas of how to be a woman. They can feel put down by men and cut off from younger women. Alice wrote 'Custom-Made Woman Blues' for women like this, caught in between, stranded in the meanwhile. She says 'It's not easy for lots of women these days, trying to find some sense and meaning to our lives after such long years of working to find it through our men or through society's definition of womanhood, which for more and more women is no longer proving to be enough.'

> Well I tried to be the kind of woman you
>   wanted me to be
> And it's not my fault that I tried to be
>   what I thought you wanted to see;
> Smiling face, shining hair, clothes that I
>   thought you'd like me to wear,
> Made to please and not to tease, it's the
>   custom-made woman blues.
>
> Yes I tried to be the kind of woman you
>   wanted me to be
> And I tried to see life your way and say all
>   the things you'd like me to say:

Loving thoughts, gentle hands, all
   guaranteed to keep a hold of your man;
Made to please and not to tease, it's the
   custom-made woman blues.

And now you say you're tired of me and
   all of those things I thought you wanted
   me to be;
It is true you want someone who knows
   how to think and do on her own?
Lord it's hard to realise the lessons I
   learned so young were nothing but lies;
Made to please and not to tease it's the custom-
   made woman blues.

Women who have been put down and conditioned into a femininity which is hostile and alien to many of their feelings as a person can become suspicious of any strong emotions with men. Hazel Dickens says when she met a man who was 'willing to accept me on an equal basis, I found it difficult to believe. Out of all these mixed feelings and ponderings I wrote "Pretty Bird" '. The song goes,

Fly away little pretty bird;
Fly fly away;
Fly away little pretty bird,
And pretty you'll always stay.

I see in your eyes a promise;
Your own tender love you'll bring;
But fly away little pretty bird,
Cold runneth the spring.

I cannot make you no promise;
Love is such a delicate thing;
Fly away little pretty bird,
For he'd only clip your wings. . . .'

The way oppression affects your innermost feelings is harder to work out and act clearly upon than the direct protest against material hardship, violence and injustice which Aunt Molly sings about. But the expression, and bringing to the surface of these mixed inner feelings is just as vital if we are to make a real home of the brave and land of the free.

8. 'Ladies Don't Stand on Picket Lines'

'Ladies Don't Stand On Picket Lines', *Miner*, September 1974. Both this article and no. 7. 'Mountain Women Blues' came out of a visit to Harlan County, Kentucky, in the summer of 1974 during the miners' strike.

The music of Aunt Molly Jackson and Hazel and Alice is issued by the Rounder Records Collective, 186 Willow Avenue, Somerville, Massachusetts 02144, USA. The story of the strike is told in the film 'Harlan County'.

Singing is a moving source for memory and mining communities all over the world have a great respect for memory.

> Though I leave the past behind I will never change my mind,
> These troubled times are more than I can bear

But we cannot settle down with memory. We must reveal and transform.

> Lord it's hard to realise the lessons I learned so young were
>   nothing but lies;
> Made to please not to tease it's the custom-made woman blues.

Sadly I must confess I cannot sing.

In September, 1973 180 miners working in the Brookside mine at Harlan in Kentucky went on strike for the right to join the United Mine Workers of America, the union which has been cleared of a corrupt leadership by the Miners for Democracy Movement. The strikers want a health programme, pensions for retired and injured miners, a better procedure for grievances and payment from the time they go underground, not from the time they start cutting.

These very basic demands carry with them much wider issues. Harlan is a town with a violent history. The coal owners employ gun thugs and a striker was shot and seriously wounded this July.

Amidst the beautiful green hills of Kentucky, the miners and their families live in company shacks, with inch-thin wooden walls and the best houses are made of corrugated iron. They are without proper lavatories, some of the houses are on stilts and the refuse gathers underneath until it is swept away when the river rises.

There is no longer any medical insurance with a union card. So a young woman in her thirties can be without teeth. The people are not just kept down by guns and poverty – power in the town is with the company. The law, the doctors and local bigwigs are company men. The school teachers, often the children of coal owners, are, with rare exceptions, hostile to the union and the history of the miners' and their wives' years of struggle for a decent life.

The grades of strikers' children mysteriously go down. A teacher tore a union button off one child and threw it to the ground. The strike divides the whole town and involves women and children as well as the men on strike.

The men had an injunction served on them and could not picket. Scabs continued to work the mines so the women held a march in support of the miners in the union. Betty Eldridge was among them.

> Most of us are just housewives and mothers. The ladies just sort of got together. We just had a march in Harlan. I didn't really know what picketing was. I didn't know they had so many people working back at Brookside. When we started picketing, the miners started leaving. The scabs, they thought we were pretty funny. We talked to them and we begged them and finally we just took sticks and switches and started whipping them.
>
> There were a lot of women at first, about a hundred. When we really started picketing we took our sticks with us. We had women from other communities come to help us. There was Lois Scott. She's real go git'em and she gives all the other ladies courage. But it's been long drawn out. By the end we didn't have a lot who picketed every day.

Minnie Lunsford, an old lady who can remember the union struggles and shootings in the thirties, went every day, whatever the weather. Betty said seeing Minnie turn out gave her courage when she longed to stay at home. Minnie dismissed this attention to her age. 'Age and looks don't count one bit. It's what you feel and what you have got in you and what you want other people to have – things that we never had – and what you believe in.'

On the first day of their picket, the state police arrived. The women realised they could not fight them, so they just lay on the ground. The police carried some of the women off to jail. There was nowhere for the children to go so they had to come, too.

Seven women spent two days in a jail with a dirt floor infested with bugs, refusing to mop the floor for their jailers and refusing to let the welfare take their children away, even though they hated having them there in such conditions.

When they came up before the court, the attitude of the men judging them was hardened for they were not only supporting strikers but taking action which placed them outside their place as women. Mary Widener, one of the imprisoned pickets, said: 'They didn't call us ladies or women or mothers, they called us females. Ladies don't stand on picket lines.'

After being arrested they formed the Brookside Women's Club to continue their support for the strike. They raised money by making coffee and doughnuts and using the money for medicine, for flowers for members of strikers' families in hospital, and for Christmas and Easter presents for the children.

The very existence of the women's club is an indication of the slow but significant changes which have occurred in women's position in the Kentucky mining community. Minnie Lunsford remembers in the thirties: 'We women had to stay in the house.'

The changes are most felt now in the personal relations between men and women and the strike and the women's club have had their effect. Betty Eldridge and Minnie Lunsford were both in favour of improvements. Betty said: 'As far as my husband's concerned, we share. Some men, they think they're God and He has given them women to slave for them. I think the women's liberation is a good thing, I do. Why shouldn't women get the same pay as men?'

Mary Widener was more doubtful, agreeing that Ray Widener had become a good coffee-maker as a result of the strike, but saying she'd been raised to be a housewife and taught to keep her place and had a husband to live with and so she couldn't say what she thought.

But her daughter Audie, aged seventeen and herself on strike as a waitress, was the most vehement of all about the effect of the strike.

9. Travellers in a Strange Country: Responses of Working-Class Students to the University Extension Movement – 1873–1910

◆◆◆◆◆◆

'Travellers in a Strange Country: Responses of Working-Class Students to the University Extension Movement – 1873–1910', *History Workshop Journal*, no. 12.' autumn 1981. This article, and the piece that follows (see p. 306), belong together not in time or in any conscious way but because both are examples of me boundary-defying and presuming to write about the feelings and ideas of a sex and class which is not my own. But the problem they tussle with is familiar, the relationship between personal rebellion and political consciousness.

'Travellers in a Strange Country' was based on my thesis on University Extension. It was greatly helped by the editing work of members of the *History Workshop Journal*.

◆◆◆◆◆◆

Introduction: The idea of fellowship

The University Extension Movement[1] – ancestor of both the Workers' Educational Association and of extramural classes today – was started at Cambridge university in 1873 by James Stuart, a young Scottish radical who was later to be the Liberal-Radical MP for the London constituency of Hackney. The initial impetus to the movement came from within the ancient universities (Oxford followed Cambridge by setting up an Extension department in 1878), and it drew on the doubts and restlessness of young university graduates. There were, for example, clergymen, such as Rev. Hudson Shaw from Oxford, influenced by a rejection of fundamentalism and dogmatism in the church, and seeking some more secular plane on which to exercise their Christian vision. Rev. Moore Ede was one of several Cambridge disciples of the economist Alfred Marshall, who took their questioning of classical economics into the early Extension classes. Then there were the early economic historians, for whom there was no place in the university curriculum, pioneering a more historical approach to economics, and practising a critique of *laissez faire*. William Cunningham and W.J. Ashley are influential examples.

Unlike the University settlement movement of the 1880s (with which it shared certain affinities), University Extension was not directed at the poor, nor even specifically at workers. Stuart's dream was that of educating all classes together. The movement proved important to middle-class women, but it never involved workers on the scale that the early organisers had hoped. They had underestimated the difficulty of educating all classes together. There was, however, success in certain centres, for instance Ancoats in Manchester. On the whole it was in the smaller industrial towns and villages that the movement took firmest root. In these places the audiences would be predominantly working class. In Hebden Bridge, for instance, a West Riding textile town, 600 people went to Hudson Shaw's history course in 1888 – out of a total population of 5,000. In places such as Hebden Bridge and Todmorden in Yorkshire, Backworth in Northumberland, Pucklechurch and Swindon in Gloucestershire, University Extension was able to build up a fairly continuous working-class constituency at its classes.

When I began work on University Extension in 1964, I knew of the sharp confrontation which had taken place earlier in the nineteenth century over political economy in the Mechanics Institutes and the later strike of the Ruskin College students in 1909. I assumed again that there would be similar evidence of an unsuccessful attempt to impose middle-class values and politics upon the working class and that there would be an outright rebellion among the worker students.

As I waded through University Extension reports and journals, biographies and collections of letters, local newspapers and cooperative bees I became more and more puzzled about this encounter between the upper-middle-class university men and the working-class students (mainly men). How was the extension of university education to be understood? Was it education for social citizenship, spiritual enlightenment through culture and fellowship?

Were worker students uplifted or 'nobbled'[2], patronised or enlightened, I wondered, as I attempted to trace their responses to the movement? I never found the decisive political rejection I had imagined would occur. I found instead a discomfort expressed in many different ways, accompanied by an excitement and a sense of liberation almost like religious conversion. I remained puzzled. Sometimes I fancied that I was sitting in some dimly lit hall and could hear a worker student's chair scraping as he came in late from shift work violating the reverent academic silence surrounding the Extension lecturer. Or perhaps there was a tension as shoulders braced against a complacent plumbiness in an upper-class voice. I could imagine these scrapings and bracings for they are still part of class, ideas, culture and language, and we live with them still.

We historians are trained to restrain our imaginations with evidence. Our craft depends not only on ears for echoes, but on a tracker's eye and a nose to sniff out the faintest footprints. Well, on one side there *was* the evidence for 'nobbling'. When University Extension was founded, the ancient universities were under attack. They needed to reform themselves in order to forestall criticism. There was concern that the new working-class voter should be steered down the paths of moderation. There was anxiety at the proposals made by Henry George for land nationalisation and later the ideas of socialists. The desire to moralise economic theory could be seen as a means of making it more acceptable to workers. The enthusiasm for the cooperative movement and for profit-sharing schemes and responsible trade unions could be interpreted as ways of countering the threat of socialism. There were enthusiasts for Empire as well as those who believed University Extension had an imperial mission.

On the other hand, there was no denying the genuinely radical beliefs of men like James Stuart and R.D. Roberts, an early organiser of the Extension movement with close links among the miners in the Northeast, or of A.H.D. Acland and Hudson Shaw. They were convinced that education was a basic democratic right which should be available to everyone. They did not regard workers as a threat but saw themselves as popular champions. 'There were too many who were afraid of the people and needlessly so,'[3] Acland told a Liberal meeting at Barnsley in 1885. Men like these honestly sought to serve 'the people', not to nobble or cajole.

Also anti-socialist sentiments could be in accord with the views of some workers. When Michael Sadler told cooperators in Wombwell in the same year that Extension lectures '. . . would be the best safeguard of the country from revolutionary and all wild socialism and would enable the people to pass from one stage of happiness to another',[4] he was not denounced but applauded. Either there were no wild Wombwell socialists yet or they had boycotted the meeting.

The liberal interest in cooperation was partly in response to socialism, but there were also internal tensions in liberalism between individualist and communitarian traditions. The Great Depression of the 1870s and '80s, and the changing shape of capitalist society undermined the faith of the liberal intelligentsia in *laissez faire*. There was a philosophical and political shift towards a more organic view of society, and some of these men and women were drawn into settlements or sometimes towards socialism. Many Extension supporters were attracted to a new social liberalism which accepted state intervention. This was not merely opportunist, it was sincerely a matter of conscience. They believed that they must combine social reforms and liberalism. They thought it was better to integrate the working class harmoniously and avoid class conflict and confrontation.

While this social liberalism was the major influence in University Extension there were other strands. There were the social imperialists like Cunningham and Ashley; anti-imperialists like J.A. Hobson. A.P. Laurie, who taught in the Northeast, was a follower of Henry George. Edward Carpenter was influenced by christian socialism, Mazzini and Walt Whitman, and was to become a buddhist and a socialist. He went into University Extension in the 1870s to merge with the mass of the people, but was frustrated to find that he mainly taught the middle class. In the 1880s Charles Ashbee was a student at King's College, Cambridge. Influenced by Carpenter, he wavered between a religious interpretation of socialism, mysticism, aesthetics and a personal longing for comradeship with workers. Graham Wallas, a Fabian, also worked in Extension.

Regardless of political objectives, the lecturers shared a great faith in the power of ideas to overcome social and economic divisions and problems. The generally stated purpose of University Extension was to uplift all classes through education. For most of the lecturers culture was inseparable from ethical improvement. This spiritual experience and intellectual expansion would infuse all aspects of social progress. It would transcend the petty materialism which fed radical envy and socialist materialism. Seekers of knowledge were to be transported together beyond the sordid circumstances of daily life.

According to the dominant ethos in University Extension the values they were trying to impart were universal values; the great truths which the working class must become sufficiently mature to inherit. The effort to control and integrate the new electorate was not too difficult to spot and resist in the superficial sense of an argument about political ideas. It was much harder to expose and unravel these lofty cultural ideals. There was a bias at work, not in the sense of a *united* plot to 'nobble', but in a profound conviction which the majority of lecturers shared that the late-Victorian upper-class male's ideals represented the highest attainment of civilisation.

However, it should also be said in fairness to some of the Extension lecturers that this confidence in the culture of the middle class was sometimes checked by an awareness of the remoteness of the Extension movement from the working class and several attempts were made to connect to workers' institutions before the formation of the Workers' Educational Association in 1903 made this an explicit policy. This really involved the beginnings of a recognition that the working class possessed its own culture and that adult education for workers involved negotiating with labour movement institutions like trade unions and coops. Sheffield Scissor Grinders bought tickets for Moore Ede's political economy classes in 1874. The Durham miners gave their support to local Extension courses in 1883. Tom Mann and John Burns spoke at Extension meetings in the early 1890s. Lecturers like A.H.D. Acland, Sadler, Hudson Shaw and Cosmo Gordon Lang were involved in the cooperative movement. Graham Wallas and J.A. Hobson worked closely with the Woolwich Independent Labour Party.

Moreover, some lecturers were in fact critical of the rather ethereal nature of the transcendent ideal of culture. There were attempts to bring it down to earth. The economic historian, Cunningham, for example, stressed education as a way of bringing more meaning to workers' everyday life, rather than trying to escape from it. Hudson Shaw and S.R. Gardiner who lectured in East London took a similar approach in their history teaching. It was implicit in popular science classes and lectures which taught miners geology and working-class women hygiene and health. C.R. Ashbee, concerned about the destructive effects of the division of labour, devised syllabuses on art history which combined aesthetics with economics, geography, science and industrial history.

Another vital impetus behind University Extension was the longing for fellowship and communication across the class divide. For Stuart and his colleagues, the object of the movement was to provide an education which dissolved class distinctions, not only in the contents of the courses, but in the very act of attending classes. Cultural enlightenment and social harmony were seen as inseparable from the personal experience of fellowship.

Consequently, the relationship between men of different classes in Extension cannot only be understood in terms of political and social or cultural values, or even as a secularised evangelicalism. The infinitely complex nuances of the British class system were always evident. This was not just a matter of the intentions of the teachers. Some of the lecturers involved with worker students were ready to criticise the limitations of a purely academic culture with its restricted values and forms of communication. But this did not always mean that they could themselves get over their ideas to working-class audiences. Tom Mann told an Extension meeting in 1893 that working men and women did not come to classes because

> The lecturers have great difficulty in setting forth the case with that vigour and simplicity of language that workmen insist upon. . . . The airiness of manner which in a common room enables him to express serious opinions without being condemned as an 'enthusiast' and a 'bore' is out of place with a popular audience.[5]

Some of the university men must have squirmed a little in their seats but they applauded all the same. Some were to take these criticisms to heart and attempt to negotiate workers' cultural experience in these personal ways, as well as seeking formal accord with the public institutions of labour.

The longing for fellowship came not only from a desire to be of service, but also because some of the upper-middle-class men were clearly unhappy in the class in which they had been raised. Sometimes they sought still an ideal; a pale pink populist chimera or some embodiment of the dignity of labour, and so it could be said that they still sought a form of control by imposing their ideal upon the working class. But the dissatisfaction and the yearning were still real enough.

Edward Carpenter wrote in a manuscript poem, while he was working in Extension in the North:

> White skin, soft hands,
> Everywhere the thrust of alienation
> The bond of redemption nowhere.[6]

He and R.D. Roberts were both influenced by Walt Whitman's love of frank comradeship. After an upper-class dinner party, Michael Sadler commented: 'There was an ice of unreality over all the folks.'[7] In the mid 1880s, Ashbee longed to 'shake off this churlish gentility'.[8] J.C. Powys, a literature lecturer in Extension, wrote of his inner spirit 'fumbling to fill itself out and round itself off by a sort of devotional transmigration of the soul into the lives of soldiers, sailors, peasants and factory hands'. More self-conscious than the earlier transmigrators, he added: 'Although you may call me a humbug, these labourers do not.'[9]

Whatever the views of Powys's 'labourers', fellowship had various meanings. Sadler hastened to explain to an Extension soirée in Hebden Bridge in 1889 that,

> . . . he did not want anyone to run away with the idea that he believed in anything like absolute equality, but . . . in the possibility of frank democratic fellowship.[10]

However, for Leonard Montefiore and Edward Carpenter in the 1870s, and for Hudson Shaw and Ashbee later, University Extension did involve equality and making important changes in how they lived. Montefiore, influenced by utopian communism in the United States, went to live in East London; Carpenter to a cottage in the country. Hudson Shaw quarrelled with the church establishment and gave up a living. Ashbee formed a guild of handicraft. Less dramatically, other more conservative Extension lecturers, like J.A.R. Marriott, W.A.S. Hewins, Rev. Cosmo Gordon Lang, were all deeply affected personally by the responses of worker students. If they entered the movement with an idealised picture of the working class, many of them learned painfully of the intricate dimensions to culture and class consciousness, which were the everyday reality of their working-class and lower-middle-class students. The worker students were not the only travellers in a strange country.

Students: 'The elite of the working class'?

For their part working-class students who became involved were not just passively 'nobbled' or passively ennobled. Their responses were far more complex.

There are many untold stories. We do not know the feelings of men and women who attended the odd lecture and went away uncomfortable or angry. We can imagine their dismay behind the shrinking numbers who attended Moore Ede's early classes on political economy. But there are many statements about the practical difficulties facing the students who remained. They have left accounts of their own sense of class position and culture, their response to lecturers politically and personally. Their own educational idealism was real enough but they could not ignore economic hardship. There was considerable confusion about knowledge and ideas on the one hand and the understandings which came from life. The purpose of education also remained unclear. Knowledge was associated with moral self-control, with power as a class, with spiritual enlightenment, with cross-class fellowship and material self-improvement. University Extension made some fervent converts but Stuart's dream of educating the classes together remained unrealised.

Extension students had to face very obvious economic and physical difficulties to attend courses. R.D. Roberts received this letter from a working man at a centre where 6s was being charged:

> How can you expect such as myself to keep a house over my head, support and keep things respectable, and be able to pay 6s down on the nail for a course of lectures out of a little over a pound a week.[11]

He had tried paying by instalments but found this was not possible. So he had paid 3s to attend just the lectures and not classes:

> I and many other working men are grasping for what fell from the lips of the German poet Goethe viz, 'More light', but when we have to purchase it so dearly I am afraid we shall have to remain in darkness.[12]

He mentioned the special problems of friends with large families. Other workers pointed out there was also the expense of books and travel on top of the courses. Shift work, overtime, fluctuations in trade, the need to change jobs made it difficult to attend regularly. With a stiffness which masked a desperation difficult to communicate to the middle-class students and teachers Joseph Emes, a miner from Pucklechurch, Gloucestershire, told the university congress in 1894:

> . . . they were exhausted by a hard day's work and there were family and domestic duties to be done in the evening; it was also detrimental to serious study to be confined with several others in one room where the necessary quietness was not to be had.[13]

Monotonous clerical work meant a different kind of exhaustion. Ramsden Balmforth, a Fabian working as a clerk for the Huddersfield Cooperative Society, wrote to Graham Wallas:

> As to the 'wider life' you speak of you make me smile sadly . . . I am *hors de combat* just now feeling quite limp and almost helpless with overwork. It is as much as I can do to scrape through the daily work which brings bread and butter — the feeling of mental weariness is quite maddening.[14]

Students walked for miles in country and pit districts to reach classes. Then they sometimes were not within reach of a library or the local free library did not stock the new books the university men put on their syllabuses.

Students who struggled through all this were clearly a rather special group within the working class. There was a sense of superiority. This was not merely a matter of income or even of occupation; learning, religion, political understanding, morality as well as family and community traditions were also involved. There were tremendous regional variations. Northern mining communities were quite different from East London. A worker in small Yorkshire and Lancashire towns had a very different cultural inheritance from someone in a small town in the South.

Hebden Bridge was a strong working-class centre with which Sadler, Cosmo Gordon Lang and Hudson Shaw were closely connected. Dissent was still a vital question. After a lecture on Oliver Cromwell in 1889 the class debated the execution of King Charles. Tempers rose high about the religious and social implications of the English Civil War. They voted on the issue with a majority of hands in favour of beheading him as a traitor.[15]

Joseph Greenwood and John Hartley were cooperators and members of the Hebden Bridge Industrial Society. As boys they could remember Chartism. Hartley had been a supporter of Feargus O'Connor's land scheme and in the 1840s had been among a group of workers planning to form a community in America. Greenwood had been influenced by Holyoake, the pioneer cooperator and and freethinker. Dissent was still a force in the workshops when they were young men. Joseph Greenwood's father had been a handloom weaver. As a child he read the Bible, *Pilgrim's Progress* and *Robinson Crusoe*. All three had left their mark. Greenwood and Hartley met through the temperance movement and both became local supporters of Extension.

Greenwood made an illuminating assessment of what constituted superiority within the local working class:

> We were fortunate at Hebden Bridge, we had two silk mills and the silk weavers were the elite of the working class. They were Radicals in advance of their time. They were temperance reformers, educationalists and cooperators, and in some way or other connected with the various places of worship and the Sunday Schools.[16]

He does not mention the women of Hebden Bridge but we know from an amusing account in Cosmo Gordon Lang's biography that they had their own views of status and etiquette. They were scandalised when young Beatrice Potter (Webb) arrived and not only walked with the men discussing cooperation but carried on when the other women, uncomfortable in their long dresses and elastic-sided boots, gave up. 'Then one guardian of the proprieties turned to another and said grimly: "the impudent huzzy" (sic).'[17]

The culture and values of the superior workers were distinct from those of the lower middle class, though sometimes through elementary education the rising generation would pass over as clerks or teachers. However, the world of the upper middle class was remote indeed. It is difficult to grasp in retrospect the impact of the encounter between these two worlds.

Although Extension students tended to be recruited from the upper working class, this could still imply a very wide range of cultural and political associations as well as differences between and within families. Samuel Fielding, another Hebden Bridge Extension student, was a member of the Calder Valley Poets, local Band of Hope, mutual improvement classes and the Good Templar Lodge. Ramsden and his brother Owen Balmforth in Huddersfield were from a Chartist and Secularist background. Owen, the elder brother, went through Secular Sunday School, the Huddersfield Republican Society, the Coop, the Liberal Association. He had attended the Mechanics Institute as well as University Extension. Ramsden was involved in Fabianism and Unitarianism.[18] Thomas Okey, a basket maker in the Whitechapel classes in the 1870s, had been influenced by secularism, republicanism and German socialists in Soho. He was sympathetic to the anarchists.[19]

The development of a national system of education was just beginning to create a new and awkward group of men and women who taught in the schools. They were frequently attracted to Extension courses. One of these students, F.H. Spencer, has described his education in his autobiography *An Inspector's Testament*. Spencer was from Swindon, a pupil teacher who eventually became an inspector but his background was that of the superior worker. He went to University Extension lectures as a boy of sixteen in his native town of Swindon, and gazed hopelessly at the beautiful twenty-year-old daughter of a Jewish watchmaker.

Born in 1872, he had been brought up according to the stern and independent tenets of the 'respectable' upper working class, and taught,

> . . . to be clean, to be proud, to respect learning, to read, to remember that there were great works of art in the world, though none to be seen in Swindon, that we must never take a penny as a tip except from relations or personal friends and that we must remember that our name was Spencer, that we were as good as anybody else and better than most, . . . and that no Tory could be a good man.[20]

However, there was always an unspoken conflict of values within the family. His father, who worked in the G.W.R. factory, was of Lancashire copyholder stock, a serious man and a radical: he was an active member of the Mechanics Institute, where he disapproved of billiards and dancing. He was interested in church architecture and insistent on tidiness in the home. His mother in contrast was dreamy, inclined to religious musing, careless about housework. Her family were all house decorators, artistic, ineffective and given to drink, eloquence and generosity. The son inclined towards his mother.

As for intellectual influences, there were a few books his father had brought from Lancashire, which included the Bible, Shakespeare, *The Ancient Mariner, The Principles of Elocution.* An evangelical watermonger sold tracts along with his water, and possibly through him, *Jessica's First Prayer* and *The Lamplighter* entered the house. Outside home, he went through the dame school, the Junior Templars run by the Primitive Methodists, the Congregational Band of Hope, and discovered the *Boys Own Paper* at Sanford St. Young Men's Friendly Society. Finally of course, there was the Board School.

Spencer progressed through the standards, through copy books to Newton's *Laws of Motion* (which he learnt by heart), army drill and bowdlerised *Henry V.* At fourteen he became a pupil teacher, soon afterwards catching the football fever. His reading was a mixture of sports papers, Shakespeare and classical novels. He possessed a fragmentary scientific knowledge and snippets of information from the *Boys Own Paper* and *Whittaker's Almanac.*

His social experience did not extend beyond the working and lower middle classes, but he learned to distinguish the extremely complicated stratifications and distinctions dividing them, and the way the various religious denominations constituted a 'horizontal classification' coinciding '. . . with the social levels of the skilled and unskilled trades'.[21]

It was really the social organisation of the chapel which did most to educate him. There were the Band of Hope dramatic entertainments, where he recited *Mary the Maid of the Inn*, performances of the *Messiah* and *Elijah.* Extremely important was the Young Men's Friendly Society debating and discussion group which met every Saturday. It consisted of the minister, the W.H. Smith bookstall man, a speculative builder and his son, a medical student, two educated engineers, the chief clerk of the locomotive works, several draughtsmen of superior rank, a carpenter, some boy apprentices and various girls and women occupied and unoccupied, married and single, 'who in those days sat appropriately silent'. While the meetings were usually on scientific topics some of them were interested in social questions, and discussed Capital, Labour and Socialism. 'Party-political' subjects were forbidden, but for most of the members radicalism went with their nonconformity. The effect of the group on Spencer was profound. It gave him the stimulus to read, the opportunity to express his ideas to an audience, and the general liberalising effect of contact with other peoples' ideas.

There were thus diverse strains of enlightenment at hand in Swindon – '. . . in this environment of an outwardly monotonous town of small working-class dwellings, run up higgledy-piggledy by speculative builders . . .'.[22]

However, his teaching took him out of Swindon, first for training and then for work. In 1894 he got a job in Woolwich, went to University Extension lectures again, and becoming friendly with C.H. Grinling, an Independent Labour Party member, he joined the study group which met in his house.

The case of F.H. Spencer illustrated well the complexities within the situation of those men and women, by origin working class, propelled through Board School and pupil-teacherdom to the periphery of the umbrella-carrying society. He combined a strong cultural identification with the 'people' and a sense of separateness from the upper middle class, with a consciousness of his own social distinctiveness from the upper strata of the working class.

Local organisers made spasmodic efforts to broaden the base of working-class support, either by starting more informal reading circles or by offering science classes which were felt to be of more practical use and likely to attract less intellectually dedicated workers. In Nottingham, for instance, the decision was taken not to hold classes in the summer as working hours were longest then. On the whole, though, even those lecturers who resisted the elitist views that higher education for the workers meant a vulgarising of culture still saw the movement as reaching only a minority of the superior sort of workman. They hoped that culture and political enlightenment would somehow percolate down to the lower classes.

There was little concern to reach working-class women or any realisation that their situation differed in significant ways from that of male workers. The occasional references to working women students were evidently exceptional. When James Stuart gave his introductory lecture at Crewe in 1867 on 'Meteors' women came with their children in their arms because they had nowhere to leave them.[23] The idea that caring for children might be an obstacle to women coming to classes did not appear to trouble Extension organisers or working-class men students. However, there was at least one attempt to think of a choice of subject for working-class women though it was men making the decision. The first classes organised by the Cambridge Society were in the North Midlands.[24] Nottingham Mechanics Institute took the initiative in asking for classes from the university and a committee of workmen did a survey of the educational situation for the working class in the town and suggested that working-class women might attend a class on the laws of health. The tutor Rev. Moore Ede reported to *Syndicate* in 1874 that six women of 'the milliner class' had been among the fifty-eight candidates in political economy and literature.[25] Very few women of the 'artisan class' had attended but a lady had given four lectures specially for women and about 250 women had come, mainly factory and warehouse hands. It is possible that working women were unable to attend the longer course for quite straightforward financial reasons. If classes were expensive for a male worker they were prohibitive for women. In Nottingham, a town of traditional female employment in the early 1870s, a male lacemaker could earn £1–5s. to £1–15s., but women were getting 8s. to 10s. Women just like the men presumably felt uncomfortable in middle-class company and as the Nottingham centre became a local college which was to be Nottingham University it became increasingly middle class. This was a pattern which was repeated whenever local centres turned into colleges. Working men as well as women were driven out. The success of the women's short course was remarkable. But I have not found any indications that it was repeated.

Women must have felt the same embarrassment about written work as the men. But it was even harder for them to do it at home because of the greater domestic demands on their time. In 1893 Hudson Shaw mentioned the difficulty of persuading students to do written work in a course which included working-class women.[26] The lack of working-class women students in Extension was undoubtedly due partly to the same reasons that it was difficult to attract men, with the added economic and social predicament of women and the prevailing assumption that there was no need to educate women. The exception were the pupil teachers because their education could be justified as vocational. The phrase 'working women' was sometimes used to include elementary teachers – a recognition that the class position of this new social group was ambiguous. Women teachers were distinct both from the 'milliner class' and from 'the ladies'. Apart from young women teachers

279

University Extension was largely confined to filling the needs of middle-class women. While this was a real and pressing need it presented quite a different educational problem than the education of women from the working class.

'The broadening of the spirit' . . .

Communities in which men worked in the same trade, like mining, or which already possessed a tradition of working-class self-education could become successful centres of Extension, but in these workers controlled both the choice of subject and the local organising. On the other hand, elsewhere there was a fierce guarding of autonomy in working-class education; in Rochdale, for instance, cooperators suspected the Extension movement, on class grounds, as education from above. Local committees dominated by the middle class could fan this suspicion with patronage and snobbery, thwarting the idealism of the young university lecturers. Or the lecturers themselves could tread on class corns.

But it was not really their politics but their personal attitudes to worker students which made them popular or unpopular. Students noted distance, arrogance, abstraction rather than ideology or politics on the whole. Though there was suspicion of the content of subjects like political economy and history, students were prepared to take issue with lecturers about their views. Indeed, many of the men who came to Extension classes were experienced in debate and disputation. It was rather the manner of the lecturer which generated hostility or support. According to *Oldham Industrial Cooperative Record*, Rev. Hudson Shaw 'won the heads and hearts of thousands of hard-headed Oldhamites, by his strong, simple, homely manner, passionate earnestness, and clear grasp of his subject'.[27]

Worker students resented complacent ignorance about working-class life but were extremely open to lecturers like Hudson Shaw, Cosmo Gordon Lang and later, Tawney, who were ready to relate and connect their subjects to the students' own experience. Hudson Shaw's version of history as the progressive unfolding of liberty and social altruism were applauded enthusiastically by radical workers in the North. He 'carried his audiences from the material to the higher things of life'.[28]

It was not a simple question of left and right for they chose their heroes and mentors from both camps higgledy-piggledy – King Alfred and Oliver Cromwell, John Wesley or William Morris, Ruskin, Dante, Carlyle, the historian J.H. Green, Thomas Hardy, Dickens. The forces of light were a mixed bunch indeed. They were important because they seemed to indicate a world which was not based on profit and gain. A Manchester socialist, a clerk in a foundry works, asserted

> I'm dead against materialism, though I've no religion in my composition. I want to live in my spirit. I want to feel more, and to see more deeply into the truth of things.[29]

Men who struggled so hard in circumstances of such difficulty delighted in intellectual stimulus and care. Joseph Emes said that before University Extension he had been 'lost in the great Forest of Ignorance'.[30] Education was valued because it was acquired so painfully, hewn out of granite, pressed into narrow crevices. It carried an inner meaning beyond words or the acquisition of knowledge. It brought with it a vague and unspecific promise of a more generous way of living, an assertion that there was more to life than work and dying, that even among the despised and neglected there was dignity and hope. According to the Manchester socialist, 'when a man begins to get education, he soon sees that the main thing in life is the broadening of the spirit'.[31] In the real world the working-class intellectual might be ignored and of no consequence but there was equality and comradeship to compensate in this world of the mind. The idealism of the university men thus met the idealism of a specific group of workers. Both came from differing sources but had enough in common for some kind of communication.

The relationship between lecturers and students was important to both as a glimpse of a relationship in which the bond was thought rather than cash. The overwhelmingly masculine composition of working-class audiences perhaps made this easier. It was quite literally an extension of the intellectual setting of Oxford and Cambridge with the same unreality superimposed upon the hidden reality of lives consumed in labour. But it provided a context in which class division could be transcended in the realm of mind. In this sense the movement came to have a personal hold on some working men because it fulfilled a genuine and urgent emotional need.

A new way of seeing . . .

University Extension never came near to a significant penetration of the corporate fastness of the working class, but it acted on individual students with a remarkable intensity. Just as it was something more than a pedagogic exercise for the lecturers, it represented for working students a whole new way of seeing, bringing qualitatively different levels of experience. The revelatory, transforming nature of higher education comes through in the quasi-religious earnestness of their response. Thus a Canning Town audience listened to the lecturer with 'almost painful attention' and were 'intolerant of any interruption' taking up his points keenly.[32] A student in the Northeast went to meet R.D. Roberts outside church to confirm whether he was really a successful candidate in an exam, exclaiming when he found it was true: 'Eh, but it's a proud man I am today.' After a geology course a Cleveland miner wrote: 'I have lived in Cleveland about eighteen years of my life, but find it true that I am now in a strange country. I mean however to know it.'[33] Higher education not only revealed the contours of a 'strange country', it brought a kind of spiritual deliverance. Men spoke of education in terms of religious conversion. In 1874 one of the early lecturers from Cambridge, T.J. Lawrence, was told by a working man student in the Midlands, Mr Day, that,

> . . . He had got into a new life, that it talked to him as he went along the street and that he had obtained a new set of ideas . . . No doubt it did make him feel a man as must result from the cultivation of that part of man which raised him above the brutes.[34]

In the early years at Hull a working joiner attended regularly for six years except when he was ill:

> I cannot tell how much I owe to these lectures. They have worked a revolution in my life. I am able to take broader views of questions and my interests are widened. My life is altogether brighter and happier. There is something about these University Lecturers different from Science and Art Classes. I can't say exactly what it is, but they do more for you and have more life in them.[35]

In 1892 Tom Mann told a conference on 'The Extension of University Teaching Among Workmen' that as a trades unionist in the Labour Movement he recognised 'a real desire not only to speak of brotherhood and sisterhood, but to strive honestly to live it'. Amidst applause he said he believed these were the aims of University Extension as well.[36]

This educational idealism could have the effect which many of the lecturers and organisers desired of making workers reject class hatred or irreligion, but such a response was complex and the process of political chastening did not necessarily mean that men ceased to be socialists or secularists. It was rather that there was some attachment to the world inhabited by the upper middle class through an attachment to the intellectual culture of that class. Admiration for aspects of a culture was difficult to disentangle from admiration for the possessors of that culture. They held the standards of what was great and grand and good in the world. How could they be evil men when they held beauty?

If the University Extension Movement provided an outlet for lecturers preoccupied with social and political unease and religious doubt, it answered a corresponding need among workers who might be influenced by free thought arguments but who were unable emotionally to accept what appeared to be the bleak world of secularism. The outer forms of religious certainty gave way but the emotional and moral responses remained bound to christianity. Among the upper-middle-class intellectuals this created an opening for the vague good will of the new liberalism in which the state was benefactor and neutral mediator between opposing interests. In religious terms this attachment to the internal idiom of faith could seek certainty in anglo-catholicism and social roots in a deep yearning for community, or move towards the tolerant erastianism of the broad church. The majority of workers were untouched by this poignant liberal agony but there was a minority of thinking and earnest men searching for an intellectual and spiritual community who were exposed in a very different context to the terror of losing their religion. Christian workers had to contend with working-class secularism. Frederick Rogers confronted this in Soho and the East End. University Extension provided him with an alternative to the materialism of the secularists and socialists and the snobbery and narrowness of middle-class churchgoers.

Rogers was a member of the original Extension committee in Whitechapel, attending lectures on science, on political economy and S.R. Gardiner's courses on history. He became a great admirer of Gardiner's work. Through the committee he developed a friendship with Leonard Montefiore. When Toynbee Hall started he became closely involved in the settlement and with Canon Barnett.[37] He was a member and officer of the Vellum Binders union and a cooperator. In 1898 he was appointed organising secretary to the National Pensions Committee and was largely instrumental in the passing of the 1908 Pensions Act.[38]

Rogers was born in Whitechapel in 1846. His father was a sailor turned linen draper's assistant. Rogers, who was educated at a dame school and a British School, said laterhe never had much elementary education. As a boy he encountered *Pilgrim's Progress* and *Sweeney Todd*. At ten he worked as an errand boy; at fourteen he was in a stationers; between sixteen and nineteen his health failed and it was really then that he began reading seriously.[39]

He learned the trade of vellum binding, the conditions of which were not unconducive to intellectual development. Not only was it an interesting craft, but the 'speed of a workshop was not set by the motor or the gas engine'. For a workman endowed with those virtues of the labour aristocrat, thrift and temperance, there was the possibility of improvement, intellectual and material. There was the precious Saturday half-holiday which Rogers spent in the Guildhall library in the winter and in Hyde Park in the summer reading Byron, Browning, Emerson and Huxley.[40]

An important influence was a free-thinking workman, Edward Baker, who brought him into contact with the Church of Progress in Langham Place, a meeting place for spiritualists, agnostics, broad churchmen, unitarians, and secularists. Baker also introduced him to a Working Men's Club, his own teetotal club in Camden Town and a free thought society in Tottenham Court Road. These were all powerful stimulants to enquiry. Rogers received some guidance too in his reading from Baker. Frederick Rogers, however, found the free thought movement emotionally unsatisfying. For several years he attended J. Allanson Picton's independent chapel in Hackney, hiding his working-class identity from the middle-class congregation when they finally deigned to speak to him. In the 1870s he was involved in various movements and activities in the East End, serving on the School Board, taking office in working men's clubs, and attending the Progressive club in Kingsland Road and Tower Hamlets Radical Club.[41]

A man of the 'superior sort', Rogers was acutely, almost painfully, aware of the thin line which divided the 'respectable' from the derelicts, and fearful lest the sober serious men should be contaminated by vice. He was uneasy about the atmosphere in radical clubs in the early 1880s: smoke, beer, dramatic presentations, melodramas, political lectures, cheap political pamphlets, periodicals like *The Dispatch, The Referee*, and *The Freethinker*. True, there were 'decent-looking' workmen of 'respectable appearance' there but many were 'dirty unshaven',[42] and, worse, some were often not too sober. Rogers was of the opinion that,

> Until the potent sway of the brewer be removed it is scarcely possible that much good, social or political, can come from such an institution . . . the more intellectual among workmen will avoid the clubs, and those who remain in them will simply play into the hands of their worst foes.[43]

He had his own species of radicalism in the 1870s and '80s which was intimately bound up with ideas of moral worth. He was excited by the idea of higher education for workers:

> Intellectual infirmity is no more Nature's law than is physical infirmity. . . . If Radicals look with contempt on false class distinctions — and he is no true Radical who does not — then the Radical pitman will give a hearty support to his appeal; for if progress means anything it means the destruction of all sham divisions of class. Real division there always will exist while men are what they are. It is a real class division that divides the sober man from the sot, or the hypocrite from the honest man. . . . These things always will and always ought to divide men. . . . Other things than these are but the survivors of our social fetish worship, and all true lovers of progress should aid in sweeping them away.[44]

He was later to respond with sympathy to what he felt was the idealism of revolutionary socialists and praised Morris and Hyndman especially. His main objection to socialism was the stress on 'materialism' which upset his religious, anglo-catholic proclivities. Vaguely attracted to the Fabians, it was Canon Barnett's amalgam of social reform and liberal christianity which finally satisfied him.[45]

Reuben George, a student in Swindon in the 1900s, had travelled into the 'strange country' by a quite different route. He was born at a boot shop in Barton Street, Gloucester in 1864. School he disliked, 'when I could dodge it I did', but he wished later his parents could have seen he needed time:

> I was a slow child, and I was put through the same hoop as my brother, Alf, who was a smart boy to whom learning was natural. But my parents came to the conclusion that I hadn't got it in me to be a scholar, just because I was slow at my books, and so they took me away from school when I was only a nipper . . .

At the age of eight he,

> . . . used to clean boots before breakfast, go to school for the morning, take out a blind man in the afternoon, sell newspapers at night, and go round with the meat of a Saturday. I was the errand boy for the district — anybody could buy me for tuppence.

Later he received some encouragement from a Sunday school teacher, and though the atmosphere at home was not particularly intellectual, he heard politics from his father, who was a 'strong liberal and . . . used to lay down the law at mealtimes'. In this way Reuben George '. . . picked up a good many notions'.

At sixteen, he went to work in the Gloucester wagon works and at twenty-three lost some of his fingers in an accident there. Needing a new job he took up the insurance business and moved to Swindon:

> I began to feel when I got to manhood a yearning for education. I knew I had missed something. I felt something inside me moving about dissatisfied and resentful. I thought to myself: 'It is time, Reuben, you began to study.' I seemed to know by instinct that my brain needed feeding — and so I saved up money and bought books. I was always buying books, picking them up here and there and everywhere . . . but of course I couldn't have found my way alone. I should have got lost in the wilderness or stuck in a bog.[46]

The University Extension lectures were a source of guidance and inspiration. His first visit to Oxford in 1907 amounted to something of a spiritual revelation.

With the beginnings of his systematic education through University Extension and the Workers' Educational Association came a profound religious and political crisis. Originally a Wesleyan methodist, by 1907,

> Rightly or otherwise I had taken a course that was to me a severe wrench. I had left the church — the church I loved; the Church loved by my forefathers. I did not object to the talk of Heaven, but what I did object to was the misery, the poverty, the ignorance and degradation down there. I felt the churches were not doing their best to mitigate these evils; that they condoned a system that was crushing to humanity. Conviction told me I ought to get out and fight this wrong, and I did so. I had also been a member of the Liberal Party, and my experience as a public man told me that it was utterly useless to look to that party for the removal of the wrongs done to mankind, and that liberalism proper finds its biggest opponents in its own ranks.[47]

Reuben George went to University Extension lectures at the Mechanics' Institute in the early 1900s, listening to Horsburgh on economics and Italian masters and Hudson Shaw on Ruskin.[48] In the exam in economics he nearly failed, but despite this managed to get himself to the summer meeting at Oxford.[49] Later he was active in the Workers' Educational Association for many years and encouraged women to come on the rambles.[50] He was involved in numerous causes and campaigns, opposing the Boer War, and the 1902 Tory education bill. A founder member of the Swindon Social Democratic Federation, he later served as a socialist councillor. At the general election in 1918 he stood as labour candidate for Chippenham with the slogan: 'You have King George, you have had Lloyd George, and all you want is Reuben George.' They didn't have him, but three years later he was a rather unconventional mayor of Swindon, not attending the civil service at the parish church, refusing to sit as magistrate because he would not judge his fellows, and touring the hospital dressed as Father Christmas.[51] For Reuben George, University Extension lectures

> . . . were my beginning of a new life. It was wonderful what they did for me. I began to see life as I had never seen it before. The beauty and mystery of Nature on one hand and the misery and wretchedness of civilisation on the other.[52]

He still, however, said 'Down with all that's up.'

Social and political regeneration

Education affected personal morality and attitudes. John V. Barrow told of two miners in the Northeast where he worked who bought tickets for a course on 'The Problems of Life and Health':

> One of them I knew to be a very intelligent man and he has supplied me with some interesting facts concerning his companion. He says that when he first knew him he was a dissolute, degraded man, caring for nothing but drink, gambling, fighting and every other thing that belongs to an evil life. They lived near to each other, and occasionally had some conversation. By and by they took walks together and questions of interest were discussed in a simple way. One by one he dropped off his evil habits and sought the society of his intelligent friend. He abandoned drink and devoted his money to the purchasing of books, he took every means that was likely to afford him information, and sought knowledge wherever it was to be found. And now he is a student at the present course of lectures, and has already earned first-class marks for his exercises . . . this man travels a distance of over five miles every Saturday evening in order to attend the lectures, and often does his exercises after a hard day's work at the mine . . .[53]

In some cases contact with the movement was not just a personal spiritual experience but modified both class consciousness and political opinions. Mr Wilson, a member of the Sheffield artisans' committee, declared in Hull that at the Sheffield centre,

> All classes of society met together at these lectures, and many persons got their prejudices rubbed down. He believed the interest of labour and capital were identical (Applause) and in their harmonious working the supremacy of the nation must be upheld.[54]

This was certainly an approved response. But even this political conversion had a personal dimension. An aspect of adult teaching which was often noted was the personal relationship between lecturers and worker students. It was felt to be quite remarkable that men of different classes simply got on.

Personal contact was charged with significance. It was to be both a political solvent and an emotional balm. For the class gulf was wide enough at a personal level for acquaintance and friendship to evoke comment. It was partly a case of getting to know men at the opposite end of the class pole. Frederick Rogers instanced the friendship of Leonard Montefiore and a workman Charles Connor in Whitechapel in the seventies:

> The cultured free-hearted Oxonian and the workman who had won his education by the sweat of his brow, came very close together and understood each others' aims and hopes. University Extension was breaking down the worm-eaten barriers of class and prejudice.[55]

These encounters were necessarily self-conscious with some romanticisation on both sides.

Albert Fearnehough went up to Edward Carpenter after one of his Extension lectures, giving the lecturer his name and address and asking him to visit him some time.

> Later meeting me in the street, he renewed the request, telling me that his friend who came with him to lectures was a young farmer who was well up in 'book-learning' (which he himself was not) — that they both lived in the country, he in a cottage on the farm of which Fox, his friend, was owner and that they would both gladly entertain me at any time that I cared for a country walk.

Accordingly Carpenter went to Bradway, four or five miles from Sheffield, where his two students lived. He describes his new acquaintances in his autobiography:

> Fearnehough was a scythe-maker, a riveter, a muscular, powerful man of about my age, quite 'uneducated' in the ordinary sense (since indeed at the age of nine he had pushed a handcart about the streets of Sheffield) but well-grown and fine built, with a good practical capacity though slow brain, and something of the latent fire and indomitableness of the iron-worker — a man whose ideal was the rude life of the backwoods, and who hated the shams of commercialism. Indeed he was always getting into coils with his employers because he would not scamp and hurry over his work as occasion demanded; and with his workmates because he would not countenance their doing so. In many ways he was delightful to me, as the one 'powerful uneducated' and natural person I had as yet in all my life met with. Moreover there was a touch of pathos in his inarticulate ways and in his own sense of inability to compete with the cheap Jack commercialism of the day.[56]

The effect, on the other side, on workers' lives, goes unrecorded and is left to our imagination. Certainly the self-educated workman was often a lonely figure reading in dinner hours or before work, wasting time copying out-of-date scientific works, painfully conscious of pronunciation when he asked a question, dragging words from pages into strange company, prickling at a young clerk's smirk, uncomfortable both in his work clothes or second-to-Sunday best in a middle-class audience. The inner revelation of the higher learning was all very well but he still lived in a different world from the middle-class student and university lecturer. After the class he had to walk home or travel by workman's ticket, to earn his living doing manual work, to study in cramped rooms, face poverty in the world outside.

Perhaps the most painful aspect of this search for education was not material hardship or even the sometimes complacent patronage of privileged people, but being forced apart from workmates and from working-class women, few of whom could share such new and alien interests. The working-class intellectual's new self was necessarily fragmented. He could never bring the two worlds together and this was accentuated when the educational agency was from above, when learning was not bound up with an emergent social movement from the working class which could bring a sense of at least political connection.

The social gulf might be overlooked in the Extension class; it could not be ignored in domestic life. Classes meant that men invariably left their wives at night. For the woman, the classes were thus part of the man's outer world, like the union or even the coop. This must have caused resentment. Yet the men felt it was so difficult to bring that outer world into the women's lives at home. The impact of adult education on domestic life did not figure in the lofty debates on education in the University Extension journals. An odd reference in private correspondence carries a glimpse of this estrangement.

An East London worker student, Frederick Hubbard, was worried about his wife's reaction if he joined C.R. Ashbee's art class in the East End. She was an uneducated girl and had recently been ill:

> I am afraid my wife will not come to the classes and will be very unhappy if I leave her alone another evening or two a week – and wish it were possible for you to come tomorrow evening and persuade her that it would be for our good but I am afraid it would be presumptuous to ask you to do so and to share our humble fare.[57]

This fragmentation was thus at once a personal, domestic matter and was also experienced in terms of cultural identification and political allegiance.

The new learning took a working-class man away from his own life and from people of his own class. He caught sight of the ways of the upper-class intelligentsia from inside, feeling some understanding as he realised how they saw the world. Their values often seemed so confident, more generous, broader than the narrowness, dogma and bitterness he often associated with his own class. It was easy to feel himself apart, feel a certain distaste for workmates, family and neighbours. A member of the Independent Labour Party said he thought many workers were narrow-minded, 'bigoted and intolerant', reading 'dreadful wash' and spending their leisure in the gin palace and low music hall.[58]

However, at the same time upper-class culture seemed superficial. It had been acquired with such ease it seemed meaningless to its possessors. He felt desperate to communicate with these languid purveyors of high culture, to touch them, make them respond like a human being, make them feel him and his world directly even for a moment. Perhaps to humble them just a little, scoop the superiority out of them, force them to acknowledge the false complacency of their class privilege. The worker student carried this knot of adulation and resentment within him for ever wriggling and twisting but unable to free himself as an individual. It was a 'personal' problem for which there was no personal solution. Listen to the representative from Newcastle, Mr Hoare, at the conference on 'The English Universities and the English People' in 1892. He demanded that lecturers should come down to the worker's level and at once qualified this:

> Mind I am not speaking of coming down to our level so as to keep us there; we want them to come down to our level so that when they have experienced our difficulties they can lift us up to the level from which they came . . .[59]

So although University Extension could have the effect its organisers desired in binding workers to the institutions and values which belonged to their rulers, it bound them still fretting and cheated. It could also make them aware of their exclusion, help them to chart the boundaries of that class privilege of learning. Its political effects were thus hard to estimate for it could leave a worker student politically acquiescent but emotionally rebellious. Alternatively, some students remained socialists but were emotionally impressed with their lecturers' life and attitudes.

There was a more specific bitterness as men became conscious of what they had missed personally and realised the way in which their class was excluded by the educational system. A Cleveland miner told Roberts:

I deeply deplore the past thirty-four years of my life in being buried in the mines since I was nine years of age, and taught to look jealously on science as being antagonistic to religion. I little thought what pleasure of thought and contemplation I lost. I have however broken loose from my fetters and am proceeding onward.[60]

A miner from Pucklechurch, Gloucestershire was aware

that the great cultural class possessed almost every available means of education; and what was worse, monopoly, prejudice, and class feeling formed a great and almost impassable gulf, separating us not only from the means of education but from the society of the educated.[61]

Mr Hoare, the Newcastle delegate to the conference on 'The English Universities' in 1892, expressed the same feeling:

. . . there is, unfortunately, or has been, a great class distinction; knowledge has been locked up to all intents and purposes within four walls; it has been made most difficult of access to the working man, who has not been able to get to it, has been placed at a higher figure than he has ever been able to command to get it, and then when he has surmounted all these difficulties he has put himself, and possibly his family, to great deprivation to get it and then has found the cold shoulder exposed to him. He has been knocked down in every shape and form, and now we want you to come down to us with open arms (Applause), we want you to feel amongst us that you are a human being the same as us (Applause). We want you to open your hearts free from all restrictions.[62]

Men could be politically moderate and still fell resentful. A sense of injustice comes through in Robert Halstead's statement, for example. Halstead was a student for many years at Hebden Bridge and a regular attender of Extension summer meetings.

To the average working man a University training, in the ordinary sense of the phrase, is about as possible as if all the Universities were situated at the north pole. Some of us have had it hammered into us by hard personal experience, or the experience of our fathers, as a curious moral anomaly in the management of national affairs, that the working class who actually form the bulk of the nation should up to the present date have been so largely ignored, and having done the lion's share of the world's work, should have been only furnished with so many kicks and so few half-pence in the practical schemes adopted for sharing out the good things of life.[63]

Halstead himself expressed a patchwork of class consciousness, radical beliefs and intellectual aspirations. He wrote several articles in the journals of the Extension Movement. When the Educational Guild (connected with the

Workers' Educational Association) was started in the early 1900s he also gave his support to the new adult education efforts.[64] Halstead was involved in various social and religious movements, national and local. He was a cooperator,[65] a supporter of labour co-partnership and profit-sharing,[66] a member of the Sunday School Union[67] and the Christian Social Union. In 1897 he gave a paper on education to the Todmorden Literary Society.[68] As a cooperator he was especially involved in the question of education. In the late 1890s he was occupied in recruiting cooperators for Extension summer meetings.[69] In 1897 he suggested forming a cooperative section, and would have liked to have seen a cooperative students' association collecting a fund for cooperators' classes.[70] In 1899 he organised a party of cooperators to attend the summer meeting. Anyone interested was asked to contact him at Hebden Bridge beforehand, and the subject for study was on labour co-partnership. Only twenty-three of the tickets offered by coops were applied for and nearly all these came through Halstead's efforts.[71]

He was a calico weaver and had begun work in a cotton mill at the age of eight, going through the various departments of the cotton industry.[72] In the 1890s he was working in the Hebden Bridge Fustian Manufacturing Cooperative Society, where he minded four looms.[73] Physically he was 'slight and frail'.[74] In politics he was cautious but capable of determined radical statements, retaining a strong class consciousness and sense of harsh realities of working-class life. On general themes he tended to fall into the rather vague and high-flown rhetoric which characterised the progressive movement at the time, but when dealing with a topic familiar to him, either from his experience of a Northern clothing community, cooperation, or simply individual hardship, he combines a great moral steadfastness with considerable dignity of expression. He had strong views on child labour, but pointed out the hardship caused by legislation while wages remained low. He had stern words for industrial capitalists who threatened to close the mills and force their work people to the workhouse while they were, '. . . helping to crowd our thorough-fares with their magnificent carriages and decorating our suburbs with splendid mansions'.[75]

As a cooperator he rejected firmly the idea of social improvement through individual self-help or education alone without material change. He was a religious man, with a strong moralising streak, concerned that the conditions of working-class life exposed men to drink, to their physical passions and to 'vigorous stimulants', but his religious faith was by no means narrow or uncritical. He was pleased to find churchmen sympathetic on social questions rather than stressing the original sin of the poor. His real moral criticism was not directed at the profligacy of the poor but against a system out of joint:

> Haunted by a suspicion that there is a fundamental moral defect in the constitution of things, that civilisation is but a product of the centuries for making the mean and selfish into millionaires, and the nobler spirits of the world into suicides, the more thoughtful and finely strung amongst us are finding it difficult to hold by the faith of our childhood. The idea that the whole fabric of law and order is a piece of imposing fetishism slowly elaborated through the ages by the intelligent few, to secure the protecting veneration and respect of the ignorant many for everyone's rights but their own, is gradually working its insidious way amongst us; and can we be condemned when our main source of knowledge on these subjects has been by getting into prison or craving the dubious benevolence of the workhouse.[76]

Behind the articulate worker's bitterness was not merely his own experience but the knowledge of so many of his fellows,

> . . . who have striven nobly to climb with him the steeps of life, if perchance they might gain some of its shining heights, but baffled and exhausted by the hardships of their lot, have fallen by his side, dying with the conviction that the very fates were against them.[77]

Here again the religious imagery is very clear.

Robert Halstead shared the peculiar strengths and weaknesses of men of his kind. Their critique of society came so much from a personal moral and emotional sense of wrong that merely encountering liberal members of the upper classes engaged in philanthropy could effectively dampen their radicalism. *They* were not evil men, *they* cared, *they* listened with respect to the ideas of working people. The whole tone of this is well expressed in Halstead's statement at the conference of the Todmorden and District Sunday School Union:

> Workmen are sometimes asked to believe that almost every scrap of political and civil advantage which they now enjoy had to be wrung from the unwilling hands of the dominant classes. In the education of the poor, such as it was, as Canon Barnett once pointed out to a few working men, amongst whom I had the honour to be present, we have an exception to this.[78]

The political implications of this concept of change being initiated by generous members of the upper classes are most apparent. Perhaps this was

293

the point through which the Extension organisers did get the essentials of their politics through. How could a society based on ruthless class conflict create members of the upper classes who cared? How could a bad system create nice men? If the men were nice perhaps the system was after all good. How could an exploiting class also be considerate? Extension students like Halstead concerned themselves with what should be, virtue rewarding the just deserts of the diligent and worthy, rather than the actual mechanism of capitalist society. Individual members of a class were thus continually confused with the position of the class as a whole. Relations between individual workers and lecturers symbolically became relations between classes. Because they accepted a view of mental learning transcending the real differences in their childhoods, their work, their family relations, their homes, they found it difficult to see ideas, values, culture, as the social creation of a particular relationship between classes.

The summer meetings

Education as the new life comes through with most intensity in the accounts from students of the summer meetings. These holiday courses were important in strengthening the personal connection to Extension. The initial idea came out of discussions about how to encourage systematic reading. The actual suggestion was Charles Rowley's, a founder of the Ancoats settlement in Manchester. Scholarships were given by private individuals and by cooperative societies to enable working-class students to attend.[79] The first summer meeting was at Oxford in 1888 and Cambridge followed on a smaller scale. The first three at Oxford were organised by W.A.S. Hewins, the economic historian and enthusiast for the Empire.[80] In the late eighties and early nineties the threat of socialism and militant unionism seemed real and powerful to many middle-class people. The ethos at Oxford was of this middle-class social awareness with a bustle of settlements and University Extension, and reference to Ruskin, Toynbee and the dignity of manual work and the nobility of sacrifice. They persuaded labour leaders like Tom Mann to come to the Oxford summer school and talk about University Extension and the working class. It is easy to be ironic about these gatherings, part educational and part social, but irony quite misses the point and makes it impossible to see the importance of this aspect of the journey into the strange country.

Summer meetings provided in microcosm the abrupt contrast between the workers' situation and an alternative way of living. Here most clearly higher education appears not simply as teaching but as the means to a new life. Men remembered the summer meeting years later. A friend of Halstead's told him, 'The memory of my visit to Oxford will never die away, it has been one of the chief events of my life.'[81] Some men returned like Halstead year after year – summer meeting 'regulars'. After his first meeting in 1907 Reuben George took his family to Oxford and Cambridge as a kind of cultural pilgrimage every year.

The university towns provided the glimpse of a qualitatively different world. Students from Manchester in 1890 went bathing at Parson's Pleasure and observed the contrast between the Isis and '. . . our rivers at home, foul stinking and used to receive the contents of drains and sewers'. They could appreciate 'three good knife and fork meals per day', and set off in search of the slums of Oxford, finding nothing as bad as Ancoats but still discovering 'places, even in Oxford, which well might be made better'. Residence in a college was a new experience for them and helped them to understand E.V. Neal's scheme for associated homes: '. . . it all seemed very practicable to us, the difficulty we felt would be to educate the working men's wives into the system. . .'.[82] They found it difficult on the basis of what they had known before to imagine what the universities would be like. Acland describes showing a group round Oxford. One man was simply amazed at the place and a companion teased him with: 'I know what you expected to see, you expected to see something like Leeds Infirmary, only larger . . .'[83]

Most important was the physical sense of uprooting and transplanting which the new environment brought to workmen.[84] Halstead watched workers for several years at summer meetings and, 'observed that almost uniformly they have experienced more or less a mental break-up and reconstruction of ideas as to life and character'.[85] A Yorkshire working man felt that workers from the northern manufacturing centres were possibly more susceptible because of the contrast with their home life where, 'the struggle for wealth is so absorbing and so keen, that if a man lose sight of the world for a time, his competitors instantly trample upon him. . .'.[86]

The physical structure of the towns brought also a feeling of connection to the past. When Joseph Emes first went to Oxford in 1891,

> . . . the glorious old city burst upon my vision, as I walked its beautiful streets and visited its magnificent colleges; and as I thought of the great and noble men who had walked its streets and studied in its halls of learning, it seemed to link me

to the Past and made such an indelible impression in my mind that I feel it will never be erased.[87]

This consciousness of a relation to the past contributed to a feeling of sympathy towards the church. Halstead said: '. . . one may feel in step with the heavenward march of ancient pilgrim and saint'.[88] Reuben George, Charles Spencer and Horace Anderson from Swindon later hearing Bishop Percival preach in the Church of St Mary the Virgin became aware of the spiritual influence of Oxford in the past.[89] Reuben George remembered later how a 'mate' from Swindon whispered in his ear,

> 'Reuben, I could pray now, and so could you; we could both pray.' Both of us were outside the orthodox faith, and we're both outside of it still, but neither of us will ever forget that sermon and the feeling that came over our souls — I've never wiped Oxford off me. I've got her all round me to this moment. I feel that she is my University, that I've taken a degree there, and that she will be my Alma Mater to the end of my days . . .[90]

It was not only the effect of the beauty and traditions of the university towns which produced this vague religious feeling. Workmen who found a narrow and fundamentalist christianity intellectually unacceptable could hear liberal churchmen providing a broad religious statement with which they could agree. The Manchester students boycotted chapel at first but as the week went by their interest grew and they all appeared for the last service when their baritone sang a solo of 'Lead Kindly Light': 'Some dozen workmen, most of whom have drifted away from Christianity itself, listening to one of their number, and all united in the desire which the hymn so well expresses for more light.' They were impressed with Rev. W. Dank's sermon, 'full of expressions of tolerance and charity towards those who feel no longer able to subscribe to the Church dogmas', and felt 'if such sermons were common, many who have left the Church and no longer believe the teachings of orthodoxy, would again place themselves within the sphere of religious influences'.[91]

Certainly these were exactly the kind of reactions which most of the Extension organisers desired, reverence for the two universities and identification with their traditions, feelings of continuity with the past which would temper the radical wish for a complete break with what had gone before, and a broadly religious sympathy which would serve to muffle the stridency of secularism.

There are hints of uneasiness but the sources for summer meeting are all official and the kind of men who wrote were probably in a sense preselected. Even so a member of the students' union in Whitechapel confessed it was impossible to suppress a feeling of bitterness:

> In spite of good intentions . . . I am filled with sallow envy after these glimpses of collegiate life. Envy of these whose good fortune has placed them in a position to pursue their studies in an atmosphere charged with the power of all that is great and noble in the history of the past and worthy to be known in the present.[92]

The contrast could make some workers muse on the possibility of creating conditions like those at the universities elsewhere. As Reuben George and his companions at Cambridge strolled round the colleges and saw 'the workshop of the student with its fine grass plot, its ivy-covered buildings, its flowers and its beauty' they thought if all this were necessary for the student, '. . . what about the workshop of the factory hand?'[93]

However, the most characteristic feature of working students accounts was not bitterness but an overwhelming gratitude at the reception the upper classes gave them. They were flattered by being consulted by lecturers, overcome at being treated as social equals – especially by middle-class women. Henry Crabtree in 1889 recounted how in response to the working students' 'felt unworthiness' Hudson Shaw said all were alike at Oxford and bade them make themselves at home.[94] Joseph Emes discovered that lecturers,

> . . . were not stiff academical pedants and strong partisans, whose only object was to suppress public opinion and denounce popular movements, but men with human sympathies. Most of them I found were desirous of soaring above party spirit and bias, and of dealing with facts. I found also that they were desirous of making the acquaintance of working men, that they enjoyed a good chat with them, and consulted their opinions on almost every point . . . Party spirit and class feeling seemed to have melted away, thus beautifully uniting us all into one. The ladies, (especially the Ladies' Committee) were not those delicate and exquisite bits of nature and art which we often meet in a railway carriage, and who are afraid of a working man's clothes to touch them, but ladies who appeared to have a mission in life, whose desire was to brighten someone's life whose lot was cast in less favourable circumstances than their own . . .[95]

The 'ladies' obviously made a striking impression on Joseph Emes. He brought them up again at the University Extension Conference that year:

> I came to Oxford expecting that no-one would take notice of me, although I

expected to be interested, but I find that I have come amongst friends and as for the ladies they are really beautiful (much laughter). I speak as a married man (renewed laughter). I think gatherings of this sort are tending more than anything else to break down the barriers which separate classes, and cannot but be a benefit to the country.[96]

For some men the summer meetings represented not only a personal means of communication but a more general social breakthrough. Robert Halstead felt that the dialogue between classes was of great social import:

Narrow provincialism of ideas and sentiments breaks down. . . . Working men discover that men and women in other walks of life are not the stilted creatures of self-conscious superiority that the poorer classes are apt to think them, and one hopes that they themselves are not invariably found to consist of incorrigible stupidity of mind, vulgarity of ambition and boorishness of manners, which their superfine and supersensitive critics would have us believe . . .[97]

The summer meeting was regarded as a means of promoting class understanding. Halstead was still making the same point in 1900 – he felt they were:

. . . calculated to teach representatives of the masses the value and pleasure of good and refined social manners, and the representatives of the classes may learn something of the stern and unceremonious realities with which the common people have to associate.[98]

But he also suggested that if University Extension could involve groups of workmen in summer meetings, it would prevent them feeling 'the social isolation into which they are apt to drift when thrown into the society of other classes'.[99] This would indicate a certain tension behind the social intercourse of the different classes. While the social aspects, both personal and on a more generalised level were undoubtedly the most significant feature of summer meetings for participants, the intellectual stimulus they provided was also extremely important. Students, in meeting each other, could exchange ideas.[100] Undoubtedly too they appreciated the contact with specialists in various disciplines who could provide teaching in depth not otherwise accessible to them. Working students told A. Zimmern in 1907, 'Snowden and Barnes we can have up for nothing . . . but this is the real thing'.[101]

Political tendencies

The whole situation of an adult working student made it impossible to disregard the social and economic framework within which the dissemination of sweetness and light operated. If one response was 'let the intellectual workman use his learning to obtain a position with enough leisure to pursue his studies', another was that 'education could be used to raise the whole class'. Very broadly one could say that there were two main political trends in all the diversity of the early years of the Extension movement. There were those who felt education was necessary to prevent the working class misusing the power they already possessed, and those who wanted them to be educated in order to obtain more power.

Lecturers who believed in education as a means of developing working-class power saw this in terms of a gradual evolutionary process. For Ashbee and Geddes it was to be through a cultural transformation in the social circumstances of the working class. For J.A. Hobson it meant a change in consciousness. For Tawney, an awakening and expansion in workers' own cultural institutions. For Tawney, a leading figure in the WEA, the real problem was the fact that education was imposed from without. Workers should be taught what they wanted to know and not what 'academic persons think they ought to want'.[102] This meant workers' control of their own education and ultimately popular control over the scandalous misuse of the capital of Oxford and Cambridge. He wanted organised labour to realise its educational heritage, and to step foward to claim it. 'In the past, education had been supplied too much by churches, philanthropic institutions, and a group of benevolent officials at Whitehall. It should be supplied by the people for the people (hear, hear).'[103]

The University Extension organisers were very sensitive to the accusation of bias. They tried to avoid 'party politics' and had learned the lessons of earlier middle-class educational movements which had provoked working-class enmity by very crude ideological indoctrinations. There remained a deep resentment of such educational 'nobbling'. Extension lecturers did not try and hammer a simple message home. They were warned not to score points off workers. On the other hand, very strong social ideals brought many of them into the movement. There was certainly an attempt to intervene, direct and improve workers' aspirations and political aims, either through holding them in check or guiding them along established, albeit radical, channels.

The whole question of relationship to the labour movement was inevitably bedevilled by accusations that the education was in some way loaded. The old suspicion that education would make workers discontented was still about. John V. Barrow parried it rather deftly in 1891. He said he thought unless discontent was interpreted as 'a clearer conception of what is right and a legitimate ambition to secure it', this was out of the question. He went on to argue that University Extension trained men to think clearly and reasonably, the employer who was opposed to Extension must be a man who did not want 'trade disputes or social difficulties to be settled on lines of reason'. Barrow was of the opinion that,

> It is the unthinking majority which too frequently precipitate deadlocks between employer and employed while the men of intelligence are noticeable for their desire to avert such conflicts and to secure a settlement on a basis of reason compatible with justice and their freedom as workmen.[104]

Ellis Edwardes, a miner student in Backworth, Northumberland, was evangelical for Extension. Like lay preachers, the Backworth men went out into the neighbouring villages reading papers and giving lectures. Edwardes was aware that they could be criticised as possessing 'only a light knowledge . . . only a smattering of different subjects', but, he reminded the Extension Congress,

> the platform in England is free to all, and . . . there was always an army of orators – socialists, anarchists, agitators and demagogues, all shades of social and political opinions, not always well informed or highly cultured – going about lecturing and speech making, and trying to force their theories and fancies upon the public.

Against such propaganda it was necessary to disseminate the higher university instruction.[105] As for any connection to the socialist movement, to many workmen in Extension this was anathema. They regarded the higher education emanating from the universities as something above and beyond opinion and interest, indeed as a corrective to partisan political propaganda:

> The great drawback to the working man at the present time is that he is largely at the mercy of political tacticians and extravagant socialists for his knowledge of history. He has to be guided by the second-hand inferences of party enthusiasts in attempting to discharge his political obligations. All the contending parties are belabouring him with one-sided arguments that prove with a bewildering conclusiveness that Providence has always been on their side. If it be possible we want access to a knowledge of all the truth without reference to any other

consideration than a right discharge of political duties in the largest sense of the word.[106]

The Workers' Educational Association, founded in 1903, was an explicit attempt to connect University Extension to the organised labour movement, and it found support both in the trade unions and among cooperators. It represented a recognition of the working class as an increasingly independent class, but educationally it kept close to the original ideals of Extension. Albert Mansbridge, the founder of the WEA, envisaged cooperators and trade unionists lifting themselves through 'higher knowledge' to 'higher pleasures'.[107] Like the liberal organisers, he felt that higher knowledge automatically produced political wisdom – which meant for him being above economic class interest:

> The deep draughts of knowledge drunk by those within the currents of correct thoughts, will provide that power and strength, which inspite of stressful and baneful days, will divert the strong movements of the people from the narrow paths of immediate interests to the broadway of that rightly ordered social life of which only glimpses have yet been seen even by the greatest of the world's seers.[108]

A much more explicitly political turn followed the formation of the Plebs League and the National Council of Labour Colleges, in the aftermath of the Ruskin College Strike of 1909. Here the ideals of non-partisan education were rejected in favour of one that had both a class character and a socialist content. The movement, which rose on the syndicalist tide of the pre-war years – a revolt by younger trade unionists – carried the influential support of the South Wales Miners and the Railwaymen's Union. For the following forty years it fought a vigorous campaign for what it called 'Independent Working Class Education', and played an important part in training the cadres of the British labour movement.

The 1900s saw a mounting attack on the ideals of University Extension. Arthur Abbot of Leeds, for instance, speaking in 1900 on the newly founded Ruskin College (a college for working men in Oxford), and urging the cooperators of Leeds to support it, claimed that movements like Extension came from 'members of a superior class extending a patronising hand' – that such men, however admirable their intentions, could not be expected 'to realise the conditions of those for whom they worked'.[109] Similarly, Mr Campbell, the representative of the Woolwich cooperative society, speaking at a conference of the Association for Higher Education,

. . . in an excited speech raised a storm of protest by declaring that there were men present who had no sympathy with the working man . . . many people get their education on the shoulders of working men and when they had got it they took their seats there and refused to move (laughter).[110]

At a less politicised level, antedating the formation of the Plebs League, there was a powerful undercurrent of suspicion and ambivalence on the part of many worker students at the education which University Extension had fostered. Sometimes they sneered at 'book-knowledge'[111] or pointed out that working men were 'extremely apt and full of ingenuity, with practical work',[112] although they could not follow the academic ways of the universities. They also pointed to the superiority of lived experience. They lived in 'a world of facts' while the university men lived in,

> a world of conjugations and declensions, of theories and aphorisms and syllogisms, and things of that kind, and sometimes when they sought to instruct working men, they were more of laughing stocks than knowledge givers.[113]

Some men put forward the view that workers were closer to nature than the upper classes and while this direct contact did not,

> . . . polish the workman's manners or increase his power of expression, it gives him a dumb insight and sensibility, which enables him to hold his own at least in his own consciousness, even when apparently vanquished by the nimble logic and the skilled articulation of the academic mind.[114]

There was too the feeling that the 'culture' of the universities was something superficial, it gave to the upper classes a polish and veneer, while the common people possessed culture in a far deeper sense. Not only did workers have a qualitatively different source of knowing, they had a different way of knowing:

> They think not in abstract and general terms of culture, but from fact to fact of their experience and recollections. These people think in the concrete; and it's no unusual thing to find men who scatter their aspirates in all directions of the linguistic compass, yet in matters of local and national politics, in questions relating to labour and social problems, reasoning as closely and as wisely as the best academic trained men of the district.[115]

While these criticisms are obviously partial and incomplete, they present an important indication of the uneasiness and dissatisfaction which University Extension sometimes could evoke and which may have been one of the less visible elements behind the revolt of the Plebs League.

Conclusions

There was a real difficulty which remained unresolved. Worker students were often saying they had been wrongly excluded from an intellectual upper-class culture while trying to assert the values and traditions existing within their own class. These were not confined to book learning but this did not mean that workers did not require book knowledge. It was hard to balance these because there were passionate emotions, echoes of childhood, the lilt of a dialect, humiliations and dignity, oppression and power bound up in education. It was reassuring to drop into the oversimple polarisation between the world of ideas and the lessons of hard experience. This distortion made it impossible to recognise that a limited upper-class experience could be part of the dominant intellectual culture, but that this did not mean it was the only part or that other aspects of this cultural heritage could not be both useful and delightful to working-class people. On the one side there was not a pure experience. Working-class experience generated its own ideas, institutions and values, though harsh circumstances often made this unnecessarily difficult.[116] A persistent vice of subordination has been the tendency to elevate scarcity into a virtue. The struggle to resist becomes an end in itself; the limitations of oppression are refined and preserved for the next generation.

In the later nineteenth century there was no clear challenge and creation of separate independent working-class institutions like the Ruskin College students' strike and breakaway from university control in 1909. There was not a sustained ideological critique of the dominant assumption in University Extension that enlightenment through education was what workers needed. The Plebs League in the 1900s was to assert against this view that education must aim at making economic and political resistance effective.[117] Nor was there in Extension a conscious critical appropriation by workers of those aspects of ruling-class culture which they desired while rejecting other class-biased values.

By the 1900s the more class-conscious socialists among the Ruskin breakaways and the Plebs League were trenchant in their criticisms. For them the Extension worker students were simply the guards at the gate of the rich man's castle, toadies and lackeys who maintained capitalist exploitation. In the later years they attacked the Workers' Educational Association in similar terms.

The aim of social harmony did mean that University Extension was yet another subtle agency within that network of influence within which the British ruling class has sought to contain and channel working-class aspiration and discontent. It can be seen to have made some contribution towards the making of those strands in the labour movement which have basically accepted the terms of their rulers.

But although such a description fits neatly over the surface, when the actual microcosm of integration is examined closely it cannot illuminate the personal sources of feeling which really bound individual students, and indeed lecturers, to the movement.

If this is to be our whole truth it leaves us with a shallow stereotype of the lecturers as very crafty hypocrites and the students as fools or self-seeking opportunists. It is clear from their own statements that this is an inadequate dismissal. There was certainly a cultivating and grooming of moderate radicals like Rogers, Halstead, Greenwood, Edwardes, Emes, Mansbridge and the rest. They were undoubtedly flattered by the attention which they ironically owed partly to the extreme statements of men whose politics they deplored. But this did not mean that they accepted all the lecturers' ideas and were prepared to deny their own experience and values. They were mostly men who chose their own ground and stood on it.

Through the Extension movement two idealisms encounter one another. One came from the sense of religious crisis and the search for a new philosophic basis to liberalism which troubled the late nineteenth-century upper-middle-class intelligentsia. Another less clearly documented working-class idealism was sustained by some strands of Christian belief, cooperation, temperance and certain radical communitarian and utopian traditions. The points where the movement touched worker students deeply were those moments in which their own lofty ideals could find a resonance in those of the lecturers. Certain aspects of this process had conservative implications. Class became a state of mind. The true elite were the moral, sober aristocrats of the intellect. Conflict appeared as an unfortunate misunderstanding. Reforms were granted by the benevolent middle class. Others had both conservative and radical elements. The rejection of immediate self-interest as a motive for action and the glimpse of a society which was not based on competition, machines and money-making carried ambiguous political meanings. The sense of intellectual fellowship and spiritual discovery which some students experienced tended to be contrasted with a caricature of materialistic, tub-thumping secularism or socialism. But the release of this free self-development was still real and deep enough. The Manchester summer school students' delight in an unpolluted river, Joseph Emes' love of architecture in Oxford, Reuben George's spiritual experience in an Oxford church, confirmed a belief that there were far greater possibilities in the human soul than worldly circumstance allowed. It could nurture the enlightened discontent which was the aim of radicals like Hobson and Tawney.

Both the ideals of education as a transcendent fellowship and the ideal of a learning which might enlighten the daily circumstances of working-class life were attractive to working-class students who often bundled them both together. They were in the movement because they did not want only education for a trade or a streamlined education which would equip them to fight capitalism. Both approaches were too narrow and utilitarian. The universities were offering them 'the best' – so they took it.

But here of course the catch came because most of the worker students remained in the material circumstances of an exploited class. There was nothing much that Dante, or King Alfred, or John Wesley or Ruskin or the Extension lecturer could do about that. Also even while they were being dazzled by the beauty and knowledge which the university was extending they could never somehow settle comfortably. Physically, emotionally and intellectually worker students remained travellers in a strange country. The tragedy of their situation was not that they were being nobbled, but that the ideals and culture which inspired them were tangled among the self-interest and prejudices of a class which held power over them and benefited from their labour.

10. Working-Class Heroes

'Working-Class Heroes', *Spare Rib* 21, 1974

This is a reflection, in the light of feminism, on the working-class novels of the fifties which affected many of us growing up in that period. It is noticeable how the class consciousness of the male characters was defined against and at the expense of the middle-class and working-class women.

The Silent Majority, A Study of the Working Class in Post-War British Fiction, Nigel Gray, Vision Critical Studies, 1974

(Books discussed, *Kes*, Barry Hines, 1968; *Billy Liar*, Keith Waterhouse, 1959; *Borstal Boy*, Brendan Behan, 1958; *Saturday Night and Sunday Morning*, Alan Sillitoe, 1958; *This Sporting Life*, David Storey, 1960; *Alfie*, Bill Naughton, 1966)

Nigel Gray explores two dilemmas – how an oppressed group can express and recognise its own perception of itself and at the same time break out of the circumstances which impose silence. These are problems of language and history but they are ultimately political and confront not only the working class but women and black and gay people too.

The atmosphere of working-class fiction in the fifties was very much one in which immediate experience was asserted against abstract phrases. There was usually a deep suspicion of politics and politicians, right or left, and a deep rage against humiliation, punishment, sexual repression and authority. The class arrogance of the upper and middle classes and the vegetable deference of older workers were both fiercely resisted.

With precision Nigel Gray distinguishes the class experience of the characters. There is Billy Liar's world, 'the dreariness of dark satanic tea shops' and Sunday tea for girlfriends, 'a baptism of lettuce and pineapple chunks', which is miles away from Arthur Seaton's pints, cracked lavatory bowls and red ochre steps. The specific way in which family and neighbourhood shape your perception of your own class relationships moves out of the sociological frozen category. In *Borstal Boy* Gray examines the distinctions between workers and how these can limit or develop class consciousness.

There is Tom who comes from the upper working class and feels himself apart from the other men in the jail. Even his crime had come out of his pride. He murdered his girlfriend out of jealousy. He is locked in his own notion of his respectability. It gives him a certain security but at the cost of despising other men and killing his love. Brendan's distinction belongs to a different tradition.

Members of his family were among the political and cultural leaders in Ireland though the family was working class. He grew up on the north side of Dublin. When Tom refers to his Borstal chinas as scum, he says, 'Sure the blokes are only working-class kids the same as ourselves.' The Irishman was imprisoned in a foreign country but his consciousness of class is not enclosed. It can connect to others.

Sillitoe's hero, Arthur Seaton, fights individually with a confidence his father couldn't have. Capitalism in the second half of the fifties needed his labour power. Sillitoe says of Arthur, 'No more short time like before the war, or getting the sack if you stood ten minutes in the lavatory reading your *Football Post* – if the gaffer got onto you now you could always tell him where to put the job and go somewhere else.'

But this cockiness depends on him staying single to spend his fourteen quid a week and working his 'backbone to a string of conkers on piece work'. The new affluent world wasn't that affluent and it wasn't equal or classless at all. Nor did the new working-class hero escape from the circumstances that had broken his father. He carried these circumstances inside him. In Nigel Gray's words:

> A house where the pressures of family living have to be contained within a limited space and within earshot of the neighbours. . . . Growing up close and warm, but bitter too, and with a fear and hatred of 'them', the authorities. With parents who have lived through the depression and the war and who have been left maimed and scarred. Parents who have lived to see a Labour government after the war, that was to be a government for the people and against the bosses, that nibbled at social inequality – and broke their hearts and their belief in political change.

It is true that in the fifties a 'working-class hero' might be becoming 'something to be'. But he emerged at a cost. He can only assert his freedom at the expense of other people, and especially at the expense of women. Arthur Seaton's sexual encounters are grabbed and furtive. He sees the women who go with him as dirty. He prides himself on being better than their husbands. Alfie is another hero who is trapped in his own sex chauvinism. He hits Annie because he can't bear her to be thinking of someone else in bed — he thinks when he likes, of course. He's furious when Gilda talks to another man: 'You've got to strike off what they call a relationship. And that can turn out to be a very intimate thing.' What a nerve. The girls are even expected to be grateful for a kiss.

But the supremacy of the working-class hero is also fragile. He faces a continual and silent subversion of thoughts and feelings. How can he ever know if his object is still loyal? He maintains his supremacy at a terrible cost. Even as he fights the deadening world of work, the numbing domesticity of the nuclear family and legal sex, he is becoming dead and numb himself — too hurt to feel and express sensitivity, love and warmth. Sex becomes combat and is surrounded by nightmare fears about achievement.

Nigel Gray describes the bitterness of this without once elevating bitterness and rage. His description of the relationship between Arthur Machin and Val in *This Sporting Life* is particularly moving. Arthur is shown trapped in his own bigness and his success as a rugger play. Val too is a woman — not a caricature with a cunt unlike so many of the women in fifties fiction. David Storey describes her fears of opening herself up to Arthur. He 'had brought the blood up in her and made it surge in parts she'd thought or felt dead'. But if he left her she would be faced with living with that rawness alone so she pushes him off . . . 'hurting herself as much as me, and building up a fire and pain between us that neither of us know how to handle. . . . Living had turned up so many bad cards for her that she was refusing any more deals. She was withdrawing and lying down.'

Val would be about fifty now. Gray describes the experience of so many women of her generation. 'A lifetime of repression and pain, a budding in her youth when she had a little independence working in the munitions factory, a marriage and the weight of two kids to bear, and suddenly the emptiness left by the central figure in her life who was suddenly no longer there.'

And then Arthur, young, untouched, cocky, rugby hero, whose sexual onslaught continually threatens to sweep away those careful boundaries of white-net-curtain head-above-water relations with the neighbours. Her tension reflects the strain. Arthur Machin has made her a 'slut', as she says it her laughter is 'strangled from her belly'.

Both men and women are caught in the tragedy of the man's resistance being at the expense of the woman. Both oscillate between violence and bemused acceptance. Val's 'body began to mount in a slow fit of rage and bewilderment. Surprise. "You're a man!" she screamed. "You're a bleeding man!" ' If this were the stopping point the sadness would be unbearable. But the tragedy is not timeless. David Storey wrote this in 1960. At the time these books expressed the feelings of writers who had been thrown up out of the working class, who were struggling to connect their memories of the world they had left with the world to which they did not belong.

The working-class heroes have grown older now. Some of them have gone to live on the hill. Their attack on class and sex taboos was individualistic and male defined. But in the context of the fifties it had radical significance. Nigel Gray has returned to these books with new eyes. For him the angry heroes are no longer young iconoclasts but simply working-class men caught at a particular crossing of sex and class conflict. From a distance of more than a decade it is clear that they wanted to conserve as much as they wanted to overthrow. 'Poor bloody women, they don't half suffer one way or another, but what can you do? You can't argue with nature.' At the time few would have argued with Alfie – the real aspirations of Gilda and Lily and Val and Annie and Brenda and Doreen have been the most thwarted and ground down of all.

Nigel Gray has written more than a book of literary criticism, he has begun to explore the experience of being a working-class man, impatient with reverence, at a time when masculine supremacy was desperate to find new holds. He does this with a consciousness which is not only delicately attuned to the nuances of class but is informed by the feminism of a generation of women who are no longer 'withdrawing and lying down'.

PART FIVE

◆◆◆◆◆◆◆◆◆

STRETCHING

INTRODUCTION

My contribution to *Beyond the Fragments* grew out of questions raised by 'Leninism in the Lurch' (see p. 119). The mild interest the article provoked prodded me to question the hold of some Leninist assumptions about organisation on the revolutionary left.

Lynne Segal raised the limitations of the emphasis on community politics which had been an important aspect of the non-Leninist libertarian Marxist alternative in the early seventies and exerted an influence on the women's movement. Hilary Wainwright pointed to the attempts of community groups to make national links sometimes with the help of political groups or parties but not under the control or direction of any one of these. She also described how local socialist centres or trades councils were assuming the role of connection in particular towns or areas. She explained too that the power of multinationals over information was being resisted by new forms of association among workers, the combine, which brought together people in several unions from different plants owned by the same big firm.

The furore which the book caused took us by surprise. Although *Beyond the Fragments* came from the particular context of British left and feminist politics in the 1970s it has had an impact in other countries.

We found ourselves landed in many more arguments than we knew the answer to – which is a good way to learn. For instance, the book raised dilemmas about what we mean when we use terms like science, theory, consciousness, skills, needs, desire, democracy, communication. How could we anticipate the socialist future when we only knew capitalism? What did we do when there was a clash of anticipations? How were we to transmit memory, overcome very different kinds of fragmentation between people? And what of the odds against us? The military and political might of the ruling class, the ravages of imperialism. The numb exhaustion and despair which Margaret Thatcher has been able to pontificate over have brought these lessons home.

Leninism tried to take on some of these problems. But its attempts at solution have caused as many dilemmas as its efforts to resolve them. To criticise the Leninist tradition is not to deny the validity of many questions Lenin tried to solve, but to break with the assumption that we should take the same course.

The matter of concern though for socialists internationally who have come to the same conclusion by many differing routes is how a democratic renewal of socialism can be created and what would this socialism mean. What forms of combination and association would be appropriate, flexible, resilient and expansive? How do we use the ideas and organisations which are our inheritance and transform them? How do we create alternatives within the here and now which make practical sense of the dream? How do we root socialism in existing needs and reach out towards the precious alchemy of desire?

In Britain now, amidst negligence, arrogant power and disintegration, there are many small groups of people meeting, often unbeknown to one another, seeking understanding, there are fragile attempts to cooperate amidst devastation, new links being made between workers and users, young and old, people of different class, race and sex. Despite suspicion and antagonism, there has been a rapid, if inchoate, developing of consciousness that we must share and develop the skills, assets and abilities which we have if we are to resist accumulative injustices.

It is, however, only an impression − now you see it, now you don't − so simple yet so elusive in capitalism. The dawning realisation that when it comes down to it, it is up to *us* to dismantle and overtake power and transform the organisation of society. Just us. Not them. It is no good waiting for them to bring us socialism. Half of them have no such intention and the others will dawdle too long, forget what they were doing and leave us to burn and perish.

No individual would be adequate for the task. And not one sex. It must be carried by many and varied hands, or be lost. A most dexterous audacity and cunning is our only chance, or the future will be grim, bitter and bleak. This is not to cry wolf − the times are indeed dangerous. When I was a child there was a Guinness advertisement in which one Guinness with a face drawn on its froth looked at the other and said, 'Don't look now but we're about to be swallowed.' It smiled the smile of nervous anticipation before succumbing to its fate. Let's hope there are enough of us to look sharp so we don't go down like that poor Guinness.

1. Harry McShane Speaking at Ruskin History Workshop, May 1976

'Harry McShane Speaking at Ruskin History Workshop, May 1976' originally published in *Cutlasses and Earrings*, ed. Michelene Wander and Michele Roberts, Playbooks 2, 1977.

From the mid-1960s the emergence of a shop stewards movement contributed to historical interest in the workers councils and the shop stewards movement. A new generation of socialists learned how, early this century in Glasgow, the Marxist theoretician and teacher, John Maclean, had lectured on Marxism to huge audiences. Workers formed economics classes to study Marx. The Russian Revolution inspired great hopes. Things were not clear-cut organisationally and politically. In Glasgow worker intellectuals debated, there were strikes, the women led a rent strike, socialist feminists gave out anti-war propaganda. There was talk of Havelock Ellis, working-class men and women became vegetarians, learned Esperanto, books on birth control circulated. There were Clarion camps, the Clarion Players, and socialist Sunday schools where John Maclean spoke.

Harry McShane remembers.

◆◆◆◆◆◆

An old man
speaks with precision
of a lost revolutionary tradition.

He tells of John Maclean
weaning Marxism
out of the pain of 1914.

Unfamiliar with a microphone,
accustomed to speaking
with his own voice,
honoured to be asked
to talk again,
conscious of the responsibility
of proletarian education.

He studies his notes.

A weariness in his shoulders
passes as he takes his bearings.

Standing,
he draws strength
from comrades long ago
and the young
who surround him now.

Remembering so many meetings
And John Maclean speaking,
Sixty years or so
passing in between.

He is still learning,
assessing consequences
analysing fragmentation,
still considering the odds
for and against
working-class emancipation.

He loves Marxism
and nods to an earlier tradition
of Scottish hairsplitting disputation.

Remembering so many meetings
and John Maclean speaking,
sixty years passing in between.

He knows we need more
than economic argumentation
more than political education
more than *The State and Revolution*.

'Communism,' he says,
'is only the beginning.'

He is pushing possibilities
bringing reality to bear on longing

bearing an earthly basis
for the dream,
holding
the dialectic
respectfully
in two hands.

Remembering so many meetings
and John Maclean speaking,
sixty years or so passing in between.

An old communist
conceives
an embryo of longing.

2. The Women's Movement and Organising for Socialism

'The Women's Movement and Organising for Socialism'. This extract was taken from my contribution to *Beyond the Fragments*, Merlin Press, 1979, shortened by Allen Hunter and Linda Gordon, and appeared in *Radical America*, vol. 13, no. 5, September-October 1979.

I see the growth of new forms of organising within the women's movement as part of a larger recovery of a libertarian socialist tradition. I think that this requires a sustained re-evaluation of the tradition of Leninism, and in Britain, because of its particular influence, of Trotskyism.[1] I will confess to being a reluctant contributor to this process, for such a realisation is still in its early days with confusion and doubt on one side and a more tenacious clutch of doctrinal purity on the other. While there is a growing muttering and mumbling among the dissatisfied it is still being met by a pother of rhetoric from the Trotskyist and neo-Trotskyist leaderships.

Not only fear at stirring the pother has restrained me but respect. Organising ideas, male dominated and handed down from above or not, are laborious creations and root themselves through usage. There certainly *are* skills which need to be passed on. There *are* things you need to learn from people who know more. Everything does not pop up in our heads. I know I have learned from both Lenin and Trotsky. Leninist ideas have obviously been well tried and sanctioned by practice. Whatever criticisms I'd make of Leninism there was always some friend at the Communist Party or one of the left groups to explain Lenin hadn't meant it like that or he'd said something different. Sometimes I feel even naming the problem as Leninism is wrong. For I know that in all left organisations there are always people with complex understandings which are lived in many dimensions. So I've thought for years perhaps it *was* best to leave well alone whatever uneasiness I felt. Why tussle and worry when you have no worked-out alternatives?

Now though, it seems to me to have become inescapably important to bring the real disagreements about how to make socialism which exist in the left and the labour movement out into the open in order to develop new understandings. We can best begin by examining our own political experience and see what might be generalised from that. We need to uncover what we have been actually doing without claiming an ascendant correctness or disguising weaknesses.

All this is just the story behind the main plot which in summary is: how I think some of the approaches to organising which go under the headings of Leninism and Trotskyism are flawed; how I think the assumptions of what it means to be a socialist carried within Leninism and Trotskyism and which prevail on the left now block our energy and self-activity and make it harder for socialism to communicate to most people; and why I think the women's movement suggests certain ways of reopening the possibility of a strong and popular socialist movement.

I want to begin to explore the challenge I think the women's movement is making to the prevailing assumptions of how revolutionary socialists should organise. These involve how theory is conceived, how the political organisation sees its relationship to other movements, how consciousness is assumed to change, how the scope of politics is defined, how individual socialists see themselves and their relationship to other people, now and in the past.

I don't see this as a matter of biological people, women, scoring off biological people, men. Feminism for me is a movement to assert the interests of women as a sex. But more than this it is a means of releasing and communicating the understandings which that subordination holds in check. The movement for women's liberation is part of the creation of a society in which there are no forms of domination, and this society cannot be separated from the process of its making.

Relationships between men and women have undoubtedly changed historically along with the great upheavals in which the production and reproduction of all the means of social life and material existence have been transformed by people in the past. This does not mean that sex-gender relations can be either dissolved into economic changes in how things are produced or seen as a function of biological difference. We know very little of the forms these relations have taken for most people in the past. But socialist feminists have begun to assert the need to look at the sexual division of labour and the power relations within kinship networks as they have appeared historically. We are not arguing then either for a biologically universal kind of relationship or for one which is totally contingent on change in the mode of production.

Potentially Marxism is a valuable means of understanding how historical transformations affect our lives and how we are both limited by these processes and help to make them. The existing shape of Marxism has itself been made by the forces and dilemmas uppermost for socialists in the past. The emergence of the women's movement has shown the underdevelopment of Marxism on relations between sexes and the connection between this and women's subordination within the left. It has meant that socialist women, both inside and outside left groups, have challenged the power of men to determine Marxism in their own image. The imperatives of feminism requires that we make many aspects of Marxism anew.

The experience of feminism has been that the specific gender oppression of women requires an independent movement in order for us to develop and assert a new collective consciousness of being female, whether this is seen as separatist or autonomous. Bea Campbell has described how this autonomy was defined in practice from the start as autonomy from men. Implicit in this though was the assertion of sex-gender relationships as an area of social conflict neglected by socialism; this went beyond any definition of femaleness. In delineating what was specific to us as a sex we were necessarily transforming the boundaries of identity.

> . . . feminism necessarily identifies both the subjective and objective condition of existence as problems of politics. In other words, the person became a political problem. This challenged a way of practising politics that treats revolutionary

personnel as agents rather than subjects.

Feminism proposes that the lived relations of subordination, the way of being subordinated, must be a central problem for revolutionary strategy. (It is not alone in doing that, but it is the most coherent and persistent of the 'new' politics.) This prompts a form that is about mass engagement, that is about a process of preparedness.[2]

The power of definitions and icons . . .

I don't mean by this subtitle the necessary effort we all make to define and distinguish different aspects of reality. I mean the false power which avoids and actually prevents us thinking about the complexities of what is happening by covering it up in a category. All references have to be in terms of the categories. Once named, historical situations and groups of people can be shuffled and shifted into neat piles, the unnamed cards are simply left out of the game. They don't exist. The named are branded 'ultra-leftist' or pensioned off as dozy but harmless 'progressive peoples'. Guilt is by association – the Stalinist use of 'social fascist' is the most notorious – but Trotskyists have their own hold over names. The game is rigged to dispose of the 'baddies'. The slots for those labelled only come in certain shapes. So criticism of particular forms of organisation has to be disposed of down one slot marked 'anarchism', questioning of a particular idea of leadership goes down into 'spontaneism', some baddies are stricken with a terrible hereditary disease and called 'middle class'. They have only one chance of survival – join the something party. It all sounds absurd when it is put like this. It is an absurd activity. But nonetheless the power of naming is a real force on the left today. It *deflects* queries about what is going on. It makes people feel small and stupid. It is a part of the invalidation of actual experience which is an inhibiting feature of many aspects of left politics now. Part of its power is in the strange lack of self-consciousness which the left has towards its own values. The power of defining is reduced as soon as it is itself described. But the silences within the Leninist language of politics make it impossible to expose these hidden sources of power. They also make it hard to see that behind, for example, the Troskyist approach to history, there is a personal vision. It is this vision which sustains certain concepts of consciousness, leadership, and the form which it is assumed that the struggle for socialism will take. It is a self-confirming system which is why it is peculiarly difficult to oppose within its own terms.

Individual intention is constantly overridden in practice and sustained by the organisation. These choices are rarely clearly stated, the opponent is dismissed as 'backward' or 'opportunist' or whatever or becomes caricatured as morally evil behind the phoney objectivity of 'reformist', 'centrist', etc. This is a language you learn. It is part of the training about how to organise. The words are some of the tools of the trade. The names do have a fascination when you try to see through them to the diverse realities which they encapsulate. But even this delight is a trick. It channels the imagination and keeps thought straining between closely defined points. It has the pleasurable intensity of theological disputes over doctrine. The game is to see how deviously you can stretch the finite bits of elastic. But absorption in the game makes you deaf to the experience of other people and blind to their capacity for self-activity. This vesicatory rigour intimidates opposition and actually contributes to the fears we all have in a competitive capitalist society about our incapacity to think and act.

Although the Leninist left eschews discussions of its personal values and self-image, it nonetheless carries a version of what it means to be a socialist in images and assumptions. All kinds of dusty icons lurk behind the public face. We need to bring them to the surface. Once we have them out in the open we can examine whether this really is how we want to be and whether it is likely to make most people want to become socialists. For example, what about all those comparisons to nineteenth-century armies marching in orderly formation and retreating smartly at the officer's command? Why is there such a horror of cosiness, as if cosiness were almost more dangerous than capitalism itself? Now it may well be true that at certain times we will all practise drill and that cosiness is inappropriate for some of the circumstances of conflict. But there seems to be an imbalance in the contempt it evokes.

The fear seems to be that cosiness means people get cut off from the 'real' politics. I think this should be put the other way round. If a version of socialism is insisted upon which banishes cosiness, given the attachment of most people, working-class men and women included, to having a fair degree of it around in their lives, this socialism will not attract or keep most people. Why should the ruling class have a monopoly of cosiness?

'During the strikes against General Electric in 1974, women at Heywood, Lancashire, made themselves a picketing base by occupying an empty house owned by the firm just outside the factory, putting in carpets and cooking apparatus and even decorated the mantlepiece with flowers. They inhabited the picket.'[3]

Values are carried not only in implicit attitudes but through the dark shadowy vision of the individual revolutionary. This individual militant appears as a lonely character without ties, bereft of domestic emotions, who is hard, erect, self-contained, controlled, without the time or ability to express loving passion, who cannot pause to nurture, and for whom friendship is a diversion. If this is our version of what it means to be a socialist, it implies that we see socialism as limited to a professional elect who can muster these eccentric qualities. Membership of this elect will for a start be predominantly male for if it attracts a minority among men, it fits even fewer women. Left to carry the burden of a higher consciousness, members of this elect will tend to see the people around them as at worst, bad, lazy, consumed with the desire for material accumulation and sundry diversionary passions, at best, ignorant, needing to be hauled to a higher level. In the hauling the faint-hearted fall by the wayside, the cuddly retire into cosiness and all the suspicions of the elect are confirmed. Being an elect they can rely on no-one and being an elect means they have to do everything. And always the weight of the burden of responsibility, the treachery and insensitivity of everyone else is bearing down on them.

It's a stark, bleak vision of sacrifice and deprivation which when stated explicitly appears to be a caricature. Nonetheless it strikes some chords of recognition on the contemporary left. It surely owes something to the strange things done to little boys in preparing them for manhood in capitalism. More particularly it presents in cameo a nostalgic and romantic yearning for the pristine clarity which is seen as 1917. How often do we need to say we are not in Russia in the early twentieth century before it becomes a felt reality? The Tsar is dead!

Even the anarchists and anarcho-syndicalists have clustered round these high points where power is seen by them as becoming coercive. They have been more concerned with the corruption of the powerful – including the communists and Trotskyists and their suppression of popular resistance. But in this critical emphasis on the leadership and on their moments of confrontation, they have nonetheless excluded most people, including most women, from their version of history. The dramatic instances of conflict are extracted from their longer term context, the toing and froing of resistance which is so evident when you focus on women's lives.

So the women's movement is contesting not simply at the level of programmes and constitutions, which is why we could never find adequate words to meet the aggressive question from men in left groups in the early days, 'Well what is it that you want?' The dispute is about an idiom of politics. It is about how we think about what we are doing; how we situate ourselves historically; how we see ourselves and one another in relation to the movement for change and how we see the forms in which we resist capitalist society. These open up fundamental disagreements about how you organise for socialism and what is the relationship of parties to other movements. They involve the power to define what is politics.

The problem of democracy

If there was an ideal equal relationship between organisations and movements we should just pool our strengths and weaknesses and get on with it. Unfortunately it is not that simple. Bolshevism has a particularly long and sinister record in these matters which I think it's too easy to foist off onto Uncle Joe. More immediately the left groups have often been wrong in the last ten years or so but this seems only to make them more certain they hold the most complete understanding. This absurd paradox might begin to be cleared but for an enormous reluctance at the centre of organisations to say simply that they were wrong, that they have learned this or resisted that out of fears and misconceptions. These seem obvious enough things for human beings to say, not as a great beating of breasts and tearing of hair but as a basis for working together as equals. But it seems to me that a Leninist approach to organisation (and here the name is important) is inconsistent with such equality regardless of the intention of individual Leninists.

For although Leninist and Trotskyist groups acknowledge the need to learn from the working-class movement, I think that secretly they feel deep down they already know better. After all why would they be there if they did not know better? What else could distinguish the member from the 'contact'? Along with this inner assumption there is an acceptance of hierarchy within the organisation itself. If members know better than non-members then the leaders know better than members and the world is felt to be an orderly place. Why else would they be leaders – mere staying power? The thought brings a rash of intolerable anxiety. Away with it – such psychologising leads into the black holes of cynicism.

But there is democratic centralism, that wonderful device without which it would be impossible for everyone to do everything at the same time. *We* know the enemy alright. Here is real socialist democracy, none of your liberal nonsense. And haven't we learned from the crimes of Stalinism? Don't we allow factions even. Don't we just!

Democratic centralism was one of the issues raised in 1956 by the men and women who left the Communist Party to form the new left. They argued that it was inherently undemocratic. Behind the versions of democratic centralism in the Trotskyist groups and the neo-Trotskyism of the S.W.P. now is the conviction that it is a neutral form which can be adapted in a non-Stalinist context. With this goes the belief that the basic problem of making socialism is primarily the making of a leadership through the creation of an 'efficient' organisation.

Richard Kuper, in 'Organizing and Participation' questions the separation between efficiency and democracy. He pointed out the way in which Leninist groups still tend to reduce the criteria of success to an old-style managerial concept of efficiency at the expense of democracy, long after the real managers have caught on to the 'efficiency' of limited forms of participation.

As for the 'efficiency' of democratic centralism he says that the question of the degree of centralisation we might decide is necessary, depends on our assessment of the nature of the task in hand. It requires also that we have a very general kind of agreement. If that is not present 'democratic centralism' is merely a tool to quell opposition. Richard Kuper argues that when it is presented as an absolute rule the concept itself tends to provide a structure which is 'uniquely vulnerable to a certain kind of degeneration and one extraordinarily difficult to regenerate'.[4]

Whether we argue for a more generous or a more scrupulous interpretation of democratic centralism, or a more relative concept of the relationship between centralism and democracy, or whether we believe with Ralph Miliband that it ' . . . has always served as a convenient device for authoritarian party structures'[5] and should be simply dumped, we have to concede that the evidence of this century indicates that it is not a 'neutral' form. There has been something very funny indeed about it in practice. This has not only been a feature of Stalinism but of the more recent experience of the Trotskyist groups in the last decade. For instance, it is a curious fact that the hard core of the leaderships of these groups, despite a series of palace revolutions, manage to tuck themselves into the centre into perpetuity and that bits of broken-off leaderships resurface within the splinters. They have a permanent advantage against all incipient oppositions because they are at the hub of communication and can organise to forestall resistance quicker than people who are scattered in different branches and districts. Also they are known – and better the devil you know!

Even if it gets a bit hot at the top now and then, there is a loophole. The members – poor old things, tramping around getting sore feet on their paper sales up and down all those concrete council flat steps, getting calloused hands lassoing elusive 'contacts' over the balconies. Well they have a tendency to get routinised. Not the leadership. It is up to the leadership to spot when this is happening and leap out towards 'the class' to knock the members into shape. Whoosh – Superman. Poor old members they look on with awe. Some get a bit grumpy. Why isn't democratic centralism binding on the leadership? Because the leaders know best. How else could they possibly be leaders? Whoosh goes Superman again, only doing his duty. How does Superman leadership know when to go whoosh towards the advanced sections of the class? Because he is leader of course. Pop go the poor members. The cosy ones fall by the wayside to seek comfort in discussion circles while the neurotic ones disappear to be cuddled in therapy groups. The intransigent form a small splinter replica. And the leaders go whoosh, whoosh all the way back to the centre.[6]

Soon they are safely ensconced again with the added authority of the patent they have out now on 'the class'. No wonder leaders of Leninist groups have staying power. They are further legitimated by the respect in Leninism due to leaders and by the assumption that just as the members know better than non-members leaders know better than opposing members. The factions can stand up democratically and be counted. They can thus be rapidly isolated. But even if the opposition is based within a campaign, a movement, trade union or community activity, there is a strong possibility that the leaders' position will prevail. The individual member will face a split loyalty between a commitment to an autonomous group and the organisation. The theory says the Party must be more important. The choice is either to get out of the organisation (which seems from within to be leaving socialist politics itself), to ignore the centre (in which case democratic centralism has proved unworkable), or to accept the line. So however unsectarian this socialist may be, he or she has very stark choices and a political ideology which sanctions accepting party discipline more than helping to develop the self-activity of other people.

I am not trying to assert against this that the women's movement has found *the* answer about how we should organise. Though it is certainly worth noting that the women's movement *has* found a means of remaining connected while growing for a decade, and that shifting and spontaneous initiatives have been taken by an extremely large number of women within the movement. But I *am* arguing that the form in which you choose to organise is not 'neutral', it implies certain consequences. This has been a growing recognition on the left since the late sixties. If you accept a high degree of centralisation and define yourselves as professionals concentrating above everything upon the central task of seizing power you necessarily diminish the development of the self-activity and self-confidence of most of the people involved. Because for the women's movement the development of this confidence and ability to be responsible for our own lives was felt to be a priority, this became part of the very act of making a movement. The enormous weight of the inner passivity which was the result of the particular nature of the subordination of the women who became involved meant that the effort to struggle , both against the personal forms of men's control and our oppression within capitalist society, became inseparable from the struggle against the ways in which these had become internalised. We had to learn to love ourselves and other women so we could trust one another without falling back on men. We inclined consequently towards small groups, circles rather than rows, centres as information and research services, open newsletters. The attempt to avoid individual women being isolated as exceptions, either as spokesperson or as freak, the need for our *own* movement and the feelings of sisterhood came from this understanding.

I am not suggesting that such concerns are unique to women or that such forms are biologically determined. Indeed, I believe that the problem of how people can overcome the passivity, self-hatred and lack of trust which is peculiar to modern capitalism is crucial for making a socialist movement – which is not to say that recognising this as central solves the problem of how to do it.

Basically the women's movement accepts a form of 'participatory democracy' which has a long tradition from democratic religious groups to the American New Left of the late sixties and the anti-authoritarian currents in the student movement. The problems about participatory democracy are evident. If you are not able to be present you can't participate. Whoever turns up next time can reverse the previous decision. If very few people turn up they are lumbered with the responsibility. It is a very open situation and anyone with a gift for either emotional blackmail or a conviction of the need to intervene can do so without being checked by any accepted procedure. Participatory democracy only works if everyone accepts a certain give and take, a respect for one another's experience, a desire and need to remain connected. If these are present it can work very well. If they are not it can be a traumatic process. Despite obvious inadequacies though, 'participatory democracy' does assert the idea that everyone is responsible equally and that everyone should participate. It concedes no legitimating respect for permanent leaders or spokespeople.

It has been modified in the practice of the women's movement by women bringing in other concepts of how to organise from tenants groups, trades councils, trade unions or from the Labour Party, the C.P. and from Trotskyist and Maoist groups. Sometimes these have been met with a defensive suspicion and dismissed as simply male-dominated. But in cases when the women's movement has been stronger and more confident we have been able to meet these ideas and recognise the validity of some of their criticisms. The resilience of the women's movement has been partly because of this openness. In practice what we have been doing is adapting several forms of organising to fit the particular circumstances we are engaged in. This does not remove the dangers of 'substitutionism', or centres losing contact with local groups, or small groups of people doing all the work, or people not knowing what other people are doing. All the problems of democracy do not magically disappear. But it does make for an approach to organisation which is prepared to test forms and discard or select according to the situation rather than asserting a universally correct mode. It also means that the 'movement' is perpetually outwards. As women encounter feminism they can make their own kinds of organising dependent on their needs. It is this flexibility which it is extremely important to maintain. It means that for example groups of women artists or groups of women setting up a childcare centre or on the sub-committee of a union can decide for themselves what structure is most useful.

The women's movement shares with the 'anti-authoritarian' movements of the late sixties a commitment to a notion of democracy which does not simply recognise certain formal requirements of procedure. Obviously the danger of this is to reject completely any understanding of how these formal procedures have historically come to be used. When the dust of the first rush of enthusiasm settles it is often handy to have them. But if we simply respond to this by dismissing 'anti-authoritarian' movements as naïve and just ignorant of the 'correct' political procedure, we miss an insistence which carries a deeper meaning of democracy. Faced with the opposition of women and workers in '*Lotta Continua*', an Italian revolutionary organisation, Adriano Sofri, its founder and undisputed leader, made a self-criticism. He said democracy involved not only formally contesting theories of organisation which left politics to the professionals. It involved examining his own inner sense of being a professional. It meant uncovering in public his own capacity to survive and not be frightened by political opponents. He could no longer take refuge in the objectivity of the socialist theoretician. His desire for power could no longer assume a paternal legitimation in a sense of responsibility. There was a strange sense of history repeating itself. He compared the confrontation that he faced to his own opposition, with others, to the Communist Party leadership in 1968. This was 'not a conflict over political line, but a conflict over what politics was all about'.[7]

The Leninist sleight of hand

Values, attitudes and forms of organising are carried and recreated by people in the ways in which they associate. We learn not only from what is said or what we read but from our relationships with other people. This process does not mysteriously stop when we desire to associate in order to create a socialist society.

Our encounters with other people in capitalism are not free, open and equal. But there are different degrees of inequality, distance and coercion involved. These differences in degree make it possible to imagine how things might change. They force the cracks which open to illuminate the soul.

If our imagination is to be sustained by our associating, the ways we meet and cooperate and feel towards one another must develop not from our experiences of the most repressive and authoritarian encounters, but from our understandings of more loving, free ways of connecting to others and acting.

A vital feature of Lenin's concept of the Party is based on its supposed capacity to bring together, spread and transcend the limited, uneven notions and experiences of an alternative to capitalism which are present in the various sections of the working class and among the groups of people who support them. Now this is obviously a real and enormous problem. We *are* limited and cut off by our specific experiences of oppression and by the conflict of interests between us. The disagreement is about how this can best be overcome.

Let's pretend for a moment that there *was* a revolutionary party in real life which did bring together all the elements most 'advanced' or developed in their opposition to capitalist society. Why does it follow from their bringing together in this pretend ideal Party that their limitations are transcended rather than partially reflected and reproduced? If there is no conscious acknowledgement of the need to create and develop political forms which seek to overcome inequalities, and release the full potentialities of all socialists, what is there to prevent power consolidating with the powerful but moral strictures? How can the real antagonisms which are the source of division between oppressed people in capitalism disappear within the Party? Isn't this assuming that the Party is an island?

If we descend from the ideal Party in the sky to more earthly groups and parties the prospect is even more gloomy. Central committees scurry like a lot of white rabbits through a series of internal and factional documents and the smaller the party the greater the hurry. In such circumstances the pressure to neglect inequalities within the organisation in pursuit of the ultimate goal are great. But the theory of what a Leninist Party should be leaves hardly any space to help people participate more equally, much less to develop their potential. Without any theory or structure it seems to me idealistic folly to expect 'the Party' to overcome rather than simply reflect and harness these inequalities of power which we are opposing in capitalism.

The argument used against these criticisms is always to deny that 'the Party' or 'parties' should be places where people experience anything other than the relationships which dominate capitalism. This gruesome state of affairs is presented as being necessary for the working class to take power. Though it is not the working class who are to be relied on to reach this conclusion but 'the Party' which by a process like apostolic succession inherits Lenin's words.

The black, gay and women's movement have been bringing the criticism more closely home, because they have raised inequalities actually *within* Leninist organisations. They have demanded that changes have to be made now. These changes involve examining how real life inequalities as opposed to ideal interpretations are disregarded and perpetuated within socialist parties. They have argued that it is not enough to declare that people should not be 'prejudiced'. The socialist organisation has to create forms of associating and relating which actively seek to overcome the sexism and racism within it. It has become more and more difficult to dismiss these demands as 'utopian'. Not only do they involve a loss of membership, but they come up again and again.

Now the problems of relationships within the Party have been discussed by Leninist organisations in the past though not in these terms. They have been seen as particular deformities which arise and have to be dealt with as they emerge. The emphasis in the Communist Party historically has been on the relationships between workers and middle-class intellectuals (mainly men). More recently it has been a tortured and painful area in the Socialist Workers Party, because of the effort to change the class basis of this organisation. Both the Communist Party and the Socialist Workers Party have relied formally upon political education and informally upon guilt to try and curb the confidence of middle-class intellectuals. Sometimes it has been used by one group of middle-class administrators against another, or by the permanent administrators against intellectuals who might challenge the central bureaucracy. It has also been used, more understandably, by working-class people as a defence against being made to feel ignorant and humiliated by the intellectuals' use of theory as a form of power against them. But whatever the reasons this negative control through the public orchestration of personal guilt has a terrible record and disastrous ramifications. It is certainly not caused by Leninism. For instance, guilt between blacks and whites, women and men, gays and heterosexuals bedevilled the American New Left in the late sixties and early seventies. Leninism serves in fact to hold the extremes of this negative response to power relations at bay. But this is not the same as providing a solution by going directly to the sources of the antagonisms producing guilt and allowing them free expression which implies trusting the imaginative capacity of human beings to enter one another's predicaments and learn from the attempt. . . .

Not until the 1960s, when the black question was raised by the growing militancy of American blacks and revolutionary movements in developing countries, was the power relationship between autonomous movements and socialist organisations seriously contested. In the course of this confrontation the need for autonomous movements of self-definition was clearly asserted. This was to be a decisive influence on the emergence of the women's liberation movement.

We have no clear alternative of how to combine the advantages of autonomous movements with the strengths of a more general combination. But at least we must now recognise it as a problem to face. Leninism does not 'know' the answer. It merely asserts an ideal transcendence.

There remains then no effective guarantee within Leninism that the groups who are in a dominant position in capitalism won't bring their advantage into 'the Party'. Worse there is an effective sleight of hand which conceals this inherent tendency in the assertion of the *ideal* of the Party transcending the interests and vistas of its sections.

This does not imply that we should deny that people can become stuck in their own grievances and not see the wood for the trees. There is always the temptation to attack the people in the same boat as you as this takes the least effort and involves the least risk. The argument is about how to overcome this. We need a form of organisation which can at once allow for the open expression of conflict between different groups and develop the particular understandings which all these differences bring to socialism. For if every form of oppression has its own defensive suspicions, all the movements in resistance to humiliation and inequality also discover their own wisdoms. We require a socialist movement in which there is freedom for these differences, and nurture for these wisdoms. This means that in the making of socialism people can develop positively their own strengths and find ways of communicating to one another what we have gained, without the transcendent correctness which Leninism fosters.

The attitude towards power relations within socialist organisations has an important bearing on how such an organisation will relate outwards. . . .

Vanguards and consciousness

It is not difficult to demonstrate that Lenin's notion of the vanguard was not devised to give comfort to bossy socialists but to illuminate the strengths and weaknesses of the forces of resistance to capitalism. In theory, it provided a means of channelling for the greatest effect all the elements in struggle, not only the economic conflict of workers against employers but all the experience of social and cultural struggles. The idea was to bring the strengths of the most 'advanced' to the assistance of the less developed through the Party.

According to one current version of this Leninist intention, 'advanced' consciousness by definition finds its way into 'the Party'. This internal definition of the vanguard tends to be a characteristic of Trotskyism. It becomes a tautology. The 'Party' is the expression of advanced consciousness, therefore advanced consciousness is to be found in the Party.

In the attempt to break with this narrow and internal idea of the vanguard various attempts have been made to locate the vanguard in struggles outside the Party. This was an argument internationally within Trotskyism after the Second World War. On the Italian left after 1968 some socialists argued that the workers in struggle are the vanguard rather than the Party. In America by the early 1970s, the vanguard was up for grabs. Everyone claimed to be the vanguard, blacks, women, gays. In fact they all fell out with one another over this.

This notion of the vanguard assumed it applied to either the most oppressed or the most foolhardy and illustrates the problem in defining the vanguard in terms of whoever is struggling. . . .

Criticisms of the Leninist idea of the 'vanguard' have tended to assume that the attempt to assess consciousness itself was at fault. I think this needs shifting into a different area of dispute. The argument is really about who has the power to define how the estimation is made and the acknowledgement that none of us are the embodiment of the pure abstract reason of correct ideas.

So in reaction against Leninism there was a tendency in both the American New Left and among British libertarians to dismiss the very attempt to assess consciousness as inherently elitist. Less clearly this dismissal of the problem has been present in the women's movement.

The trouble is that if you disregard all attempts to work out who is likely to stick their neck out in particular circumstances and who can sustain attack in particular places you are left wide open. Without any historical and social estimation of different kinds of consciousness you are left with only static categories of the oppressed. You have no means of deciding how various sections are likely to respond to change. As your oppressed constituency is both enormous and inert and as there is no difference between the oppressed category and conscious politics there is nothing to stop you acting on their behalf. There is not even the awareness that is present within Leninism of the dangers of 'substitutionism'. Here a sleight of hand appears in an over-generalised concept of a static condition of oppression. A politics of example by self-appointed small groups has often been the undemocratic consequence of a critique of differentiation as elitist. This has bedevilled anarchism historically and was a paralysing feature of libertarian Marxism in the early 1970s. It has been a rumbling source of confusion in the women's movement.

Instead of examining the actual social composition of our movement and the forces and experiences which have radicalised certain groups of women, the feminism of the women's liberation movement can be presented as the consciousness of women in general. This makes it impossible to begin to work out the relationship of the movement to women not already involved. Their absence is in fact being dismissed and explained away. They need simply to be reached and enlightened by the propaganda of the movement. Any opposition they might make is because they have been hopelessly brainwashed by men. Under a 'false' non-feminist consciousness sits a 'true' natural feminism in every woman. Feminists just need to plumb the depths of this well of common sense to reach what every woman knows. It is true that every woman knows, but we happen to know somewhat differently depending on our circumstances and the openings created by the process of change. We need to examine what is specific as well as what is shared by women in differing situations. If circumstances and consciousness are concertinaed we fold an abstract category 'Woman' into a particular historical movement which has emerged out of changes in the life of some women.

Thus if we are to distinguish the various ways in which women approach their situations we need to understand the different nature of the power relationships which enmesh us. This means that we do not present relations in the family simply as the equivalent of relations on the cash nexus, or assume that the condition of a sex is the same as class relations. It also means we need to assess very carefully changes in class composition and their impact on women's consciousness.

Some socialist feminists in America have been drawn to analyses of class in which professional, service, administrative and communications workers are equated with the working class. This recognises the emergence of new kinds of work closely connected to the welfare of people and the communication of values which have become crucial areas in modern capitalism. It also focuses on the radicalisation of men and women in these jobs. But it makes it difficult to understand the specific ways in which changes in class composition have affected various groups differently. In Britain the emotive force of class has led to similar elliptics in practice. For example the IS Rank and File groups and Working Women's Charter tended to emphasise the similarity between white-collar trade unionists and manual and lower-grade service workers. They were all trade unionists. This was important to assert against the traditional suspicion in the trade union movement of white-collar workers and the dismissal on the left of women. But this meant that other important power relationships were dismissed. These were in fact vital to an understanding of consciousness which could avoid fatalism, a notion of an intact true consciousness or an external vanguard bringing understanding. The 'Red Collective' pointed out in a criticism of the Charter in 1974 that the simple assertion of a common trade unionism denied ' . . . the experiences that brought these women into women's liberation, and the difficulties they must meet in their jobs as "handlers" of people which ought to make them aware of other divisions, based on a hierarchical division of labour'.[8]

While resistance to 'handling' was certainly part of the personal experience of women in local Charter groups and also in the real rank and file of 'Rank and File', it was not accepted as part of the theory of organisation and consciousness of the IMG and IS who had hegemonic positions in these groupings. So individual understandings were passed over as by the way. But in fact the women's movement and the whole process of radicalisation among people in these jobs were providing vital clues to the puzzle of how to oppose modern capitalism and how to go about a more complex assessment of consciousness.[9]

The women's movement has broken the circle in the concept of a vanguard Party by questioning the criteria used in assessing the meaning of 'advanced' and 'backward' and arguing that this assessment is not a neutral and objective process but a matter of subjective control.

The women's movement's criticisms of the ways in which the Leninist left assess activity and the manner in which consciousness changes have come not from a completed theory of organisation but from the experience of a particular group of women's lives. The wide-ranging areas of women's oppression, the complexity of the subordinated relationship with men, and the deep personal hold of women's sense of secondariness have combined with significant changes in class composition and social relations.

It is not enough for left groups to simply widen the range of subjects which can be discussed in their publications or meetings – the crucial question is what significance is given to these subjects and how is that estimate reached? If a political or economic scale is used the same judgements of advanced and backward forms of consciousness can be retained with a few sexual political frills. But if you take into account other kinds of struggle like resistance to the domestic control of the state which has been part of a wide range of community politics or the emotional personal challenge to sexual domination, the old scale of measuring consciousness becomes ungainly because you are moving in several dimensions at the same time. People can be so backward and so forward at the same time that the scale won't work any more. There is no way of marking consciousness off on a straight line to assess it in this clear and simple way.

Of course Leninism recognises that consciousness is uneven. But this still assumes that it can reach one level. The notion of the vanguard suggests a tough poky thing moving in the same direction at the same time. The approach to consciousness in the women's movement has uncovered many aspects of experience neglected by socialist politics but it also has the aware-ness that formal theoretical or practical public abilities are not the only important areas for growth. Our personal relationships with our families and friends, how we connect to other women in the movement and our inner spiritual and sexual life are never separate from our feminism. Indeed as we resist subordination most strenuously in one area it has a way of creeping up on us from some completely different direction. The feminist approach to consciousness perceives its growth as many-faceted and contradictory. The model of the vanguard doesn't fit into this way of thinking. It's not even like trying to put a square peg into a round hole. It's like dropping it down a well. The criteria used for 'advanced' and 'backward' elements can no more be applied to this more complex view of political consciousness than a spirit level can be used for assessing an electrical current. This does not mean that we should abandon the attempt to estimate the consequences of different forms of consciousness at various times. But it means we need a much more delicate kind of socialist theory to gauge them. The Leninist approach simply blots out immense but fragile processes of transformation.

Left organisations, particularly since the Bolsheviks, have assumed a kind of pyramid of levels of activity. Near the top are struggles for political power and conflict at the work place. Community struggles follow, traditionally seen mainly as the housing question and tenants movements. After them education, welfare and cultural issues may be considered with an optional cluster of sexual politics, 'personal' politics, ecology and whatnot under a rather dusty heading of 'quality of life'.

Feminists have criticised these levels, arguing particularly against the over-emphasis on wage work, which excludes many women. The problem can't be solved by recognising demands for a changing quality of life and just widening the areas of activity.

We also need to challenge the notion of consciousness which is behind this approach to activity. For consciousness is also being chopped up into categories of significance. The women's movement has enabled us to understand that such divisions do not reach the roots of oppression. Presenting consciousness in the compartments of political, economic, cultural, social, personal, makes it impossible to begin to see how the different forms feed and sustain one another. Feminism has shown how consciousness spills over these boundaries. I don't think this need imply that particular groups of socialists should not make certain forms of activity a priority given resources of time, energy and skill, and the forces of opposition. For example, it would be evidently absurd to expect that the possibilities present for women in a democratic capitalist society would be the same as the narrower options for resistance under fascism. It is not an absolute moral principle which is involved but the power to challenge the criteria in which priorities are decided. . . .

Conclusion

It has required a big argument on the Leninist left to take up even one aspect of 'personal' power relationships – the question of inequality between men and women within socialist organisations themselves. The feminist movement has challenged this reproduction of inequality within the left. After nearly a decade sexism (like racism) is now admitted to exist even within left parties themselves by most organisations on the left. This used to be denied or it was said that it was utopian to expect anything else until after socialism. The ground has shifted because men and women affected by sexual politics have been saying both inside and outside socialist groups that we can't wait. We have to find effective ways of struggling against these inequalities for they are not only wrong in themselves, they paralyse many socialists and restrict our communications with many people who can see little difference between socialist and right-wing organisations. They also block understandings vital for the making of socialism.

However, the implications of this recognition are still not followed through. The assumption within left groups has continued to be that the remedy for inequalities was the exhortation to improvement. It is presumed that within the organisation itself change can be a result of an effort of pure reason. It is true that we can change our minds when confronted with 'facts' and argument. But they are inadequate on their own to touch the full extent of the problem. This emphasis on reason and will is the reverse side of the coin to the fatalism which denies the possibility of prefigurative change before socialism. Leninists are saying at once no change is possible and yet all changes necessary can be made by political education in the Party.

Feminists have been arguing a form of politics which enables people to experience different relationships. The implications of this go beyond sex-gender relationships, to all relationships of inequality, including those between socialists. Leninist organisations *have* made piecemeal concessions to the women's movement and the gay movement under pressure. They have been affected also by the contradictory pulls in modern capitalism which have led to questioning certain areas of control in everyday life. But they have resisted the implications of these social changes and movements as a more general challenge to their notion of politics. The notion of organisation in which a transforming vision of what is possible develops out of the process of organising questions some of the most deeply held tenets of Leninism. The weight of Leninist theory (Gramsci apart) and the prevailing historical practice of Leninism is towards seeing the 'party' as the means by which the working class can take power and these 'means' have a utilitarian narrowness. Other considerations consequently have to be deferred until the goal of socialism is reached. But socialist feminists and men influenced by the women's movement and gay liberation have been saying that these are precisely the considerations which are inseparable from the making of socialism. These involve considerable disagreement about the meaning of socialist politics and what it means to be a socialist.

So I don't believe it is a matter of adding bits to a pre-existing model of an 'efficient' 'combative' organisation through which the working class (duly notified and rounded up at last) will take power. You need changes now in how people can experience relationships in which we can both express our power and struggle against domination in all its forms. A socialist movement must help us find a way to meet person to person – an inward as well as an external quality. It must be a place where we can really learn from one another without deference or resentment and 'theory' is not put in authority.

This will not just happen. It goes too deeply against the way of the world.

We really cannot rely on common sense here. We need to make the creation of prefigurative forms an explicit part of our movement against capitalism. I do not mean that we try to hold an imaginary future in the present, straining against the boundaries of the possible until we collapse in exhaustion and despair. This would be utopian. Instead such forms would seek both to consolidate existing practice and release the imagination of what could be. The effort to go beyond what we know now has to be part of our experience of what we might know, rather than a denial of the validity of our own experience in face of a transcendent party. This means a conscious legitimation within the theory and practice of socialism of all those aspects of our experience which are so easily denied because they go against the grain of how we learn to feel and think in capitalism. All those feelings of love and creativity, imagination and wisdom which are negated, jostled and bruised within the relationships which dominate in capitalism are nonetheless there, our gifts to the new life. Marxism has been negligent of their power, Leninism and Trotskyism frequently contemptuous or dismissive. Structuralist Marxism hides them from view in the heavy academic gown of objectivity. For a language of politics which can express them we need to look elsewhere, for instance, to the utopian socialists in the early nineteenth century, or to the Socialist League in the 1880s, or Spanish anarcho-syndicalism. We cannot simply reassert these as alternatives against the Leninist tradition. There are no 'answers' lying latent in history. But there is more to encourage you than meets the Leninist eye. We have to shed completely the lurking assumption that Leninism provides the highest political form of organising and that all other approaches can be dismissed as primitive antecedents or as incorrect theories.

The versions of Leninism current on the left make it difficult to legitimate any alternative approaches to socialist politics which have been stumbling into existence. These Leninisms are difficult to counter because at their most superficial they have a surface coherence, they argue about brass tacks and hard facts. They claim history and sport their own insignia and regalia of position. They fight dirty – with a quick sneer and the certainty of correct ideas. At their most thoughtful intensity they provide a passionate and complex cultural tradition of revolutionary theory and practice on which we must certainly draw. Socialist ideas can be pre-Leninist or anti-Leninist. But there is no clear post-Leninist revolutionary tradition yet. Leninism is alive still, whatever dogmatic accoutrements it has acquired. The argument is about the extent of its usefulness for making socialism now.

I know that many socialists who have lived through the complicated and often painful encounters between sexual politics and the left in the past few years believe we must alter Leninism to fit the experience gained in sexual political movements. I have been edged and nuzzled and finally butted towards believing that what we have learned can't be forced into the moulds of Leninism without restricting and cutting its implications short. Moreover, the structures of thought and feeling inherent in Leninism continually brake our consciousness of alternatives. I don't see the way through this as devising an ideal model of a non-authoritarian organisation but as a collective awakening to a constant awareness about how we see ourselves as socialists, a willingness to trust as well as criticise what we have done, a recognition of creativity in diversity and a persistent quest for open types of relationships to one another and to ideas as part of the process of making socialism.

3. More Than Just Cogs in the Machine

'More Than Just Cogs in the Machine', *New Society*, 11 September 1980.

Mike Cooley, *Architect or Bee?: the Human/Technology Relationships*, Langley Technical Services, c/o 95 Sussex Place, Slough, 1980
Marianne Herzog, *From Hand to Mouth: Women and Piecework*, Penguin, 1980

'People are trouble,' ran a headline in the *Engineer* in 1978, 'but machines obey.' As people cannot simply be eliminated, the answer to trouble must be to build as many human skills as possible into the machines while ensuring that machine-like qualities take over the people. For the misfits, the recalcitrant, the worn-out or the unwanted, there is always unemployment.

Such logic and such practices are not, of course, entirely new but Mike Cooley argues that these long-term processes are reaching new intensity in modern capitalism. This denial of humanity also no longer focuses only on the manual worker. While manual workers become redundant, clerical and administrative staff are 'surplus to requirements' and scientists and technologists are most politely 'technologically displaced'. As Cooley says, it amounts to the same thing – 'the good old-fashioned sack'.

Of course, the labour movement has opposed unemployment. But the assumption has been that more planning or, on the left, that public ownership – possibly with workers' control – is the answer. In *Architect or Bee?*, Mike Cooley draws on his experience as an engineer in the Aerospace industry and argues that none of these solutions goes far enough. For they share the assumption that science and technology are neutral. He believes that they are not. The values of the conquering White Male Warrior are historically bound up with apparently objective and scientific ideas about the rational organisation of work, the very design of jobs, machines and computers. He does not believe this means dismissing all aspects of a scientific approach but that it should always be seen as merely complementary to experience and nurtured by the imagination.

It is not only the loss of freedom involved in the physical and mental subjection of human beings to the machine which is at issue. There is an argument about how you design machines, about what they produce and the forms in which production is organised. Mike Cooley develops the idea of workers' control and questions existing assumptions about what socialism involves. In many societies which have attempted to make socialism, faith in the neutrality of science and technology has meant there has not been a clear recognition of the need consciously to challenge discipline and hierarchy in the work process or the emphasis upon the product rather than the person producing. These have important political consequences.

'If a worker is constrained through Taylorism at the point of production it is inconceivable that he or she will develop the self-confidence and the range of skills, abilities and talents which will make it possible to play a vigorous and creative part in society as a whole.'

In *Architect or Bee?*, Cooley describes some living sources for this creativity. He tells how Lucas Aerospace workers discovered that with the skills they possessed they could make many things which were needed. For example, they designed a 'hobcart' so children with spina bifida could move around, a simple portable life-support system to keep victims of heart attacks going until they reached hospital, and came up with various energy-conserving products and ideas.

Work begins to take on a new meaning when the social results of labour can be personally seen and understood. Such a sense of value has been the preserve of the more privileged professions in capitalism. It has been glimpsed as a common condition for humanity only in precious moments by visionaries, artists and democratically minded philosophers. The practical assertion of the value of human skill as a vital part of our culture challenges the power of the machine and indeed the mechanical fatalism of theories presenting social change simply in terms of objective laws which deny human efforts.

However, I think this leaves us with some important snags around the sense of value which skills carry. Cooley recognises that the abilities valued in Western science and technology deny qualities which are often socially connected with women. He mentions intuition, subjectivity, tenacity and compassion. Perhaps it would be more accurate, though, to see these as qualities often associated with oppressed people. They are the sources of resistance from within subordination. For the Great White Male Warrior is not merely male but white and ruling class as well. All men have not had an equal part in the making and the use of science and technology. On the other hand, all workers have not had an equal power to define what they do as a skill.

This is not just an old battle between skilled and unskilled, but between men and women within the working class itself. It is true that it has often been those workers who have had their skills eroded – the early nineteenth-century handloom weavers, engineers early in this century, intellectual workers in our own day – who have found the spirit to rebel. A position of privilege can give you a sense of your own worth and, when this is challenged, leave the strength to assert alternative values to the logic of inevitable 'progress'. However, the possessors of skill often sought to exclude others. The implication of *Architect or Bee?* is for the creation of a non-exclusive notion of skill.

But what of the people, many of whom are women, who have not been able to assert the skill in what they do? There are, for instance, not only the most alienated kinds of factory work, but the lower grades of service work, labour-intensive home industry and the unwaged activities, housework and childcare. Moreover, feminists have long struggled with a dilemma which is now clearly relevant to workers.

If you try and redefine skills and assert their real social value from within the existing sphere of oppression, a contained space can open up when you manage eventually to exert sufficient political pressure. Thus early-twentieth-century feminist emphasis upon the craft of housewifery produced classes for girls in domestic economy but did not challenge the division of work in society. Human creativity could be confined again within the limits of the assertion of the skill present in what was already done. An important argument of the contemporary feminist movement has been not only the need to resist the devaluation of housework and childcare but to insist that nobody should have to do them all the time. Surely the same must be true of the skills of computer design and aerospace engineering?

Just as Mike Cooley contests the idea that automation automatically means progress, Sally Alexander, in her introduction to Marianne Herzog's *From Hand to Mouth*, questions the benign faith in gradual improvement which is a feature of many commentaries on women's work. She quotes a manager of a shell factory in the First World War. He said of the dilutees whose presence threatened the skilled engineers, 'We put the brains into the machines before the women began.' These are precisely the circumstances which Marianne Herzog encounters in a German engineering factory in the 1970s.

From Hand to Mouth approaches the problem of finding a sense of value from the situation of unskilled women workers, and so her perspective is in a sense more pessimistic than that in *Architect or Bee?*. The image of work as a prison recurs in her account. Accidents happen but the machines do not stop. The rhythm of the work process is everything. 'Collect, collect, collect, wait, stare, wait, collect, collect, collect and again collect, wait, stare, collect wait, stare, collect.' In these conditions there is no clear sense of having been valuable, of a tangible skill which has been eroded or any memory of worth denied.

The women doing piecework are caught in a tight web of dependence. 'When Frau Shuster gets home she is faced with three children. She's not allowed to moan, the children want everything from her all over again.'

Even though the conditions of labour described are so alienated, and the women are not able to take collective action, Marianne Herzog notes how they still contrive to make space for their desires and feelings. There are dreams which raise alternative possibilities of what life could be: 'Frau Winterfeld dreams of an ice-cream parlour of which she is the proprietor. She imagines pastries and ice-cream sundaes and invents names for them. . . . Frau Lange dreams of the relationships that she had before marriage.'

It is true that such dreams will not bring capitalism to its knees, but within them lurks a troublesome vision of self-definition and freedom. Herzog also describes a culture of mutual care which has a fragile existence amid the competition of piecework rates. An old male worker massages the shoulders of a woman while she pauses in her work. Ritual and celebration enter the factory. There is practical help and that thoughtful attention to detailed needs which is such an important part of existing skills among women. Bargains are brought to work. Clothes and shoes are given among friends. There are also the discussions about children's schoolwork or personal relationships.

Though Marianne Herzog's account of her work in Germany is desolate, the machine is still not in total control. Yet there is no possibility for these German factory women of active rebellion. Sally Alexander reminds us that this should not be seen as the general predicament of all women workers. For in the last decade there have been many struggles for union recognition, equal pay, crêches among women and important instances of male support. But *From Hand to Mouth* is a stark reminder of the inhuman conditions in which a significant section of the labour force spends its days.

Marianne Herzog concludes with a description of another more hopeful experience in the Lip factory in France which workers occupied in 1973. During the occupation a sense of an alternative culture became not merely a matter of defence and survival but a defiant release, a certainty that life could be different. The workers discovered a people's culture of realism and humour, a freedom from conformity and punctuality, the value of living collectively. Even when they returned under the old regime, one woman says, there was still the memory of the victory, and 'the great friendship which arose during the struggle is still alive. . . . We no longer worry about whether someone is working in production or in an office. . . . We must preserve it for it will be our strength.'

4. Planning From Below

'Planning From Below', (with Charlie Owen), *Beyond the Fragments Bulletin*, no. 3, January 1982.

When we were planning the *Beyond the Fragments* conference in 1980 it seemed clear that the response to the book came from a wide range of grass-roots groups and campaigns and from people who felt politically isolated and without any voice.

Since then there have been tremendous shifts in the whole political spectrum, the struggle of the Bennite left in the Labour Party, the growth of the SDP, the anti-nuclear movement, opposition within the Tory Party.

Those of us who have continued the *Fragments* network, producing the bulletin, meeting nationally to discuss our experience and to try and work through ideas, have, like many other people on the left, been caught up by these large-scale changes. We have landed rather puffed and bewildered in a new situation. Many of us have been startled to find ourselves hanging on fragile ropes slung across a series of chasms between local non-aligned politics and Labour councils, between rank-and-file union struggles and the official trades union structure, or personal politics and state power. Even more alarming, the chasms themselves have been moving.

It is not a particularly comfortable predicament. Crucial rule of thumb approaches, for instance the distinction between seeing Labour councillors as 'providers' and 'enablers', the desire for a politics which allows 'individual exploration and flexible discussion', the need for our politics to affect how we live and what we do, can easily be marginalised and dismissed as some kind of 'utopian purity' or as 'unrealistic'.

There is also the danger that the struggle for control over social resources and resistance to relations of authority in everyday life, which has been such a vital feature of the socialist movement in the 1970s, could be overwhelmed. The effort just to survive and the difficulty in defending one another has become the main thing. The failure to prevent Mike Cooley being sacked from Lucas Aerospace is a recent bitter defeat.

On the other hand, the extremity of the new circumstances can provoke a stubborn spirit. So it is idle to regret that times have changed. The onslaught also brings new connections and understandings.

People whose politics have for so long been 'agin' all the established political structures, including the Labour Party, have been forced to examine the simple reflex of opposition. Partly because all the familiar signposts are wobbling frantically. Partly because of the changes in the Labour Party and the opening up towards movements outside the Labour Party.

It is no longer enough to repeat what we don't like, we have to work out 'what sort of society do we want. . . .'

To develop such a general conception we have to overcome the divisions between economic, personal, social, and political areas which have been part of our fragmentation. We have to find ways of doing this by direct action from below, else we will find the ground taken from under our feet. But this will not mean we solve the knotty old problem of how these forms of organising find coordinated power, or how direct action can be carried through the delegation of power in structures like the Labour Party.

It is apparent that real unity can only be developed when we can be frank both about differences in our situations and actual conflicts among people who want change in capitalism. This has been a recurring theme in the various feminist criticisms of the starting point of the debate around the Alternative Economic Strategy. Men become 'the working class' in general, rather than one half of a working class which has two sexes. However, the need for coherent strategy is resulting in proposals for feminist social policy. Again we find ourselves facing both ways. These have to be taken up by the Labour Party and the official trade union structure but this will only have real power if they are also part of a widespread democratic movement against sexual inequality and oppression in every sense. It must be working-class women who change the labour movement to fit their needs. Power cannot be given from on top – which is not to say that it cannot be 'enabled'.

Things are moving so fast there has not been much time to think out the implications. But we cannot ignore that the need to give shape and substance to what kind of socialism we want is inseparable from a fundamental examination of what we mean by socialism.

Such big propositions make most people's thoughts seize up completely. But if planning from below means anything it means we all have to chew thoughts in larger chunks than we've been accustomed to.

The familiar notion of planning is that done by experts, with scientific knowledge. We have seen the results of that rational planning: tower blocks, food additives, valium – the list of horrors is endless.

Socialist planning, in both its Fabian and Communist forms, took this form of planning to extremes. The radical science movement of the 1930s, for instance, actively promoted a pervasive optimism in the ability of science to solve social problems once freed from the constraints of capitalism. They saw the inevitable outcome of science and rationality as progress, whereas today we see repression, exploitation, and weapons.

This form of planning requires no consultation with those on the receiving end, because they lack the abstract knowledge required for understanding: they only have their 'experience' or their 'emotions' to go on. It is no accident that this dimension of (valued) abstraction and (devalued) experience is also a characteristic of masculinity versus femininity.

To break out of this planning as social control requires new forms of democracy which allows social priorities to come from below and the expression of needs; it requires a new relationship between experts and planning; and it requires a re-examination of the social basis of our ideas of rationality and objectivity, and their relation to masculinity.

In order to get things clearer in our own minds it's a help to start off from what we know from our own experience and then begin to interrogate what we take for granted. For example, words like 'needs', 'science', 'planning', 'realism', 'reason', 'rationality', 'skill', 'technology' are shaped by the world as it is on the terms of people with various kinds of power. We have continually to extract and appropriate their radical meaning while revealing in practical ways how elements within these words adhere to and confirm the status quo. The renewal and recreation of socialism requires a dismantling process if old truths are to find new light.

5. Feminism and the Making of Socialism

'Feminism and the Making of Socialism', *Beyond the Fragments Bulletin*, no. 3, January 1982. The response to *Beyond the Fragments* helped me to learn about movements and ideas which I had not known about in any detail before.

The discussions which have continued within the loose network which developed out of the conference at Leeds in summer 1980 have directed my thoughts away from the argument about political organisation. We have been working our way round wider questions of relationships at work and in the community, the effect of unemployment, the question of the state and centralised and decentralised executive power. Discussing planning from below leadership, democracy and the reasons for the unpopularity of socialism we have begun to realise how the meaning of socialism itself has been taken for granted, as if the purpose of all our struggles and endeavour was either too obvious or too large to explain and examine.

In the midst of this and the attack of the right upon the old sanctities and securities of socialist politics, I have found myself like many other people on the left really forced to begin to express what kind of socialist society we seek. Somehow we need to find ways of making our rather vague suppositions take on practical shapes.

This means beginning with what exists, what has been done, without deluding ourselves that these are anything other than fragile growths. A vital strand in this was the practical creation of a simple and startling idea which the Lucas workers initiated, and was carried on in the attempts to develop workers' plans. The idea is that the people who experience exploitation and oppression can find the means of resistance by sharing their skills, abilities and creativity. This means challenging the control of employers and managers and of the financial power structure internationally. The idea has become a plan. The plan means that instead of a group of workers bargaining simply for money or even seeking control over conditions and relationships at work there is a challenge to what is actually produced. This involves an onslaught on the values and assumptions which enhance the power of capital. Why do we produce things such as armaments which harm one another but make profits for a few? Our livelihoods could be better made. On balance, given the choice, most people would be happier spending their lives in ways that brought pleasure rather than distress, sorrow, despair.

This led to another idea. Why do we hand over so much power to plan aspects of our lives to people who lack the experience of how things work out in practice for thousands of people? Why are we not all raised on the assumption that we must be the architects of our society? For this is imparted to the children of the ruling class, especially to the little boys, from an early age, fostered in the public schools and emanates from the élite universities (and includes the aspiring oddballs from other classes who make it through the gates). Privilege reinforces itself.

However, it is best attacked from both sides. The privileged have a real contribution to make in repaying opportunities gained at the expense of the labour of others. Among these debts to be settled when the toilers of hand and brain come asset-stripping is the exposure of the fraud, which gives some people the confidence to assume they should govern others. This is as much of an outrage against people's humanity as taking their lifetimes and hopes from them by living off their labour.

These subversive ideas and alternative plans which came from a group of workers at Lucas Aerospace in the mid 1970s meet others which have been developed by health workers, women's health groups, radical scientists, nursery workers and users, tenants, builders, alternative energy groups, teachers and parents, transport workers and users, radical architects and tenants and perhaps others of which I am ignorant.

The odds against the making of a cooperative commonwealth are stacked in favour of the existing holders of power. It is not always the case that where there's a will, there's a way. And Margaret Thatcher and her ilk are adroit politicians in the interests of their class. They understand the will and how to sap the spirit of rebellion.

On the other hand, revolutionary guerrilla armies fighting for a cause worth the trouble are redoubtable opponents. True we face great powers. But it is worth remembering they too came from small beginnings. The accumulation of capital itself was but a robbery here, an encroachment there, a good idea, concentrated ambition, perseverance, thrift, an aspiration to travel on the high seas, to leave villages and the constraints of community, to seek freedom and fortune, questioning why the world should go on just as it was. Not evil qualities in themselves but bringing exploitation, death and pain in their wake. So the power which defends them now has to be contested by all the means we can muster.

This is a stern task and must be worth the trouble. There must be no remaking of corruption, bureaucratic callousness, sneaking privilege and dishonourably calling it socialism.

But a socialism which could create, root and develop a transformation and renewal of that old friend of the people, democracy. Well, that would be worth the trouble.

◆◆◆◆◆◆

The book *Beyond the Fragments* explored some of the practical and theoretical connections between feminism and other radical social movements mainly in relation to organising. This means not only asserting the interests of women as a group but understanding the political implications of feminism for our understanding and making of socialism.

Discussions since the book was published, in the planning for the Leeds conference and in the network which grew from this, have begun tentatively to tackle the problem of what kind of socialism and how it is to be made.

The areas in which these connections keep appearing seem to me to be the following:

1. Questioning the division between economic necessity and social need.

2. And between producers and consumers or makers and users.

3. Extending the idea of political and industrial democracy into social and personal life.

4. Challenging the limitations of 'rationality', e.g. money is the only snag, strategic nuclear warfare.

5. Breaking down and redistributing the power involved in expert knowledge, e.g. professionalism, craft skill, technology, planning from on top.

6. Challenging the division of labour in capitalism which also permeates socialist organising, i.e. intellectuals think, workers provide muscle, women care, children play. We can all do with less of what we're meant to do and more of what we're not meant to do.

7. Transforming our understanding of creativity to mean not only ideas and artistry in making, but the capacity to nurture human life and growth.

6. Reclaim the Moon

'Reclaim the Moon' spring 1981. Uncomfortable at being dragged by circumstance to think about power and feeling sometimes, even among my socialist feminist friends, a frivolous, soppy and moonish creature, I stake a claim for romance, in the new moral world.

I am serious, but embarrassed, because sensibility does not meet analysis.

So I act the fool and make doggerel. Politics makes comics of us all. Or we would weep. How else could we bear to reclaim the moon?

Well we the wise ones
have disowned the moon
to spoon
in June
is not our tune.

And as for Hecate's pale spell,
the healing glade
or loving dell,
They are the patriarchal sell,
just signs and symbols of our plight.
So nymphs take flight
abandon myth,
objective science is the tryst
for feminist materialists.

And yet, and yet and yet and yet,
there is the odd moment of regret.
This mumbo-jumbo moonish stuff
is ideologically pretty tough.

Or do I lapse
to think that p'raps
the moon and love
are not all guff.
If lapse I do

then I should rue
this world we hew.

Let us lay claim
to our birthright,
liberty, love
and delight.

7. Against the Grain

Mutterings need to be voiced to get some air. Criticising wrongs done in the name of socialism has bruised many souls. That is bad enough. To criticise the doings and sayings of the feminists slices the soul. But to remain silent is to criticise by implication the reasons many of us spent all those hours, days, months, years, writing, speaking, leafletting, encouraging, listening, learning, changing, loving, babysitting, arguing, fighting, voting, shouting and discovering over and over again the power of the idea of liberation. So let us take seriously enough what we have done to speak our minds and protest when something is done in the name of women's liberation which we think is wrong.

For, however distressing, however uncomfortable, it would be lax and irresponsible to imply that socialists made all the mistakes and feminists knew all the answers.

We women have insisted on the right to make our own mistakes. So now we must take responsibility for them, or else they will land us in the mud.

As the old Russian peasant women told the Bolsheviks, 'If you like tobogganing, you must be prepared to pull your sledge uphill.'

Banners flicker heroically in the wilderness. Reason, memory, imagination and courage set off to seek democracy, freedom and the commonweal. Huge contingents cross bridges as far as the eye can see. The bands are playing and the people singing. We march together, salt of the earth and solid against the power of the ruling class.

Oh, for a grand, great day of reckoning. The battle of battles. But it is not that simple. For the ruling class does not sit pretty to be expropriated, or line up for a clean fight to the finish. The battles are everyday and rarely grand or great. As soon as we reflect upon the political past we can see them, tedious, messy, time-consuming, negotiated compromises and trails to social security.

Then there is that one step forward and several back in which we strive and struggle for some gain, only to lose something we took for granted.

In a sense, everything *is* simple, and we should not forget love, equality and freedom. But we cannot thus be simpletons. We have to have wit enough to express uncomfortable thoughts. It has become possible, just about, to do this about socialism in Britain. This is an advance. But about feminism it is harder, and even though feminist ideas have reached many people, socialist feminists are fighting on several fronts and feeling beleaguered.

We could not have imagined the growth in the impact of the ideas of women's liberation which has occurred since the early 1970s. Many of us who were involved in the early days have done things which would have surprised us then.

However, the women's liberation movement has not turned the world inside out and upside down. Dreams have been disappointed. On an International Women's Day march in the early seventies I carried a placard saying 'Equal pay is not enough. We want the moon'. It was only partly in earnest. My pre-1968 Marxism meant that I had been trained to scepticism about impossibilist demands. I knew, moreover, all the arguments about how equal pay legislation would be evaded by employers well before there was even a law to be crafty about. Marxists have this irritating habit of knowing the general and missing out on the particular: ho, ho, I told you so – which does not encourage in people the energy to do much in particular in the meanwhile.

But desire for the moon still flickered. May '68 in France touched the lonely fantasy and infused it with a collective energy. In the emerging women's movement in Europe, for better or worse, the May uprising in France and the student movements it helped to generate were 'borning struggles', like American civil rights. To demand the impossible was part of resisting the inducements of an expanding capitalism to play the game. Even in the grim capitalism of the 1980s, where inducements are thin on the ground, I incline to the partial truth in this – the assertion of a challenge to the terms of the powerful, a refusal to accommodate to the definitions of privileged interest over what must be.

But the challenge of the impossible encourages a certain insensitivity to the physical wear and tear of everyday existence, impatience with the significance of snags, scorn towards the handiness of the patch or darn, a blindness to the patterns of the past. If you ignore the humdrum you fall into arrogance. Arrogant dreamers turn into poseurs and thus end up playing the game after all. In middle age they become cynics.

The initial strength of women's liberation was an implicit connection of dream and reality. Our immediate political heritage from the sixties meant that we took for granted that changes we made now could prefigure a less oppressive future. But still the pressing needs of our material circumstances and the social relationships we experienced as women meant that we did not forget that we lived in the present. In good times this combining of need and desire has enabled us to ride the waves, move the heart, meet the eyes, resuscitate the spirit and, within certain confines, change the world.

But it has to be said that there is a seedy side. The tension between present and future persists and makes for a certain discomfort. An irritation with the world's incongruence, an impatient yearning for resolution itches away. It can result in political stances which are frenzied, dismissive, over-simple, dogmatic and plain dishonest. These may keep fears and anxieties at bay for a while but they lead us down blind alleys.

Well, feminism is no more exempt from these than any other political movement. To claim the purity of our sex would be to declare ourselves above politics, which would simply be to accept the idealised place male power has allowed us. If we are not content with closed and sacred groves, with sacrificial dells and still pools where we can contemplate our own image, stagnant with the inwardness which avoids flux, then we have to face the hurly-burly of battle, draw clarity from real muddles and learn from our mistakes.

We have lost our innocence as a political movement. The first flush of sisterhood is no more. This in itself is not such a disaster – no good crying over spilt milk. Innocence is sweet but not when it is guarded. It turns into prurience, unable to brave the rub of circumstance, incapable of admitting to daftness, too stiff with rectitude to delight in absurdity. Innocence is not to be preserved. Instead we can, thank goodness, claim some maturity as a political movement. The blemishes of error, creases of time and scars of battle are not to be covered in shame. They are the marks of history and should make some tales worth telling to those granddaughters. Not for nostalgia's sake: we got neither equal pay nor the moon and have no space for nostalgia.

Nor can we be sanctimonious. Dangerously, our movement has begun to forget the habit of open discussion and self-criticism. It increasingly appears to remember only its innocence. 'I am Innocent. I am the Victim. I cannot be criticised. Therefore I can be a bully.'

No false innocence, then. Sisterhood has bloomed and it has also taken a knocking, and not only from men. It still hurts to say it. It is more comforting to keep the enemy clearly out there. But this is only part of the truth, and we take responsibility or mock our own origins.

I am not pretending that this is an easy course. The pain of disconnection between men and women is destructive – between women it eats at the soul of hope. No false optimism then. But unless feminists find the courage to say that our movement has carried love but that there are deep political divisions, smugness, competition and no longer free and honest communication but fears and resentments, we will dwindle into a sect muttering privately. Unstated taboos paralyse.

The open affirmation which marked our origins as a political movement has faltered. We have only expressed part of the truth – sisterhood and resistance to the power of men. It has become comforting to tell the same story. The record turns in the same groove. This may bring comfort and consolation amidst loneliness and fear, but it does not stretch the intellect and the imagination. It does our feminism no dishonour to say that change is awkward, that it is not linear or always pleasant and positive. We seek to make, in my opinion anyway, a movement for the liberation of all women, not a movement of liberated po-faced hypocrites who seek to rein in the intellect and would have the shears out on fancy if they could but find this devious, elusive, subversive. We, the feminists I mean, are not the pure embodiment of everything that is not tainted by the evil of masculinity. Nor in any case is all evil to be found in another biological grouping, or even in the concept of what is masculine. Nor is any particular man person simply the incarnation of a historical concept of masculinity. A fixed moral rectitude is incapable of negotiating with history. It knows no past, no present, cannot move into a future. Blown up with its own conceit, it heads for entrances and fills them with guilt as authority. 'Sorry, you can't get through here any more', 'You must have made a mistake', 'Who told you there was a door?', 'It'll be down the snake for you, I'm afraid', 'Well, she can't be a feminist', 'Feminists don't', 'She must have been colluding', 'Some women have shit in their heads'. When you hear remarks like this, sound the alarm, blow those whistles, bang the dustbin lids as loud as you can and shout back, 'Roll up, roll up. Let's enlarge the entrance on either side of her. Whoopsy daisy, through we all go.'

There have been evasions and silences about this for too long, and mine among them. The difficulty of trying to change the world and arguing among yourselves is well known to socialists. Evasion, silence, hearing only what you want to hear, even justifying actions to quiet unease have all been responses by people in the name of religion, revolution and socialism. Let's not do them under the cover of feminism.

It is not easy. How can we be self-critical, acknowledge real division between women and affirm our need to connect? How do we face conflict, dependence, domination between men and women without denying loving friendship and passionate desire? I am not sure how. There are no role models in my particular neck of the woods. But a culture shifts when people persevere.

I would not presume to map out the political 'way forward'. There is a deep and strong recognition within women's liberation that leadership is not a matter of individual pronouncements but a collective responsibility. This means every person saying what they think and contributing what they can. It means that what we have developed through action and ideas has always to be subject to reassessment. Otherwise dissatisfaction and disappointment turn inward and go into retreat.

The sources for reassessment are there in the uncharted repercussions of the women's liberation movement. As Sara Evans wrote of the American movement in *Personal Politics*, 'As the women's movement dispersed, splintered, formed and re-formed, its importance lay less and less with the specific groups who initiated it and more with the kind of responses it made possible . . . The experiences which had provoked and formed a feminist consciousness in the first place re-created themselves not only beyond the new left, but beyond the middle class as well.'[1]

In the early 1980s in Britain many feminists are to be found struggling against low pay and unemployment, resisting coercion from police and army, violence in the home and on the streets. They are part of the attempt to democratise welfare, halt the cuts, make local government more responsive to people's needs. They are helping to develop workers' plans, contesting the allocation of council housing, creating alternative forms of heating, forming cooperatives, still campaigning for abortion and childcare. There are therapy and health groups, adult education courses, job-sharing projects. There are black feminist groups, groups of Filipino and Asian women, Latin American women's groups, feminist theatre, films, poetry, publishing groups, magazines and journals.

All this, then, is our collective responsibility, and more – not to tell the same story over again but to assimilate and learn anew from the wider context of struggle which changing circumstances present.

We have made, amidst error, a movement seeking bread and roses. This is no mean quest: it is a source of strength, the stuff of life, worth handing on, not to be forgotten, very precious, a beautiful engagement present for anyone just becoming interested in feminism. Good luck to you, and it's a pleasure, etc.

I would, though, tie a little label to the bread and roses I deliver to your door. Just a small message from a medium old-timer. Take care not to dismiss aspirations which do not fit the outer pattern of politics – even a politics which knows the personal is political. For over the power to decide boundaries one has to be constantly vigilant.

We women lack practice in this alertness. Home bodies, hampered by many pressing duties and obligations, we have not been accustomed to the heroic quest. Grails and dragons have not been our cup of tea.

There is much that is unclear and unknown in the making of a new culture. But this much is certain. We cannot close down the possibility of human transformation or waste the transcendent creativity which is the precious radical heritage of feminism and of socialism. For this is the dream – that all human beings can be more than present circumstances allow. And the dream is not to be appropriated and confined.

This, then, is the dilemma – how should we act? How can we change circumstances to give substance to the dream? The times are going to require some energetic stretching. Have we got it in us? To be honest, at this point in time I do not know. But my ears are flapping; I would like to be convinced.

I hope these essays help substantial dreamers to find tracks through the past. If they stir the heart, bring a few smiles, knuckle the spirit, leave some puzzles and bring in a few quid, I will be sustained to elbow with you, still resolute, towards our future. (I mean the one where there are no masters of course.)

NOTES

PREFACE

[1.] Thalia Doukas, in *One Foot on the Mountain*, ed. Lilian Mohin, Onlywomen Press, 1979, p. 229.

PART ONE. BEGINNINGS: THE ORIGINS OF WOMEN'S LIBERATION

INTRODUCTION

[1.] Quoted in Sara Evans, *Personal Politics, The Roots of Women's Liberation in the Civil Rights Movement and the New Left*, Knopf, 1979, pp. 86–7.
[2.] Helke Sander, Action Committee for the Liberation of Women, SDS Conference Frankfurt, September 1968, translated by John Birtwhistle, unpublished.

1. 'WOMEN'S LIBERATION AND THE NEW POLITICS'

[1.] E.E. Evans-Pritchard, 'The position of women in primitive societies and other essays in social anthropology', 1965, p. 56.
[2.] Edith Thomas in *The Women Incendiaries*, 1963, describes this in connection with the Paris Commune. Wilhelm Reich's *The Sexual Revolution*, 1967, contains an account of the hostility to the Women's Club after the Russian Revolution as well as the whole dilemma of the Bolsheviks about their approach to sexuality. Helen Foster Snow's *Women in modern China*, 1967, mentions similar hostility in China.
[3.] E.J.P. Mayer, *The Recollections of Alexis de Tocqueville*, 1959, pp. 132–3.
[4.] See Karl Mannheim, *Ideology and Utopia*, 1965, parts 4 and 5. F. Graus, 'Social utopias in the middle ages' in *Past and present*, 1967, no. 38. Any biography of worker students, e.g. Thomas Bell, *Pioneering Days*, 1941; Thomas Cooper, *The Life of Thomas Cooper Written By Himself*; Gwynn A. Williams 'Rowland Detroisier, a Working-Class Infidel 1800–1834'; University of York, *Borthwick Papers*, no. 28, 1965.
See also E.P. Thompson, 'Education and Experience', Fifth Mansbridge Memorial Lecture, 1968.
Frantz Fanon, *The Wretched of the Earth*, and Black Power literature in general, especially Stokely Carmichael in *The Dialectics of Liberation*, ed. David Cooper, and Eldridge Cleaver's *Soul on Ice*.
[5.] This section is taken from my article, 'Women, the struggle for freedom', *Black Dwarf*, 10 January 1969.
[6.] Mao Tse-Tung, 'Investigation of the peasant movement in Hunan: the movement of the riffraff', *Selected readings*, 1967.
[7.] Beryl Smalley, *English Friars and Antiquity in the Early Fourteenth Century'*, 1960, pp. 17–18.
[8.] Simone de Beauvoir, *The Long March*, 1958, p. 139.
[9.] Valerie Solanas, 'S.C.U.M. Manifesto', 1968.

[10.] W. Butler-Bowden, ed., *The Book of Margery Kempe*, 1954, pp. 15–16.

[11.] See Thomas, 'Women in the Civil War sects', op.cit.

[12.] Ellen MacArthur, 'Women petitioners and the Long Parliament', *English Historical Review*, vol. 24.

[13.] Roger L'Estrange, *The Woman as Good as the Man, or the Equality of Both Sexes*, 1677.
For a strong dose of anti-feminism see 'The women's fegaries showing the great endeavour they have used for obtaining of the breeaches', anonymous, c. 1675.

[14.] Hannah Wooley quoted in M.S. Storr, *Mary Wollstonecraft et le mouvement feministe dans la literature anglaise*, 1932.

[15.] Christopher Hill, 'Clarissa Harlowe and her times', in *Puritanism and Revolution*, 1962, pp. 367–94.

[16.] See J.A. and Olive Banks, *Feminism and Family Planning*, 1964.

[17.] See David Mitchell, *Women on the Warpath*, 1966, and George Dangerfield, *The Strange Death of Liberal England*, 1961, for accounts of the suffragettes. For a contemporary criticism of bourgeois feminism see A.M. Kollontai's 'Critique of the feminist movement' in R.A.J. Schlesinger, 'Changing attitudes in Soviet Russia', *The Family*, 1949.

[18.] See Juilet Mitchell's 'Women: the longest revolution' in *New Left Review*, no. 40, November-December 1966, for a brief account of socialist and Marxist approaches to the family and the reaction. The literature is voluminous, but apart from Engels, *The Origin of the Family* see especially A. Bebel, *Women in the Past, Present and Future*, 1887; Alexandra Kollontai, *Communism and the Family*, 1920; Lenin on *The emancipation of Women*; Alexandra Kollontai, *Free Love*; Leon Trotsky, *Problems of Life*, 1924.

[19.] Since Barbara Castle's Equal Pay Act in 1970, employers have already begun to find ways round an increased wages bill. They have introduced job evaluation schemes and redefined skills. They have also considered replacing labour-intensive female work by machines, or keeping men's wages down in order to pay for the women.

[20.] See PEP Report, 'Women at work'; 'Women's wages' in *Labour Research*, August 1968; Sabby Sagall, 'Interview with Rose Boland', *Socialist Worker*, 21 September 1968; Audrey Wise, 'Equal pay is not enough', and 'Lil Bilocca and Hull trawlers', *Black Dwarf*, 10 January 1969; 'Working-class girls', *Black Dwarf*, 2 May 1969; Sabina Roberts, 'Equal pay, the first step', *Socialist Woman*, March-April 1969; Kath Fincham and Sabina Roberts, 'The struggle for democracy — who says women can only do unskilled work'; Sue Pascoe, 'Conference of London and Westminster Trades Council on equal pay for women', *Socialist Woman*, May-June 1969; 'Woman's Rights: account of equal pay demonstration and information about the various women's groups which exist', *Black Dwarf*, 1 June 1969.

[21.] Since this was written there have been a few changes — although they've been painfully slow. Women's Liberation has made open contempt impossible. But there is a new danger now. Men on the left can pigeonhole certain questions as 'women's lib' without examining how ideas in the women's movement mean they must reassess their own politics.

[22.] 'I.C.A. Woman', Women's Liberation Workshop, *Black Dwarf*, 14 June 1969. Nelbarden swimwear, *Shrew*, no. 3, July 1969.

[23.] Trotsky, *Problems of Life*, op.cit., p. 99.

8. 'PROBLEMS OF ORGANISATION AND STRATEGY'

[1.] *Stalin*, Isaac Deutscher, Pelican, 1966, p. 51.

PART TWO. MAKING TRACKS: WOMEN'S LIBERATION 1972–82

5. 'WOMEN WORKERS AND CLASS STRUGGLE'

[1.] The information about particular strikes is taken from 'Striking Progress 1972–1973', *Red Rag*, no. 5, which was originally compiled from the *Morning Star* and *Socialist Worker*. Information about strikes between July 1973 and August 1974 comes from an unpublished chronology collected by Dave Phillips from back numbers of *Socialist Worker*. We are grateful to him for allowing us to make use of this. Other information comes from the files of the *Morning Star*. For information and suggestions we are indebted to Mick Costello and Jean Gardiner.

[2.] Sylvia Greenwood, interviewed by Sheila McGregor, *Socialist Worker*, 10 August 1974.

[3.] See, for example, articles published in *Radical America*, vol. 7, nos. 4 and 5. The collection of papers from the Women's Liberation and Socialism Conference, London, 22/23 September 1973.

[4.] See Bob Rowthorn, 'Unemployment in Britain,' in *Marxism Today*, February 1972.

[5.] Richard Hyman, 'Industrial Conflict and the Political Economy,' pp. 105–6 in Ralph Milliband and John Saville, ed., *The Socialist Register 1973*, Merlin Press, 1974.

[6.] For an account of this strike see Huw Beynon, *Working for Ford*, Penguin, 1973; and John Matthews, *The Ford Strike*, Panther, 1972. For the effect on the women's movement see Sheila Rowbotham, 'The Beginnings of Women's Liberation in Britain', in Michelene Wandor, ed., *The Body Politic: Women's Liberation in Britain 1969–72*, Stage 1, 1973.

[7.] 'Fakenham Occupation', *Socialist Woman*, summer 1972; and *Shrew*, October 1972, vol. 4, no. 5.

[8.] Jim Roche, 'The Leeds Clothing Strike', *Trade Union Register, 1970*; and the account by Gertie Roche in Sheila Rowbotham, *Woman's Consciousness, Man's World*, Penguin, 1973.

[9.] For details of this strike see Richard Hyman, 'Industrial Conflict and the Political Economy', op.cit., pp. 148–9.

[10.] *Case Con, Women's Issue*, spring 1974. Includes articles on the reproduction of labour power, women in white-collar unions, the sexist ideology of case work, women in prisons, adolescent girls, battered women. See also Elizabeth Wilson, 'Women and the Welfare State', *Red Rag*, pamphlet 2.

[11.] Sections of the 'Nightcleaners', *Shrew*, were reprinted in *Radical America*, vol. 7, nos. 4 and 5, and in Michelene Wandor (ed.), *The Body Politic*. A more recent account is Sally Alexander, 'The Nightcleaners, an Assessment of the Campaign', *Red Rag*, no. 6.

[12.] 'Sacked for Fighting Three-Day Week', *Women's Voice*, no. 9.

[13.] An example of union apathy is described in 'Scrooge and Stooge: Company and Union v. The Workers of Cheeseborough Ponds', Notting Hill Women's Liberation Workshop. See also Alexander, 'The Nightcleaners', on the attitude of the trade union officials.

[14.] Beatrix Campbell, 'Equal Pay: the Results of an Action', *Link*, winter 1973, no. 4, gives a fuller account of this strike.

[15.] 'Danger: Women at Work', Report of the conference organised by the NCCL, 1974.

[16.] *Socialist Worker*, 10 August 1974.

[17.] Audrey Wise, 'Women and the Struggle for Workers' Control', Spokesman pamphlet, no. 33.

[18.] Audrey Wise, 'Trying to Stay Human', *Red Rag*, no. 3, p. 5.

12. 'WOMEN, POWER AND CONSCIOUSNESS'

[1.] Diane Gold, 'Leeds Tailoring Workers', unpublished Mss., quoted by Sally Alexander in her introduction to Marianne Herzog, *From Hand to Mouth, Women and Piecework*, Penguin, 1980, pp. 31–2.

[2.] Sylvia Greenwood quoted in Bea Campbell and Sheila Rowbotham, 'Women Workers and Class Struggle', *Radical America*, vol. 8, no. 5, September-October 1974, p. 56.

[3.] Maria O'Reilly, 'Netherley United Women Take on the Housing Corporation', *Spare Rib*, no. 56, March 1977 p. 13.

[4.] Barbara Castle, 'Coming Alive Hurts', *Women in Collective Action*, ed. Ann Kurno *et al.*, Association of Community Workers, 1982.

[5.] Cynthia Cockburn, *The Local State, Management of Cities and People*, Pluto, 1977.

[6.] London to Edinburgh Weekend Return Group, *In and Against the State*, Pluto, 1977.

[7.] *What We Want for Hackney*, conference papers, October 1981.

[8.] Rape Crisis Centre, First Report, March 1977, p. 1.

[9.] Annette quoted in Ingrid Muir 'Refuge for Dundee', *Spare Rib*, no. 50, September 1976, p. 24.

[10.] Women's Aid Paper, 'You're Either Someone's Daughter or Someone's Wife', Women's Liberation Conference, 1977, p. 2.

[11.] Lesley Merryfinch and Jill Sutcliffe, 'Street Hassles', *Shrew*, Women and Violence Study group, summer 1978, p. 24.

[12.] Amrit Wilson, *Finding a Voice, Asian Women in Britain*, Virago, 1978, p. 167.

[13.] Quoted in Vicky Seldon, 'Violence Against Women, Male Power in Action', *Shrew*, August 1981, vol. 25, no. 8, pp. 14–17.

[14.] Merryfinch and Sutcliffe, op.cit., p. 34.

[15.] 'Why Do We Emphasise Small-Group Discussions?', *Shrew*, Women's Liberation Workshop, no. 6, October 1969.

[16.] *ibid.*, p. 4.

[17.] Nell Myers, Annie Mitchell, Adah Kay and Val Charlton, 'Four Sisters', *Red Rag*, no. 11.

[18.] Peter Anderson and Martin Steckelmacher, 'The Labour Party and Beyond, An Interview with Raymond Williams', *Revolutionary Socialism*, Big Flame Magazine, summer 1980, p. 17.

[19.] Kenric, in 'A Guide to Lesbian Groups', *Spare Rib*, no. 74, September 1978, p. 27.

[20.] Monty Johnstone, interview with Lech Walesa, *Marxism Today*, vol. 25, no. 10, October 1981, p. 14.

[21.] Anton Pannekoek, quoted in Holloway, Pannekoek and Gorters, *Marxism, Capital and Class*, no. 7, spring 1979, p. 154.

[22.] Sheila Rowbotham, Lynne Segal, Hilary Wainwright, *Beyond the Fragments*, Merlin Press, 1979.

[23.] *A Declaration, Popular Planning for Social Need, An Alternative to Monetarism from Shop Stewards Combine Committees and Trades Councils*, September 1981, p. 9.

[24.] Anna Coote, 'The Sexual Division of Labour and Relations in the Family', paper given at Conference on Alternative Strategies for the Labour Movement, October 1981, extracts in *Beyond the Fragments Bulletin*, no. 3, January 1982.

[25.] Victor Anderson, paper at Conference on Alternative Strategies for the Labour Movement, October 1981.

[26.] National Childcare Campaign, Conference Papers, July 1980.

[27.] Mandy Merck, 'The City's Achievements', in ed. Susan Lipshitz, *Tearing the Veil, Essays in Femininity*, Routledge and Kegan Paul, 1978, p. 112. Mandy Merck quotes the lecture sequence of Laura Mulvey and Peter Wollen's film *Penthesies*: 'their weapons and strategy are men's weapons and strategy. They offer a solution which is magical not political.'

[28.] Sandra McNeill, reproduction workshop paper at National Socialist Feminist Conference, January 1978, *Scarlet Women*, 6/7, p. 4.

[29.] Betty McArdle, 'Ballad of a Single Woman', *Spare Rib*, no. 95, June 1980, p. 35.

[30.] Mary Kelly, 'Sexual Politics, Art and Politics', *Proceedings of a Conference on Art and Politics*, April 1977, first impression 1980, p. 68.

[31.] Felicity Edholm, Olivia Harris, Kate Young, 'Conceptualising Women', *Critique of Anthropology*, Women's Issue, 9 and 10, vol. 3, 1977, p. 126.

[32.] Joan Kelly, 'The Doubled Vision of Feminist Theory: A Postscript to the "Women and Power" Conference', *Feminist Studies*, vol. 5, no. 1, spring 1979, p. 221.

[33.] Michele Barratt, *Women's Oppression Today*, Verso, 1980, pp. 58–60.

[34.] Anna Coote and Peter Kellner, *Hear This Brother, Women Workers and Union Power, New Statesman* Report 1, 1980.

[35.] Anna Coote and Jean Coussins, 'Family in the Firing Line', Poverty Pamphlet, 51, Child Poverty Action Group and National Council for Civil Liberties, March 1981.

[36.] Margaret Walters, review of Juliet Mitchell, *Psychoanalysis and Feminism, Spare Rib*, 1974.

[37.] Women and Fascism study group pamphlet, 'Breeders for Race and Nation'.

[38.] Quoted in *ibid.*, p. 23.

[39.] Eve Fitzpatrick, 'To My Father', *Spare Rib*, no. 55, February 1977, p. 38.

PART THREE. HOLDING TRANSIENCE: MARXISM, FEMINISM AND HISTORY

INTRODUCTION

[1.] Karl Marx, Preface to the Second Edition of *Capital*, vol. 1, 1873. Translated by Samuel Moore and Edward Aveling. Allen and Unwin, 1957, p. xxxi.

2. 'SEARCH AND SUBJECT, THREADING CIRCUMSTANCE'

[1.] One of these papers has been published: Jo O'Brien, *Women's Liberation in Labour History*, Spokesman Pamphlet no. 24, Nottingham, n.d.

[2.] Eileen Power, *Medieval People*, London, 1924, p. 1. For the influence of Marx on the development of social and economic history, see E. J. Hobsbawm, 'Karl Marx's Contribution to Historiography' in Robin Blackburn, ed., *Ideology in Social Science*, New York, 1973.

[3.] Alice Clark, *The Working Life of Women in the Seventeenth Century*, London, 1968 (first edition 1919), Preface.

[4.] *ibid.*

[5.] *ibid.*, p. 308.

[6.] Mary Beard, *Woman as a Force in History*, New York, 1971 (first edition 1946), Preface.

[7.] Karl Marx and Frederick Engels, *The German Ideology*, London 1965, vol. 1, p. 31.

[8.] *ibid.*, p. 39.

[9.] *ibid.*, pp. 50–51.

[10.] These arguments are developed in Jean Gardiner, *Political Economy of Female Labour in Capitalist Society*, paper delivered at the British Sociological Association Conference, Aberdeen, 1974.

[11.] See Michelle Zimbalist, Rosaldo and Louise Lamphere, eds., *Woman, Culture and Society*, Stanford, 1974.

[12.] For the historical background of Engels' views, see Joan Bamberger, 'The Myth of Matriarchy' in *ibid.* See also chapter 13, 'Socialism, the Family and Sexuality', below.

[13.] For a more detailed statement of these currents in anthropology, see Raymond

Firth, 'The Sceptical Anthropologist, Social Anthropology and Marxist views of Society', *Proceedings of the British Academy*, vol. LVIII.

[14.] 'The Disenchantment of the World', *New York Review of Books* 2 (1971).

[15.] Christopher Hill and Lawrence Stone, *The Listener*, October 4, 1973.

[16.] Marilyn Clark, 'Interview With My Mother-in-Law', unpublished interview.

[17.] *The Household Account Book of Sarah Fell*, Norman Penney, ed., Cambridge, 1920.

[18.] 'Lucy Larcom's Factory Experiences', from *Lucy Larcom: A New England Girlhood*, Boston, 1889, quoted in Nancy F. Cott, ed., *The Root of Bitterness*, New York, 1972, p. 139.

[19.] Alice Walker, 'In Search of Our Mothers' Gardens', *Radcliffe Quarterly* vol. 60, no. 2 (June 1974), pp. 4–5.

[20.] *The Politics of Sexuality in Capitalism*, Red Collective Pamphlet.

3. 'WOMEN AND RADICAL POLITICS IN BRITAIN, 1820–1914'

[1.] Barbara Taylor, 'The Woman-Power, Religious Heresy and Feminism in Early English Socialism' in Susan Lipshitz, ed., *Tearing the Veil: Essays in Femininity*, Routledge and Kegan Paul, 1978, p. 121.

[2.] *ibid.*, p. 129.

[3.] *ibid.*, p. 128–9.

[4.] *ibid.*, p. 133.

[5.] *ibid.*, p. 134–5.

[6.] *ibid.*, p. 138.

[7.] *ibid.*, p. 139.

[8.] Dorothy Thompson, 'Women and Nineteenth-Century Radical Politics: A Lost Dimension', in Ann Oakley and Juliet Mitchell, eds., *The Rights and Wrongs of Women*, Penguin, 1976, p. 114.

[9.] *ibid.*, p. 113.

[10.] *ibid.*, p. 119.

[11.] *ibid.*, p. 122.

[12.] *ibid.*, p. 120–21.

[13.] *ibid.*, p. 135.

[14.] *ibid.*, p. 136.

[15.] *ibid.*, p. 137.

[16.] Jill Norris and Jill Liddington, *One Hand Tied Behind Us: The Rise of the Women's Suffrage Movement*, Virago, 1977, p. 133.

[17.] Geoffrey Mitchell, ed., *The Hard Way Up*, Virago, 1977, p. 130.

[18.] Norris and Liddington, p. 216.

[19.] *ibid.*, p. 214.

[20.] *ibid.*, p. 235.

5. 'THE TROUBLE WITH "PATRIARCHY" '

[1.] For critical accounts of how the word 'patriarchy' has been used: Paul Atkinson, 'The Problem with Patriarchy', *Achilles Heel* 2, 1979. Zillah Eisenstein and Heidi Hartman, *Capitalist Patriarchy and the Case for Socialist Feminism*, ed. Eisenstein, Monthly Review, 1978. Linda Gordon and Allen Hunter, 'Sexual Politics and the New Right', *Radical America*, November 1977, February 1978. Olivia Harris and Kate Young, 'The Subordination of Women in Cross-Cultural Perspective', *Patriarchy Papers*. Roisin McDonough and Rachel Harrison, 'Patriarchy and Relations of Production', *Feminism and Materialism*, ed. Kuhn and Wolfe, Routledge, 1978. Gayle Rubin, 'The Traffic in Women', *Towards an Anthropology of Women*, ed. Rayna Reiter, Monthly Review, 1975. Veronica Beechey, 'On Patriarchy', *Feminist Review*, 3, 1979.

[2.] and [3.] See *Capitalist Patriarchy and the Case for Socialist Feminism*.

PART FOUR. MEMORY AND CONSCIOUSNESS

INTRODUCTION

[1.] Susie Fleming and Gloden Dallas, 'Jessie', *Spare Rib*, no. 32, February 1975.
[2.] Barbara Taylor, *Eve and the New Jerusalem, Virago*, 1983, p. vi.
[3.] E.P. Thompson, 'Postscript 1976' to William Morris's *Romantic to Revolutionary*, Merlin, 1977, p. 792.
[4.] *ibid.*, p. 792.

6. 'IN SEARCH OF CARPENTER'

[1.] Arthur Calder-Marshall, *Havelock Ellis*, London, 1959, p. 71.
[2.] *ibid.*, p. 74.
[3.] E.P. Thompson, 'Homage to Tom Maguire' in Asa Briggs and John Saville, ed., *Essays in Labour History*, London, 1960.
[4.] Kate Salt is described in Stephen Winsten, *Salt and his Circle*, London, 1951.
[5.] The friendship is mentioned in Charles Ashbee Memoirs, mss. Victoria and Albert Museum; in Charles Ashbee, *Journal*, and in G. Lowes Dickenson, *Correspondence*, King's College, Cambridge.
[6.] Ed. Gilbert Beith, *Edward Carpenter, An Appreciation*, London, 1931, p. 36.
[7.] Edward Carpenter, *Love's Coming of Age*, 12th edition, 1923, p. 22. The first edition of the book appeared in 1896.
[8.] Edward Carpenter, *My Days and Dreams*, London, 3rd edition, February 1918, pp. 195-6.
[9.] Carpenter, *Love's Coming of Age*, pp. 69–85.
[10.] I owe these comments on Carpenter's views of homosexuality to Graeme Woolaston, 'Edward Carpenter on Homosexuality', Gay Culture Society, London School of Economics, duplicated paper.
[11.] London, 1971.
[12.] E.M. Forster, *Maurice*, Terminal Note, London, Penguin, 1975, p. 217.
[13.] Carpenter, *My Days and Dreams*, p. 321.
[14.] 'England Arise', in Carpenter, *Chants of Labour, A Song Book of the People*, 6th edition, 1922, pp. 18–19. The first edition of the book appeared in 1888.
[15.] Carpenter, *My Days and Dreams*, p. 322.

9. 'TRAVELLERS IN A STRANGE COUNTRY'

1. On the University Extension Movement generally, see James Stuart, *Reminiscences*, London, 1911; H.J. Mackinder and M.E. Sadler, *University Extension: Past, Present and Future*, London, 1891; R.D. Roberts, *Eighteen Years of University Extension*, Cambridge, 1891; W.H. Draper, *University Extension: A Survey of Fifty Years*, Cambridge, 1923; N.A. Jepson, 'A Critical Analysis of the Origin and Development of the University Extension Movement between 1893 and 1902, with special reference to the West Riding of Yorkshire', Ph.D. thesis, Leeds, 1955; Brian Simon, *Education and the Labour Movement 1870–1918*, London, 1965, pp. 86–96. On the background to the social theories of the movement see D.A. Winstanley, *Later Victorian Cambridge*, Cambridge, 1947; Melvin Richter, *The Politics of Conscience: T.H. Green and his Age*, London, 1964; Gareth Stedman Jones, *Outcast London: A Study in the Relationship between Classes in Victorian Society*, Oxford, 1971.

2. R.H. Tawney, 'The Labour Movement and the W.E.A.', Rochdale Education Guild Notes, Item 14, newspaper cutting *Rochdale Observer*, 28 May 1910, in Rochdale Public Library.

3. A.H.D. Acland at a liberal meeting in Barnsley, *Barnsley Independent*, 11 April 1885.

4. Michael Sadler, 'The Cooperative Society Educational Movement', *Barnsley Chronicle*, 21 March 1885.

5. Tom Mann, *Oxford University Extension Gazette* (hereafter *Gazette*), August 1893, p. 152.

6. Edward Carpenter, Poem Mss., *3–8 Carpenter Collection*, Sheffield Local History Library.

7. Michael Sadler, *Michael Ernest Sadler: A Memoir by his Son*, London, 1949, p. 65.

8. C.R. Ashbee, *Mss. Journal*, April 1886, Kings College Cambridge MSS.

9. J.C. Powys, *Autobiography*, London, 1949, pp. 184–5.

10. Michael Sadler, *Todmorden Advertiser*, 29 March 1889.

11. R.D. Roberts, *Eighteen Years of University Extension*, Cambridge, 1891, pp. 30–31.

12. R.D. Roberts, *ibid.*

13. Joseph Emes, *University Extension Reports*, London, 1894, pp. 73–4.

14. Ramsden Balmforth to Graham Wallas, *Wallas Papers*, 22 December 1892, London School of Economics.

15. *Todmorden Advertiser*, 22 February 1889.

16. Joseph Greenwood, 'Reminiscences of Sixty Years Ago', *Copartnership*, July 1910, p. 103.

17. J.G. Lockhart, *Cosmo Gordon Lang*, London, 1949, p. 49.

18. Information from Mr D. Wright and Mr R.K.B. Aldridge, Huddersfield Public Library.

19. See Thomas Okey, *A Basketful of Memories*, London, 1930.

20. F.H. Spencer, *An Inspector's Testament*, London, 1938, p. 67.

21. *ibid.*, p. 104–5.

[22.] *ibid.*, p. 104–16.

[23.] James Stuart, *Reminiscences*, London, 1911, p. 166.

[24.] *Cambridge University Review*, 27 May 1873.

[25.] Rev. W. Moore Ede, *Report presented to the Syndicate for Conducting Lectures in Populous Places*, Cambridge, printed at the University Press, 1875, p. 19.

[26.] *Gazette*, June 1893, p. 125.

[27.] *Oldham Industrial Society Record*, vol. 11, no. 19, July 1913, p. 223.

[28.] *Oldham Industrial Society Record*, vol. 11, no. 19, July 1913, p. 223.

[29.] Harold Begbie, *Living Water, Being Chapters from the Romance of a Poor Student*, London, 1918, p. 110.

[30.] Joseph Emes, *Gazette*, October 1892, p. 4.

[31.] Harold Begbie, *Living Water*, p. 110.

[32.] *Journal*, December 1892, p. 134.

[33.] R.D. Roberts, *Eighteen Years of University Extension*, p. 27.

[34.] T.J. Lawrence, *Derbyshire Times*, 28 November 1874.

[35.] R.D. Roberts, *Eighteen Years of University Extension*, p. 31.

[36.] *Gazette*, October 1892, p. 5.

[37.] Frederick Rogers, *Labour Life and Literature*, London, 1913, p. 10, pp. 76–91, 99–102, p. 142. See also, *East London Observer*, 27 April 1879. Frederick Rogers, 'Twenty Years of Social Movement', *The Progressive Review*, June 1897, pp. 203–10.

[38.] Frederick Rogers, *Religion an Answer to the Problem of Life, Labour and Religion* by Ten Labour Members of Parliament and Other Bodies, London, 1910, p. 28.

[39.] Frederick Rogers, *Labour Life and Literature*, pp. 1–13; Frederick Rogers, 'Education and Working Men III, What Working Men are doing for it', *Weekly Dispatch*, 24 February 1884.

[40.] Frederick Rogers, *Labour Life and Literature*, pp. 41–4.

[41.] *Labour Life and Literature*, pp. 23–73.

[42.] *Labour Life and Literature*, pp. 100–110.

[43.] Frederick Rogers, 'A Sunday Morning at a Radical Club', *Pall Mall Gazette*, 1 June 1883, pp. 3–4.

[44.] Frederick Rogers, 'Education and Working Men III', *The Weekly Dispatch*, January 1883.

[45.] *Labour Life and Literature*, p. 119, p. 140; Frederick Rogers, *Religion an Answer to the Problem of Life*, p. 28, p. 82.

[46.] J. Lee Osborn, *Reuben George, An Appreciation*, reprinted from the *Wiltshire and Gloucestershire Standard*, 13 June 1936. See also *Reuben George is Dead, Tragic Last Illness of Under Dog's Champion*, reprinted from *Evening Advertiser*, 5 June 1936, Wiltshire Pamphlets 8.

[47.] William Davidson, *Reuben and I*, Swindon, 1922.

[48.] Reuben George, *The Path We Trod, Twenty Years' Comradeship with the W.E.A.*, reprinted from the *Swindon Advertiser*, 31 March 1933, Wiltshire Pamphlets 103.

[49.] J.A.R. Marriott, Examiners' Report on E.L.S. Horsburgh's course on Political and Social Problems, Swindon, Michaelmas 1907, *Oxford University Extension Delegacy Examiners Reports*, 1907.

50. Albert Mansbridge, *Fellow Men*, London, 1948, pp. 44–5.

51. William Davidson, *Reuben and I*; Albert Mansbridge, *Fellow Men*, pp. 43–4.

52. Harold Begbie, *Living Water*, p. 4.

53. John V. Barrow, 'The English Miners and University Extension', *University Extension*, Philadelphia U.S.A., vol. 1, no. 6, December 1891, pp. 188–9.

54. Cambridge University Extension in Hull, *Hull News*, 25 March 1876.

55. Frederick Rogers, 'Twenty Years of Social Movement', *The Progressive Review*, June 1897, pp. 205–6.

56. Edward Carpenter, *My Days and Dreams*, London, 1918 (1st ed. 1916), pp. 102–3.

57. Frederick H. Hubbard to C.R. Ashbee, 9 February 1897, *C.R. Ashbee-G. Lowes Dickinson Papers File 2*, Kings College, Cambridge.

58. *Gazette*, December 1894, p. 26.

59. Mr Hoare, 'The English Universities and the English People', *Oxford University Extension Delegacy Minutes*, 1892, p. 18.

60. R.D. Roberts, *Eighteen Years of University Extension*, p. 32.

61. 'Impressions of the Summer Meeting VIII', by a Gloucestershire Miner, *Gazette*, October 1892, p. 4.

62. Mr Hoare, *Oxford University Extension Delegacy Minutes*, 1892, p. 18.

63. Robert Halstead, 'Working Men and University Extension', *Gazette*, May 1893, p. 108.

64. *Todmorden Advertiser*, 24 September 1909.

65. *Todmorden Advertiser*, 7 July 1899. See also Robert Halstead to the Secretary of the Rochdale Education Department, 4 July 1894, *Rochdale Pioneers Education Department Papers Item II*, Rochdale Public Library.

66. Robert Halstead, 'The Stress of Competition from a Workman's Point of View', *Economic Review*, vol. 4, p. 55, 1894; Mansbridge, *Fellow Men*, p. 193.

67. *Todmorden Advertiser*, 25 October 1895.

68. Robert Halstead, *The Economic Review*, vol. 4, 1894.

69. Robert Halstead to the Secretary of the Rochdale Education Department, 4 July 1896, *Rochdale Pioneers Education Department Papers Item II*.

70. Arthur E. Teasdill, Report Oxford Summer Meeting, *Leeds Cooperative Record*, 238, October 1897, pp. 2–3.

71. *Journal*, October 1899, pp. 2–3.

72. Robert Halstead, *The Economic Review*, vol. 4, 1894, p. 44.

73. Robert Halstead and Samuel Fielding, 'University Extension and County Council Grants', *Gazette*, February 1894, p. 56.

74. Albert Mansbridge, *Fellow Men*, p. 19.

75. Robert Halstead, *The Economic Review*, vol. 4, 1894, pp. 55–6.

76. *Economic Review*, 1894, p. 54.

77. *Economic Review*, 1894, p. 58.

78. *Todmorden Advertiser*, 25 October 1895.

79. W.H. Draper, *University Extension*, Cambridge 1923, pp. 48–9, 121–2.

80. W.A.S. Hewins, *Apologia of an Imperialist*, London, 1929, pp. 19–20.

[81.] Robert Halstead, 'Impressions of the Summer Meeting', *Journal*, October 1894, p. 16.

[82.] 'Working Men at the Summer Meeting', *Gazette*, October 1890, pp. 5–6.

[83.] A.H.D. Acland, Address at the Annual Meeting of the Chelsea Centre, November 28 *Journal*, December 1892, p. 136.

[84.] Charles Owen, 'Impressions of the Summer Meeting', *Journal*, November 1899, p. 21.

[85.] Robert Halstead, *Journal*, October 1894, p. 6.

[86.] Extracts from a letter from a Yorkshire working man, Summer Meeting 1890, *Gazette*, October 1890, p. 2.

[87.] 'Impressions of the Summer Meeting VIII', *Gazette*, October 1892, p. 4.

[88.] Robert Halstead, *Journal*, October 1894, p. 5.

[89.] Reuben George, *The Path We Trod*, Wiltshire Pamphlets, 103.

[90.] Harold Begbie, *Living Water*, p. 12.

[91.] 'Working Men at the Summer Meeting', *Gazette*, October 1890, p. 5.

[92.] 'A Pilgrimage to Oxford Communicated by One who Went', *Journal*, July 1890, p. 69.

[93.] Reuben George, 'The Worker at Cambridge', *University Extension Board*, Cambridge Section 1908, no. 4, Michaelmas Term, p. 14.

[94.] Henry Crabtree, 1889 Summer Meeting, *Todmorden Advertiser*, 20 September 1889.

[95.] 'Impressions of a Summer Meeting VIII', by a Gloucestershire miner, *Gazette*, October, 1892, p. 4.

[96.] Joseph Emes, 'The Universities and the English People', *Oxford University Extension Delegacy Minutes*, 1892, p. 22.

[97.] Robert Halstead, *Journal*, October 1894, p. 6.

[98.] Robert Halstead, *Journal*, December 1900, p. 39.

[99.] Robert Halstead, *Journal*, December 1900, p. 39.

[100.] Joseph Owen, *Journal*, November 1891, p. 21.

[101.] A. Zimmern, 'The Worker at the Summer Meeting', *The Oxford Magazine*, 24 October 1907, in H.R. Smith, *Labour and Learning*, Oxford, 1956.

[102.] R.H. Tawney, 'On the Guild Work', *Rochdale Observer*, 13 January 1909.

[103.] R.H. Tawney, 'Workers and Education – Mr Tawney's appeal to Organised Labour', *Rochdale Observer*, 14 April 1910.

[104.] John V. Barrow, *University Extension*, Philadelphia U.S.A., vol. 1, no. 6, December 1891, p. 186.

[105.] Ellis Edwardes, *Journal*, October 1894, p. 91.

[106.] Robert Halstead, *Gazette*, May 1893, p. 109.

[107.] Albert Mansbridge, *Journal*, March 1903, p. 53.

[108.] Mansbridge, *Journal*, 1903, p. 85.

[109.] Arthur Abbott, 'The Ruskin Hall Educational Movement', *Leeds Cooperative Record* 269, May 1900, p. 4.

[110.] Conference at Ilford on the Higher Education of Working Men, *Ilford Recorder*, 10 March 1905.

[111.] J.L. Boards, *Todmorden Advertiser*, 29 March 1889.

[112.] Ellis Edwardes, *Journal*, February 1904, p. 68.

[113.] Mr Jackson, 'Conference at Ilford on the Higher Education of Working Men', *Ilford Recorder*, 10 March 1905.

[114.] Robert Halstead, *Journal*, April 1903, pp. 100–101.

[115.] 'Persona, Culture and Progress', *Woolwich Labour Journal*, August 1902, pp. 1–2. Henry Stewart Wishart attacked him and defended University Extension, *Woolwich Labour Journal*, October 1902, p. 16.

[116.] E.P. Thompson, 'Education and Experience', 5th *Mansbridge Memorial Lecture*, Leeds, 1968.

[117.] Brian Simon, *Education and the Labour Movement*, pp. 296–342.

PART FIVE. STRETCHING

2. 'THE WOMEN'S MOVEMENT AND ORGANISING FOR SOCIALISM'

[1.] For a discussion of Trotskyism as an identifiable political tradition see Geoff Hodgson, *Trotsky and Fatalistic Marxism*, Spokesman Books, 1975. Jim O'Brien's summary of the histories of American Leninist groups makes for an interesting comparison with Britain. Jim O'Brien, 'American Leninism in the 1970s', New England Free Press, 1979. This article originally appeared in the November 1977/February 1978 issue of *Radical America*.

[2.] Bea Campbell, 'Sweets From a Stranger', *Red Rag*, no. 13, p. 28.

[3.] Bea Campbell and Sheila Rowbotham, 'Women Workers and the Class Struggle', *Radical America*, vol. 8, no. 5, September-October 1974, p. 63.

[4.] Richard Kuper, 'Organizing and Participation', *Socialist Review*, July-August 1978, p. 36. (Ed: This is the British S.W.P. journal.)

[5.] Ralph Miliband, 'The Future of Socialism in England', *Socialist Register*, 1977, p. 50.

[6.] For a recent example of whooshing see Chris (Super) Harman, 'For Democratic Centralism', *Socialist Review*, July-August 1978, p. 39.

[7.] Adriano Sofri, *Italy 1977–78: Living with an Earthquake*, Red Notes pamphlet, no date, p. 95. See also the criticisms made by women in '*Lotta Continua*' of the leaderships' response to feminism.

[8.] Red Collective, 'Not so much a charter, more a way of organizing', mimeograph, 1974. (The Red Collective were a small group of men and women concerned to relate socialism and sexual politics.) This statement is quoted in Barbara Taylor, 'Classified: Who Are We? Class and the Women's Movement', *Red Rag*, no. 11, p. 24.

[9.] See, for example, *Case Con*, Women's Issue, spring 1974, and *London Educational Collective in Women and Education*, no. 2, 1973–4, on Rank and File's resistance to taking up women's subordination in education.

8. 'AGAINST THE GRAIN'

[1.] Sara Evans, *Personal Politics, The Roots of Women's Liberation in the Civil Rights Movement and the New Left*, Knopf, 1979, pp. 226–7.

INDEX